WHAT HAS WITTE

WHAT HAS WITTENBERG TO DO WITH AZUSA?

Luther's Theology of the Cross and Pentecostal Triumphalism

By

David J. Courey

Bloomsbury T&T Clark
An imprint of Bloomsbury Publishing Plc

B L O O M S B U R Y
LONDON • OXFORD • NEW YORK • NEW DELHI • SYDNEY

Bloomsbury T&T Clark
An imprint of Bloomsbury Publishing Plc

Imprint previously known as T&T Clark

50 Bedford Square
London
WC1B 3DP
UK

1385 Broadway
New York
NY 10018
USA

www.bloomsbury.com

First published 2015
Paperback edition first published 2016

British Library Cataloguing-in-Publication Data
A catalogue record for this book is available from the British Library.

ISBN: HB: 978-0-567-65630-8
PB: 978-0-567-67189-9
ePDF: 978-0-567-65631-5
ePub: 978-0-567-65632-2

Library of Congress Cataloging-in-Publication Data
Courey, David J.
What has Wittenberg to do with Azusa? : Luther's theology of the cross and pentecostal triumphalism / by David J. Courey.
pages cm
ISBN 978-0-567-65630-8 (hbk) – ISBN 978-0-567-65631-5 (epdf) –
ISBN 978-0-567-65632-2 (epub) 1. Pentecostalism–North America.
2. Pentecostalism. 3. Theology of the cross.
4. Luther, Martin, 1483–1546. I. Title.
BR1644.5.N7C68 2015
232'.4–dc23
2014033316

Typeset by Newgen Knowledge Works (P) Ltd., Chennai, India

CONTENTS

PREFACE

I was not born a Pentecostal. I suppose the pioneers of Azusa might say, 'No one was. After all, God has no grandchildren!' I came to Pentecostalism after a dramatic conversion experience at the age of 19, which, like the best testimonies, rescued me from a life of sin, degradation and eventual oblivion. At that point, I had never heard of Pentecostals, and when the fellow who had picked me up as I was hitchhiking shared his experience of Christ with me something life-changing took place. When he prayed with me and spoke in tongues, I just assumed it was a foreign language. It literally sounded like Greek to me!

Early in my Christian experience I had been warned to stay away from Pentecostals. All manner of spiritual havoc could ensue. But the first time I walked into a Pentecostal service, about a year and a half after my conversion, I knew I had come home. The tears that streamed down Winifred Anderson and Ethel Neal's cheeks as they sang 'It is Well with My Soul'; the outstretched arms peppered around the small auditorium; the abandon of passionate worship – these all seemed commensurate with the experience in that Volkswagen Beetle on Highway 401.

From that moment I began an intense search for what made this church different from others. These were the heady days of charismatic renewal. It was 1976 and there were Full Gospel Businessmen's breakfasts to attend, Bob Mumford and Judson Cornwall tapes to hear, and especially books from Logos Press. Real Holy Spirit stuff like Dennis Bennett's *Nine O'Clock in the Morning*, and particularly Harold Hill's *How to Live Like a King's Kid*, let alone the Pentecostal classics like Smith Wigglesworth's *Ever Increasing Faith* from Gospel Publishing House. But beneath the zeal and palpable electricity of Spirit-filled life were the constantly nagging questions. Where were the miracles on magnitude with Hill and Wigglesworth? Were these not intended as models to follow and not hagiographic tales of the especially sainted? And were all the experiences we touted as divine intervention really all that divine? All was well as long as one suspended judgement, and warded off critical questions.

A crisis of faith was brewing. It took place after a seminar with 'The Happy Hunters', an older polyester couple from the Full Gospel circuit. They had taught us how to heal. It was quite ingenious how over a thousand people who had never complained of arm or leg problems had both appendages miraculously lengthened in one mass healing. In the hours after the session, the dam broke loose, and I had yet another life-shaping question to face. Could I continue as a charismatic, as a Pentecostal (for I felt in many ways I was by now both of these), or would I abandon all the genuinely supernatural encounters I believed I had?

I have since gone on to 30 years of ministry in the Pentecostal Assemblies of Canada. I have pastored two churches that I would characterize as generally more conservative in their Pentecostal expression than I, and confess that, in spite of some modest success, I have yet to see what I have longed for, and believe is still possible in terms of divine intervention. Over the intervening years since the 'Happy Hunters' experience, I have found comfort in trusting in God's sovereignty and his wisdom. I have learned to live within the reality of my limited human capacity: 'Lord, I believe . . . help my unbelief!' And I have found great solace in Martin Luther. His passion, commitment, and self-awareness as well as his glaring imperfections are stunning testimony to the fact that God can use whomever he deigns to do supernatural things. And in this reality, I find the courage and peace to continue as pastor, preacher and student.

This is the journey out of which the following pages arise. I set out as a young believer to change the world. Now, I am grateful for the God who is changing me . . . and for the promise that *he* is changing the world and that I can begin to live now out of that coming kingdom. I think that's a healthier place from which to serve. And somehow I manage to do it . . . on my best days.

I wish to express gratitude to my academic mentors. Dr Bob Kelly at Waterloo Lutheran Seminary was the first Luther scholar I encountered. His introduction to the great Reformer was both exhilarating and enlightening. Dr Steve Studebaker has been a patient, and diligent supervisor. I have never known a more incisive reader, who can assess any piece from Augustine and Edwards down to my humble efforts and offer insight, and critique, and do it so quickly. I also want to mention Dr Gord Heath, whose affable warmth welcomed me to McMaster Divinity College. His impeccable organization as a teacher, and his encouragement as a scholar have been of great help. Beyond these I have appreciated the conversations I have had with faculty at MDC. From Dr Mark Boda to Dr Stan Porter, Principal of the school, I have been grateful for time and wisdom they have shared with me from busy schedules. One particularly hot summer, Lois Dow taught me Greek while she herself was in the midst of a move. This kind of helpfulness characterizes the collegiality at the school. Special thanks are extended to Nina Thomas, whose very long title indicates that it is she, in fact, who oversees the regular operations of the college. Her advice and encouragement have been invaluable. I here express gratitude to Dr Bill Faupel whose sensitivity to the spirit of this project has been of such encouragement.

I wish also to mention one particular mentor who shaped my zeal to connect the academy and the church and to embody passionate spirituality and disciplined scholarship in Pentecostal ministry. Dr Ron Kydd has been an inspiration to hundreds if not thousands of pastors-in-training. Ron has lived out a genuine commitment to thorough scholarship and an infectious spirituality since long before I came across his short booklet *I'm Still There* and long after our initial meeting when I accosted him at my first District Conference as a Bible College graduate. I thank him for his investment in my life and his consistent encouragement every time we have met or spoken on the phone. Along with Ron, I have greatly appreciated my interactions over the years with Dr Van Johnston and Dr John Stephenson both of whom have been catalytic models. Finally I mention my sermon-buddy and long-time mentor Bruce Martin who has prayed, encouraged, and pushed me along longer than both he and I care to recall.

This book was born in the crucible of ministry, the highs and lows of real people who experience real life before a real God. I have been part of the problem described in these pages, I have also strived to be part of the solution. I have stood shoulder to shoulder with some great pastors at Calvary Pentecostal Assembly, in Cambridge, Ontario. There have been too many great friends along the way to mention. But I have been especially grateful for my small group who gathered biweekly to pray, study and ask, 'When is the dissertation going to be finished?' I thank my personal assistant Veda Newell for her encouragement and hard work, and Liz Vanner for her tireless photocopying. I wish to express gratitude to the Board of Calvary for their longsuffering patience with me during this journey, which included a major building expansion along with doctoral studies, and the congregation who have by now heard enough Luther stories and are quietly awaiting publication. In the midst of it all, we left the church we had loved for 20 years as Eileen and I took on the role of global workers, at Continental Theological Seminary in Brussels, Belgium where I serve as dean of Graduate Studies.

I wish to thank the fine folk at Bloomsbury T&T Clark for their kind patience, and helpful suggestions. Of particular note, I express appreciation to Miriam Cantwell and Anna Turton for getting this project to publication. I must also mention my son, Michael Courey, doctoral student in sociology at the University of Western Ontario who assisted with bibliographic details.

Final words of appreciation go to my family. On this long journey I worked on Bonhoeffer as Rebecca entered the joys and challenges of adulthood; I read Althaus while visiting Sarah and Leighton in Saskatchewan and I cracked *The Crucified God* as we prepared for Michael and Kristina's wedding. Jazmyn was born as I agonized over whether chapter five should be one or two chapters (it turned into two as I held the newborn!). Rachel and I worked on Midrash and Moltmann together over Christmas (she finished first!). And Jonathan and I noshed, talked the benefits of vinyl over digital, and grooved on Zappa and the Beatles as I plodded through Luther. Micah, Zephaniah and Isaac have never known a grandfather without homework, and little Jade is sitting on my lap as I type these words. Everett and Felix raced around the apartment as I edited, while Kaya quietly kept her distance. In the end, it really is a family project, isn't it?

But it's Eileen who put up with my dreaming in German, lamenting over deadlines, and lost paragraphs, because even if Jesus saves, others not so much. We made a home together, filled the walls with laughter and sold the house to move to Europe. She has endured salary adjustments, an extra year's tuition, and the general commotion of living with me: husband, pastor and student. To her I dedicate this work.

To whom I owe the leaping delight
That quickens my senses in our wakingtime
And the rhythm that governs the repose of our sleepingtime,
The breathing in unison.

—T. S. Eliot

LIST OF ABBREVIATIONS

Luther Resources

BC	Tappert, Theodore G. ed. *The Book of Concord: The Confessions of the Evangelical Lutheran Church*. Philadelphia: Fortress Press, 1959.
LSC	*Luther: Letters of Spiritual Counsel*. Library of Christian Classics, Volume 18. Edited and translated by Theodore G. Tappert. Philadelphia: Westminster, 1960.
LW	*Luther's Works*. Philadelphia: Fortress Press, 1999.
WA	*D. Martin Luthers Werke: Kritische Gesamtausgabe*. Weimarer Ausgabe. Weimar: Hermann Böhlau, 1883– .
WA Tr	Weimarer Ausgabe Tischreden [Table Talk].

Pentecostal Resources

AF	*The Apostolic Faith* (Apostolic Faith Mission, Azusa Street, Los Angeles)
BM	*The Bridegroom's Messenger* (International Pentecostal Assemblies)
CE, WE, PE	Publications of the Assemblies of God
	Christian Evangel (19 July 1913–6 March 1915)
	Weekly Evangel (13 March 1915–18 May 1918)
	Christian Evangel (1 June 1918–4 October 1919)
	Pentecostal Evangel (18 October 1919–9 June 2002)
	Today's Pentecostal Evangel (16 June 2002–19 July 2009)
	Pentecostal Evangel (26 July 2009–)
PT	*The Pentecostal Testimony* (Official Organ of the Pentecostal Assemblies of Canada)
TF	*Triumphs of Faith* (Carrie Judd Montgomery)

Periodicals and Dictionaries

AQ	*American Quarterly*
AR	*Archiv für Reformationsgeschichte*
BDWP	*The Blackwell Dictionary of Western Philosophy*. Edited by Nicholas Bunnin and Jyuan Yu. London: Blackwell, 2004.
CC	*Christian Century*
CH	*Church History*
CMM	*Canadian Methodist Magazine*
Concern	*Concern: A Pamphlet Series for Questions of Christian Renewal*

CT	*Christianity Today*
CTJ	*Calvin Theological Journal*
CV	*Communio Viatorum*
DCA	*Dictionary of Christianity in America*. Edited by Daniel G. Reid, Robert D. Linder, Bruce L. Shelley and Harry S. Stout. Downers Grove: InterVarsity, 1990.
dialog	*dialog: A Journal of Theology*
DJG	*Dictionary of Jesus and the Gospels: A Compendium of Contemporary Biblical Scholarship*. Edited by Joel B. Green, Scot McKnight, and I. Howard Marshall. Downers Grove: InterVarsity Press, 1992.
DPCM	*Dictionary of Pentecostal and Charismatic Movements*. Edited by Stanley M. Burgess, Gary B. McGee and Patrick H. Alexander. Grand Rapids: Regency/Zondervan, 1988.
EA	*Ex Auditu*
EDT	*Evangelical Dictionary of Theology*. Edited by Walter A. Elwell. Grand Rapids: Baker, 1984.
EJ	*Enrichment Journal*
ER	*The Ecumenical Review*
ET	*Ecumenical Trends*
GDT	*Global Dictionary of Theology: A Resource for the Worldwide Church*. Edited by William A. Dyrness and Veli-Matti Kärkkäinen. Downers Grove: InterVarsity, 2008.
HJ	*Heythrop Journal*
HTR	*Harvard Theological Review*
IBMR	*International Bulletin of Missionary Research*
IJFM	*International Journal of Frontier Missions*
IJPR	*International Journal for the Psychology of Religion*
IRM	*International Review of Mission*
JBV	*Journal of Beliefs & Values: Studies in Religion & Education*
JEPTA	*Journal of the European Pentecostal Theological Association*
JES	*Journal of Ecumenical Studies*
JETS	*Journal of the Evangelical Theological Society*
JPS	*Journal of Pentecostal Studies*
JR	*The Journal of Religion*
JSSR	*Journal for the Scientific Study of Religion*
MH	*Medical History*
MQR	*Mennonite Quarterly Review*
MT	*Ministry Today*
NIDPCM	*The New International Dictionary of Pentecostal and Charismatic Movements: Revised and Expanded Edition*. Edited by Stanley M. Burgess and Eduard van der Maas. Grand Rapids: Zondervan, 2003.
Pneuma	*PNEUMA: The Journal for the Society of Pentecostal Studies*
Proc Am Ant Soc	*Proceedings of the American Antiquarian Society*
RRR	*Reformation and Renaissance Review*
SA	*Sociological Analysis*

SHE	*Studia Historiae Ecclesiasticae*
SJT	*Scottish Journal of Theology*
SR	*Studies in Religion/Sciences Religieuses*
TB	*Tyndale Bulletin*
TJ	*Trinity Journal (New Series)*
TT	*Theology Today*
W&W	*Word and World*
WTJ	*Wesleyan Theological Journal*

Introduction: Evaluating Contemporary Pentecostalism

I. The Problem with North American Pentecostalism

The advent of Pentecostalism was one of the top religious news stories of the twentieth century.[1] Surely the globalization of Pentecostalism will prove to be one of the top stories of the twenty-first.[2] But in North America, the place of its birth, Pentecostalism is in trouble – at least if numbers tell the tale.[3] This fact stands in tension with its own triumphal self-interpretation as an end-time revival movement – a vision that has yet to find fulfilment, at least in its North American

1. In fact the Azusa Street Revival made the top ten for both stories of the century and the millennium, according to the Religion Newswriters Association; Richard N. Ostling, 'Reporters Name Reformation Millennium's Top Religious Event', *Moscow-Pullman Daily News* (10 December 10 1999), p. 9A.

2. The brute numbers augur for a view of Pentecostalism that sees it as a 'new Reformation' of the church. By the year 2050, Philip Jenkins claims, the number of global Pentecostals should reach the 1 billion mark; *The Next Christendom: The Coming of Global Christianity* (New York: Oxford University Press, 2002), p. 8. Regardless of whether we follow Jenkins in including indigenous churches, or Allan Anderson (*An Introduction to Pentecostalism: Global Charismatic Christianity* (New York: Cambridge University Press, 2004), pp. 9–14) in rejecting them, Pentecostal growth in the majority world remains an impressive phenomenon.

3. All references to North America encompass only English-speaking North America. The situation in Canada is easily discerned from the 2001 Canadian Census: 'Pentecostals recorded the second largest decline, their numbers falling 15% to almost 369,500'; Statistics Canada. *2001 Census: Analysis Series Religions in Canada* (Ottawa, 2003) Online: http://www12.statcan.ca/english/census01/products/analytic/companion/rel/pdf/96F0030XIE2001015.pdf (Accessed 4 July 2014), p. 7. The 2010 General Conference Report of the Pentecostal Assemblies of Canada noted a 41 per cent decline in conversions between 2004 and 2008 based on individual church reports submitted to the denomination; Pentecostal Assemblies of Canada, *Rooted in Relationship: General Conference, 2010* (Mississauga: PAOC, 2010), p. 30. Perhaps pointing to the fickleness of census data, the 2011 census shows a 29.6 per cent increase among Pentecostals to 478,705; *National Household Survey, Canada, 2011* (Ottawa, 2014) Online: http://www12.statcan.gc.ca/nhs-enm/2011/dp-pd/prof/index.cfm?Lang=E (Accessed 4 November 2014).

locus of initial ascendancy. Instead, questions have been raised as to its future viability in the West. These include issues of acculturation, institutionalization and thorny concerns about its relationship to Evangelicalism.[4]

Aware of the current malaise in North American Pentecostalism, Edith Blumhofer commented poignantly that 'the Assemblies of God will be stronger when it finds the courage to raise theological questions for which it may not have ready answers'.[5] This is a challenge that poses vexing questions for both global and North American dimensions of Pentecostal reality. While Blumhofer's insight will eventually confront the emerging global Pentecostalism, which will at some point require greater theological precision; addressing this challenge is immediately critical to the future of North American Pentecostalism.

Appropriating Canadian theologian Douglas John Hall's paradigm of expectation and experience, I contend that contemporary North American Pentecostalism finds itself at an impasse at three levels: the grassroots of Pentecostal spirituality, the more reflective level of its theological contemplation and ultimately at the institutional level. In order to elaborate the contemporary crisis of Pentecostalism, I will survey historical tensions in Pentecostal theology, experience, and rhetoric to demonstrate that Pentecostalism (as it has developed, though not necessarily inherently) contains within it a basic contradiction between the expectation raised by its promise of power, and the frustration of disappointed experience. While the ensuing disillusionment is painful at the personal level, it receives palliation at the institutional level through sustained rhetoric, and the substitution of organizational success for personal disenchantment.

This book is an effort to follow Blumhofer's prescription by addressing this internal tension within Pentecostal theology, piety and practice in light of Martin Luther's theology of the cross. Following Blumhofer's prescription, I will address this internal tension in light of Martin Luther's theology of the cross. Luther may at first appear an unlikely dialogue partner for Pentecostals. He is rarely mentioned in early Pentecostal literature or in current Pentecostal discussion, except as a hero of restorationism. But he is an appropriate interlocutor, first, because Luther actually demonstrates remarkable sympathies of heart with Pentecostalism. As a premier existential theologue, Luther shares a concern for spiritual experience, including the supernatural and the eschatological. Beyond this, though, Luther continues to be one of the most fertile, enigmatic and remarkably adaptable thinkers in the history of the church. Mark Noll chose Luther as a key figure in the history of Christianity, in large measure because of the enduring value of the theology of the cross as his supreme contribution.[6] The final reason I have selected Luther

4. Eric Patterson and Edmund Rybarczyk (eds), *The Future of Pentecostalism in the United States* (Lanham, MD: Lexington, 2007).

5. Edith Blumhofer, *Restoring the Faith: The Assemblies of God, Pentecostalism and American Culture* (Champaign: University of Illinois Press, 1973), p. 273.

6. Mark A. Noll, *Turning Points: Decisive Moments in the History of Christianity* (Grand Rapids: Baker, 2000), pp. 164–73.

is precisely this aspect of his thought. Luther's theology of the cross will serve as a lens to consider the situation both historically and theologically in which Pentecostalism finds itself. What follows is a work of constructive theology that places Martin Luther's *theologia crucis* in dialogue with Pentecostal spirituality and theology. By bringing these two apparently divergent theological trajectories into conversation, I believe Luther's venerable theology will find a fresh milieu in which to make its contribution to a vital and popular form of Christianity. At the same time, as a practicing Pentecostal, I fear that Pentecostalism carries within its pragmatic triumphalism the seeds of its own demise, seeds that can be counterbalanced by a judicious application of the theology of the cross.

a. Assessing the Problem

Despite its global success, then, Pentecostalism seems to contain an inherent conflict. The Pentecostal narrative suggests that once one has experienced true salvation, and fullness of the Spirit, the result should be 'the victorious Christian life'. The corporate story extrapolates this victory narrative to the Spirit-filled community whose collective quality of life, and effective witness will ensure that many will receive Christ in the great end-time harvest that will precede the Lord's return. The failure of this narrative at the existential level, as well as historically; coupled with the contemporary suspicion of totalizing metanarratives makes this matter vitally important as Pentecostalism faces the future. Using Hall's expectation-experience critique, I will examine the apparently limitless extent of Pentecostal promise ('all things are possible!') against the critical reality of Pentecostal eventuality (how those 'things' actually happen). This dialectic, I will argue, exists in some measure in all forms of North American Pentecostalism. It occurs both at the level of Pentecostal spirituality and the popular theology that funds it, as well as at the denominational level where Pentecostal rhetoric reinterprets promise in institutional terms. Whether in terms of 'the victorious Christian life', 'the power of Spirit-filled living', or the success of 'the fastest growing denomination in the world', Pentecostalism as experienced inevitably falls short. In brief, Pentecostalism promises, as Nietzsche said of Christianity, more than it can deliver.[7] At its centenary, it seems that Pentecostalism finds itself at an impasse between expectancy and experience that can be resolved through an application of Luther's theology of the cross, which will liberate it to continued development as a viable expression of Christianity in the twenty-first century.

By Pentecostalism, I refer particularly to North American Pentecostalism. It will simplify the process to concentrate on this one locus of the Pentecostal world, for two primary reasons. First, the shape of global Pentecostalism is only now being probed, and its versatile character, tempered with divergent cultural contexts, doctrinal variances, and variegating expressions, is just now beginning

7. Cited in Douglas J. Hall, *Lighten Our Darkness: Toward an Indigenous Theology of the Cross* (Philadelphia: Westminster, 1976), p. 109.

to appear.[8] The application of this study to the global dimension would be both premature and perhaps a little too daunting. Still, I have little doubt that the approach suggested here would yield useful results at the level of world Pentecostalism(s). Second, the specific constellation of issues confronting North American Pentecostalism warrants its own consideration. Some of these matters are endemic to Pentecostalism, others to the North American context. Extricating these two dimensions from one another is both challenging, and unnecessary, if one seeks to treat both historical and theological forces as this thesis proposes.

But Pentecostalism, even limited to its North American expression, has ramified since its inception at the turn of the twentieth century. While this dissertation is written from the perspective of a much later institutionalized Classical Pentecostalism, it also has in view the larger charismatic community. This discussion adopts the now well-known and still useful 'three wave' distinction first proposed by C. Peter Wagner in 1988.[9] This definition views the Pentecostal revival in North America as occurring in three stages: the Classical with its origin at the beginning of the twentieth century; the second phase which comprehends the splinter groups following the 'Latter Rain Movement' of the 1940s, and the emergence of the charismatic movement; the third development is the rise of the 'signs and wonders' movement usually associated with the Vineyard churches, and commonly referred to as the T Third Wave. Together these three streams form a diverse movement linked by a common worldview.[10] For our purposes, then, the term Pentecostal will remain general, referring to any Christian group espousing an existential supernaturalism, often mediated by 'the baptism in the Holy Spirit' and focusing on 'the gifts of the Spirit'.[11] The cross-pollination and overlap of these streams of renewal confuses the elegant three-wave distinction proposed by Wagner, but while all three exhibit different origins, varying emphases, and distinctive modes of expression, they share a common yearning for spiritual transcendence through pneumatic and

8. A growing literature includes, for instance, Karla Poewe, *Charismatic Christianity as a Global Culture* (Columbia: University of Carolina Press, 1990); David Martin, *Pentecostalism: The World Their Parish* (Oxford: Blackwell, 2002); Anderson, *An Introduction to Pentecostalism*; Donald Miller and Tetsunao Yamamori, *Global Pentecostalism: The New Face of Christian Social Engagement* (Los Angeles: University of California Press, 2007); and Steven M. Studebaker (ed.), *Pentecostalism and Globalization* (McMaster Theological Studies Series, 2. Eugene, OR: Pickwick, 2010); and Robert W. Heffner (ed.), *Global Pentecostalism in the 21st Century* (Indiana: Indiana University Press, 2013).

9. Peter C. Wagner, *The Third Wave of the Holy Spirit* (Ann Arbor: Vine Books, 1988), p. 15.

10. Daniel E. Albrecht, *Rites in the Spirit: A Ritual Approach to Pentecostal/Charismatic Spirituality* (Sheffield: Sheffield Academic Press, 1999), pp. 28–29, see especially n. 8: '[A]mid the many Pentecostal spiritualities there is a *core* spirituality, as experience in and of the Spirit that unifies the vast variety.'

11. That is, what David Martin has well termed 'Pentecostalism and its vast charismatic penumbra'; Martin, *Pentecostalism*, p. 1, cf. xvii.

charismatic experience; that is, a hunger for divine immediacy.[12] And, more to the point of this study, a similar pathology of triumphalism affects them all.

II. The Critical Issue: Triumphalism

Triumphalism is an inherent weakness in North American Christianity, affecting some expressions more than others but still infecting the whole. In order to get a fix on this term, and to gain an entry to Luther's *theologia crucis*, I wish to consider triumphalism as contemplated by Canadian theologian Douglas John Hall, perhaps the foremost contemporary exponent of the theology of the cross as a tool of social and theological criticism. Hall defines triumphalism as:

> the tendency in all strongly held world views, whether religious or secular, to present themselves as full and complete accounts of reality, leaving little if any room for debate or difference of opinion and expecting of their adherents unflinching belief and loyalty. Such a tendency is triumphalistic in the sense that it triumphs – at least in its own self-estimate – over all ignorance, uncertainty, doubt, and incompleteness, as well, of course, as every other point of view.[13]

Hall positions his diatribe against the liberal theological tradition of which he confesses to be a part. While he occasionally takes shots at Fundamentalists, biblicists and televangelists, Hall is chiefly concerned with the inherent triumphalism of mainline Protestantism. Still, his critique hits the mark in describing the totalising rhetoric of Pentecostal/charismatic spirituality.[14]

12. As late Vineyard leader John Wimber, noted, the third wave was not so much 'another development of the charismatic renewal. Perhaps both Pentecostal and charismatic movements are part of one great movement of the Holy Spirit in this century. In this perspective the similarities between the movements outweigh the differences'; John Wimber and Kevin Springer, *Power Evangelism* (London: Hodder and Stoughton, 1985), p. 122.

13. Douglas J. Hall, *The Cross in Our Context: Jesus and the Suffering World* (Minneapolis: Fortress, 2003), p. 15.

14. The totalizing potential of the Pentecostal worldview is illustrated in these words from Jackie Johns. 'The Spirit-filled believer has a predisposition to see the transcendent God at work in, with, through, above, and beyond all events. Therefore, all space is sacred space and all time is sacred time'; Jackie D. Johns, 'Yielding to the Spirit: The Dynamics of a Pentecostal Model of Praxis', in *The Globalization of Pentecostalism*, pp. 70–84 (p. 75). As we shall see, paradigms like 'the Latter Rain' provided a lens for early Pentecostals to understand their place in the unfolding and eternal plan. This sort of interpretive paradigm is not unusual as a means for discerning the significance of one's experience. This continued in recent times with the 'Toronto Blessing', itself a paradigmatic term that created a way of seeing reality, and provided significant jargon such as 'the River', 'soaking', 'carpet time', and 'catch the fire' as the map to boundary-marker experiences.

Early Pentecostal self-interpretation envisioned an end-time revival movement, empowered by the Holy Spirit 'to usher in the second coming of Christ'. This conceptualization functioned at the grassroots level to mobilize a remarkable expression of Christian fervour and missional effort. With incipient institutionalization, the end-time revival became a powerful tool of Pentecostal rhetoric fuelling denominational success. Triumphalism at both these levels forms the concern of this study.

The common posture of Pentecostal spirituality provides a ready example of Pentecostal triumphalism. Reality, for the faithful, is a black-and-white affair. The Pentecostal experience is one of divine immediacy: to this extent it is a mystical experience. The early Pentecostal saw herself as a Spirit-filled witness to the unsaved, as a wise virgin with oil-filled lamp waiting for the soon return of the Lord (Mt. 25.1–13), and as a prayer warrior in ongoing cosmic combat with the world, the! flesh and, often pre-eminently, the devil; a battle she was sure to win, as long as she stayed 'under the spout where the glory comes out!' This tendency to oversimplification and reductionism characterizes Pentecostal spirituality, and indeed all triumphalism, and leads to an assertion of ultimacy for its vision, and a rejection of all that negates its claims.[15]

Eventually, however, such a posture forces a denial of reality. When the stubborn facts of existence refuse to comply with its proposed worldview, either reality must be reinterpreted or one is left to suspend judgement with a simple, 'I don't understand.' This tacit admission that one's theological system does not offer categories for expressing the reality one is experiencing is often held at enormous emotional and intellectual cost. Consider the case of Brittany, a 9-year-old who succumbed to death after a long slow decline.[16] Almost half of Brittany's short life had been taken up with disease. But there was one 'saving grace': her family was devoutly Christian. Between hospitals and healing lines, skilled healthcare professionals, and Spirit-filled, caring believers, she had somehow made it through an intense and rare form of leukemia punctuated with periods of blessed remission, each hailed, with decreasing certainty and joy, as a miracle. Her grandmother, a veteran of the healing revival of the 1950s kept 'rebuking the devil', 'pleading the blood' and 'claiming the victory'. Her aunt, a faithful supporter of several TV 'health and wealth' preachers, secretly blamed her parents and their Pentecostal church for lacking the faith for 'complete deliverance'. Her parents, having survived the funeral, are at the end of their emotional rope, too numb to think about God or anything else. Her siblings, though, the teenager and the young adult, try to

15. Douglas J. Hall, *Confessing the Faith: Christian Theology in a North American Context* (Minneapolis: Fortress Press, 1996), p. 234.

16. Brittany's story is a composite of several actual situations I have encountered in 30 years of pastoral ministry. This is not to say that the number of confluent issues represented here exaggerates her story. Rather, no one narrative allowed me to draw together all the theological factors that Brittany's does. Though as a composite, this anecdote is not atypical.

process all of this theological confusion along with their own mass of conflicting emotions.

Bringing matters to the existential level sharpens the focus. Pentecostal triumphalism, like Hall's broader Christian version, 'instinctively draws away from the sufferer, except where it can play the role of the benefactor and miracle worker, because every unresolved negation calls into question its ideology of triumph'.[17] Such negations undermine the sense of existential immediacy with the divine on which Pentecostal triumphalism operates. Thus 'it drives its adherents to try always to *make* the world conform to its theory'.[18] The result, then, as Hall terms it, is 'world-denial', which in its Pentecostal permutation is masked by a veneer of 'prophetic' spirituality; with a rhetoric of personal perfectionism; or through 'apostolic' systems of authority that repackage reality in more palatable forms, redefining triumph in institutional terms. The Assemblies of God and the Pentecostal Assemblies of Canada both attempted this in the 1990s with initiatives to 'reboot' institutionally, termed the 'Decade of Harvest' and the 'Decade of Destiny' respectively. This kind of 'world-denial' in Pentecostalism, both in terms of its spirituality and in its institutional behaviour will be the subjects of this study, as it seeks a theological category to understand the tension between Pentecostal expectation and experience.[19]

At the heart of Christian triumphalism, Hall contends, is a kind of 'resurrectionism' that animates the inevitability of Christian victory, motivating its sense of 'manifest destiny'.[20] By resurrectionism, Hall refers to the tendency to dispense with the cross as a mere preliminary in the face of the resurrection triumph and, for Pentecostals, 'the power of Pentecost'.[21] It represents the immediate embrace of the entire victory of the resurrected Christ with little recognition of the world of tensions and ambiguities in which the church is called to offer her witness.

17. Douglas J. Hall, *Thinking the Faith: Christian Theology in a North American Context* (Minneapolis: Fortress, 1989), p. 29.

18. Hall, *Confessing the Faith*, p. 233. Hall sees this as clearly in the Nazi and Stalinist drive for conquest as in the Christian impetus to 'conquer the world for Christ'.

19. Hall, *Thinking the Faith*, p. 29.

20. Hall differentiates between resurrectionism and resurrection: 'I use the term "resurrectionism" intentionally to distinguish this phenomenon, which is a blend of cultic-folkloric heroism, New World optimism, and religious triumphalism from the Christian theology of the resurrection of Jesus Christ'; Douglas J. Hall, *Professing the Faith: Christian Theology in a North American Context* (Minneapolis: Fortress, 1993), p. 96, n. 3.

21. One need not follow Hall the entire distance in order to appreciate his critique of Christian triumphalism. In his appraisal of traditional theology's 'God of power', Hall seems to call into question the attributes of omnipotence, omniscience, and omnipresence, and prefers, instead, to think of God as limited, constrained and, in some ways, weak. In his discussion of the consummation, he rejects any concept of apocalyptic judgement, and sees motifs of 'power and glory' as accretions arising from the human proclivity to triumphalism. See ibid., pp. 95–99 and pp. 526–29 and Hall, *The Cross*, pp. 224–30.

Thus resurrectionism propels that peculiar species of Pentecostal immediacy that accesses heaven in the here and now, and focuses on the positive, the victorious, the successful – the divine – without reckoning with the ambiguity of earthly existence: resurrection victory, yes, but still mired in sin, sorrow and suffering, in short, still coping with the human. 'The triumphalistic spirit . . . replaces the dialectical Already/Not Yet with a straightforward Already. It produces a gospel that consists primarily in the *overcoming* of the experience of evil and negation, a gospel whose "Yes" disqualifies the "No" of human existence.'[22] Thus, evil, sorrow, and suffering are dispensed with in the victorious Christian life, along with sin, struggle and doubt. The Spirit-filled Christian is a paragon of confident assertion, overcoming faith, unwavering commitment and profound sensitivity to the voice of the Spirit. Above all, the Pentecostal is convinced that when you 'do your best, God will do the rest'.

Faith placed in slogans, formulae and verses brings the reductionist nature of Pentecostal triumphalism most clearly into focus. The populist appeal of Pentecostalism lends itself to simplistic solutions to multifaceted issues. Triumphalism thrives on its proffered security, its assured success and its steadfast repudiation of any ambiguity or relativity. Hall suggests that the only remedy to this pathology is to encourage 'doubt and self-criticism to play a vital role in the life of faith'.[23]

Of course this kind of critical stance, this attitude of uncertainty is problematic. It undermines what Pentecostalism perceives as the proper posture of faith best prepared to receive its experience. Pentecostal boldness stands in a position of immediacy to the divine by faith. But, is it not, rather, the appropriate humility of uncertainty; the admission of the inaccessibility of the divine; the existential awareness of the limits of human fallenness that locates the believer in the position of divine possibility? This, at least, is the teaching of the Beatitudes: 'Blessed are the poor in spirit.' Hall charges the church with imagining that God shares its own triumphalist assumptions, and as a result entertaining the 'quite ludicrous tendency on the part of moral and spiritual mediocrity to think itself worthy of ultimacy'.[24] The hubris of such triumphalism brings focus to Blumhofer's question concerning 'the courage to raise theological questions for which it may not have ready answers'. Or, to put the question more bluntly within the present context: Is Pentecostalism more than the sum of its triumphalist assertions?

a. Pentecostal Triumphalism in Its Evangelical Context

Sharing the Puritan legacy with other heirs of the Great Awakening, the evangelical genealogy includes a broad swath of nineteenth-century movements including the perfectionist revivalism of Charles Grandison Finney, and the

22. Hall, *Lighten Our Darkness*, p. 205.
23. Hall, *The Cross*, p. 18.
24. Hall, *Confessing the Faith*, p. 517.

Wesleyan Holiness movement, the activism of social reformers such as Theodore Weld, and Frances Willard, and the reformed scholasticism of Princeton's Charles Hodge and B. B. Warfield. It is also represented by the Restorationist stream, beginning in North America with the ministries of Barton Stone and Alexander Campbell. By the end of the nineteenth century many forms of popular Christianity were touting the recovery of apostolic faith, from the radical fringes of the Holiness movement, to the practitioners of healing by virtue of the atonement, and those who shared the premillennarian expectation of the Prophetic Conferences that proliferated in the last quarter of the century. Springing into being from grassroots revivals in various locations across the United States, Pentecostal preachers shared the essential world of thought of other proto-Fundamentalists.[25] It was these movements that, through a variety of combinations, gave rise to Fundamentalism and led to the neo-Evangelicalism and even the Pentecostalism of the present day, which shares similar commitments but includes a more profoundly existential experience of the Holy Spirit, beyond initial conversion. Indeed Evangelicalism should not be thought of as one form of Christianity but as an amalgam of different streams that hold to what has been described as the Bebbington quadrilateral: conversionism, activism, Biblicism and crucicentrism.[26] It is difficult to conceive of Pentecostalism apart from this schema. Thus this dissertation argues that Pentecostalism is that stream of Evangelicalism that added to the rationalism of its original proto-Fundamentalist source an existential supernaturalism that made it particularly successful in the late modernity that characterized the twentieth century. This distinction notwithstanding, both expressions imbibed the same triumphalist assumptions that formed the Protestant consensus, however differently they expressed them. These assumptions, it will be shown, arose from an underlying perfectionism and restorationism that influenced the shape of emerging Evangelicalism.

Nineteenth-century Jacksonian optimism and the growing positivistic scientism of the age led also to a secular notion of triumphalism. Protestantism in general and Pentecostalism specifically were shaped by cultural forces that emerged at the end of the nineteenth century. American intellectual life, which had its roots in

25. Donald W. Dayton, *Theological Roots* (Grand Rapids: Zondervan, 1987).

26. David Bebbington, *Evangelicalism in Modern Britain: A History from 1730s to the 1980s* (London: Unwin Hyman, 1989), p. 3; elaborated, 2–17 (This definition will be probed in Chapter 1). William Menzies summarized the evangelical roots of Pentecostalism in this way: 'This revival, although so startling in some of its implications that it was often referred to as the "Latter Rain," was in reality an extension of common strands evident in American Evangelicalism at the turn of the century'; William W. Menzies, 'The Challenges of Organization and Spirit in the Implementation of Theology in the Assemblies of God', in *Church, Identity, and Change: Theology and Denominational Structures in Unsettled Times* (ed. David A. Roozen and James R. Nieman; Grand Rapids: Eerdmans, 2005), pp. 97–131 (pp. 97–98).

the Great Awakening, developed a perfectionist strain through the 'New Divinity' of Nathaniel Taylor and the rise of New School Presbyterianism.[27] Ultimately perfectionism became the driver of the Oberlin theology of Charles Finney. The transformation of this perfectionism in the hands of Phoebe Palmer and the emerging holiness movement contributed to the unique genre of Pentecostal triumphalism. Related to perfectionism is the emergence of restorationism, an effort to recapture the vitality of New Testament Christianity, by returning to apostolic ways. According to Richard Hughes this took place through a search for early church structures in terms of governance and forms of worship, or by the call to biblical standards in behaviour, or, as in Pentecostalism in the quest for apostolic power.[28]

Of course, other cultural forces were at work and contributed to the formation of Pentecostalism. Three can be named in passing. Progressivism, with its positivist assumptions arising out of Darwinian evolution, and its social agenda drawn from the reform programme of the earlier Protestant consensus made an impact both negatively and positively. Moulded by the economic depressions of the 1890s, Progressives had roots in the postmillenniallism of the 'benevolent empire'. While in many ways the fundamentalism of both the revivalist and rationalist strain was a reaction against progressivism, neither side could avoid imbibing some of its triumphalist qualities. An ally of progress was its philosophical companion pragmatism. While Pentecostals were far removed from the thought of Charles Sanders Peirce, John Dewey or William James, the implications of their thought for American entrepreneurialism, and the rise of scientific management marked the transition into the late modernism of the twentieth century and also had a profound influence on Pentecostalism. While Pentecostals reacted against some dimensions of modernity, they were not above applying its pragmatic solutions to the problem of evangelistic growth. But it was the populist reaction to eastern elites and their imposition of a cultured, moderate and liberal Evangelicalism that forged disparate strands of these movements together and created the atmosphere that gave rise to the Pentecostal revival as one response to the demise of the nineteenth-century Protestant consensus.

These cultural forces will be encountered obliquely in the treatment here, but they were of significance. Each of these interlocking pieces proposes its own form of triumphalism, and the amalgam of these emphases contributes to the triumphalism of the conservative Protestant response to the full-blown modernism of liberal

27. Douglas A. Sweeney, *Nathaniel Taylor, New Haven Theology, and the Legacy of Jonathan Edwards* (Religion in America Series. New York: Oxford University Press, 2003); and Charles G. Finney, *Finney's Lectures on Systematic Theology* (ed. J. H. Fairchild, 1878, Reprint, Grand Rapids: Eerdmans, 1957).

28. Richard T. Hughes, 'Christian Primitivism as Perfectionism: From Anabaptists to Pentecostals', in *Reaching Beyond: Chapters in the History of Perfectionism* (ed. Stanley M. Burgess; Peabody, MA: Hendrickson Publishers, 1986), pp. 213–55.

Christianity. If, in its evangelical dimension, Pentecostalism may yet be shown to have affinities to modernism, it is equally true that its spirituality of immediacy and its pragmatic fluidity grants it great potential for the postmodern world as well.[29] Still, whether at its modern or postmodern interface Pentecostalism carries the pathology of triumphalism, which must be addressed, if it is to move into the future.

b. A Theological Remedy for Triumphalism: Luther's Theologia Crucis

Returning for a moment to the story of Brittany, our composite 9-year-old, will set the problem this dissertation addresses in its starkest terms against the theology of the cross. At its heart, early Pentecostalism offered a simple solution to the problem of Brittany. Nancy Hardesty calls it 'the most vexing issue concerning divine healing'. The logic of healing required that reasons for its failure be found in the person requesting it. Sin, a lack of faith or demonic activity were the three most obvious causes.[30] At some point living in sickness might be easier than getting healed![31] Healing belonged to those who could meet the requirement. In more recent years, Pentecostal denominationalism has backed away from such extreme positions.[32] Whatever the consequences of this distancing, though, it has not led to the kind of theologizing that has responded to the need. In Blumhofer's words, denominational Pentecostalism has failed to raise 'theological questions

29. David Martin speaks of the ambiguity of Pentecostalism as its strength. It can be seen as part of 'a wave of fundamentalism sweeping world religions in a last-ditch defence against modernity. Or you can see it as an adaptable form of heart-work and spiritual self-exploration breaking free of the restrictive protocols of enlightened reason into a New Age of post-modernity'; Martin, *Pentecostalism*, p. 169. The emergence of Pentecostalism is, in significant ways, a function of its interaction with modernity, and thus with modernity's inherent triumphalism. This triumphalism and its Pentecostal permutations must be jettisoned not only on theological grounds, but also because they are an unwelcome posture in a postmodern world.

30. Nancy A. Hardesty, *Faith Cure: Divine Healing in the Holiness and Pentecostal Movements* (Peabody, MA: Hendrickson, 2003), pp. 130–34.

31. According to Hardesty, Holiness healing advocate R. Kelso Carter held that God maintained high standards before healing could be simply claimed. Believers might find forgiveness for sins but still be taken from the world because of them, and many workers 'sin frightfully through intemperance in the marriage relation'; ibid., p. 132.

32. Assemblies of God, *Divine Healing: An Integral Part of the Gospel* [Position Paper] (Springfield, MO, 2010). Online: http://ag.org/top/Beliefs/Position_Papers/pp_downloads/PP_Divine_Healing.pdf (Accessed August 15, 2014); Pentecostal Assemblies of Canada, *Miracles and Healings* [Position Paper] (Mississauga: PAOC, 2007). Online: https://paoc.org/docs/default-source/Fellowship-Services-Docs/credential-resources/Forms-Documents/miracles-and-healing---11-07.pdf?sfvrsn=0 (Accessed 14 August 2014).

for which it may not have ready answers'. In the present case, it has failed to articulate a distinctive spirituality of suffering or an encompassing theology of healing. In the broader context, it has not broached the triumphalism that plagues so much of North American religion, particularly in its Evangelical and Pentecostal context.

Enter Luther, venerable father of the Reformation, and great grandfather to the variegated expressions of contemporary Protestantism. Even the multifaceted Pentecostal movement of the twenty-first century is in his debt and shares some affinities with him. At the centre of Luther's thought stands the *theologia crucis*; the great Reformer's uncompromising declaration of the limits of human pretension and the extent of divine hiddenness.[33] Juxtaposed to a theology that claims as powerful access to the divine, and as optimistic a perspective on human potential as Pentecostalism, Luther's theology of the cross makes a probing interlocutor. It does so by posing its questions at the very heart of Pentecostal pretension, for the central assertions of Pentecostal triumphalism stand at direct variance with the very nature of Luther's theology.

In spite of the broad applicability of his thought, Luther was a medieval man facing a distinctly medieval problem. Scholasticism was a system of reasoning that had arisen through the Middle Ages. It was particularly optimistic about human potential to apprehend and make at least the first faltering step to God. Luther's personal battles with assaults of doubt, terror and condemnation raised serious questions about the speculative nature of scholastic theology. He wrestled with the theological and philosophical implications of these questions in some very pointed writings between 1517 and 1518. These included his famous 'Ninety-Five Theses' (1517), the 'Disputation against Scholastic Theology' (1517) and especially the 'Heidelberg Disputation' (1518). Initially intended as a benign set of resolutions to stimulate non-controversial debate at the triennial meeting of the general chapter of the German Augustinians, the Heidelberg Disputation actually contains the revolutionary building blocks of Reformation theology.[34]

The Disputation's resolutions are often set forth in typically paradoxical form (the good works of humans are sinful, but the threatening works of God are good).[35] The Disputation is broken into two sections, theological and philosophical, the former aimed at the Scholastic system, and the latter at its Aristotelian basis. The basic dialectic that characterizes Luther's theology, however, is affirmed in the four

33. Bernhrad Lohse offers a survey of major interpretations on centrality of the theology of the cross in chapter 6 of his *Martin Luther: An Introduction to His Life and Work* (trans. Robert C. Schultz; Philadelphia: Fortress, 1986).

34. Grimm, 'Introduction to the Heidelberg Disputation' (1518), *LW* 31:37–38.

35. Theses 3 and 4, 'Although the works of man always seem attractive and good, they are nevertheless likely to be mortal sins. Although the works of God always seem unattractive and appear evil, they are nevertheless really eternal merits'; 'The Heidelberg Disputation' (1518), *LW* 31:39, 43–44.

groups of theological theses.[36] Anticipating at the outset what Luther will clarify in the third section, these assertions are best considered as a faceoff between triumphalism, what Luther will call the theology of glory, and the revelation of God in the Crucified, or Luther's theology of the cross. The accumulated force of Luther's argument will be to decimate every human pretension, and all human devices to manipulate the divine in the face of the stunning reality of the cross.

The burden of the first 12 theses is to describe the tension between God's works and human works: the demands of God's law and human powerlessness to fulfil it. These are calculated to demonstrate the bankruptcy in the assertion of self so central to the theology of glory. The highest and best human pretensions performed outside the fear of God only prove the depth of human arrogance and its denial of divine grace. The second section (Theses 13 through 18) is concerned with the limits of free will. While all agree that sin poses the fundamental problem of the human predicament, the theologian of glory proposes that God will surely not withhold his grace when humans do the best they can (*facere quod in se est*). The theology of the cross regards this as a soul-destroying presumption that can only be dismantled when we 'utterly despair of [our] own ability' (Thesis 18). What hope, then, can exist for men and women caught between the threatening law of God (Thesis 1) and the inviting love of God (Thesis 28)? This Luther elaborates in Theses 19 through 24, where he explores the divergent paths of glory and the cross. The theologian of glory searches for God where he might naturally expect him, in 'wisdom, glory, power, and so on' (Thesis 21). Only the theologian of the cross understands that God has preferred to reveal himself supremely where he has hidden, in 'suffering and the cross' (Thesis 20). The folly of the theology of glory is that it twists God's revelation in nature (Thesis 24). Luther explained:

> Because men misused the knowledge of God through works, God wished again to be recognized in suffering, and to condemn wisdom concerning invisible things by means of wisdom concerning visible things, so that those who did not honor God as manifested in his works should honor him as he is hidden in his suffering.[37]

Thus the theology of the cross introduces a hermeneutic of suspicion concerning all human projects that seek to systematize God, to use him, or to capture his power and glory. Luther's *theologia crucis* can be used to critique triumphalism in its broad evangelical form, which endeavours to limit God by capturing him in the Bible, and its specific Pentecostal incarnation, which seeks to tame God's power through human channels. The final section (Theses 25–28) takes up the relationship

36. This fourfold division of the theological theses is followed by; Martin Brecht, *Martin Luther: His Road to the Reformation, 1483–1521* (trans. James L. Schaff; Minneapolis: Fortress, 1985), pp. 231–35; and Gerhard Forde, *On Being a Theologian of the Cross: Reflections on Luther's HeidelbergDisputation, 1518* (Grand Rapids: Eerdmans, 1997).

37. 'Proof of Thesis 20, Heidelberg Disputation', *LW* 31:52.

between faith and works, law and gospel. Here the gospel overturns the very core of Scholastic theology. The righteousness that God seeks does not come to those who 'do', but to those who believe (Thesis 26). Or, put more passionately, the love of the cross extends, not where goodness is found, but where goodness is lacking, and creates it (Thesis 28). Either way, the freedom of divine grace performs what the machinations of human effort cannot.

At this point the Heidelberg Disputation makes its attack the more stinging because rather than probing the basest dimensions of human existence; it makes its assault on the highest aspirations of the human spirit.[38] The theology of the cross is offensive because 'unlike other theologies, it attacks what we usually consider the best in our religion'.[39] Indeed, the theology of the cross is not so much concerned with what is obviously bad, sinful or evil in us, but much more with the pretensions of our perfectionist triumphalism, and the empire of self. What sorrow can be more profound? What realization can be more desolating? – than the moment of recognition that one's entire fantasy of autonomy and self-aggrandizement has been shown to be hollow, inert, impotent. The crisis, though, does not remain private and existential. It extends from the individual to the church, society, and indeed, the world. The theologian of glory 'does not know Christ' and therefore does not know 'God hidden in suffering'.[40] People who do not know the cross, but rather hate it, 'necessarily love the opposite, namely, wisdom, glory, power, and so on'.[41] And so as Christianity itself becomes subservient to the longing for earthly power, godless glory, and worldly wisdom, it, too faces the censure of the cross.

One painful evidence of this in North American Christianity is surely the triumphalism of the Evangelical/Pentecostal church with its paint-by-numbers programmes, its promise of '*Extreme Makeover*-like' personal transformation, and its present-day icon, the perpetually growing megachurch. The onward and upward sweep of North American Evangelicalism is rooted in the soil of the 'muscular Christianity' of the progressive era, and its emphasis on manliness and success.[42] After a survey of American success literature, Robert Kelly offers this observation: 'With Augustine and Luther, we believe that it is just when we are at our hardworking, positive-thinking, people-influencing best that we are at our arrogant worst and farthest from God.'[43] But the critique cannot end at the church. As the structure of one's tightly packed worldview is confronted by the

38. Forde, *On Being a Theologian of the Cross*, pp. 32 and 42.

39. Forde, *On Being a Theologian of the Cross*, p. 2.

40. 'Proof of Thesis 21, Heidelberg Disputation', *LW* 31:53.

41. 'Proof of Thesis 22, Heidelberg Disputation', *LW* 31:53.

42. For a fascinating introduction and its early and developing role among conservative churches see Clifford Putney, *Muscular Christianity: Manhood and Sports in Protestant America, 1880–1920* (Cambridge, MA: Harvard University Press, 2001), pp. 9–10 and 206.

43. Robert Kelly, 'Successful or Justified? The North American Doctrine of Salvation by Works', *CTQ* 65 (2001), pp. 224–54 (p. 244).

cross; the entire house of cards collapses. The easy triumphalism of Evangelicalism leads to the confusion of Christianity with culture, and ultimately with nation, race and class. Witness the rise of the religious right in American politics in which Pentecostals have played an active part.[44] In the 1970s conservative Christians were more likely to be Democrats than Republicans, yet by 2004 most pundits would agree that religion was a significant factor in the Republican victory.[45] But Luther's theology of the cross brings all such collusion into question. *Crux probat omnia*, Luther says.[46] No area of human endeavour, no totalizing system of human device can escape the probing force of the cross. It cuts its swath at the existential, the ecclesial and even the social level.

c. Rephrasing Hall's Paradigm for Engagement with Pentecostal Triumphalism

Turning Douglas John Hall's model to a consideration of Pentecostal triumphalism may create the kind of postmodern dialectic required to refocus Pentecostalism for the future, because as it stands, Pentecostalism forms an excellent case in point of Hall's 'officially optimistic religion'. At the centre of Hall's project is the recurring dilemma of expectation and experience. 'Human life', Hall claims, 'is a dialogue between expectation and experience'. Expectation 'deliver[s] us from bondage to the past', but experience keeps us in touch with reality.[47] And, as Luther says, 'A theologian of the cross calls the thing what it is.'[48] The dialogue between expectation and experience drives human endeavour, and depends on the imbalance that one imposes on the other, at some times with expectancy in the ascendency, at others with experience. Hall sees North American culture as obsessed with the continual promise of 'bigger and better', terming it the 'officially optimistic society'. He proposes that the officially optimistic society offers a series of expectations that cannot be sustained, and are constantly being called into question by the harsh reality of disappointed experience. This is the course of North American triumphalism with its roots in postmillennial optimism. 'Every day and in every way, I am becoming better and better', ran a slogan that became contagious in the

44. From Classical Pentecostals such as John Ashcroft to charismatics such as Pat Robertson, and neocharismatics such as former National Association of Evangelicals president Ted Haggard, Pentecostals have proved to be centrally involved in the Christian Right.

45. Richard G. Kyle, *Evangelicalism: An Americanized Christianity* (New Brunswick, NJ: Transaction Publishers, 2006), p. 168. The sixth chapter, 'God is a Conservative', treats the issue of the white, middle-class, religious power base.

46. 'The cross tests all things' or 'The cross is the criterion of all things' (*WA* 5.279.31; '*CRUX sola est nostra theologia*' or 'The cross alone is our theology' from the opening poem found in *WA* 5.176.32–3; capitals in the original).

47. Hall, *Lighten Our Darkness*, p. 19.

48. 'Heidelberg Disputation: Thesis 21', *LW* 31:53.

1920s.[49] In the aftermath of the Great War, it seemed to be a truism all America could cling to. By the end of the decade, though, the stock market crash reminded Americans of the realistic limits of positive thinking.

The role of religion in Hall's paradigm is to act as arbiter in the essential dialectic of expectation and experience. Hall states, 'Expectancy demands of experience that it actually offer what is longed for. Experience requires of expectancy that it provide the guarantee that evil would not come of what it desires.'[50] In the conflict between the two, religion should offer experience the possibility of hope that there may yet be something new under the sun. But it must also remind expectancy of the limits of existence this side of the consummation. Ideally, religion should maintain an equidistant critique of both unbridled expectation and unrelenting experience. Hall's contention is that post-Constantinian Christianity has failed in its purpose. He suggests, 'Through the reduction and domestication of hope, on the one hand, and by accentuating the positive aspects of experience, on the other', triumphalist Christianity has compromised its opportunity to redeem individuals, societies and the world.[51] Faced with the ruthless actuality of the abortive human project, it becomes the function of the official religion of the officially optimistic society to reaffirm hope within the system, rather than pointing to the eschatological hope that will transcend it. It does this by propounding an experience coterminous with the goals of society. Hall concludes that North American Christianity has '*ceased to be a forum for the meeting of experience and expectancy*'. He proposes Luther's corrective, the theology of the cross as a remedy.

I find Hall's model highly suggestive for an assessment of the current state of North American Pentecostalism. My contention is that Pentecostalism finds itself at an impasse between expectation and experience that can be resolved through an application of Luther's theology of the cross that will liberate it to continued development as a viable expression of Christianity in the twenty-first century. What arguably began as a protest to modernity has instead become one of the most potent purveyors of late modernity. Theological innovations within Pentecostalism, such as its emphasis on Spirit empowerment, embodied spirituality, and experience-oriented theology, have all too easily given way to power dynamics, unabashed materialism and a pragmatic theology of convenience. The question inevitably arises whether Pentecostalism is inherently and irretrievably a theology of glory.

Early Pentecostalism arose to challenge the triumphalism of complacent churches, but perhaps in spite of itself, developed its own form of triumphalism.

49. The phrase, intended to be repeated as a kind of mantra, is attributed to the French pharmacist and popularizer of auto-suggestion, Emile Coué. As June Bingham notes in her biography of Reinhold Niebuhr, in the late twenties every fashionable New York City businessman 'wore a small round gold ornament on his watch chain bearing the pre-Peale positive thinking of Dr. Coué'; June Bingham, *Courage to Change: An Introduction to the Life and Thought of Reinhold Niebuhr* (New York: Scribner, 1961), p. 154.

50. Hall, *Lighten Our Darkness*, p. 21.

51. Ibid., p. 21.

Pentecostalism matured into a particularly successful expression of Evangelicalism, especially suited for the age of late modernity. Its history and origins show how Pentecostalism is the culmination of a number of currents that also nourished Evangelicalism, and that made it on the one hand, a particularly useful adaptation of evangelical piety for the twentieth century, but have in turn, created its own crisis of expectation and experience. Pentecostal restorationism, along with Latter Rain anticipation created an expectation of divine immediacy that raised the bar on an experience of the divine. Perfectionist salvation, absolute divine healing, prophetic anointing, and victory over the world, the flesh and the devil became marks of God's end-time people. But in the ensuing years outside the wildfire of revival whether at Seymour's Azusa Street, at Durham's Chicago mission, or at Tomlinson's Cleveland camp meetings, Pentecostal expectation eventually ran against the wall of harsh experience. One cannot possibly have experienced Pentecostalism whether in its classical, charismatic or neocharismatic forms without contending with disappointed expectation.

How this crisis is encountered is of paramount significance for the future of Pentecostalism. The standard strategy of Pentecostal denominationalism has been denial, and the clever redefinition of experience to an institutional paradigm of success. The cultural changes of the early twenty-first century only exacerbate this condition. Demands for authenticity, less rigid doctrinal formulations and a suspicion of human institutions all conspire to aggravate the current crisis. North American Pentecostalism appears to be a revival movement that experienced exceptional growth in the heyday of the modern era and twilight of Christendom, but is now discovering that its expectation of 'Pentecostal power' and consequent growth and expansion does not reflect the reality on the ground. As a result Pentecostalism finds itself at a loss to navigate the future. Its misplaced expectation, and its easy triumphalism betray a theology of glory that leaves it ill-suited to deal with its crisis of experience: the disappointment of its third and fourth generations; its failure to re-invent itself for a postmodern world; and the resultant reality of declining churches in Post-Christendom North America. By looking beyond its nineteenth-century roots; by reaching past its Wesleyan legacy, and returning to its Reformation heritage, through a recovery of Luther's theology of the cross, Pentecostalism may discover the resources to resolve this crisis, and continue to develop as a viable expression of Christianity in the twenty-first century.

III. The Argument

This work consists of three movements, the first primarily historical, the second, an exploration in historical theology, and the third an endeavour in constructive theology seeking to bring Luther's theology of the cross into dialogue with Pentecostal spirituality, its underlying doctrinal apparatus and contemporary theology. Part I probes the problem of Pentecostalism: how did Pentecostal triumphalism emerge? The first chapter endeavours to establish Pentecostal triumphalism as specific variant of a more general evangelical malady. It does so by examining the evangelical credentials of Pentecostalism and asserting this in opposition to a new conventional wisdom in Pentecostal scholarship that Pentecostalism is essentially a unique phenomenon. The first chapter locates the source of Protestant triumphalism in motifs of perfectionism and restorationism. It pursues this trajectory and concludes that the Pentecostal version is an extreme form of evangelical triumphalism.

Chapter 2 considers the uniqueness of this Pentecostal triumphalism and discovers its emergence in an unabashed sense of divine immediacy. As the movement institutionalized, a synthesis between its incipient organizational dynamic and its radical/revivalist roots resulted in a kind of attenuated immediacy, which negotiated its relationship with Fundamentalism and, later, Evangelicalism. The result of this attenuated immediacy was to soften the inevitable impasse between expectancy and experience, but even as revised by institutionalization, it could not eradicate the tension entirely.

Part II introduces Martin Luther as a conversation partner, and his theology of the cross as a paradigm for revisioning Pentecostalism. Luther seems on the surface to be an unlikely interlocutor for twenty-first-century Pentecostalism, but an unbroken line leads back through Methodism and Pietism, to the often overlooked Reformation roots of Pentecostalism. The third chapter examines this heritage by revealing several areas of resonance between Luther and Pentecostals. These include Luther's notion of the supernatural, the revolutionary idea of the priesthood of all believers, his vivid apocalypticism, and especially Luther's concept of spiritual experience.

These resonances assist in introducing the theology of the cross as a resource for Pentecostalism. Chapter 4 opens by exploring the cross as a critique of both personal and institutional glory. Luther's *theologia crucis* is occasionally seen as dour, pessimistic and foreboding; but this is a misunderstanding. The resurrection, too, is a part of the theology of the cross. A consideration of the reciprocal relationship between Jürgen Moltmann's theology of hope and his theology of the cross is helpful for recasting Hall's notions of expectation and experience in a way that honours Luther, and points the way forward for Pentecostalism.

The final movement brings Luther and Pentecostalism into dialogue. The fifth chapter crafts a lens for examining Pentecostalism through the theology of the cross. It begins by defining the three dimensions of Pentecostal spirituality, doctrine and theology that are essential to a proper appreciation of the problem. It then moves to a description of the theology of the cross well suited to the Pentecostal conversation. By expressing Luther's cross in terms of *pneumatologia crucis* and *eschatologia crucis*, Spirit baptism emerges as the nexus of these two dynamics.

Chapter 6 applies the paradigm developed in the previous chapter to a consideration of three major issues in Pentecostal theology: the nature of spiritual experience, the question of human perfectibility and the issue of the supernatural. By appropriating Luther's theology of the cross, Pentecostalism may retain an optimistic expectation, shorn of its bold human-centred assertions.

The heart of Luther's theology of the cross is a head-on confrontation with reality. A concluding section clarifies the potency of Luther's theology of the cross to address the fundamental issues facing North American Pentecostalism as it enters its second century. Part of the problem of Pentecostal triumphalism has been its successful use of rhetoric to redefine harsh realities. It is in 'calling the thing what it is' that Pentecostalism will find its liberation from the crisis of expectation and experience. But 'calling the thing what it is' is also the key to the continued embrace of that experience of the transcendent breaking into everyday life that is the core of Pentecostal hope.

Part I

Probing the Pentecostal Problem: The Sources and Development of Pentecostal Triumphalism

Chapter 1

''TIS A GLORIOUS CHURCH': ANTECEDENTS OF PENTECOSTAL TRIUMPHALISM

'Tis a glorious Church without spot or wrinkle
Washed in the blood of the Lamb.

—Ralph E. Hudson (1843–1901), 'Tis a Glorious Church'

Here the church is looked on as already cleansed when saved, but not yet perfectly holy, or without spot or wrinkle. So the Lord desires it to go on in holiness or sanctification so that he might 'present the church to himself a glorious church, not having spot or wrinkle or any such thing; but that it should be holy and without blemish', Eph. 5.27.

E. N. Bell, Assemblies of God General Superintendent, 1914, 1920–23
'Questions and Answers', *WE*, No. 216 (27 November 1917), 8.

I. Introduction: The Sources of Pentecostal Triumphalism

Pentecostals intended to be that 'glorious church'. By sheer dint of determination they would be among the wise virgins whose lamps were trimmed and ready for the Bridegroom's coming.[1] This strain of the Pentecostal urgency to 'be ready' and all that it implied for the life of the Spirit-filled believer runs deep in the Pentecostal ethos and informs the underlying triumphalism that infects contemporary Pentecostalism. Triumphalism, I contend, is not an essential feature of Pentecostal experience, though it seems ubiquitous in its North American

1. Typical of the era was the conviction that the church had been asleep for centuries, but that the slumber had now ended. 'The Coming of the Bridegroom and the Marriage Supper of the Lamb was the great theme of the early Church . . . When the Bridegroom tarried, they all slumbered. This is an historical fact. In the Apostles' Creed formulated in the fourth century there is no mention of the Lord's return. The dear believers in the fourth century did not have the Blessed Hope in view because the virgins all slept. They slept centuries long' ('The International Pentecostal Convention, Amsterdam, Holland', *PE* Nos 386–87 (2 April 1921) 9).

manifestation. In order to properly assess Pentecostal triumphalism, in this chapter I locate it in the larger context of American religious history, then in the next I will determine its essence at the earliest stratum of Pentecostal experience, and trace its institutional development historically from there. The discussion takes place within the context of a significant debate regarding the relationship between Pentecostalism and Evangelicalism. On the one side are those who propose a kind of Pentecostal exceptionalism, that is, a sufficient uniqueness of the Pentecostal ethos that it should not primarily be considered a subset of Evangelicalism. On the other are those who perceive Pentecostalism as being thoroughly built upon evangelical presuppositions, but offering a fresh perspective informed by pneumatological experience.[2] One of this book's goals is to provide an analysis of Pentecostal triumphalism as a case in point of the larger evangelical story. A measure of its usefulness will be lost if its insights are limited to Pentecostalism alone. Underlying this assertion, however, is a fundamental assumption regarding the essential nature of Pentecostalism and its relationship to Evangelicalism.[3] A core premise of this study is that Pentecostalism is a specific variety of North American Evangelicalism.

Though understanding Pentecostalism as a form of Evangelicalism has become a disputed issue in the area of Pentecostal studies, this chapter will explore the continuities between the two, showing how Pentecostalism came to inherit triumphalism from its evangelical heritage. Again, definitions are crucial: it may be better to speak of Evangelicalism*s*, just as the global situation has required scholarship to discern between Pentecostalisms. Neo-Evangelicalism as currently experienced is a broad coalition of theologically conservative Christian groups, and while intentionally including Pentecostalism, is, in fact

2. See Kenneth Archer, *A Pentecostal Hermeneutic for the Twenty-first Century: Spirit, Scripture and Community* (London: T&T Clark, 2004), p. 6, who suggests that the former is the minority position among Pentecostal scholars, the latter the majority. My suspicion is that the lines are mainly generational, and that the former position is in ascendency. Archer situates his thesis regarding a distinctive Pentecostal hermeneutic within the debate about Pentecostalism's relationship with Evangelicalism.

3. Evangelicalism is notoriously difficult to define. Rather than considering it as one monolithic movement, the position taken here is that Evangelicalism is made up of several varieties that share a common core. Robert Webber listed 14 evangelical subcultures including both Pentecostal Evangelicalism and charismatic Evangelicalism; *Common Roots: A Call to Evangelical Maturity. Contemporary Evangelical Perspectives* (Grand Rapids: Zondervan, 1978), p. 32. A good working definition is David Bebbington's, which locates four principal dimensions to evangelical self-definition over the centuries: '*conversionism*, the belief that lives need to be changed; *activism*, the expression of the gospel in effort; *biblicism*, a particular regard for the Bible; and what may be called *crucicentrism*, a stress on the sacrifice of Christ on the cross'; *Evangelicalism in Modern Britain*, p. 3; elaborated, pp. 2–17.

antedated by Classical Pentecostalism.[4] Still, both had their roots in the soil of the American Christianity that culminated with the Evangelical Alliance of the late nineteenth century.[5] First, I will raise serious questions about the assertion of Pentecostal exceptionalism. I will then elaborate the broad historical background of evangelical triumphalism, and the specific antecedents of its Pentecostal variety as they emerged towards the end of the nineteenth century. Though revisiting these may seem to be covering old territory, they are essential to uncovering the undergirding restorationism and perfectionism which give rise to Pentecostal triumphalism. Next, I will argue, by exploring its antecedents, that Pentecostalism shares much in common with the very movements from which some seek to distinguish it. I will relate the development of Radical Evangelicalism and Pentecostalism to the emergence of Fundamentalism and neo-Evangelicalism. Pentecostalism, it will be asserted, fits very centrally in the taxonomy of Evangelicalism, and for that reason, solutions for the problem of Pentecostal triumphalism will have significant ramifications for contemporary Evangelicalism.

II. Triumphalism and the Question of Pentecostal Exceptionalism

Pentecostal triumphalism, I assert, is a species of the larger genus of evangelical triumphalism. Its essence, though in some ways unique, and perhaps, extreme, does not arise separately from its antecedents, nor has it developed over time in a way unconnected to its fellow travellers. Considerable energy has been spent in Pentecostal academia to distance Pentecostalism from two other historically significant movements: Fundamentalism and Evangelicalism. William Faupel, for instance, claimed in 1992 that Pentecostalism was at a crossroads. It must

4. Contemporary Evangelicalism had its roots in the protest of so-called neo-Evangelicals against the Fundamentalism that resulted from the confrontation of orthodox Protestantism with the liberalizing religious tendencies of nascent modernism. See George Marsden’s chapter 2, ‘Evangelicalism since 1930: Unity and Diversity’, in *Understanding Fundamentalism and Evangelicalism* (Grand Rapids: Eerdmans, 1991), pp. 62–82.

5. The Evangelical Alliance was an interdenominational group of Protestant denominations, originating in London in 1846, and finding a distinctive American embodiment in 1867. In the last third of the nineteenth century the Evangelical Alliance demonstrated the underlying unity of American Protestantism, until rent by the internal dissent of radical Evangelicals such as the Holiness come-outers, and external pressures such as modernism. The Evangelical Alliance eventually gave way to a more liberal, progressivist Federal Council of Churches that formed in 1908; R. R. Mathisen, ‘Evangelical Alliance’, in *DCA*, pp. 408–9. Radical Holiness revivalism from which Pentecostalism arose was, in part, a reaction to the respectability of Methodist participation in the Evangelical Alliance; Roger G. Robins, *A. J. Tomlinson: Plainfolk Modernist* (Religion in America Series; New York: Oxford University Press, 2004), pp. 14–15.

choose between two 'competing visions:' one seeing Pentecostalism as a subgroup of Evangelicalism, the other as a movement with 'its own mission, its own hermeneutic, and its own agenda', separate from Evangelicalism.[6] The novice to Pentecostal studies may be bewildered by this insistence, because without fully understanding the reasoning behind such clear assertions of independence, the superficial historical connections will appear decisively to the contrary. But solutions to this quandary are not simple. They depend on shifting definitions, and nuanced understandings of the terms employed.[7] First I will inquire as to the reasons for stressing Pentecostal exceptionalism, and then turn to an exploration of its historical basis.

At some point one might inquire as to the use to be made of the conclusion drawn in the matter of Pentecostal exceptionalism. Is the question simply one of historical accuracy, or is there some teleological point that the conclusion serves? Does one's interpretation of the historical data depend on some utilitarian application to be made of the conclusion? Arguments along several trajectories have made use of the notion of Pentecostal exceptionalism, that is, that Pentecostalism is primarily neither a form of Fundamentalism nor of Evangelicalism, but is, at its heart, something essentially different than either. The earliest Pentecostal historiography tended to explain the Latter Rain outpouring with reference to prophecy and eschatology. From B. F. Lawrence's *The Apostolic Faith Restored*, the first 'history' of Pentecostalism, published by the Assemblies of God (AG) in 1916, to Carl Brumback's suggestively titled *Suddenly . . . from Heaven*, published in 1961, the notion was perpetuated that the Pentecostal revival was simply an act of God, entirely discontinuous from historical or social factors, to restore primitive

6. D. William Faupel, 'Whither Pentecostalism? 22nd Presidential Address, Society for Pentecostal Studies, November 7, 1992', *Pneuma* 15 (1993), p. 26. Faupel argues that to understand Pentecostalism as a subset of Evangelicalism is to read Pentecostal history 'selectively' and to abandon many of the 'initial Pentecostal assumptions'. The same issue of *Pneuma* featured an article by Cecil M. Robeck, in which he raises the concern that involvement with the National Association of Evangelicals has 'led to the change or compromise of certain Pentecostal distinctives as [Pentecostals] have become more assimilated into the Evangelical subculture'; 'Stock of Pentecostalism: The Personal Reflections of a Retiring Editor', *Pneuma* 15 (1993), p. 55.

7. Historically, the earliest stratum of Pentecostalism preceded both Fundamentalism, and Evangelicalism. The publication of the 12 tracts entitled *The Fundamentals* (1910–15) is often considered to have coalesced the Fundamentalist movement; and the formation of the National Association of Evangelicals in 1942 formally inaugurated the neo-Evangelical split with Fundamentalism; R. A. Torrey (ed.), *The Fundamentals: A Testimony to the Truth, Volume I-XII* (Chicago: Testimony Publishing Co., 1910–15). But the currents which led to both run deep into nineteenth-century Protestantism, and neither development can be understood without some appreciation of these roots. The same, I contend, is true of Pentecostalism.

Christianity.[8] Clearly the point of Pentecostal exceptionalism in these accounts was to underscore that this was God's movement, and no one else's. However, as time moved on, other agendas also made the claim. Robert Mapes Anderson's 1979 book *Vision of the Disinherited* found in Pentecostal exceptionalism a case in point for his elaboration of the church-sect hypothesis, demonstrating that Pentecostalism could be understood primarily as a movement of the socially deprived and discontented.[9] The remarkable flattening of historical and religious realities made by such a reductionist approach is stunning, but it is supported by an appeal to Pentecostal exceptionalism.[10]

Another example of the ideological need to invoke some sort of Pentecostal exceptionalism is found in the work of Margaret Poloma. In her effort to assess the knife-edge balancing act the Assemblies of God (AG) has performed to maintain intact the tension of charisma and institution, she has emphasized as a danger signal the growing ambiguity that pastors feel between their Pentecostal identity and their self-identification as Evangelicals. The ultimate threat for Pentecostalism, it seems, would be an uncritical drift into Evangelicalism in which case it would obviously have sustained the loss of the charisma.[11] 'These cultural Pentecostals',

8. B. F. Lawrence, *The Apostolic Faith Restored* (St. Louis: Gospel Publishing House, 1916); Carl Brumback, *Suddenly . . . from Heaven: A History of the Assemblies of God* (Springfield, MO: Gospel Publishing House, 1961); Stanley Frodsham, '*With Signs Following*': *The Story of the Latter Day Pentecostal Revival* (Springfield, MO: Gospel Publishing House, 1926) and Frank Bartleman, *Azusa Street (How 'Pentecost' Came to Los Angeles – How It Was in the Beginning* (1925, Reprint, Plainfield, NJ: Logos, 1980). See Augustus Cerillo, 'The Beginnings of American Pentecostalism: A Historiographical Overview', in *Pentecostal Currents in American Protestantism* (ed. Edith L. Blumhofer, Russell P. Spittler and Grant A. Wacker; Urbana: University of Illinois Press, 1999), pp. 229–59 (pp. 229–30); and Grant Wacker, 'Bibliography and Historiography of Pentecostalism (US)', in *DPCM*, pp. 65–76 (pp. 69–74).

9. Robert M. Anderson, *Vision of the Disinherited* (New York: Cambridge University Press, 2004), p. 228. Despite its shortcomings, Anderson's work stands as a landmark piece of social history.

10. Cerillo summarizes a number of the criticisms of Anderson's work, including the questionable value of models of psychological maladjustment and deprivation for explaining the maladaptive response that led to Pentecostal excess (ibid., p. 236). But *contra*, see Sean McLoud, *Divine Hierarchies: Class in American Religion and Religious Studies* (Chapel Hill: University of North Carolina Press, 2007) which argues for the usefulness of deprivation theories, and proposes a new approach to rehabilitating the notion of class in religious study.

11. Margaret M. Poloma, 'Charisma and Structure in the Assemblies of God: Revisiting O'Dea's Five Dilemmas', in *Church, Identity, and Change: Theology and Denominational Structures in Unsettled Times* (ed. David A. Roozen and James R. Nieman; Grand Rapids: Eerdmans, 2005), pp. 45–96 (54–60); Poloma is concerned that 'pragmatic decisions to accommodate multiple services, to make services more inviting for non-Pentecostals, and to deal with time-conscious Americans have produced a ritual in many churches that is indistinguishable from non-Pentecostal evangelical services' (ibid., p. 60).

Poloma states, 'are proclaiming a distinct identity but looking more and more like evangelicals in their beliefs and religious practices'. This is a common concern shared by observers, participants and leaders including Harvey Cox, Walter J. Hollenweger, Russell Spittler and former General Superintendent Thomas Trask, who exclaimed, 'The Assemblies of God was raised up to be a Pentecostal voice. I have great respect and love for evangelical churches, but we are more than evangelical; we are Pentecostal!'[12]

Perhaps the most ideologically driven use of Pentecostal exceptionalism is in the discussion surrounding Pentecostal hermeneutics, which will be considered more fully in the next chapter. In this debate much is made of certain features of early Pentecostalism such as the use of narrative theology, particularly with regard to the Latter Rain but also with its preoccupation with the Book of Acts; the centrality of personal experience of the Spirit, orality, and the function of testimony; and the role of the community in regulating experience and interpretation. Among theologians and biblical scholars who see in these marks of early Pentecostalism the beginnings of a postmodern hermeneutic, Kenneth Archer has made the most complete statement of early Pentecostal exceptionalism.[13] He implies that early Pentecostalism lost its way when, in the period of institutional development,

12. Harvey Cox, *Fire from Heaven: The Rise of Pentecostal Spirituality and the Reshaping of Religion in the Twenty-first Century* (Reading, MA: Addison-Wesley, 1995), pp. 302 and 310. See Walter Hollenweger's chapter on 'Pentecostalism and Evangelicalism', in *Pentecostalism: Origins and Developments Worldwide* (East Lynn, MA: Hendrickson, 1997), pp. 190–200. Russel Spittler claims the period between the Second World War and Vietnam saw the evangelicalization of Pentecostalism; 'Are Pentecostals and Charismatics Fundamentalists? A Review of American Uses of These Categories', in *Charismatic Christianity as Global Culture* (ed. Karla Poewe; Columbia: University of South Carolina Press, 1994), pp. 103–16 (p. 112). Thomas E. Trask and David A. Womack, *Back to the Altar: A Call to Spiritual Awakening* (Springfield: Gospel Publishing House, 1994), p. 25; cited in Gary B. McGee, '"More Than Evangelical": The Challenge of the Evolving Identity of the Assemblies of God', in *Church, Identity, and Change: Theology and Denominational Structures in Unsettled Times* (ed. David A. Roozen and James R. Nieman; Grand Rapids: Eerdmans, 2005), pp. 35–44 (p. 40). McGee, seeing Trask's statement as too great a concession, comments, 'It is this ideal of being "more than Evangelical" that presents the greatest challenge to the denomination as it enters the twenty-first century' (ibid., p. 40).

13. I refer here, not only to scholars related to the Pentecostal Theological Seminary of the Church of God (Cleveland, TN) such as John Christopher Thomas, 'Women, Pentecostals and the Bible', *JPT* 2 (1994), pp. 41–56; 'Reading the Bible from within Our Traditions', in *Between Two Horizon: Spanning New Testament Studies and Systematic Theology* (ed. Joel B. Green and Max Turner; Grand Rapids: Eerdmans, 2000), pp. 108–22; John Christopher Thomas and Kimberly Ervin Alexander, '"And the Signs Are Following": Mark 16:9-20 – a Journey into Pentecostal Hermeneutics', *JPT* 11 (2003), pp. 147–70; and Kenneth Archer, *Pentecostal Hermeneutic*; but also to individuals as diverse as Mark D. McLean, whose seminal 1984 paper ('Toward a Pentecostal Hermeneutic', *Pneuma* 6

Pentecostals first entertained the presuppositions of Fundamentalism and entered evangelical seminaries where they imbibed the more rationalist and modernist assumptions of historical-critical scholarship. For Archer, it is the modernist search for authorial intent and objective meaning from the text which must be eschewed if Pentecostals are going to be true to their roots, and return to a truly Pentecostal reading of the text which places meaning in a dance between the Spirit, Scripture and the Pentecostal community. This, he claims, was the way of the first Pentecostals.[14] But easy parallels between early Pentecostals and the emerging concerns of postmodern hermeneutics are both anachronistic and deceptive. Such comparisons are superficial at best. For instance, Timothy Cargal's assertion that the truth claims of a Pentecostal hermeneutic lie on a higher 'pneumatic' level without necessary reference to historicity, would scandalize early Pentecostals who, despite their narrative theology, and less rationalistic paradigms, had a remarkably literal sense of what actually took place in the Bible.[15]

Often, then, what is assumed regarding Pentecostal exceptionalism drives an ideological agenda. Whether the spiritual schema of a heaven-sent revival; social and historical models of class deprivation; a sociological paradigm of institutionalism; or issues of postmodern hermeneutics, Pentecostal exceptionalism serves a chief functional role in making the argument. I wish neither to defend nor deny the reality of Pentecostal exceptionalism. The issue is far from clear to adjudicate. If there was no difference between Pentecostals and Fundamentalists or Evangelicals,

(1984), pp. 35–56) led the way in exploring the relationship between Pentecostalism and postmodern hermeneutics, and Veli-Matti Kärkäinnen, 'Pentecostal Hermeneutics in the Making', *JEPTA* 8 (1996), pp. 76–115. See also Amos Yong's, *Spirit-Word-Community: Theological Hermeneutics in Trinitarian Perspective* (Ashgate New Critical Thinking in Religion Theology and Biblical Studies Aldershot, UK: Ashgate, 2002); which transcends Pentecostal and Evangelical spirituality to include a distinctly Orthodox Trinitarianism.

14. Archer contrasts the view that 'Pentecostals need to use evangelically and academically acceptable methods (a modified historical-critical approach of modernity) which attempts to avoid "sectarian" epistemological categorization and strive for universally acceptable rationalistic foundations' with a position that 'recognizes Pentecostalism as an authentic Christian movement whose identity cannot be submerged into Evangelicalism without losing important aspects of Pentecostal identity'; Archer, *Pentecostal Hermeneutic*, p. 6. I believe Archer is wrong on two counts, first that contemporary evangelical hermeneutics cannot so easily be labelled 'rationalistic' and second that Evangelicalism is not a monolithic unity into which Pentecostalism is in danger of being swallowed. See also Archer, *Pentecostal Hermeneutic*, pp. 174–80 and pp. 195–208.

15. Timothy B. Cargal, 'Beyond the Fundamentalist-Modernist Controversy', *Pneuma* 15 (1993), pp. 167–68 and 184–85. For an opposing response, see Robert P. Menzies, 'Jumping Off the Postmodern Bandwagon', *Pneuma* 16 (1994), pp. 115–20. Cargal asks Pentecostals to jettison Evangelical approaches for explicitly postmodern methods but without reference to postmodern parallels in early Pentecostalism.

there would be no discussion to begin with. I want, however to place the matter within a historical and theological context, to acknowledge that there is indeed a Pentecostal uniqueness, but that this exceptionalism cannot be simply asserted in opposition to either Fundamentalism or Evangelicalism, but is better seen in a larger measure of continuity with these. In providing a more nuanced notion of exceptionalism, I argue that Pentecostal triumphalism is best understood as a form, an extreme one, perhaps, but still a variety of the triumphalism that has plagued the broader Evangelical enterprise at least since the arrival of the Puritans in the new world.

This approach derives inspiration from the 'Re-forming the Center Project', and before that the work of Laurence Moore, Jon Butler and Catherine Albanese.[16] Under the leadership of Douglas Jacobsen and William Vance Trollinger, Jr, several scholars contributed essays to Re-Forming the Center, contending that the standard 'two-party' picture of Euro-American Protestantism developed originally by Martin Marty, and based on the work of his graduate student Jean Miller Schmidt, does not adequately demonstrate the religious realities on the ground.[17] David Harrell argues that the conventional representation of the church divided along liberal and conservative lines obscures the story of large numbers of Christians, including the African-American churches, the churches of Christ, Nazarenes and even Pentecostals.[18] So, while the Fundamentalist-Modernist controversy provides a useful paradigm for understanding one portion of twentieth-century religious history, it can also become a hindrance to getting the full picture. Applying these insights to the question of Pentecostal exceptionalism may provide a fuller sense of Pentecostal origins that gives place to the uniqueness of the Pentecostal perspective, without necessarily disconnecting it from its links to nineteenth-century Radical Evangelicalism and other proto-Fundamentalists. But first, it will be necessary to locate Pentecostal triumphalism within the broader taxonomy of Evangelicalism.

16. Douglas Jacobsen and William Trollinger (eds), *Re-Forming the Center: American Protestantism, 1900 to the Present* (Grand Rapids: Eerdmans, 1998). The work of Laurence Moore, *Religious Outsiders and the Making of America* (New York: Oxford University Press, 1986); Jon Butler, *Awash in a Sea of Faith: Christianizing the American People* (Studies in Cultural History; Cambridge: Harvard University Press, 1990); and Catherine Albanese, *America: Religions and Religion, 3rd Edition* (Belmont, CA: Wadsworth, 1999); each provide insights to a more eclectic, more diverse religious history than that proposed by traditional interpretations emphasizing the centrality of Puritanism in the American religious psyche.

17. Martin E. Marty, *Righteous Empire: The Protestant Experience in America* (New York: Dial Press, 1970); *Nation of Behavers* (Chicago: University of Chicago Press, 1976); and Jean Miller Schmidt, *Souls and Social Order: The Two-Party System in American Protestantism* (Brooklyn: Carlson, 1991).

18. Douglas Jacobsen and William Trollinger, Jr, 'Introduction', in *Re-Forming the Center*, pp. 1–14; and David E. Harrell Jr, 'Bipolar Protestantism', in *Re-Forming the Center*, pp. 15–30.

III. The Emergence of Evangelical Triumphalism

Pentecostalism's peculiar brand of triumphalism has historical antecedents, beginning with its Puritan roots, stretching through the 'Benevolent Empire' of the nineteenth century, and down to the splintering of the evangelical consensus in the wake of incipient liberalism. One might say Pentecostals came by their triumphalism honestly, for they are simply heirs to the broader tendency as it has developed in American Christianity. Indeed, Evangelicalism is a persistent movement in North American culture, and triumphalism has been a significant motif in its North American expression. While Douglas John Hall traces Christian triumphalism to the Constantinian watershed, the North American variety of triumphalism has its roots in the Puritan vision that shaped America.

Sailing to the Promised Land in 1630, John Winthrop, architect and founding governor of the Massachusetts Bay Colony, mused:

> if the Lord shall please to heare us and bring us in peace to the place wee desire then hath he ratified this Covenant and sealed our Commission . . . for wee must Consider that wee shall be as a Citty upon a Hill, the eis of all people are uppon us.[19]

In the generation that followed, sons of planters lamented the apparent failure of the Puritan dream in sermons that inveighed the wrath of God and read the signs of impending doom in the dire circumstances of the day.[20] Their titles tell the tale. From Michael Wigglesworth's poem, *God's Controversy with New England* (1662) to John Higginson's *The Cause of God with His People in New England* (1663); Samuel Danforth's *A Brief Recognition of New England's Errand into the Wilderness* (1670); and Increase Mather's *The Day of Trouble is Near* (1673), a new, and perhaps the first truly American genre of literature was birthed: the jeremiad.[21] Fear that New England had betrayed its God-given mission may sound far from triumphalistic, but the underlying purpose of such admonishments was to reawaken New England to its divine calling as Elect Nation. Even commercial Virginia was in part defined

19. Aboard the *Arabella* en route to the Massachusetts Bay Colony, 1630; John Winthrop, 'John Winthrop's Model of Charity', in *American Christianity: An Historical Interpretation with Representative Documents, Vol. 1. 1607–1820* (ed. H. Shelton Smith, Robert T. Handy and Lefferts A. Loetscher; New York: Scribners, 1960), pp. 98–102 (pp. 101–2).

20. Perry Miller relates the story engagingly in his classic essay *Errand into the Wilderness* (Cambridge: Belknap Press of Harvard University Press, 1956), pp. 1–15.

21. Perry Miller, *The New England Mind: From Colony to Province* (Cambridge: Harvard University Press), pp. 27–30. The influence of this genre in American literature is explored in James A. Bercovitch, *The American Jeremiad* (Madison: University of Wisconsin Press, 1978). The jeremiad had its origin in Europe, but 'was transformed both in form and content by the New England Puritans, persisted through the eighteenth century, and helped sustain a national dream through two hundred years of turbulence and change'; ibid., p. ix.

by its role as an extension of God's Kingdom. In 1613 Alexander Whitaker, the Anglican curate at Henrico on the James River reminded the Virginia Company in England of their sacred responsibility. 'Awake you true hearted English men, you servants of Jesus Christ', Whitaker cried:

> Remember that the Plantation is Gods, and the reward your Countries. Wherefore aime not at your present privat gaine, but let the glory of God, whose Kingdome you now plant . . . so farre prevaile with you . . . that you would more liberally supplie for a little space, this your Christian worke which you so charitably began. . . .[22] The emerging American ethos is difficult to separate from the notion of divine commission.

In a masterful and wide-ranging study, Ernest Lee Tuveson charted the roots and course of this American sense of destiny in *Redeemer Nation*, where he demonstrated the religious roots of America's role as Elect Nation. As a chosen people, America was to pursue its divine mandate to prosecute the conflict of righteousness (later defined as republicanism and still later as progress) against the forces of evil (the retrograde forces of monarchism, Catholicism, slavery and foreign incursion).[23] The interplay of America's millennial role with the later conflicting currents of isolationism and manifest destiny make for the peculiarly American flavour of what the British called 'the white man's burden'.[24] Indeed, the notion of America as Redeemer Nation resonates throughout its history, with reverberations that reach to the present. Tuveson recalls Henry Steele Commager's words before the US Senate Foreign Relations Committee in February of 1967, that it is a sense of New World innocence before Old World corruption that leads America to 'transform our wars into crusades'.[25] Political affinities aside, one need only remember President George W. Bush's war for the liberation of Iraq, and the repeated post-9–11 refrain, 'God bless America', words that take on an ominously apocalyptic tone in the present context.

This notion of America's redemptive role makes sense in the context of a broadly postmillennial matrix of thought that transcended various specifically religious contexts. Indeed this was the situation that prevailed in the days before the Civil War, with the advent of the Evangelical Alliance, and the so-called benevolent empire that brought Protestants together across a wide swath of denominational interest to bring about the reform of America.[26] That premier revivalist of the

22. Whitaker, Alexander, 'Good News from Virginia', in *American Christianity*, pp. 45–48 (p. 48).

23. Ernst Lee Tuveson, *Redeemer Nation: The Idea of America's Millennial Role* (Chicago: University of Chicago Press, 1968).

24. See the poem 'The White Man's Burden' by Rudyard Kipling, who addressed it as a critique of American policy in the newly acquired Philippines.

25. Tuveson, *Redeemer Nation*, p. viii.

26. The working out of America's sacred mission was more than spiritual, as Robert T. Handy demonstrated in *A Christian America: Protestant Hopes and Historical Realities*

mid-nineteenth century, Charles Grandison Finney proclaimed in 1835 that 'if the Church will do all her duty, the millennium may come in this country in three years'.[27] Americans actively pursued the establishment of the millennium until the twentieth century, when immigration, urbanization and modernism brought about the dissolution of the Protestant consensus.[28] Nevertheless, triumphalism continued unabated, finding different incarnations.

While Finney spoke from the centre of New School revivalism, which was restructuring the boundaries of an older Calvinist consensus, his ideas found broader application through Julia Ward Howe and her apocalyptic anthem, *The Battle Hymn of the Republic*. Howe was no Evangelical. She was a companion of transcendentalists Ralph Waldo Emerson, and Oliver Wendell Holmes, a parishioner of Unitarian Theodore Parker. As such, her circles were not those from which one might expect to find Protestant triumphalism expressed in millennial tones. But by her own testimony, inspired by the grim images of soldiers encamped on the Potomac, Howe chose the metaphors closest at hand for the great conflagration of righteousness and wickedness marked by the Civil War.

Mine eyes have seen the glory
Of the coming of the Lord;
He is trampling out the vintage
Where the grapes of wrath are stored;
He hath loosed the fateful lightening
Of his terrible swift sword;
His truth is marching on.

The language of Armageddon and the eventual triumph of the American experiment were images so iconic as to transcend religious boundaries.[29]

(New York: Oxford University Press, 1971; 2nd rev. edn and enlgd, 1984). Through tracts, temperance and a variety of Bible and missionary societies a network of reform known as 'the benevolent empire' rose into prominence. See Timothy Smith, *Revivalism and Social Reform: American Protestantism on the Eve of the Civil War* (New York: Harper & Row, [1957] 1965); Charles, Foster I., *An Errand of Mercy: The Evangelical United Front 1790–1837* (Chapel Hill: University of North Carolina Press, 1960); and for a critique of American imperialism in missionary venture; William R. Hutchison, *Errand to the World: American Protestant Thought and Foreign Missions* (Chicago: University of Chicago Press, 1987).

27. Charles Finney, *Lectures on Revival of Religion* (ed. William G. McLoughlin; Cambridge: Belknap Press of Harvard University Press, 1960), p. 306. Indeed, Finney imagined that if there had been less opposition and more support over the previous ten years, 'the millennium would have fully come into the United States before this day', ibid., p. 305.

28. Handy, *A Christian America*.

29. Tuveson, *Redeemer Nation*, pp. 197–202. The same use of iconic apocalyptic metaphor recurs in our day at the popular level in blockbuster movies such as *Knowing* (2009); *2012* (2009); *The Book of Eli* (2010); *Legion* (2010); *The Road* (2010); *World War*

American religious and cultural triumphalism found further expression among the Progressives who nurtured the social gospel, the liberal Christianity of the twentieth century, and, surprisingly, an American civil religion.[30] Given the centrality of Christian imagery in the American psyche, secular versions of the Christian victory were certain to proliferate. Both historian Sidney Mead, and sociologist Robert Bellah came upon this stream of secularized triumphalism at about the same time. Mead developed the concept of a 'religion of the Republic' in which Enlightenment Deism along with sectarian pluralism created a quasi-religious political consensus that enshrined religious freedom.[31] Mead's 'religion of the Republic' was similar to Bellah's 'civil religion'. Bellah had proposed that 'there actually exists alongside of and rather clearly differentiated from the churches an elaborate and well institutionalized civil religion'.[32] The content of this public faith was unmistakeably Christian according to Bellah. 'Behind the civil religion at every point lie biblical archetypes: Exodus. Chosen People. Promised Land. New Jerusalem. Sacrificial Death and Rebirth.'[33] Bellah substantiated his hypothesis by demonstrating a recurring religious motif in presidential inaugural addresses.

While Christian triumphalism makes sense in its postmillennial form, and even its secular incarnation, how may one think of triumphalism within a distinctly premillennial matrix such as that which informed the Radical Evangelicals prior to the Azusa Street revival, and the newly constituted Pentecostals afterward? The Pentecostal paradigm was largely built around a premillennial narrative framework at the centre of which was the 'Latter Rain' theology.[34] The 'Latter Rain' was a highly typological abstraction of an artefact of Palestinian meteorology. The term 'Latter

Z (2013); and *Edge of Tomorrow* (2014) with 'end of the world' scenarios in Christ-less dystopias that pit good against evil with varying results.

30. See Marsden's chapter on the 'Great Revearsal' regarding the shift from evangelical benevolence to an almost total repudiation of social agenda, while liberals picked up the theme of 'Social Christianity'; *Fundamentalism and American Culture: The Shaping of Twentieth Century Evangelicalism, 1870-1925* (New York: Oxford University Press, 1980), pp. 85–93. For parallel movements in Canada see; Richard Allen, *The Social Passion: Religion and Social Reform in Canada, 1914–28* (Toronto: University of Toronto Press, 1971) and; Fraser, *The Social Uplifters: Presbyterian Progressives and the Social Gospel in Canada, 1875–1915* (Waterloo: Wilfrid Laurier University Press, 1988) which demonstrates the emergence of a liberal Evangelicalism that led to progressivism, and the social gospel.

31. Sidney E. Mead, *The Nation with the Soul of a Church* (New York: Harper & Row, 1975).

32. Robert Bellah, 'Civil Religion in America', in *American Civil Religion* (ed. Russell E. Richey and Donald G. Jones; New York: Harper & Row, 1974), pp. 21–44 (p. 21).

33. Bellah, 'Civil Religion in America', p. 40.

34. William D. Faupel, *The Everlasting Gospel: The Significance of Eschatology in the Development of Pentecostal Thought* (Sheffield: Sheffield Academic Press, 1996), pp. 30–41; see also Archer, *Pentecostal Hermeneutics*, Ch. 2 'Pentecostal Story'.

Rain’ applied literally to the later of two rainy seasons occurring in the Middle East; spiritually to the contemporary outpouring of the Spirit, and prophetically to the eschatological climax, which would culminate with the return of the Jews to Israel, and the coming of the Lord.[35] The outpouring of the Holy Spirit in copious fullness just as at Pentecost ensured that Spirit-filled disciples would be empowered to bring in the end time harvest by evangelizing the nations before the great and dreadful Day of the Lord. As healing evangelist turned Pentecostal, Maria Woodworth-Etter declared,

> The Lord has poured out the Holy Ghost as He promised He would in the last days with ‘signs and wonders’ following. He said He would give the latter rains of the Spirit before the notable Day of the Lord came. This was to be given to gather in the last harvest of souls before Jesus comes in the clouds.[36]

The assurance of effective evangelization through the fullness of the Spirit spurred an urgent mobilization of Pentecostal missionaries, all equipped with the necessary language tools through the gift of tongues. The earliest Pentecostals understood tongues primarily as a missionary gift and anticipated that the ‘foreign heathen’ to whom they were sent would recognize the untaught languages they spoke. The experience of A. G. Garr and his wife Lillian was not unique. The Garrs were among the first missionaries to leave Azusa, arriving in Calcutta in early 1907, only to find that they were unable to speak Bengali.[37] The ‘Latter Rain’ theology continued, for the initial years prior to institutionalization, as a powerful paradigm for Pentecostal triumphalism. In the decades following the original revival, it continued as a potent tool in the Pentecostal worldview and its rhetoric.

Pentecostalism, then, achieved a peculiar triumphalism of its own, but not independently of its roots in American Christianity. Pentecostalism is a variety of American Evangelicalism, nourished by its common heritage with both Fundamentalism and the broader neo-Evangelicalism that arose from it. The critique of triumphalism applied in its specifics to Pentecostalism in this work can likely be applied in general to popular Evangelicalism, but such an undertaking is beyond the scope of this project. In this regard, Pentecostalism here may be regarded as a case-study of the triumphalist malaise shared by North American Evangelicals more generally. For instance, Pentecostals have participated with other Evangelicals in the last quarter century in concerted attempts to recover elements of fading Christendom, and

35. Wesley Myland, *The Latter Rain Covenant* (Springfield, MO: Temple Press, n.d), pp. 1 and 100–1.

36. Maria Woodworth-Etter, *A Diary of Signs and Wonders* (Tulsa: Harrison House, [1916] n.d.), p. 37.

37. Gary B. McGee, ‘Garr, Alfred Goodrich, Sr’, in *NIDPCM*, p. 660, and ‘Missions, Overseas’, in *NIDPCM*, pp. 887–88. Parham and his followers claimed tongues to be xenolalia (foreign languages). Garr was among the first to contradict this and to focus on tongues as prayer.

especially in America, to see explicitly Christian values enshrined in state institutions such as the Supreme Court and the educational system. The conservative, moralist assumptions of the so-called culture wars have become synonymous with evangelical and Pentecostal triumphalism. The legitimate extension of the basic critique provided here is based on the relationship between the two, which is substantiated by their mutual religious roots and the common historical contexts that gave rise to both. Indeed both Evangelicalism, and Pentecostalism, as one of its expressions, may benefit from a consideration of Luther's theology of the cross.

IV. The 'Physiography' of Early Pentecostalism

There is considerable discussion regarding the immediate antecedents of Pentecostalism, and this touches significantly on the question of triumphalism and its varieties.[38] A geological metaphor may help in understanding the interrelationships of various traditions, and how they blend together to account for North American Pentecostalism. On the external level, one might think of local variations in geography. A drive from Ottawa, to Sudbury and then on to Thompson, Manitoba is bound to provide sightseers with an awesome assortment of formations, and this itinerary covers only a portion of the Laurentian Shield. Sitting on the Shield are a variety of geological features, but beneath them is the vast primeval plateau which undergirds them all. The Shield itself, however, is one of a number of continental phenomena including the Appalachians, the Prairies, and the Rockies, and under them all lay tectonic plates which shift at their own rhythm most often without direct reference to the surface features. One may trace the basic contours of early Pentecostalism by considering its external features: who are these people and where do they come from? But a better sense of the nature of Pentecostalism is to be gained by studying the underlying phenomena. Once one accounts for the vast diversity of early Pentecostals, there are at least four physiographical features upon which early Pentecostalism lay: the Holiness movement, premillennialism, the

38. The classic treatment, and, in many ways, still the best is Donald Dayton's *Theological Roots of Pentecostalism*. See also D. William Faupel's, *The Everlasting Gospel*. A good companion to Faupel, Steven Land's, *Pentecostal Spirituality: A Passion for the Kingdom* (Journal of Pentecostal Studies Supplement Series; London: Sheffield Academic Press, 1993), serves a similar purpose with a more theoretical goal. Vinson Synan's, *The Holiness-Pentecostal Tradition in the United States 2nd Revised Edition* (Grand Rapids: Eerdmans, [1971] 1996), the earliest of these, remains a seminal treatment of Wesleyan antecedents. Augustus Cerillo's historiographic essay offers a useful introduction to the topic. The theological presuppositions of the various leaders of early Pentecostalism and their antecedents, are explored in; Douglas Jacobsen, *Thinking in the Spirit: Theologies of the Early Pentecostal Movement* (Bloomington, IN: Indiana University Press, 2003). Grant Wacker provides a fascinating 'ground-up' look in *Heaven Below: Early Pentecostalism and American Culture* (Cambridge: Harvard University Press, 2003).

healing movement, and revivalism. Beneath these, however, were the two massive plates whose motions gave rise to nineteenth-century Radical Evangelicalism, and to Pentecostalism. These are perfectionism and restorationism.

a. The Holiness Movement

A look at the backgrounds of three of the earliest leaders in the Latter Rain revival is, in itself, revealing in classifying the variety of its surface features. Vinson Synan has shown persuasively the Holiness-Wesleyan roots of Pentecostalism. These are represented by Charles Fox Parham, arguably the first to connect glossolalia to the Holiness category called 'baptism in the Holy Spirit'. Parham had received and preached entire sanctification as a Methodist, but by 1895 had become a Radical Holiness 'come-outer', decrying all denominational ties. After the events of New Year's Day 1901 at the informal Bible School he began in Topeka Kansas, he carried his holiness experience as a second-blessing, and taught Spirit-baptism as a third encounter.[39] Continuing to survey the Pentecostal topography, a second feature of the early movement was first promulgated by the venerable Walter Hollenweger. He has long contended that the global popularity of Pentecostalism is due to its 'black root'. Its orality, and embodied spirituality; its democratized participation; and its supernaturalism are personified in William Seymour.[40] The black, one-eyed, Holiness preacher, and Parham's one-time student, presided over the Azusa Street Mission and represents the African-American spirituality which added its spontaneity and passion to the holy-roller prostrations of the Holiness movement. Seymour came to Los Angeles to preach in a black Holiness mission, under Julia W. Hutchins. When the doors were locked to him after his first sermon there, he was welcomed into the homes of Edward S. Lee, and then Richard and Ruth Asberry.[41] These meetings led to the Azusa Street Revival. William Menzies, and Edith Blumhofer have both demonstrated that early Pentecostalism had non-Welseyan features as well.[42] Overseeing his own centre of Pentecostal revival at his North Avenue Mission in Chicago, William Durham was a straight-talking, deeper-life preacher. In 1911 he almost ousted Seymour from the Azusa Street

39. Synan, *Holiness-Pentecostal Tradition*, pp. 89–92.

40. Hollenweger, *Pentecostalism*, pp. 18–19. For an argument that Seymour was the 'father of Pentecostalism' including a first-hand report of early events at Azusa Street, see also Leonard Lovett, 'Black Origins of the Pentecostal Movement', in *Aspects of Pentecostal-Charismatic Origins* (ed. Vinson Synan; Plainfield, NJ: Logos, 1975), pp. 123–41.

41. Craig Borlaise, *William Seymour: A Biography* (Lake Mary, FL: Charisma House, 2006), pp. 97–98 and 102–4.

42. William Menzies, 'Non-Wesleyan Origins of the Pentecostal Movement', in *Aspects of Pentecostal-Charismatic Origins* (ed. Vinson Synan; Plainfield, NJ: Logos, 1975), pp. 81–98; Blumhofer, *Restoring the Faith*; and under her maiden name, Edith Waldvogel, 'The "Overcoming" Life: A Study in the Reformed Evangelical Contribution to Pentecostalism', *Pneuma* 1 (1979), pp. 7–19.

Mission, and virtually single-handedly instigated the Finished Work controversy that called into question second-blessing sanctification. Durham is adequate proof of the so-called Reformed' roots of Pentecostalism.[43]

This brief survey suggests the early Pentecostal movement appeared to be a catch-all for refugees from all manner of backgrounds. Amid this diversity of place, race and spiritual space, there were some unifying factors, some larger underlying features that connected them all. The first of these is the Holiness bias. In fact, these three leaders, Parham, Seymour and Durham, provide clues to mapping the breadth of the nineteenth-century Holiness movement.[44] Whether Wesleyan or not, virtually all early Pentecostals were preoccupied with holy living. Many of them had already received an experience they called the baptism of the Holy Spirit, though they brought with them varied definitions of the term.[45] Some experienced it through a Wesleyan concept of entire sanctification, claimed by faith at the altar, as Phoebe Palmer taught it, without any necessary immediate outward expression.[46] Others experienced it as a dynamic crisis experience such

43. Jacobsen, *Thinking in the Spirit*, pp. 141–58; Blumhofer, *Restoring the Faith*, pp. 123–42 and Robeck, *The Azusa Street Mission and Revival: The Birth of the Global Pentecostal Movement* (Nashville: Thomas Nelson, 2006), pp. 315–17. I prefer to think of 'baptistic roots' rather than 'Reformed roots'.

44. Much as the charismatic movement spilled out of classical Pentecostalism, the Holiness movement was a loosely connected group of interdenominational ministries united in its pursuit of 'Scriptural holiness' as originally called for by John Wesley. Nancy Hardesty provides a definition: 'When I write of "Holiness movements" I mean Wesleyan Holiness as it was developed in Methodist circles by Phoebe Palmer, Oberlin Perfectionism as it was developed at Oberlin College by President Asa Mahan [Congregationalist/Presbyterian], and theology professor Charles G. Finney [Presbyterian], and Keswick or Reformed Holiness, as it was formulated in England by Americans William Boardman and Mary Boardman [Methodist] and Hannah Whitall Smith and Robert Pearsall Smith [Quaker]. All stressed some form of sanctification, or the development of a holy life subsequent to salvation', *Faith Cure*, p. 1.

45. Donald Dayton traces the emergence of the expression 'baptism of the Holy Ghost' from early Methodist John Fletcher to Phoebe Palmer; and to Charles Finney and Asa Mahan's Oberlin perfectionism; Donald Dayton, 'From "Christian Perfection" to "Baptism of the Holy Ghost"', in *Aspects of Pentecostal-Charismatic Origins* (ed. Vinson Synan; Plainfield, NJ: Logos, 1975), pp. 40–54. Timothy L. Smith credits Finney as the person most 'responsible for the adoption among holiness people in America and England of the terms "filling" or "baptism of the Holy Spirit" to describe entire sanctification'; Timothy Smith, 'Introduction', in *The Promise of the Spirit: Charles G. Finney on Christian Holiness* (ed. Timothy L. Smith; Minneapolis: Bethany House, 1980), pp. 3–6 (p. 3).

46. Phoebe Palmer, *The Way of Holiness with Notes by the Way; Being a Narrative of Religious Experience Resulting from a Determination to be a Bible Christian* [Printed for the Author] (New York: N.p., 1854), pp. 40–45.

as B. H. Irwin urged in the Fire-Baptized Holiness Church.[47] Some had received an enduement of power after the fashion of the Keswick movement in England – power to live above sin, and power for service.[48] The late-nineteenth-century Holiness movement included all these variations, and more. It comprised a wide spectrum of people from the bland to the blatant. R. G. Robins sensitively lays out the cultural map of the movement.

> By the last decade of the nineteenth century, the holiness movement had come to resemble a set of overlapping templates or intersecting spheres. Beneath a firmament of luminaries such as D. L. Moody, A. J. Gordon and Reuben Torrey, networks of lesser-known and often more militant saints moved in asymmetrical orbits, ranging from a moderate region occupied by groups like A. B. Simpson's Christian Alliance to a 'torrid zone' where aggressive confederations like B. H. Irwin's Fire-Baptized Holiness Association held sway. Meanwhile back in the mainline denominations, thousands of beleaguered holiness sympathizers tenaciously held to their denominational loyalties.[49]

For Wesleyan Pentecostals it was clear that the Holy Spirit could only fill a cleansed (read 'entirely sanctified') vessel. Behind the zeal for 'Scriptural Holiness' was a transparent form of triumphalism that entertained the possibility of sinless living,

47. See Robins, *A. J. Tomlinson*, p. 44. Earlier, Mahan had suggested that the reception of the Holy Ghost should be dramatic: 'where the Holy Ghost is *received*, such a change is wrought in the subject that he himself will become distinctly conscious of the change, and of the cause of the same – a change observable to those around'; Asa Mahan, *The Baptism of the Holy Ghost* (New York: George Hughes, 1870), p. 39.

48. Dayton clarifies the difference in emphasis between Wesleyan and Keswick notions of 'second blessing' by terming the Wesleyans 'eradicationists', while the Keswick teachers were 'suppressionists'. Keswick enjoyed a significant influence over many American Evangelical leaders including D. L. Moody, and A. B. Simpson, both of whom invited Keswick speakers to their respective conferences at Northfield, MA, and Old Orchard Beach, ME. While Moody and R. A. Torrey's concept of Spirit-fullness was mainly concerned with empowered service, the Keswick message included both service and holiness, but stopped short of Wesleyan perfectionism. A. B. Simpson absorbed this double-edged Keswick notion of baptism into his 'four-fold gospel', Dayton, *Theological Roots*, pp. 104–6.

49. Robins, *A. J. Tomlinson*, pp. 18–19. While distinctions could be made between Wesleyan and non-Wesleyan approaches to holiness, the similarities were often celebrated. The *Canadian Methodist Magazine*, for instance, claimed that Higher Life advocates were 'rendering familiar, outside the pale of Methodism, a great truth', which Fletcher and Wesley had taught a hundred years earlier; C. H. Fowler, 'The Higher Life –An Entire Consecration', *CMM* 6 (1877), pp. 80–83 (p. 80).

and if a possibility, then also the responsibility of living beyond the pale of human fallenness.[50]

The ministry of John Wesley brought the doctrine of sanctification to centre stage much as Luther's emphasis on justification revolutionized that discussion. But the journey from Wesley's concept of Christian perfection to the Holiness movement's appropriation of 'Baptism of the Holy Spirit' is by no means clear. Debate has focused on whether Wesley's Christian perfection entailed a significant pneumatological element in addition to its strongly Christological focus. In the work of Wesley's younger protégé, John Fletcher, however, there appeared, in a fully 'Pentecostal' sense, an instantaneous experience of perfect love based on a post-conversion reception of the Spirit.[51] In Wesleyan circles, the path certainly makes its way through Phoebe Palmer, whose 'altar theology', steeped in the symbolism of sacrifice, involved a three-step process of wilful consecration of oneself, trusting faith that the work had been accomplished, and the ratification of that faith by testimony. Palmer spoke in highly Pentecostal terms often equating holiness with power.[52] Along non-Wesleyan lines, talk of the Pentecostal Baptism made its way through the Oberlin theology of Asa Mahan and Charles Finney. Timothy L. Smith argues that nineteenth-century New School Presbyterianism and the New England theology began to look and sound a lot like Methodism, only in Calvinist garb, if not content.[53] Finney's 'baptism of the Holy Spirit' was an

50. As early as 1832, Richard Watson noted declension in Methodist ranks, and made the connection from possibility to responsibility, 'If the doctrine of Christian perfection as taught by Mr. Wesley and Mr. Fletcher be true, as we all believe it is, I fear we do not give that prominence to it in our preaching which we ought to do; and that some of us do not seek to realize it in our experience, as it is our privilege and duty'; Thomas Jackson, *Memoirs of the Life and Writings of the Rev. Richard Watson, Late Secretary of the Wesleyan Missionary Society, Second Edition* (London: John Mason, 1834), p. 582.

51. See the considerable (and occasionally acrimonious) discussion between Laurence W. Wood, Donald W. Dayton and Randy L. Maddox regarding the origins of pneumatological interpretation of Christian perfection. Details in the bibliography.

52. Charles E. White, *The Beauty of Holiness: Phoebe Palmer as Theologian, Revivalist, Feminist, and Humanitarian* (Grand Raids: Francis Asbury Press, 1986), pp. 126–29 and 135–40. Dayton claims Palmer's use of Pentecostal imagery may have been influenced by William Arthur's *The Tongue of Fire or, The True Power of Christianity, New and Revised Edition* (New York and Nashville, Abingdon-Cokesbury, n.d.), a phenomenally popular book. For a comparison between Wesley's concept of 'Christian Perfection' as goal, and Phoebe Palmer's notion of 'holiness' as presently available, see Charles E. Jones, *Perfectionist Persuasion: The Holiness Movement and American Methodism, 1867–1936* (ATLA Monograph Series, No. 5; Metuchen, NJ: Scarecrow, 1974), pp. 4–6.

53. Timothy Smith, 'The Doctrine of the Sanctifying Spirit: Charles G. Finney's Synthesis of Wesleyan and Covenant Theology', *WTJ* 13 (1978), pp. 92–113 (pp. 95–97). The road ran both ways, though. After Finney's lectures on sanctification appeared in the *Oberlin*

experience so couched in covenantal terms that it made entire sanctification more palatable to non-Wesleyans. Increasingly, though, the Oberlin theology moved from an emphasis on purity to power.[54] By the time 'baptism of the Holy Spirit' terminology is found in the likes of D. L. Moody and his associate R. A. Torrey, the primary emphasis is on its enduement for service.[55] But, still, the Holiness bias growing throughout the nineteenth century represents one of the continental formations that underlay the diversity of early Pentecostalism.

b. Premillennialism

As late as 1859 the *American Theological Review* could claim with authority that postmillennialism was the 'commonly received doctrine among American Protestants. By 1936 postmillennialism had declined so precipitously that premillennial systemacist Lewis Sperry Chafer could write with near accuracy that it was without "living voice"'. Indeed by mid-century a new form of premillennial doctrine called dispensationalism had become so dominant in the popular evangelical mind that older forms of millenarianism were thought of as novel by most lay people.[56] How this came to be is connected in a fascinating way to the massive transformations North America underwent as it entered the twentieth century – changes that brought about the Fundamentalist-Modernist controversy, and more to the point, the emergence of Pentecostalism. A number of sociocultural changes had upset the postmillennial dynamic, along with some intellectual shifts that threatened to undermine the foundations of Evangelical Christianity.

Rapid urbanization was a fact of turn of the century life. Between 1850 and 1910 the number of cities in the United States with populations over 100,000 increased

Evangelist in 1839–40, Smith claimed, 'the transfer of Finney's [Pentecostal] language into American Methodism was direct and immediate'; Smith, 'The Sanctifying Spirit' p. 106.

54. Dayton shows how Mahan's emphasis shifted from 'Christian Perfection' and purity in 1839 to 'Baptism of the Holy Spirit' and power in 1870; Donald Dayton, 'Asa Mahan and the Development of American Holiness Theology', *WJT* 9 (1974), pp. 60–69 (pp. 64–67). See also John Gresham, *Charles G. Finney's Doctrine of the Baptism of the Holy Spirit* (Peabody, MA: Hendrickson, 1987), pp. 40–48.

55. 'The baptism with the Holy Spirit is not . . . primarily for the purpose of cleansing from sin, but for the purpose of empowering for service'; R. A. Torrey, *The Baptism with the Holy Spirit* (New York: Fleming H. Revell, 1895), p. 15.

56. Moorhead, 'The Erosion of Postmillennialism in American Religious Thought, 1865–1925', *CH* 53 (1984), pp. 61–77 (p. 61) and Robert G. Clouse, 'Millennium, Views of', in *EDT*, pp. 714–18 (p. 714). The best accounts of the premillennial resurgence are Marsden, *Fundamentalism and American Culture*; Ernest Sandeen, *The Roots of Fundamentalism: British and American Millenarianism, 1800–1930* (Chicago: University of Chicago Press, 1970); and Timothy B. Weber, *Living in the Shadow of the Second Coming: American Premillennialism, 1875–1982* (Contemporary Evangelical Perspectives; Grand Rapids: Academic Books, 1983).

from 9 to 50; the number with populations between 25,000 and 100,000 went from 58 to 369.[57] Urban growth was abetted by massive industrialization, and by two waves of European immigration, one peaking in the 1880s, the other between 1900 and 1910. By 1910 foreigners made up 78.6 per cent of the population of New York, 77.5 per cent of Chicago, 74.2 per cent of Boston and 56.8 per cent of Philadelphia. The vast majority of these were Roman Catholic, and a resurgence of anti-Catholic nativism followed each new influx of immigrants.[58] Such dramatic growth was bound to create an overload on municipal governments, which in turn led to graft and the corruption of boss politics. Ghettoization, organized vice and the failure of the churches to reach the city core were all factors that contributed to a process of urban demoralization.

These sociocultural shifts were accompanied by a significant intellectual revolution driven in part by Darwinian evolution, 'the acceptance of which', Richard T. Ely claimed in 1903, 'we must recognize as the distinguishing character of the nineteenth century'.[59] The scientific, philosophical, and eventually popular adoption of evolution had significant ramifications for the postmillennial consensus which had managed to blend faith, science, Bible morality and Americanism into one homogenous substance. Evolutionary thought threw the delicate equilibrium off kilter. In theological circles the upheaval came in the form of 'higher criticism' a means of approaching the Bible as an evolving body of documents rather than a uniquely given divine disclosure. In a 1906 book entitled *The Finality of the Higher Criticism or the Theory of Evolution and False Theology*, premillennialist, and eventual Fundamentalist leader William Bell Riley correctly identified the link between the two. At the 1914 prophetic conference in Chicago, with apocalyptic fervour Riley, denounced 'Higher Criticism' as 'the theological forerunner of the Antichrist'.[60]

57. Howard Chudacoff, Judith Smith and Peter Baldwin, *The Evolution of American UrbanSociety, Seventh Edition* (Boston: Prentice Hall, 2010), pp. 77–78; for a brief consideration of ecclesial responses to urbanization, see Robert D. Cross (ed.), *The Church and the City, 1865–1910* (American Heritage Series, vol. 61; Indianapolis: Bobbs-Merrill, 1967), pp. xi–xiv.

58. Chudacoff, *American Urban Society*, pp. 102–10 and Sydney E. Ahlstrom, *A Religious History of the American People* (New Haven: Yale University Press, 1972), pp. 330–34.

59. As the economist of the Social Gospel, Ely saw Christianity itself as pivotal transition in the process of evolution in a book significantly titled; *Studies in the Evolution of Industrial Society* (New York: Chatauqua Press, 1903), p. 4.

60. William B. Riley, *The Finality of the Higher Criticism or the Theory of Evolution and False Theology* (New York: Garland, [1906] 1988), and William B. Riley, 'The Significant Signs of the Times', in *The Coming and Kingdom of Christ: A Stenographic Report of the Prophetic Bible Conference Held at the Moody Bible Institute of Chicago, Feb. 24–27 1914* (Chicago: The Bible Institute Colportage Association, 1914), pp. 98–109 (p. 103). The Prophetic Conference movement began in earnest in 1875 with an annual conference which eventually settled at Niagara-on-the-Lake, Ontario, and became the model for a multitude of others which were held for decades; Timothy Weber, 'Bible and Prophetic Conference Movement', *DCA*, p. 136.

As the postmillennial dream crumbled, two new ways to respond emerged. One was the social gospel, which traded the old hope of the personal conversion of multitudes for a new, secularized one: the cultural and moral transformation of the social order. 'The millennial hope', trumpeted Walter Rauschenbusch, 'is the social hope of Christianity'.[61] Diametrically opposed was the premillennial view of Princeton professor and eventual moderator of the Northern Presbyterians, Charles R. Erdman. 'The hope of the world', Erdman retorted in an essay in *The Fundamentals*, 'is not a new social order instituted by unregenerate men, not a millennium made by man . . . but a kingdom established by Christ'.[62] While postmillennialism had projected a gradual process of Christianization which in many ways may have looked like what the social gospel envisioned, premillennialism proposed an unveiled supernaturalism, complete with signs in the heavens, dramatically fulfilled prophecies, a living incarnation of evil in the antichrist and a miraculous intervention in the form of the rapture. The emergence of premillennialism was a militant answer to a rapidly secularizing, modernizing world. It gave forceful response to evolution and its spawn, higher criticism, spouting instead, devotion to a literal interpretation of a divinely inspired Scripture. Moreover, it reacted to the urban crisis and the social solutions provided by the new liberal consensus by proposing an eschatology consistent with the social and religious disintegration it perceived to be taking place. Things must continue to deteriorate until the coming of Christ. This premillennial expectancy, social pessimism and escalating supernaturalism became the core of Pentecostal immediacy through the matrix of the Latter Rain narrative.

c. The Healing Movement

The healing movement as it arose in North America after 1870 owes much to both the Holiness movement and the prophetic conferences. Seen in this way, the emphasis on divine healing represents the logical extension of Christian perfection, not only for the soul, but for the body as well, while on the other hand embodying,

61. Jean B. Quandt, 'Religion and Social Thought: The Secularization of Postmillennialism', *AQ* 25 (1973), pp. 390–409; and Walter Rauschenbusch, *Christianity and the Social Crisis* (New York: MacMillan, 1909), p. 106. It would be wrong to assume that social gospellers had immediately dispensed with personal conversion. In this very context Rauschenbusch continues to say, 'To the individual Christianity offers victory over sin and death, and the consummation of all good in the life to come. To mankind it offers a perfect social life, victory over the evil that wounds and mars human intercourse, and satisfaction for the hunger and thirst for justice, equality and love . . . A perfect religious hope must include both: eternal life for the individual, the kingdom of God for humanity'; Rauschenbusch, *Christianity and the Social Crisis*, pp. 106–7.

62. Charles R. Erdman, 'The Church and Socialism', in *The Fundamentals: A Testimony to the Truth, Volume XII* (ed. R. A. Torrey; Chicago: The Testimony Publishing Company, n.d.), pp. 108–19 (p. 119).

like premillennialism, yet another supernaturalist reaction to the incursions of modernity. The Holiness roots of 'the faith cure', as it was called, are not difficult to trace. Dr Charles Cullis, an Episcopalian homeopath from Boston became a catalytic figure in the emergence of the healing movement. Cullis had become persuaded of entire sanctification as an instantaneous work in 1862.[63] Responding to the social imperatives of the early Holiness movement, he opened his first home for the proper care of consumptives in 1864. Cullis' 'faith work' grew into a large network of health reform initiatives including three more consumptive homes, an orphanage and a dispensary for out-patient work.[64] Initially his concern was to provide for those who were refused care within the systems available to them. But after reading the *Life of Dorothea Trudel*, a woman who had operated a faith cure home in Männedorf, Switzerland, Cullis began to practise healing prayer according to James 5. In 1873, following a four-month visit to Männedorf, now in the hands of the late Trudel's assistant, Samuel Zeller, Cullis was convinced.[65] Through his publishing arm, and his faith conferences at Old Orchard Beach, Maine, Cullis propagated the 'faith cure' throughout, and beyond the Holiness movement. In time he had personally initiated an influential circle of Holiness leaders, including John Inskip (first president of the National Camp Meeting Association for the Promotion of Holiness), William E. Boardman (author in 1857 of *The Higher Life* which gave impetus to the British Keswick movement), Adoniram J. Gordon (founder of Gordon College), Hannah Whitall Smith (along with Boardman, a leading instigator of Keswick) and A. B. Simpson.[66]

The doctrinal development of the 'faith cure', however, shows even more clearly its Holiness affinities. Dayton argues that all roads to divine healing in the last half of nineteenth-century America lead through the Holiness movement. Divine deliverance from sickness was a corollary of divine deliverance from sin.[67] The increasingly emphatic assertion of the soteriological basis of divine healing began, perhaps with A. B. Simpson, who claimed that 'If sickness be the result of the Fall, it must be included in the atonement of Christ which reaches "far as the curse is found"'. Simpson called for the rejection of all medical means, if one expected

63. Dayton, *Theological Roots*, p. 123 and; Raymond J. Cunningham, 'From Holiness to Healing: The Faith Cure in America, 1872–1892', *CH* 43 (1974), pp. 499–513 (p. 500).

64. Cunningham, 'Ministry of Healing: The Origin of the Psychotherapeutic Role of the AmericanChurches', (Ph.D. dissertation; Johns Hopkins University, 1965), p. 6.

65. Cullis also came under the influence of Pietists such as J. C. Blumhardt (by his writing), and Otto Stockmayer (personally); Paul Chappell, 'Healing Movements', in *DPCM*, pp. 353–74 (p. 358); and Cunningham, 'From Holiness to Healing', p. 501. For a brief account of Trudel's ministry and methods, see Thomas S. Kydd, *The Great Awakening: The Roots of Evangelical Christianity in Colonial America* (New Haven: Yale University Press, 2007), pp. 142–53.

66. Chappell, 'Healing Movements', pp. 358–59.

67. Donald Dayton, 'The Rise of the Evangelical Healing Movement in the Nineteenth Century America', *Pneuma* 4 (1982), pp. 1–18 (p. 15).

to avail oneself of healing. 'If that be God's way of healing, then other methods must be man's ways, and there must be some risk in deliberately repudiating the former for the latter.'[68] Another voice, more radical than Simpson's, was that of Robert L. Stanton, a former Presbyterian Church moderator, and President of Miami University in Ohio. His debate with M. R. Vincent, in the pages of the Presbyterian Record underscores the widespread interest in the topic. With perfectionist leanings, and having written a persuasive book on divine healing titled *Gospel Parallelisms*, Stanton was a formidable defender of the doctrine. His untimely death in 1885 en route to an international healing conference in London, was brought about by his refusal to receive medical aid for malaria.[69] Events such as Stanton's passing, and Cullis' through a heart attack; and the inability of even the saintliest missionaries to withstand tropical sicknesses by faith alone began to raise serious questions about the certainty of healing in the atonement, and caused interest to ebb towards the end of the century. But among the more radical fringes of the Holiness movement, divine healing continued to flourish.[70]

The Christian 'divine healing movement' did not arise in a historical vacuum. It must be set in the context of incipient high modernity and the rise of the sciences, and situated within the intersecting matrices of a proto-holistic health movement and a growing emphasis on spiritual healing techniques.[71] Medicine, as practised in the republic, had a questionable reputation connected to therapies of uncertain value such as bloodletting, purgatives and emetics. As medicine increasingly came into its own as a scientific discipline, through the nineteenth century the image of the physician was recast from a shadowy figure of some public disrepute to white-robed doctor as icon of the marvels of modern science. Several protest movements arose throughout the nineteenth century as a reaction

68. A. B. Simpson, *The Gospel of Healing, Revised Edition* (Harrisburg, PA: Christian Publications, [1915] n.d.), pp. 32 and 68.

69. Cunningham, 'From Holiness to Healing', p. 506.

70. Dayton, 'Evangelical Healing', p. 16.

71. Essentially, the thesis of Raymond Cunningham's 1965 Johns Hopkins doctoral dissertation 'Ministry of Healing', is that the emergence of a fully Christian field of pastoral psychology can be traced back to Christian Science, one of the plethora of mind cure techniques that flourished in the nineteenth century; but for more on these healing techniques, see also; James William Opp, *The Lord for the Body: Religion, Medicine, and Protestant Faith Healing in Canada, 1880–1930* (Montreal and Kingston: McGill-Queen's University Press, 2005), and standard treatments of medical development in the nineteenth century such as; William G. Rothstein, *American Physicians in the Nineteenth Century: From Sects to Science* (Baltimore: Johns Hopkins University Press, [1972] 1992), and John S. Haller, *American Medicine in Transition, 1840–1910* (Urbana: University of Illinois Press, 1981); P. S. Brown, 'Nineteenth Century American Health Reformers and the Early Nature Cure Movement in Britain', *MH* 32 (1988), pp. 174–94, adds a fascinating chapter to the story with his discussion of the influences of this movement on the emergence of British natural health practice.

to the professionalization of medicine, as well as an anti-intellectual response to the scientism of modernity.[72] Botanist and entrepreneur Samuel Thomson created, in the late 1820s and 1830s, a network of Friendly Botanical Societies that propagated his programme of botanical medicine, particularly among the frontier population, and much to the consternation of the medical establishment.[73] With New School modifications to the older Calvinist consensus, notions of divine benevolence increasingly displaced Calvinistic concepts of passive resignation which read physical affliction as divinely ordained. This translated into what historian James Whorton calls a 'physical Arminianism': the idea that health was the divine will, and that humans had a greater responsibility to keep healthy and to expect divine help in the process.[74] Coincident with Thomson was Sylvester Graham, a Presbyterian minister, who became known for his advocacy of fresh air, sexual continence, the drinking of water, and a healthy diet, including vegetables, and grains, particularly as prepared in the cracker that bears his name.[75] The perfectionism of 'physical Arminianism' was exemplified by Graham and in the next generation it was followed by Seventh Day Adventist John Harvey Kellogg, whose boundless pursuit of health therapies resulted, among other things, in the now famous 'corn flake'.[76]

For prosperous urban populations, homeopathy formed a more professional response to the scepticism concerning medical science. Cullis, of course, was a homeopath but the late nineteenth century saw a blossoming of homeopathic arts, again to the chagrin of medical doctors.[77] The intersection between the

72. Cunningham, 'Ministry of Healing', p. 2. Whorton, mentions the rise of Jacksonian anti-intellectualism along with the disdain of professional physicians; James C. Whorton, *Nature Cures: The History of Alternative Medicine in America* (New York: Oxford University Press, 2002), p. 34.

73. Thomson represented a kind of populist reaction. Rothstein, *American Physicians*, pp. 125–51. See also chapter 2 in Whorton, *Nature Cures*, pp. 25–48.

74. 'Physical Arminianism', a term coined by Whorton, was 'a belief that bodily salvation might be open to all who struggled to win it, and that disease and early death were an ineradicable part of the earthly passage'; James C. Whorton, *Crusaders for Fitness: The History of American Health Reformers* (Princeton: Princeton University Press, 1984), p. 15. For the tension between this view and a Calvinistic fatalism with regard to disease, see ibid., p. 30.

75. Hardesty, *Faith Cure*, p. 3; and Rothstein, *American Physicians*, pp. 159–60.

76. For Kellogg's close relationship with mentor, and Adventist prophet, Ellen G. White, see; Ronald L. Numbers, 'Sex, Science and Salvation: The Sexual Advice of Ellen G. White and William Harvey Kellogg', in *Right-Living: An Anglo-American Tradition of Self-Help Medicine and Hygiene* (ed. Charles E. Rosenberg; Baltimore: Johns Hopkins University Press, 2003), pp. 206–26; and Ronald L. Numbers, *Prophetess of Health: A Study of Ellen G. White, Third Edition* (Grand Rapids: Eerdmans, 2008), pp. 177–83, for White's patronage of Kellogg's work.

77. Rothstein, *American Physicians*, pp. 152–74.

spiritual, psychological and physiological spheres created a unique opportunity for divine healing in the Christian sense and a variety of other mental, holistic and spiritualistic approaches. Boston, the home of Charles Cullis and Adoniram J. Gordon, was also the centre of Mary Baker Eddy's Christian Science.[78] Opp, whose interest is in the body itself and its historical significance, comments:

> Instead of conceding the body as simply answerable to the physical laws of medical science, faith healing redeemed it as a site for experiencing the divine.
>
> The reconstruction of the body as being 'naturally' infused with the divine drew upon a variety of contemporary discourses, including, but not restricted to: holiness, perfectionism, health reform and homeopathy.[79]

In this environment it was to be expected that genres of mental healing such as theosophy, New Thought and Christian Science would emerge as alternatives to the evangelically oriented divine healing movement.[80] All, however, shared a common notion of human perfectibility, that is, the capacity to cooperate with divine principles to effect 'divine health'.

While the emphasis on divine healing began to wane in the 1890s, having promised much more than it could deliver, the more radical segments of the Holiness movement continued to pursue its elusive aspirations. Though somewhat tempered in Simpson's Alliance, it continued as part of his fourfold gospel. And among the more alienated sections of Wesleyan Holiness, it continued as a focus, indeed a rallying cry, along with premillennialism, in spite of restrictions in the National Holiness Association, and resistance from the increasingly sophisticated denominational Methodism of the urban establishment.[81] When early Pentecostalism took up these doctrines, it had not so much rediscovered them, as repackaged them within the third-blessing wrapper.

78. For example, 'Gordon worked out his teachings on healing in dialogue with the emerging "Christian Science" of Mary Baker Eddy, but he clearly shared most features of the Holiness ethos'; Dayton 'Evangelical Healing', p. 13.

79. Opp, *The Lord for the Body*, p. 33. Rather than seeing divine healing at loggerheads with the ascendency of medical science, Opp suggests that 'divine healing emerged at an important historical disjuncture between medical pluralism, which allowed religious and medical understandings of the body to inform and reinforce each other, and the therapeutic revolution, which transformed the role of medicine in society' (ibid., p. 34).

80. Ibid., p. 33.

81. Jones illustrates this alienation in the ministry of Holiness leader Martin Wells Knapp whose prospective disaffection with the Methodist Episcopal Church and the National Association led him to found the International Holiness Union and Prayer League, and the International Apostolic Holiness Union, associations that led to the formation of the Pilgrim Holiness Church; Jones, *Perfectionist Persuasion*, pp. 101–5.

d. Revivalism

The last of the four geological formations upon which the early Pentecostal movement stands is the revivalist tradition which flows deep and long in American religious historiography.[82] In fact the study of revivalism and religious awakenings has led to extensive debate, and a publishing bonanza.[83] The exploration of religious awakening as a widespread phenomenon has led to the investigation of revival, its local expression, and an inquiry into the role of human agency in what, at the time of Edwards, was certainly regarded as a sovereign, sudden and 'surprising work of God'.[84] Studies such as Harry Stout's account of George Whitefield, Michael Crawford's *Seasons of Grace* and Frank Lambert's *Inventing the 'Great Awakening'* all examine the human manufacture, promotion and 'branding' of 'revival' through affective preaching, the innovative use of the media and new forms of worship. Throughout the nineteenth century a steady Arminianizing, or perhaps, better, Methodizing of the Puritan roots of Protestant America proceeded apace.[85]

82. Indeed Dolan has even explored the Roman Catholic adoption of revivalistic techniques in the nineteenth century in the fascinating work; Jay Dolan, *Catholic Revivalism: The American Experience, 1830–1900* (Notre Dame, IN: University of Notre Dame Press, 1978).

83. So says Jerald Brauer, 'Revivalism Revisited', *JR* 77 (1997), pp. 268–77 (p. 268). Brauer claims no other topic in the study of religion has received such treatment from American scholars, except the topic of 'Jesus'. This should alert us to the deeper significance of revivalism, as an underlying factor in the development of American spirituality. In 1983, the pages of *Sociological Analysis* featured a symposium, edited by Roger O'Toole, discussing the social and quantitative basis for the assertion that American history has been punctuated by seasons of spiritual revitalization. The lively debate in the 'Symposium on Religious Awakenings' raises significant methodological and definitional issues regarding the nature of revival, and its very existence; Roger O'Toole (ed.), 'Symposium on Religious Awakenings', *SA* 44 (1983), pp. 81–122. The issues in this debate are still open to question, and discussion has continued. See Jon Butler, 'Enthusiasm Described and Decried: The Great Awakening as Interpretative Fiction', *American History* 69 (1982), pp. 305–25; Frank Lambert, *Inventing the 'Great Awakening'* (Princeton, NJ: Princeton University Press, 1999); and Thomas Kidd, *The Great Awakening*.

84. Mark A. Noll, *The Rise of Evangelicalism: The Age of Edwards, Whitefield and the Wesleys* (A History of Evangelicalism: People, Movements and Ideas in the English-Speaking World; Downers Grove: InterVarsity, 2003), pp. 141–42. See classic treatments in Bernard Weisberger, *They Gathered at the River: The Story of the Great Revivalists and Their Impact upon Religion in America* (Boston and Toronto: Little, Brown and Company, 1958); Smith, *Revivalism and Social Reform*; and William G. McLoughlin, *Revivals, Awakenings, and Reform: An Essay on Religion and Social Change in America, 1607–1977* (Chicago History of American Religion; Chicago: University of Chicago Press, 1978); and the more recent Keith J. Hardman, *Seasons of Refreshing: Evangelism and Revivals in America* (Grand Rapids: Baker, 1994).

85. The earliest use of this term that I have located is, Melvin E. Dieter, *The Holiness Revival of the Nineteenth Century* (Studies in Evangelicalism, No. 1; Metuchen, NJ:

The place of the human element was increasingly acknowledged and even advanced. Revival as it took place at Cane Ridge, Kentucky in 1801, in Rochester in 1830, and in New York in 1857 looked considerably and increasingly different than it did in Northampton in 1733. The journey from Edwards' New Light Calvinism to Finney's New Measures made significant changes in the self-perception of revivalists, and their understanding of what is taking place in revival.[86] The novel innovation of the First Great Awakening was conversionist expectation; an awareness of the necessity of 'the new birth'. While in Edwards' day, the process of conversion seemed a long, tortured affair, the modifications brought on by frontier Methodists and Baptists, made short work of conviction and demanded conversion now. By the time conversionism was being proclaimed by Finney, it could be reduced to an intellectual assent to the facts of the gospel, and a volitional determination to act accordingly.[87]

These differences between Edwards and Finney are made clear in a comparison of their definitions of revival, the chief means of amassing conversions. Edwards, who experienced an intense season of about 300 conversions in a 6-month period between 1734 and 1735, claimed that

> This seems to have been a very *extraordinary* dispensation of providence; God has in many respects gone out of, and much beyond, his usual and ordinary way. The work in this town, and some others about us, has been extraordinary on account of the *universality* of it . . .
>
> This dispensation has also appeared very extraordinary in the numbers of those on whom we have reason to hope it has had a saving effect . . .
>
> This has also appeared to be a very extraordinary dispensation, in that the Spirit of God has so much extended not only his awakening, but regenerating influences, both to elderly persons, and also to those who are very young. It has been heretofore rarely heard of, that any were converted past middle age; but now we have the same ground to think, that *many such* have at this time been savingly changed, as that *others* have been so in more early years . . .
>
> God has also seemed to have gone out of his usual way, in the quickness of his work, and the swift progress His Spirit has made in his operations on the hearts of many . . .

Scarecrow, Press, 1980); and Melvin E. Dieter, 'The Development of Nineteenth Century Holiness Theology', *WTJ* 20 (1985), pp. 61–77 (p. 65). Conforti also uses the term a number of times, see; Joseph Conforti, *Jonathan Edwards, Religious Tradition, and American Culture* (Chapel Hill: University of North Carolina Press, 1993).

86. For a nuanced discussion see Sweeney, *Nathaniel Taylor*. See also Conforti on 'The Edwardsian Revivalistic Tradition from the New Divinity to New Measures', in *Jonathan Edwards*, pp. 11–35.

87. Finney claimed, 'When an individual actually *chooses* to obey God, he is a Christian'; *Lectures on Revival*, p. 374.

> God's work has also appeared very extraordinary in the degrees of his influences; in the degrees both of awakening and conviction, and also of saving light, love, and joy, that many have experienced. It has also been very extraordinary in the extent of it, and its being so swiftly propagated from town to town.[88]

While the features Edwards described were not substantially different in Finney's day, Edwards' definition makes clear who was perceived as the main actor in revival. While the Great Awakening saw itself as dependent on divine sovereignty, and supernatural agency, by 1833, when he wrote his Revival Lectures, Finney's definition placed responsibility squarely on human shoulders.

> [A revival] consists entirely in the *right exercise* of the powers of nature. It is just that and nothing else. When mankind become religious, they are not *enabled* to put forth exertions which they were unable before to put forth. They only exert powers they had before, in a different way, and use them for the glory of God . . .
>
> [A revival] is not a miracle, or dependent on a miracle, in any sense. It is a purely philosophical result of the right use of the constituted means – as much so as any other effect produced by the application of means.[89]

The distinction between these two approaches, even though both depended in some way on the mystery of joint divine and human agency; makes the difference between what Iain Murray has called 'revival' and 'revivalism'.[90] Murray claims that with the frontier camp meeting revivals of the early 1800s there emerged a more human-centred appeal to personal volition as the ultimate arbiter of spiritual matters. The camp-meeting, as it degenerated from an annual communion-season gathering of scattered churches into an unbridled, frenzied evangelistic event, had, itself, become one of the means of the production of revivals, or in Murray's terms, a tool of revivalism.[91] Emotionalism, physical manifestations, and supremely, altar

88. Johathan Edwards, 'A Faithful Narrative', in *Jonathan Edwards, The Great Awakening* (ed. C. C. Goen; in *The Works of Jonathan Edwards, Volume 4* (ed. John E. Smith; New Haven: Yale University Press, 1972), pp. 99–211.

89. Finney, *Lectures on Revival*, p. 13.

90. Murray contends that after 1860, what had formerly been seen as divinely granted '"seasons of revival" became "revival meetings". Instead of being "surprising" they might now be even announced in advance, and whereas no one in the previous century had known of ways to secure a revival, a system was now popularized by "revivalists" which came near to guaranteeing results'; Iain Murray, *Revival and Revivalism: The Making and Marring of American Evangelicalism, 1750–1858* (Edinburgh: Banner of Truth, 1994), p. xviii.

91. For the annual 'communion gathering' background to camp-meetings; see Leigh E. Schmidt, *Holy Fairs: Scotland and the Making of American Revivalism, Second Edition* (Princeton: Princeton University Press, 2001); for background on frontier camp meetings;

calls, were innovations designed to raise spiritual concern and to ‘separate the penitents . . . from the congregation so that they could be made more easily and more intensely subject to the psychological and social pressures of the minister and of the community of the converted’.[92] This Methodized revivalism became the means of propagating both the New School non-Wesleyan Holiness movement and the Arminian Wesleyan movement as it became enshrined in the National Camp-Meeting Association for the Promotion of Holiness which formed in 1867.[93]

Though the Holiness movement had experienced the genteel hospitality of Phoebe Palmer’s parlour at her ‘Tuesday Meetings for the Promotion of Holiness’, larger, well-organized, revivalistic meetings were also a part of her ministry. Palmer believed God blessed her meetings simply because she employed God’s methods.[94] As the Holiness movement became increasingly differentiated from established Methodism, however, its expression took on progressively more demonstrative manifestations. After 1867 Holiness revivalism adapted an institutionalized form of the camp meeting. In many ways, camp meetings looked and sounded like Azusa Pentecostalism. Dieter captures the ethos movingly, summing it up as a ‘glorious confusion’.[95] The tone of Holiness revivalism was one of spiritual vitality, experiential focus and agitated expectation. In this kind of environment, ecstatic signs were to be expected. Vinson Synan reported the acceleration of reports of glossolalia in Holiness literature after 1890. These took place primarily on the periphery of the movement, among predominantly rural populations, and the increasingly radicalized fringes, such as the Fire-Baptized Holiness Association.[96]

Towards the end of the century, Dwight Lyman Moody became the acknowledged heir of the American revivalist tradition.[97] Moody’s meetings

see Paul K. Conklin, *Cane Ridge: America’s Pentecost* (Curti Lecture Series; Madison: University of Wisconsin Press, 1990); and Ellen Eslinger, *Citizens of Zion: The Social Origins of Camp Meeting Revivalism* (Knoxville: University of Tennessee Press, 1999).

92. Quoted words; Richard Carwardine, *Transatlantic Revivalism: Popular Evangelicalism in Britain and America, 1790–1865* (Studies in Evangelical History and Theology; London: Paternoster, [1978] 2007), p. 13; but see also; Murray, *Revival and Revivalism*, pp. 183–87.

93. Holiness historian Melvin E. Dieter proposes that a full understanding of the ‘American Holiness Movement’ requires not only a grasp of the Wesleyan roots, but of the American roots as well, which he locates in the Edwardsian tradition, and Oberlin perfectionism; Dieter, *Holiness Revival*, pp. 18–23.

94. White, *Beauty of Holiness*. For a description of the Tuesday Meetings, see pp. 161–67; for a discussion of Palmer’s revival methodology, and her position as a transitional leader between Finney and Moody, see pp. 167–86.

95. Dieter’s description is found in *Holiness Revival*, p. 114.

96. Synan, *The Holiness-Pentecostal Tradition in the United States 2nd Revised Edition* (Grand Rapids: Eerdmans, [1971] 1996), pp. 108–11.

97. Findlay charts the rise of the ‘professional revivalist’ as an impassioned lay person, close to the people, with an emotive message from circuit riders, and Baptist farmer-preachers, leading to Finney as the model for appreciating Moody; James F. Findlay Jr,

were the culminating result of a closely coordinated system of fund-raising with Christian capitalists, interdenominational networking and carefully cultivated public relations campaigns. Moody had no reservations about applying business principles to the business of revivalism. Like the promoter he was, he instructed his advance teams to create 'a spirit of excitement among the people' so that they might 'expect a blessing of unusual magnitude'. Moody did this by rallying the churches behind him, but he was not beyond using the press, or advertising to market his message as well. Indeed, credibility with the press seemed dependent on good relations with the local churches. He recognized that increasingly in a newly urbanized world, the gospel was in direct competition with secular amusements such as the theatre and other leisure recreations, and that the press was essential to his business strategy. Clearly, there were critics to this apparently newfangled merchandising of the gospel. 'This is the age of advertisement', Moody remonstrated, 'and you have to take your chance'.[98] But as Harry Stout demonstrated in his biography of George Whitefield, marketing use of the print media was a growing phenomenon over a hundred years earlier.[99] As Moody put it, 'It seems to me a good deal better to advertise and have a full house, than to preach to empty pews.'[100] His well-oiled machine brought him impressive success both in North America and Britain.

Pentecostalism imbibed deeply of both these strains of revivalism. It would be simplistic to assume that only the Radical Holiness ethos was observable in the early Pentecostal movement, which it surely was. In many ways Azusa Street, Bethel Bible School in Topeka, Kansas, and the 1908 General Assembly of the Church of God where A. J. Tomlinson received the baptism he had sought for a full year were all extensions of Holiness revivalism. But the savvy entrepreneurialism of Moody also left its mark, ultimately to be displayed in the dazzling crusades of Aimee Semple McPherson, but also in the earlier ministry of Maria Woodworth Etter. Etter had enjoyed wide popularity as a healing revivalist, especially in Holiness circles, before experiencing Pentecost. Both experiential and pragmatic aspects would mark the emergence of Pentecostalism indelibly.

Dwight .L. Moody: American Evangelist, 1837–1899 (Grand Rapids: Baker, [1969] 1973), pp. 136–45.

98. Moody's words are found in; Bruce J. Evensen, *God's Man for the Gilded Age: D.L. Moody and the Rise of Modern Mass Evangelism* (New York: Oxford University Press, 2003), pp. 21 and 25–27. Evensen is particularly concerned to show the partnership between revivalism and the media; ibid., p. 12.

99. Stout invites us to consider Whitefield's innovative use of publicity, the New England press, and even controversy, to support his ministry; Harry S. Stout, *The Divine Dramatist: George Whitfield and the Rise of Modern Evangelism* (Grand Rapids: Eerdmans, 1991), pp. 113–17.

100. Evensen, *God's Man*, p. 25.

V. The Methodization of American Protestantism

The Methodization of American Protestantism had been substantially accomplished by the middle of the nineteenth century. The Methodist church, only formally organized in America in 1784, had by 1840 become the largest denomination, surpassing the colonial denominations (Presbyterian, Congregational and Anglican), thus creating a significant market adjustment. The Calvinistic orthodoxies of the eighteenth century had been significantly Arminianized and the methods and means of religious progress had been reduced to a series of principles that were largely subscribed to across a wide swath of the evangelical consensus.[101] The four underlying physiographical formations that contributed so much to the emergence of Pentecostalism, Holiness, premillennialism, divine healing and revivalism left their mark on mainstream Evangelicalism as well. The broad features of this consensus were probably best exemplified by the Moody-Torrey synthesis, and included conversionism, revivalism, premillennialism, and a Keswick-style optimism that invoked the overcoming life, and power for service. While the Moody-Torrey synthesis did not include a significant emphasis on divine healing, the extremes of that element had begun to be tempered in all but the most radical circles by the nineties.[102] Protestant Christianity, of course, was larger than this consensus. Groups like the churches of Christ, and other branches of the Stone-Campbell movement were not directly connected, nor were Lutherans, substantial parts of Anglicanism and of course the Old School Presbyterians. But, certainly all Protestantism was affected by the evangelical consensus as it was represented by the Moody-Torrey synthesis.

Beneath the surface though, the factions that made up this broad consensus were not always comfortable with one another. It would take the growing pressures of modernism, its effects in terms of biblical criticism, the response to evolution, and the increasing secularization of an urbanizing and industrializing society to shift the tectonic plates above which the evangelical consensus lay. As the tectonic plates that created this alliance began to move, cleavages between heart and head, between urban and rural, between elites and the grassroots were creating tensions that would eventually bring to an end any vision of a 'united Evangelical front'. In the 'received' narrative this takes place through the Fundamentalist-Modernist controversy. It has been customary to separate the white hats and the black hats on one side or the other along this rift according to one's theological inclinations. But the lines were not so clear, particularly in the years leading to

101. See Smith's discussion of the process at mid-century; *Revivalism and Social Reform*, pp. 88–92.

102. Torrey was a believer in divine healing and had experienced a few marvellous instances of it in his ministry. He published a book entitled *Divine Healing*, advocating a moderate approach to the subject; Roger Martin, *R.A. Torrey: Apostle of Certainty* (N.p.: Sword of the Lord Press, 1976), pp. 70–72, see n. 5, 75.

Azusa. Divisive issues arose over dispensational and more historic approaches to premillennialism, the effectiveness of divine healing and Keswick versus Holiness approaches to sanctification.[103] The emergence of Holiness denominations not only spelled a final break with organized Methodism, but the appearance of a new radicalism that would substantially contribute to Pentecostal formation and the specific triumphalism associated with it.

Canadian Methodist, Nathanael Burwash, sometime scientist, sometime theologian and eventually Chancellor of Victoria University in Toronto, is an example of this blurriness. Far from being crushed under the load of scientific progress and higher criticism of the Bible, Burwash's revivalist spirituality remained vibrant, and in fact was nourished by them. The Methodist emphasis on experiential Christianity served for Burwash's generation of academics to dichotomize personal piety and intellectual objectivity. Hence Burwash was the chief promulgator of biblical criticism in Methodist circles on the one hand, and the anointed preacher of religious certainty through the witness of the Spirit on the other.[104] This kind of liberal Evangelicalism eventually drove the social gospel movement which was a natural outgrowth of the social reform tendencies of revivalism.[105]

The inconsistency of such accommodations with the outright rejection of Darwinism and higher criticism among the more conservative elements of Evangelicalism meant the two could not long survive together. Similarly, tensions between urban and rural populations, intellectual northern elites and anti-intellectual midwestern and southern populists created further rifts that would lead to inevitable divisions. R. G. Robins captured the breadth of the Evangelical consensus and the conflict it created in his description of *The Christian Herald*. Robins calls it the late-nineteenth-century version of *Christianity Today*, *Newsweek*, *People*, and *National Geographic*, meeting the needs of 'middle-class evangelicals who possessed enough sophistication and leisure to be curious about the world they were bent on saving'. The *Herald* purposed to propagate premillennialism, divine healing, and the higher life, carrying articles by the luminaries in these areas including Charles Cullis, A. B. Simpson and William Boardman. It also featured the Archbishop of Canterbury, Henry Ward Beecher, that silver-tongued, proto-liberal orator of the gilded age, and William Rainey Harper, Old Testament higher critic at the University of Chicago. It was this highfalutin' breadth that annoyed the plainfolk audience outside of the urban centres and the circles of

103. Timothy Smith, *Called Unto Holiness: The Story of the Nazarenes: The Formative Years* (Kansas City, MO: Nazarene Publishing House, 1962) p. 25.

104. Van Die, *An Evangelical Mind: Nathanael Burwash and the Methodist Tradition in Canada, 1839–1918* (McGill-Queen's Studies in the History of Religion 3; Montreal: McGill-Queen's University Press, 1989), pp. 3–13 and 58–64. Burwash's concepts of conversion, revival and Christian perfection underwent some modification, but were not unrecognizable to mainline Methodism.

105. Van Die, pp. 175–76 and 193–94; and Allen, *The Social Passion*.

the elite.[106] The gentrification of mainstream Evangelicalism led to a careful avoidance of the 'controversial extremes' of holiness, healing and dispensational premillennialism. As a result, *The Christian Herald* increasingly polarized these tensions and progressively alienated the plainfolk on the social periphery. It was out of this dialectic that Radical Evangelicalism emerged.[107]

Timothy L. Smith points out that by 1885 two distinct groups were coalescing that in turn would give birth to about a dozen Holiness denominations. On the one hand was a highly emotive group, primarily rural (though urbanizing through migration to the cities), more rigid in terms of outward compliance to standards of holiness and more restive towards denominationalism. On the other was a more intellectual, more urban segment, less unyielding in terms of standards, and more aware of the need for national organization to pursue its vision of 'spreading Scriptural holiness throughout the land'.[108] The former of these 'come-outers' created the cultural matrix which gave rise to early Pentecostalism. All the initial leaders of the Pentecostal revival came directly from Holiness groups of this kind.[109] And while the later ranks of early Pentecostal leaders were made up of a diversity of free-spirited, creative, spiritual entrepreneurs, there can be little doubt they had strong affinities with the Radical 'come-outers' of the Holiness movement.

106. Robins uses the term 'plainfolk' to describe 'a swath of popular culture not limited to any single region . . . from ranks of society low enough to have grounds for discontent with the status quo, but high enough to aspire to reshape it'; *A. J. Tomlinson*, p. 31.

107. Ibid., pp. 11–18.

108. Smith, *Called unto Holiness*, pp. 26–33.

109. Charles Fox Parham whose early ministry included the holiness message, a healing home in Topeka and a weekly paper, *The Apostolic Faith*, available for a dollar a year, shared the Radicals' general suspicion of denominational structure; Goff, *Fields White unto Harvest: Charles F. Parham and the Missionary Origins of Pentecostalism* (Fayetteville, AR: University of Arkansas Press, 1988), pp. 33–48. Frank Bartleman was an itinerant Holiness evangelist who ministered in several radical groups including the Salvation Army, the Pillar of Fire, and the Peniel Mission; Robeck, 'Bartleman, Frank', in *NIDPCM*, p. 366. William Seymour appears to have been involved with Daniel Warner's Evening Light Saints, and Martin Wells Knapp's God's Bible School before finding his way to Parham's Bible School in Houston in 1905; Robeck, 'Seymour, William Joseph', in *NIDPCM*, pp. 1054–55. Sources on this part of Seymour's life are fragmentary. William Durham, the instigator of the Finished Work controversy, nevertheless originally adhered to 'a fairly standard holiness message of salvation and sanctification'. After the passing of his wife in 1909, and daughter in 1910, he began to teach that salvation was complete at the cross, and one could seek the newly styled baptism of the Spirit immediately after conversion, without the so-called second-blessing; Jacobsen, *Thinking in the Spirit*, pp. 138–39, See also Blumhofer, 'William Durham: Years of Creativity, Years of Dissent', in *Portraits of a Generation: Early Pentecostal Leaders* (ed. James R. Goff and Grant Wacker; Fayetteville, AR: University of Arkansas Press, 2002), pp. 123–42 (pp. 126–28, 136–37).

a. Triumphalism and the Two Tectonic Plates

Revivalism, the recovery of divine healing, a call to primitive holiness, a return to the premillennialism of the early church, all share two essential characteristics, and the vast consensus of nineteenth-century Evangelicalism rested on these two somewhat unstable assumptions. They are restorationism and perfectionism. As these two tectonic plates scraped against one another, they created potential for eruptive change. From the abrasion of nineteenth-century restorationism and perfectionism arose the Fundamentalist-Modernist controversy, the emergence of Holiness churches, and perhaps the most extreme of its seismic shifts, Pentecostalism. Only this last result can concern us here, but its relation to the others is essential to understanding its place and the specific form of its triumphalism.

1. Prospective Triumphalism: Perfectionism The first tectonic plate upon which our entire discussion so far rests is perfectionism. William G. McLoughlin charts the centrality of what he terms 'pietistic-perfectionism' as a key to understanding the American character.[110] Far from simply being a construct of Christian theology, perfectionism has a lengthy philosophical pedigree, which informs its theological meaning. Philosopher Thomas Hurka defines it as a moral theory that situates an objective concept of the good within the capacity of human nature, and demands our best efforts to develop its dimensions to the highest degree.[111] Biblically the call for perfection emanates from both Yahweh and Jesus (Lev. 11.44–45, 19.2; Mt. 5.48).[112] And historically, the church has struggled in its various incarnations to come to terms with that call. The Christian Platonism of Clement of Alexandria and Origen formed an early response, blending Hellenistic philosophy with the Scriptures and arriving at a kind of Christian Gnosticism that separated saving faith, available to all, from the development of gnosis which led to a higher spirituality for the elite who entered into it. This duality between the ordinary and the elite anticipated the monasticism that would soon define higher Christian spirituality for a millennium.[113] The debate that ensued between Augustine and Pelagius in the fifth century on the question of human ability has since defined the parameters of the theological discussion of perfectionism by setting it in its most extreme terms. In the centuries that followed, the argument about human perfectibility has played itself out between these two poles of absolute ability and inability. In the nineteenth-century climate the debate was most dynamically alive between New School Presbyterians and the Old School Princetonians. It led to

110. William G. McLoughlin, 'Pietism and the American Character', *AQ* 17 (1965), pp. 163–86.

111. Thomas Hurka cites Plato, Aristotle, Aquinas, Kant, Hegel and Marx as perfectionists; *Perfectionism* (New York: Oxford University Press, 1993), pp. 3–5.

112. Of course, much hangs on the interpretation of *qadosh* and *teleios* in these verses. I am not here contending for any particular position.

113. R. L. Shelton, 'Perfection, Perfectionism', in *EDT*, pp. 839–43 (p. 840).

an eventual split between the two in 1837, which was finally healed in an 1869 reunion as New Schoolers returned to a more orthodox position.[114] The polemic against perfectionism in the Old School continued for years. It culminated in the work of B. B. Warfield who wrote a number of essays critiquing the perfectionist impulse that were published posthumously in 1932 in two volumes.

Warfield found claims of perfectionism in much of nineteenth-century Protestantism from German liberal theology to John Humphrey Noyes and the Oneida Community; and all points in the Evangelical spectrum between.[115] Warfield discovered in all of these a fundamental anthropological flaw concerning human ability, and charged them with varying degrees of Pelagianism.[116] ‘If Oberlin Perfectionism is dead’, Warfield claimed, ‘it has found its grave not in the abyss of non-existence, but in the Higher Life Movement [according to Warfield’s account, begun by Hannah Whitall Smith, and her husband Robert Pearsall Smith in the 1870s, and represented by A. B. Simpson later], the Keswick Movement [the British form of perfectionism which sprang from the Smiths’ revivals], the Victorious Life Movement [Charles G. Trumbull, W. H. Griffith Thomas], and other kindred forms of perfectionist teaching’.[117]

The salient point that Warfield’s cataloguing of perfectionists makes, however, is that all these groups anticipated some kind of triumph over the vicissitudes of the human condition. All were possessed of a vision of the Christian experience that reached forward to the *eschaton* in order to make real in the present the ultimate triumph of Christ. When considering the nature of perfectionist triumphalism, perhaps it may be best termed prospective triumphalism, because it finds it dynamic by drawing from the future. This sets it apart from restorationism. Prospective triumphalism is an over-anticipation in the present, a misunderstanding or a misuse of the assured triumph of the cross of Christ.

114. W. A. Hoffecker, ‘New School Theology’, in *EDT*, p. 768. See Marsden, *The Evangelical Mind* which charts the tale of division and reunion between New School and Old School Presbyterians. The so-called Princeton theology extended far beyond Old School Presbyterians, reaching among Episcopal, Congregational, Baptist and other denominations; Ernest R. Sandeen, *The Origins of Fundamentalism: Toward a Historical Interpretation* (Philadelphia: Fortress, 1968), p. 12.

115. Noyes’ is but one of several examples of the perfectionist communities that arose mid-century, from Robert Owen’s secular utopia, New Harmony, to the continuing efforts of the Shakers to reproduce Mother Ann Lee’s eighteenth-century vision of Christian communalism. These became models to a multiplicity of perfectionist communities including some Holiness groups significant to the emergence of Pentecostalism such as Frank Sandford’s Shiloh, and Alexander Dowie’s Zion City. For an overview of utopian communities, see; Robert S. Fogarty, *All Things New: American Communes and Utopian Movements, 1860–1914* (Chicago: University of Chicago Press, 1990).

116. Benjamin Warfield, *Studies in Perfectionism, Volumes I and II* (Grand Rapids: Baker, [1932] 2003).

117. Ibid., p. 213.

2. Retrospective Triumphalism: Restorationism Restorationism is the second tectonic plate upon which much of nineteenth-century Evangelicalism lay. It represents an expression of dissatisfaction with the current state of the church, and posits as a solution to this quandary, a return to the ancient path, a subverting of history that reaches back to a romantic and idealized past in which the church was unpolluted by the accretions of time and human imperfection. Richard T. Hughes calls it a kind of perfectionism in which the goal is to strive for a perfect church, modelled after the apostolic archetype.[118] For the present purpose I will call it a form of triumphalism, in that it represents a denial of human fallenness, an idealization of the apostolic church that fails to come to terms with its imperfections, and a triumphal declaration that at last 'the key' to repristination has been discovered.[119] Restorationism, then, is flawed on two counts: first for claiming that such an impeccable Golden Age exists, and secondly for assuming that it may be recovered by flawed individuals in the broken present.[120] The anthropological questions raised by the essential premise of restorationism are indeed overwhelming, let alone the historical problem it poses. For these reasons, then, I call it triumphalism. Because it derives its dynamic from the past, and it calls us to reach back, I call it retrospective triumphalism.

The Holiness Radicals and the early Pentecostals shared a common worldview in this regard, and may be characterized in similar ways on a number of criteria. Steven Ware provides four general characteristics of the restorationism shared by Holiness

118. Hughes posits three kinds of primitivism: the *ecclesiastical* kind, which is mainly concerned with forms and ritual, and is exemplified by Stone-Campbell movement, Baptists and Mormons; an *ethical* primitivism that focuses on lifestyle, such as displayed by the Holiness movement; and an *experiential* primitivism, concerned with the recovery of apostolic gifts as expressed by Pentecostalism; Hughes, 'Christian Primitivism as Perfectionism', pp. 213–14. Dieter situates the Holiness movement between a reformationist/traditionalist trajectory derived from Wesley, and a restorationist/traditionalist orientation which he illustrates by discovering all three of Hughes' varieties of primitivism within the movement; Dieter, 'Primitivism', pp. 78–91. Blumhofer suggests four restorationist impulses that significantly informed Pentecostalism: first, a purification of forms and practices according to the New Testament, second, an attitude of Christian unity and simplicity, third, eschatological orientation, and finally anti-denominationalism; Blumhofer, *Restoring the Faith*, pp. 13–14.

119. Ware calls this last facet, recovery of 'the key', spiritual restorationism and sees it as essential to the Radical Holiness movement, and to Pentecostalism; S. L. Ware, *Restorationism in the Holiness Movement in the Late Nineteenth and Early Twentieth Centuries* (Studies in American Religion; Lewiston, NY: Edwin Mellen Press, 2004), pp. 35–39.

120. Hughes' critique here is incisive. '*At its inmost core,* restitution [restoration] *depends on human potential and the ability to discern and implement the ancient Christian traditions, and often results in postures of profound self-reliance*'; Richard T. Hughes, 'Are Restorationists Evangelicals?', in *The Variety of American Evangelicalism* (ed. D. W. Dayton and R. K. Johnston; Downers Grove: InterVarsity, 1991), pp. 109–34 (p. 111).

'come-outers', which seem to define Pentecostals equally well.[121] The first was the *apostasy narrative* of the church, charting the decline of Christianity to its nadir in the medieval church. Along with its yearning to reach back, was the critique of the current state of the church as being in some measure of apostasy, though it had been experiencing gradual restoration since the Reformation. The Holiness movement, with its recovery of entire sanctification, was the culmination of this repristination of the church.[122] This kind of restorationism was certainly a dimension of early Pentecostal self-definition, a movement whose central claim that God was restoring to the church apostolic gifts, and whose central icon was called the Apostolic Faith Mission.

Intense *premillennial anticipation* also characterized these Radical Evangelicals.[123] Holiness believers saw their personal sanctification as part of the Bride's preparation, and the church's recovery of holiness as a latter day sign.[124] The same eschatological expectation motivated early Pentecostals as well, since they borrowed the 'Latter Rain' narrative wholesale from Simpson and the Alliance.[125]

The third characteristic of Radical Evangelicals was a *passionate experientialism* that revealed itself in outward demonstration and the figurative language employed to describe it. Holiness radical W. E. Shepard described an Alliance meeting in Ohio where 'the power came down, and the shouting and running about and leaping and laughing was simply grand . . . Glory to God, I like it. Deliver me from stagnation meetings'.[126] 'The fire fell', 'the Comforter had come', there was 'a glorious outpouring

121. These four aspects of the thought of Radical Holiness 'come-outers' form the substance of Steven L. Ware, *Restorationism*. Ware seeks to establish a connection between Holiness restorationism and that found among early Pentecostals.

122. The recovery of 'entire sanctification' was a mark that all had been restored; ibid., pp. 35–36; see also pp. 17–19.

123. A notable exception was Daniel S. Warner, leader of the Church of God restoration movement, which eventually became the Church of God (Anderson, IN); ibid., p. 69.

124. Even non-Wesleyan A. B. Simpson claimed, '[T]he more fully we know our Lord in his indwelling presence [read "sanctifying presence"] the more sincerely we will long for his personal return. Indeed, this doctrine and hope are intimately connected with the subject of Christian Holiness, and the revival of both these doctrines has been simultaneous in the last century. It is because the Bridegroom is at hand that his Bride is summoned to make ready for the Marriage of the Lamb'; A. B. Simpson, *The Gospel of the Kingdom: A Series of Discourses on The Lord's Coming* (New York: Christian Alliance Publishing Company, 1890), p. 24.

125. Simpson used 'Latter Rain' terminology in speaking of 'the signs of the end'. Among these were revival signs, that is, 'the special outpouring of the Holy Spirit upon the world, and the conversion of great multitudes to God. This is called the latter rain'; ibid., p. 214. The 'Latter Rain' concept received its classic Pentecostal expression in *The Latter Rain Covenant*, the work of Wesley D. Myland, former Alliance District Superintendent.

126. W. E. Shepard, 'The Meeting at Findlay, Ohio', *Nazarene Messenger* 6, No. 11 (12 September 1901) 4; cited in Ware, *Restorationism*, pp. 107–8.

of the Spirit'. The language of Pentecost occurs frequently in both Holiness and early Pentecostal writings, and always denotes intense pneumatic experiences.

Finally, Holiness restorationism was characterized by its intractable *biblicism*. The Bible was fully reliable in a rigidly literal sense, but more than that, it could be the means by which God spoke to individuals personally and existentially, and its very words might carry multiple meanings to the Spirit-informed intellect.[127] This complex hermeneutic was equally fruitful for most of the evangelical world of the time, having informed the burgeoning premillennialism of the day, the healing movement and most certainly the emerging Pentecostal movement. Clearly Holiness radicalism and early Pentecostalism were both rife with restorationist fervour. This form of retrospective triumphalism gave the marginalized radicals the sense of belonging to a community more significant than denomination or state, for they were in contact with the apostolic age. As will become clear in the next chapter, it is a theme that will develop in early Pentecostalism with even greater intensity.

The continuity between Radical Holiness and the earliest Pentecostals is well illustrated by the case of A. G. and Lillian Garr, among the first whites to speak in tongues at Azusa Street, and among the first missionaries from that Mission. The Garrs were leaders in the Metropolitan Church Association (MCA), a particularly aggressive Holiness group begun in 1894, which advocated communal living and the abolition of private property. Garr had gone to Los Angeles to assist and eventually give direction to the Burning Bush Mission, an MCA ministry there. After experiencing tension with MCA leadership, he chose to close the mission and urged his followers to participate in meetings at the mission down the road, the Apostolic Faith Mission. When the Garrs went there, it was not for them a departure from the Holiness movement, but a move between one mission and another in a world already full of internecine conflict.[128] The language, expression and anticipation one experienced in the most radical circles of Holiness were no different than what one might have encountered at Azusa. MCA churches experienced highly demonstrative worship with shouting, dancing and running the aisles.[129] Holiness evangelist Seth Rees published *The Ideal Pentecostal Church* in 1897. His description of the ideal was based on Acts 2. It was a church that included demonstrative worship, divine healing, and where 'the love of God shed abroad in the human heart . . . [would] deplore and denounce all sin, and rebuke

127. The words of A. B. Simpson were programmatic for a generation: 'It has been reserved for others in the succeeding generations [since the Reformation] to unfold the fullness of the Gospel of the grace of God, the healing life and power of Christ, and the Gospel of the kingdom. *There is no addition to the Bible, but our vision is enlarged to see more in its pregnant word*'; Simpson, *Gospel of the Kingdom*, pp. 10–11, emphasis added).

128. See chapter 7 in; William Kostlevy, *Holy Jumpers: Evangelicals and Radicals in Progressive Era America* (New York: Oxford University Press, 2010), pp. 127–44.

129. Ibid., pp. 131–32. Indeed in the MCA, jumping may have been the evidence *par excellence* of the baptism in the Holy Spirit; see also pp. 84–87.

worldliness [and] compromise’. It was a place where ‘old-fashioned conversions resulting in old-fashioned shouting’ were the order of the day.[130]

Pentecostalism, thus, was an amalgam, a specific permutation, of the raw materials that went into the general formation of all popular Evangelicalism at the end of the century. The Holiness movement, premillennialism, the healing movement and revivalism all combined in different ways to impact the assorted varieties of the Protestant tradition. The result, I argue, is dependent on the underlying tectonic plates of perfectionism and restorationism. A grasp of these antecedents, therefore, is essential for getting at the fundamental nature of Pentecostal triumphalism. It has been suggested by some that all Protestantism is, in a sense, restorationist, in that its commitment to the Bible in the face of tradition, institution and the world continually calls it to a retrospective triumphalism. Likewise, one might propose that the perfectionist impulse is intrinsic to Christian hope, and that prospective triumphalism is endemic to faith. Whatever conclusion one draws about such matters, it is clear that late-nineteenth-century Evangelicalism was substantially impacted by the motions of these large plates upon which its very moorings were built.

The emergence of Radical Evangelicals was clearly a result of the interaction of retrospective and prospective triumphalism. During the nineteenth century the emphasis in Christian perfection shifted from goal (Wesley) to gateway of Christian spirituality (Palmer). The restorationist power of recovering the apostolic secret; and the perfectionist assurance that in entire sanctification one was tasting the first fruits of eternity in the here and now; both were sufficient to countervail the growing animosity of lesser saints. Premillennial hope and the power of healing promoted a double-edged triumphalism – both retrospective and prospective. Both operated as appeals to the supernatural in an age of increasing secularity. As such, they reached back to the apostolic continuity that so empowered religious outsiders generally. But as deployed among Radical Evangelicals, they also drew the initiated forward into the *eschaton* as signs of the coming age. The recovery of divine healing, it will be recalled, had been predicated on the basis of a ‘physical Arminianism’: it anticipated the perfectibility of humanity, and with the joyful consistency of biblical literalism, it expected in the immediate present, the perfection not only of spirit but of body as well. The eschatological power of premillennial triumphalism was tied to the ‘Latter Rain’, that endtime outpouring that would empower the church to successfully complete its missionary task before the coming of the Lord. And the vehicle for all this was endless revival; finding a way to remain perpetually in the power of the Spirit. The retrospective triumphalism of Radical Evangelicalism provided the assurance of the apostolic imprimatur on the innovations restorationists emphasized. On the other hand, growing confidence in human ability, human potential, even; drove the prospective triumphalism of perfectionism to greater excesses. As the next chapter demonstrates, Pentecostalism was the most extreme of these results.

130. Ibid., pp. 28–29.

VI. Placing the Pentecostal Piece into the Puzzle of Emerging Neo-Evangelicalism

In the locale of the Moody/Torrey synthesis, the result of plate tectonics was the Fundamentalist-Modernist controversy. While the received version places this upheaval at the centre of the Protestant narrative, it sits at the periphery of the tectonic version of history proposed here. The retrospective triumphalism of Fundamentalism did not express itself in the form of pure restorationism, that is, the quest for a return to the golden founding age for the sake of purity. Rather, Fundamentalism, as Scott Appleby argues, is a utilitarian version of restorationism that seeks to use the past to control the present.[131] Thus Princetonians and Dispensationalists found common cause in order to reassert Christian ascendancy in a quickly secularizing world. As much contempt as B. B. Warfield felt for Moody and his 'coterie' of higher life enthusiasts, the Princeton theology was beset by a much more devastating enemy in theological liberalism, with its attendant higher criticism, its unbridled scientism and its Darwinian presuppositions. Politics, as the saying goes, makes strange bedfellows; and religious politics even stranger. The response to the modernist assault came from a realignment of the Evangelical wing of Protestantism.

For the better part of a century Princeton had been odd man out in the Methodizing of Protestantism. It had stood squarely behind the now-outmoded Calvinism of the New Lights. But the crisis of the First World War brought things to a head in the battle with both secularizing tendencies in the world and modernizing tendencies in the church. The emergence of a new generation of urbanized, liberated youth, some just back home from a debilitating war; the availability of automobiles, radios, and the shift in popular culture and mores that these brought, had forged a new morality in the mainstream. Now the forces of conservative Christianity must come together to make a bid for the soul of the nation.[132] Dispensationalists (the centre of the Moody/Torrey synthesis of the late nineteenth and early twentieth centuries) and Princetonians (conservative Reformed Christians, and other traditionalists) joined hands. The bridge between the two may have been the Prophetic Conference movement, which upheld a view of Scripture as high as Princeton, and, in the face of the Modernist attack, was somewhat dependent on the Hodge-Warfield theology of biblical authority. Furthermore, some Princeton men (Charles Erdman, and Samuel Kellogg, for instance) had presented papers on non-dispensational premillennialism there. As a result, cordial relations existed between some main proponents of dispensationalism and Princeton.

131. This applies the thesis of Appleby who develops it in terms of global fundamentalisms in; R. Scott Appleby, 'Primitivism as an Aspect of Global Fundamentalism', in *The Primitive Church in the Modern World* (ed. Richard T. Hughes; Urbana and Chicago: University of Illinois Press, 1995), pp. 17–33 (pp. 28–29).

132. This summary of factors is indebted to Marsden, *Understanding Fundamentalism and Evangelicalism*, pp. 53–56.

The project that first brought them together was the publication of a series of 12 pamphlets, between 1910 and 1915 with essays on a series of topics including the deity of Christ, the Virgin Birth, and the atonement; a full third of them on the authority of the Scriptures in the face of higher criticism; and others on several –isms: socialism, Catholicism, Darwinism. It brought together American and British scholars, dispensational and Reformed writers (even Warfield, himself), from a wide variety of backgrounds, intended to demonstrate the breadth of the Evangelical coalition. Bankrolled by oil tycoons, Lyman and Milton Stewart, titled *The Fundamentals* (hence the term, fundamentalism), the booklets were made available, free, to pastors and Christian workers across the nation. They formed the first salvo in a protracted battle.[133] Before it was over the conflict would split denominations and bring increasing acrimony between those who stayed and those who left. Ultimately it spelled the demise of any real Protestant consensus. Fundamentalists were marked by their own brand of triumphalism: the hubris of absolute certainty, and the nadir of brotherly love and tolerance.[134] The issues may have been real, but the solution was ultimately flawed.

a. Fundamentalism, Radical Evangelicalism and Pentecostalism

Were Radical Evangelicals fundamentalists? The question is complicated by the nuances of the term. Do we mean, ‘Were they fully engaged in the Fundamentalist-Modernist controversy as it unfolded before 1920?’ The answer is flatly, ‘No.’ During the 1890s virtually every denomination endured at least one heresy trial over modernist issues. The same period saw Radical Evangelicals ‘coming out’ of denominations, and forming missions, sects and associations. Incipient modernism through the 1870s and 80s may have been part of a much larger issue in the alienation of Radicals, but it was not yet universally felt. Indeed, Sandeen notes ‘the great majority of the pastors and laymen had not yet been forced – as they would later be – to choose sides . . . and many Christians felt they could live comfortably in both camps’, though quite surely not the Radicals.[135]

On the other hand, Radicals generally held to a high view of Scripture, though at this time not yet nuanced in terms of higher criticism or inerrancy, and most were intense premillenarians, though their dispensationalism was not fully consistent. One might ask to what extent they fulfil Ernest Sandeen’s definition that early Fundamentalism was an alliance of Princetonian inerrancy, and dispensational premillennialism.[136] Or could they fit Ferenc Szasz’s parameters of the controversy:

133. Material on *The Fundamentals* from ibid., pp. 118–23.

134. For a discussion of separatism from a Fundamentalist perspective see; Ed Dobson and Ed Hindson, *The Fundamentalist Phenomenon: The Resurgence of Conservative Christianity* (ed. Jerry Falwell; Garden City, NY: Doubleday-Galilee, 1981), pp. 143–73.

135. Sandeen, *Origins of Fundamentalism*, p. 18.

136. Ibid., pp. 3 and 24.

evolution, higher criticism and comparative religion?[137] Again, it becomes difficult to assess Radicals before the 1920s on these issues. Perhaps the Fundamentalist-Modernist controversy is not the best lens to give a sharp image of the Radical Evangelicals, who were, in any event, far more interested in the transforming power of the Word than its rationalist defence.[138] Suzie C. Stanley claims that the Wesleyan/Holiness movement was defined by its pursuit and proclamation of holiness, and deliberately eschewed the label 'Fundamentalist'.[139]

Nevertheless, in the years following 1920, as the controversy heated up, and in the wake of the famous Scopes trial of 1925, both Holiness denominations and Pentecostalism were in their institutionalizing period. *The Herald of Holiness*, a Nazarene publication, began after 1920 to pursue the matter of biblical reliability and higher criticism assiduously. Paul Merritt Bassett counted a ten to one ratio of editorials in support of the authority and inspiration of Scripture over the person and work of Christ in 1920, while he found the two topics at parity in 1914.[140] The same was true of Pentecostals who by the 1920s were establishing the infrastructure theologically and organizationally to consolidate the fruits of the earlier revival.

Often Pentecostal history is written as though Pentecostals opted out of Fundamentalism altogether. Archer claims that Pentecostal interest in inerrancy arose when Assemblies of God was prevailed upon to change its Statement of Fundamental Truths to include the term so that they could find acceptance in the newly forming National Association of Evangelicals.[141] But as early as 1924, Stanley Frodsham, writing a promotional letter for the *Evangel* proclaims unabashedly.

> A few weeks ago I heard a brother testify, 'I praise God that I am a Fundamentalist, and that I am a Pentecostal Fundamentalist.' That is what we all are. I do not know of a Pentecostal person anywhere who questions the inerrancy of the Scriptures, or one who doubts the virgin birth, the miracles, the physical resurrection, the

137. Theodore, Szasz, *The Divided Mind of Modern Protestantism, 1880–1930* (Tuscaloosa, AL: University of Alabama Press, 1982).

138. Holiness advocates might have their own notions of biblical authority. 'For Wesleyans, the authority of Scripture depended to some degree upon its own authentication, but more importantly, experience of the authenticating voice of the Living Word clinched the matter'; Paul M. Bassett, 'The Fundamentalist Leavening of the Holiness Movement', *WTJ* 13 (1978), pp. 65–91 (p. 69).

139. Susie C. Stanley, 'Wesleyan/Holiness Churches: Innocent Bystanders in the Fundamentalist/Modernist Controversy', in *Re-forming the Center: American Protestantism, 1900 to the Present* (ed. Douglas Jacobsen and William Vance Trollinger, Jr; Grand Rapids: Eerdmans, 1998), pp. 172–93 (pp. 173–77) see especially footnote 9.

140. Bassett's argument is that while the heart of Wesleyan Holiness was not by nature drawn to the type of rationalist polemic of the Princetonian Calvinists, in the event, they supported the Fundamentalist position; Bassett, 'Fundamentalist Leavening', pp. 72, 82–85.

141. Archer, *Pentecostal Hermeneutic*, pp. 87–88.

> Deity, or the efficacy of the blood atonement of our Lord Jesus Christ, nor one who has the slightest sympathy for the unproved theories of the evolutionists that are being propounded everywhere by the 'learned ignoramuses' of the earth today. We go further and affirm that the signs and wonders that our Lord Jesus Christ said should follow 'them that believe' (Mk 16.17, 18) will assuredly follow as a result of faith in Christ today.[142]

This sense that Pentecostals were 'Fundamentalists with a difference', in Blumhofer's words, is fairly consistent in the writings of this period, complete with the objection that if other Fundamentalists were consistent, they would be Pentecostals too.[143]

J. Roswell Flower complained that Pentecostals were caught between two extremes: 'Modernism does away with the supernatural; Fundamentalism believes in the supernatural, provided it is in the past, but it does not believe in it in the present'.[144] Yet when the World's Christian Fundamentals Association passed a resolution affirming its opposition to Pentecostalism in the spring of 1928, Stanley Frodsham reported the news in a somewhat hurt tone in an editorial note titled 'Disfellowshiped!'

> Although the Fundamentalists have by this action disfellowshiped a great company of us who believe in all the fundamentals of the faith as much as they themselves do, we will, by the grace of God, continue to love and fellowship every child of God, especially those who stand as we do in teaching that the whole Bible is verbally inspired . . .[145]

It appears then that Pentecostal self-perception in the 1920s placed Pentecostals as Fundamentalists-in-spirit; more consistent Fundamentalists, perhaps; Fundamentalists 'outside the camp' (to use Frodsham's phrase); but Fundamentalists nonetheless. One might pause to note the commitments to inerrancy, verbal inspiration and basic Fundamentalist doctrine affirmed by these early institutional leaders.

And yet there is a case to make that Pentecostals were not fully Fundamentalists as well.[146] They arose from the epicentre of the late-nineteenth-century seismic shift between the plates of restorationism and perfectionism. While it has been

142. Stanley Frodsham, 'Dear Evangel Reader', *PE* 541 (1924), p. 15.

143. Blumhofer, *Restoring the Faith*, pp. 5–6. See for example J. S. McConnell, who complains, 'I fail to see how any man can consistently call himself a fundamentalist, and reject any one of these fundamental truths as taught by Christ. Yet there are thousands who claim to be fundamentalists that reject divine healing'; 'The Principles of the Doctrine of Christ', *PT* 9 (1927), p. 18.

144. J. Roswell Flower, 'The Present Position of Pentecost', *PE* 601 (1925), p. 8; see also William Menzies, *Anointed to Serve: The Story of The Assemblies of God* (Springfield, MO: Gospel Publishing House, 1971), pp. 178–81.

145. Stanley Frodsham, 'Disfellowhiped!' *PE* 760 (18 August 1928), p. 7.

146. See especially Spittler, 'Are Pentecostals . . . Fundamentalists?'

customary to place the Fundamentalist-Modernist controversy at the centre of the story of emerging twentieth-century Evangelicalism, another reading of history suggests that Fundamentalism itself may be a dead end. More germane to the evangelical narrative may be the transformations taking place in Radical Evangelicalism. Rather than privileging Fundamentalism, a story that elevates J. Gresham Machen, and the rationalist Calvinism of Princeton and Westminster, perhaps the hero of the evangelical story is someone like A. B. Simpson.

Simpson was intensely interested in being identified as an Evangelical, and pursuing ecumenical ties within this framework. The Alliance was not at first intended as a denomination, but a loose association of like-minded believers and workers.[147] He took his basic doctrinal statement from the Evangelical Alliance, but wished also to be distinguished by the Four-fold Gospel of Jesus as Saviour, Sanctifier, Healer and Soon-Coming King.[148] Still, Simpson, though a Presbyterian, was what one might call a proto-Pentecostal. After the Azusa Street revival, Simpson's policy towards glossolalia, the only perceivable difference between the two groups, was one of general acceptance, except for his disapproval of 'evidential tongues', the doctrine that speaking in tongues was the necessary evidence of having received the baptism in the Holy Spirit. In the 1907 Annual Report of the Alliance, Simpson wrote that as 'essential evidence', tongues had 'led to division, fanaticism, confusion, and almost every evil work'.[149] Some Pentecostals stayed with Simpson, but many moved over. Numbers of early AG leaders including Frank M. Boyd, J. Roswell Flower and A. G. Ward flooded into the Pentecostal revival from the Alliance.[150] Certainly, Simpson may be regarded as a central figure, and a key to

147. The failure of this vision was difficult for Simpson, and after his death a second generation of Alliance leaders saw to it that the CMA would become 'a generic evangelical denomination with an emphasis upon foreign missions', by 'opting for denominationism over ecumenism, foreign missions over holiness, and fundamentalism rather than "forward movements" [of the Spirit in the End Days]'; Daniel G. Reid, 'Toward a Fourfold Gospel: A. B. Simpson, John Salmon, and the Christian and Missionary Alliance in Canada', in *Aspects of the Canadian Evangelical Experience* (ed. G. A. Rawlyk; Montreal and Kingston: McGill-Queen's University Press, 1997), pp. 271–88 (pp. 277–78).

148. Bernie Van De Walle, *The Heart of the Gospel: A. B. Simpson, the Fourfold Gospel, and Late Nineteenth-Century Evangelical Theology* (Princeton Theological Monograph; Eugene, OR: Wipf and Stock, 2009), pp. 4, n. 12, 4 n. 13, 5.

149. Blumhofer, *Restoring the Faith*, pp. 103–4. 'Evidential Tongues' was by no means a fully embraced concept in the early movement. Charles Nienkirchen demonstrates persuasively, however, that Simpson's later views may have included a tongues-evidenced Spirit-baptism. It seems certain he sought for a more powerful encounter with God as his life drew to a close; *Simpson and the Pentecostal Movement: A Study in Continuity, Crisis, and Change* (Eugene, OR: Wipf and Stock, [1992] n.d.), pp. 102–7.

150. Menzies, 'Non Wesleyan Origins', p. 89; see Nienkirchen, *A. B. Simpson*, pp. 29–41 for other non-AG leaders.

understanding Pentecostalism, but is it too much to make him into a central hero of the entire Evangelical story?

One might well ask whether contemporary Evangelicalism looks more like the Reformed, confessional Presbyterianism of Warfield, or the revivalism of Finney, Moody, Billy Sunday and Billy Graham. Simpson stood in this line, but Warfield and Machen did not.[151] The prospective triumphalism of the Holiness movement unveiled itself in such perfectionist classics as Hannah Whitall Smith's *The Christian's Secret of a Happy Life*, or Oswald Chambers' *My Utmost for His Highest*, books that still have a shelf-life in twenty-first-century Evangelicalism. A. B. Simpson was a popularizer and disseminator of the prospective triumphalism of holiness, healing, and the fullness of the Spirit to reach the world before the soon-coming of Christ. In many ways he is more at the centre of the contemporary story than Warfield, Machen, or even Torrey and Moody. His influence may have been stymied, or at least blunted in the Alliance after his passing, but it was amplified, and polarized in Pentecostalism.

With the emergence of Pentecostalism there came changes in the circles of Radical Evangelicalism. Precursors to Pentecostalism certainly existed. In the mid-1890s in the Ottawa Valley and along the St Lawrence, Ralph Horner found himself in regular contravention of the Montreal Conference of the Methodist Church. Horner held meetings characterized with an enthusiasm that offended the respectability of established Methodism and eventually began his own Holiness Movement Church which espoused a third experienced he called ‘the baptism of the Holy Ghost and fire’.[152] B. H. Irwin and the Fire Baptized Holiness Association arose in 1895, and proclaimed not one or two, but multiple encounters of Spirit-fullness.[153] Vinson Synan claims that Holiness groups which formed prior to 1894 were much less susceptible to Pentecostalism, but Holiness groups in the South, particularly after the Southern Methodist Church adopted an anti-holiness policy, were vulnerable to the new Pentecost. These included the Church of God (Cleveland), the Church of God in Christ and several other smaller groups.[154] As a result of the Pentecostal revival Wesleyan Holiness groups began to eschew the term ‘Pentecostal’ which they had loved so well. The Pentecostal Church of the Nazarene became the Church of the Nazarene, and Alma White's Pentecostal Union became the Pillar of Fire. Eventually Wesleyan groups left ideas of Spirit-

151. The following discussion owes much to Donald Dayton's ‘Preface’ to Van De Walle's *The Heart of the Gospel*, pp. ix–xvi.

152. Whitely, ‘Sailing for the Shore: The Canadian Holiness Tradition’, in *Aspects of the Canadian Evangelical Experience* (ed. G. A. Rawlyk; Montreal and Kingston: McGill-Queens University Press, 1997), pp. 257–70 (pp. 261–63).

153. Robins, *A. J. Tomlinson*, p. 44; Synan, ‘Irwin, Benjamin Hardin’, in *NIDPCM*, pp. 804–5; and Synan, ‘Fire-Baptized Holiness Church’, in *NIDPCM*, p. 640. It appears Irwin at first advocated a third-blessing ‘baptism of fire’, and several other baptisms as well.

154. Synan, *Holiness-Pentecostal Tradition*, pp. 69–71.

baptism as empowerment to Pentecostals, and focused on increasingly moralistic notions of sanctification.[155]

'Re-forming the center', then, allows for a different definition of Evangelicalism that is less Calvinistic, less rationalist, and less alien to Pentecostalism, particularly in its institutionalized form.[156] When assessing the groups that eventually formed the National Association of Evangelicals (NAE) in 1942, Donald Dayton suggests that one might well posit the Holiness movement and the emerging Pentecostals as the 'paradigmatic cultures' to understand contemporary Evangelicalism.[157] When Pentecostals were first admitted to the NAE, they formed 10 per cent of the delegates at the first exploratory meeting, by 1993 they represented some 60 per cent of the membership. In fact a look at the list of the ten largest groups in the NAE in 1999 put Holiness and Pentecostal groups by far in the ascendancy.[158]

While willing to admit the benefits membership in the NAE has provided, Mel Robeck laments also the losses. He perceives a pentecostalizing of Evangelicalism, but not without an evangelicalizing of Pentecostalism. This critique seems endemic to Pentecostal scholarship that fears that Pentecostalism is being reduced to 'Evangelicalism plus tongues'.[159] But it is necessary to define this evangelicalization. Robeck lists the loss of the early pacifist stance, the erosion of support for women in ministry, the addition of evangelical doctrinal concerns to the Pentecostal agenda (particularly inerrancy), and opposition to ecumenism as results of an evangelicalizing process that took place as a direct result of membership in the NAE. To adduce these changes, whether for good or ill, to involvement with

155. Ware, *Restorationism*, pp. 160–3.

156. *Re-forming the Center* (Jacobsen and Trollinger, eds) is the title of an edited book published by a group of scholars rejecting the two-party model of American Protestantism as divided into liberal and conservative camps resulting from the Fundamentalist-Modernist controversy. See p. 30.

157. As Dayton suggests, most observers would see the Christian and Missionary Alliance as closer to the centre of contemporary Evangelicalism than Machen's Orthodox Presbyterian Church; Dayton, 'Preface', p. xi. It should be noted that the NAE does not include the strongly Evangelical Southern Baptist Convention, which is the single largest Protestant denomination in America, numbering over 20 million, and alone making up some 7 per cent of the population of the United States; Bruce T. Murray, *Religious Liberty in America: The First Amendment in Historical and Contemporary Perspective* (Amherst, MA: University of Massachusetts Press, 2008), p. 28.

158. Cecil M. Robeck, 'National Association of Evangelicals', in *NIDPCM*, pp. 922–25 (p. 922); and 'Taking Stock', p. 55. Robeck claims the total Pentecostal component of the NAE was 56 per cent.

159. Faupel asserts that when the Pentecostal Fellowship of North America formed in 1948, and adopted a statement of faith identical to the NAE with the one doctrinal addition of the baptism in the Holy Spirit evidenced by tongues, 'the shaping of Pentecostal doctrine and self-understanding in Fundamentalist categories was complete'; Faupel, 'Whither Pentecostalism?', p. 25.

Evangelicals is simplistic, and reductionist. Other issues, to be explored in the following chapter, informed change in institutionalizing Pentecostalism. They amount to an inevitable rationalization of charismatic propensities in the wake of institutionalization.

Questions that were superfluous in the heat of revival became essential with the leisure of theological reflection, and answers were to be found from those with like-minded commitments to Scripture, and faith. Faupel, who shares Robeck's concern, acknowledges that if classical Pentecostals had not chosen this path, they 'might well still be regarded as cultic, and may not have been able to play the role within Christendom that [they] have in the past forty years'.[160] But if one recognizes the paradigmatic role of the Holiness and Pentecostal movements in the formation of Evangelicalism there are other ways to account for the current crisis of Pentecostal identity. Perhaps, in the words of Walt Kelly's Pogo, 'we have met the enemy and he is us'. The Evangelicalism which has so watered down the pristine Pentecostalism of the founding age may in fact be the very institutionalized Pentecostalism it has become!

Conclusion

Pentecostalism, then, emerges as a genuine form of Evangelicalism, like many other parts of the Evangelical family, with its own distinctives. As both Robert Webber and Norman C. Kraus remind, Evangelicalism has never been monolithic, but has always been a loose association of orthodox Christian bodies with similar commitments to some core beliefs and practices. It becomes apparent that there are indeed many Evangelicalisms.[161] Bebbington's quadrilateral of conversionism, activism, biblicism and crucicentrism defines the essence of Evangelicalism well and certainly situates Pentecostalism within it. But Pentecostalism reinterprets its evangelical roots into a unique form of triumphalism. This distinctiveness is best seen when one interprets the *fin de siècle* crisis of American Evangelicalism from a different perspective than the standard Fundamentalist-Modernist paradigm. Tracing the nineteenth-century history of perfectionism and restorationism through the Holiness movement, the rise of premillennialism, the divine healing movement, and the development of revivalism affords us a better perspective for understanding the emergence of Pentecostalism. The retrospective triumphalism of the restorationist perspective provided a sense of continuity with the apostolic age that Pentecostalism seized upon and pursued with great intensity. On the other hand, the prospective triumphalism deriving from the demise of New Light Calvinism, and the increasingly pervasive notion of human ability, became a

160. Ibid., p. 25.

161. Robert Webber, *Common Roots*, pp. 30–34; Norman Kraus, 'Evangelicalism: The Great Coalition', in *Evangelicalism and Anabaptism* (ed. Norman Kraus; Scottdale, PA: Herald, 1979), pp. 39–61.

driver of both theological and institutional triumphalism as Pentecostalism drew from this heritage.

Thus the question of exceptionalism becomes significant in resolving issues of the antecedents of Pentecostal triumphalism. Pentecostalism arrived at its specific synthesis of triumphalism from its Evangelical heritage, however it drew these strands together in an innovative and extreme way. Issues of the evangelicalization of Pentecostalism are complicated by shifting the centre of the Evangelical story away from the Fundamentalist-Modernist controversy. On that view, it is possible to construe Pentecostalism as following a separate trajectory. But with the Fundamentalist-Modernist controversy displaced, the lines separating Evangelicalism and the Holiness-Pentecostal Movements become blurrier, and the Radical Evangelical story becomes clearer. This, perhaps, is what makes it such a good paradigm for exploring the broader issue of Evangelical triumphalism, since not only has Pentecostalism become evangelicalized, but, not unlike the Methodizing of the nineteenth century, Evangelicalism over the twentieth century has been pentecostalized as well. The following chapter will detail the specific nature of Pentecostal triumphalism.

Chapter 2

'Living on the Hallelujah Side': The Emergence and Development of Pentecostal Triumphalism

> Oh, glory be to Jesus, let the hallelujahs roll;
> Help me ring the Savior's praises far and wide,
> For I've opened up tow'rd heaven
> All the windows of my soul,
> And I'm living on the hallelujah side.
>
> —Johnson Oatman Jr (1856–1922), 'The Hallelujah Side'

> ... when I saw [my daughter] Agnes, her nostrils were working in death, and her eyes were sunken and black. But oh, her face was lit up with glory, and she was singing the Heavenly Anthem as I have never heard it ... I heard her sing, as it were, the most beautiful singing and lovely music. All this time the Hallelujahs were sounding through the house more beautiful than tongue can tell or words express ... The following Sunday night at 11 o'clock I was resting on a cot at her side when I heard her shouting in other tongues, which she interpreted as, 'Jesus is coming, Jesus is coming.' Since then she has been well. Praise God. On August 9th, 1914, we were both baptized in water. ... Hallelujah!
>
> Mrs A. Shirlaw, 'A Healing and a Revelation of the Soon Coming of Jesus', *PT*, No. 129 (12 May 1917), 4

Pentecostals, by definition, are an expectant people and Pentecostalism has always been a Hallelujah experience. Pentecostals have been saved, sanctified and living in victory for over a century. While the triumphalist rhetoric has taken different forms over the decades, it has a long and deep history in the Pentecostal ethos, and profound antecedents in American religious history. The problematic of triumphalism has become endemic to Pentecostalism. The unwritten measure of true Spirit-fullness among Pentecostals is not so much speaking in tongues, as it is indomitable faith: the confident assertion that, whatever the circumstance, God will come through; and, its necessary corollary for the Pentecostal, by faith I will overcome. Often the expression of this kind of faith is the most common form the average person experiences of Pentecostal triumphalism. This chapter considers early Pentecostal triumphalism, assuming its historical antecedents in nineteenth-century Evangelicalism, and the seismic shifts of the tectonic plates of perfectionism and restorationism, the two underlying dynamics that shaped popular Evangelicalism.

The prospective and retrospective triumphalism of these plates created in Pentecostalism a unique form of triumphalism characterized by an unabashed sense of divine immediacy. By Pentecostal immediacy I mean a direct experience of God through the Spirit, marked by an acute eschatological expectancy, a sense of proximity with the apostolic age, and a 'can-do' attitude derived from an awareness of the Spirit's empowerment. The emergence of this specifically Pentecostal form of triumphalism informed every dimension of early Pentecostalism. As the movement institutionalized, a synthesis between its incipient organizational dynamic and its Radical Evangelical roots resulted in a kind of attenuated immediacy, which negotiated its relationship with Fundamentalism and the neo-Evangelicalism of the twentieth century. The result of attenuated immediacy was to soften the inevitable impasse between expectancy and experience, but it could not eradicate the tension entirely. North American Pentecostalism, whether in its roots, its earliest incarnation, or its institutional expression, represents a unique and extreme form of evangelical triumphalism.

At the beginning of the twenty-first century, however, Pentecostalism is facing an identity crisis. Just what does it mean to be Pentecostal, especially in this post-denominational age?[1] This disorientation is not unique to Pentecostals, but reflects a general suspicion of institutions facing denominations in the contemporary postmodern environment.[2] In each circle of influence this suspicion calls into question the particular form that triumphalism, as a distinguishing mark of American Protestantism, has taken in that particular denominational milieu. The

1. Sociologists of religion have noted the decrease of denominational cohesiveness and related it to the postmodern fragmentation upsetting the enlightenment consensus in various disciplines. See Terri Martenson Elton, 'Corps of Discovery', in *The Missional Church in Context: Helping Congregations Develop Contextual Ministry* (ed. Craig van Gelder; Grand Rapids: Eerdmans, 2007), pp. 143–45; and David A. Roozen and James R. Nieman, *Church, Identity, and Change: Theology and Denominational Structures in Unsettled Times* (Grand Rapids: Eerdmans, 2005), pp. 1–4. For a Canadian perspective, see also Sam Reimer, *Evangelicals and the Continental Divide: The Conservative Protestant Subculture in Canada and the United States* (McGill-Queen's Studies in the History of Religion; Montreal and Kingston: McGill-Queen's University Press, 2003), p. 6, whose statistics show that 75 per cent of respondents, American and Canadian, preferred to identify themselves as 'Christian', rather than as affiliated with a tradition or specific denomination, though by 'Christian' most seemed to mean broadly Evangelical.

2. The day of all-comprising national denominations may be past. Postmodern societies create an atmosphere of discourse which 'only give[s] rise to institutions in patches – local determinism'; Jean-Francois Lyotard, *The Postmodern Condition: A Report on Knowledge* (trans. Geoff Bennington and Brian Massumi; Minneapolis: University of Minnesota Press, [1979] 1984), p. xxiv.

amalgam of social and religious forces that combined to produce North American Pentecostalism gave birth, in the process, to a distinctive form of triumphalism that is neither a sufficient nor necessary element in Pentecostal formation.

I. The Identity Crisis in Contemporary Pentecostalism

In recent years the debate regarding identity has focused on the field of hermeneutics. As far back as 1994, French L. Arrington declared, 'The real issue in Pentecostalism is hermeneutics.'[3] Proponents of this view argue that Pentecostalism, from its earliest strata, provides a distinctive hermeneutical model that transcends the tired old paradigms of historical-critical study, and focuses on a more interactive,

3. French L. Arrington, 'The Use of the Bible by Pentecostals', *Pneuma* 16 (1994), pp. 101–7 (p. 101). The hermeneutical discussion began with a series of critiques, the first made by Walter Hollenweger in a chapter entitled 'Back to the Bible: The Pentecostal Understanding of Scripture' in his seminal *The Pentecostals: The Charismatic Movement in the Churches* (trans R. A. Wilson; Minneapolis: Augsburg, 1972), pp. 291–310. This was followed in quick succession by more exegetical works such as Frederick Dale Bruner's magisterial *A Theology of the Holy Spirit: The Pentecostal Experience and the New Testament Witness* (Grand Rapids: Eerdmans, 1970); and James Dunn's two volumes *Baptism in the Holy Spirit: A Re-Examination of the New Testament Teaching on the Gift of the Spirit in Relation to Pentecostalism Today* (Philadelphia: Westminster, 1970); and *Jesus and the Spirit: A Study of the Religious and Charismatic Experience of Jesus and the First Christians as Reflected in the New Testament* (London: SCM, 1975). The weightiest early response to these salvoes came from Gordon Fee in a self-critical essay; 'Hermeneutics and Historical Precedent – A Major Problem in Pentecostal Hermeneutics', in *Perspectives on the New Pentecostalism* (ed. Russell P. Spittler; Grand Rapids: Baker Book House, 1976), pp. 118–32. With the ripening of Pentecostal scholarship in the eighties came a fuller response in the form of Harold M. Ervin, *Conversion-Initiation and the Baptism in the Holy Spirit: A Critique of James D. G. Dunn, Baptism in the Holy Spirit* (Peabody, MA: Hendrickson, 1984); and Roger Stronstad, *The Charismatic Theology of St. Luke* (Peabody, MA: Hendrickson, 1987). French L. Arrington offered a sweeping analysis of the historical development of Pentecostal and charismatic hermeneutics 1988; 'Hermeneutics, Historical Perspectives on Pentecostal and Charismatic', in *DPCM*, pp. 376–89. In the early nineties, two entire issues of *Pneuma* were dedicated to a discussion of hermeneutics and the possibility of a specifically Pentecostal hermeneutic (vol. 15, Fall, 1993 and vol. 16, Spring 1994). This has led to a fruitful discussion both among Pentecostals and in the broader guild. For more recent Pentecostal discussion see the following selection: Kärkäinnen, 'Pentecostal Hermeneutics'; two pieces by Bradly T. Noel, *Pentecostal and Postmodern Hermeneutics: Comparisons and Contemporary Impact* (Eugene, OR: Wipf and Stock, 2010) and 'Gordon Fee and the Challenge to Pentecostal Hermeneutics: Thirty Years Later', *Pneuma* 26 (2004), pp. 60–80; William Atkinson, 'Pentecostal Hermeneutics: Worth a Second Look?', *Evangel* 21 (2003), pp. 49–54; John C. Poirier and Scott Lewis, 'Pentecostal and Postmodernist Hermeneutics: A Critique of Three Conceits', *JPS* 15 (2006), pp. 3–21; Mark Cartledge, 'Empirical Theology: Inter- or Intra-

reader-based – dare we say, postmodern approach, which liberates it to provide a contemporary word from God for the present-day reader.[4] At the heart of this project lies the recovery of the *mentalité* of the earliest Pentecostals and of a so-called Pentecostal hermeneutic that fuelled the primitivist supernaturalism of the earliest leaders of the revival. The argument suggests that this hermeneutic distinguished Pentecostals from proto-Evangelicals. Its loss was the result of assimilation with Evangelicals, and its recovery will mark the repristination of true Pentecostalism. I maintain that efforts to uncover this early interpretive grid, while of great historical interest, miss the mark of locating either Pentecostal self-definition, or the hermeneutic that propelled Pentecostal growth before the Second World War. Using this early Pentecostal mindset to fund a postmodern Pentecostal hermeneutic, and to support an argument for Pentecostal exceptionalism is both anachronistic and utilitarian.

I do not wish to imply that the earliest stratum was no different than the Pentecostalism that blossomed in the period of denomination building, but, rather, that Pentecostal triumphalism was its most blatant in this raw, revivalist Pentecostalism, and that the later organizational expressions of the movement sought to tame this triumphalism for institutional purposes. The 'Latter Rain outpouring of the Holy Ghost' cultivated a triumphalist sense of divine immediacy that animated early Pentecostal spirituality. But the wildfire Pentecostalism of Azusa Street had been tempered considerably by the days of institutional formation, and through the routinization of the Pentecostal 'charisma'.[5] The calmer, more even-tempered hermeneutic that defined institutional Pentecostalism, while similar to that makeshift hermeneutic quickly forged in the fire of revival,

disciplinary?', *JBV* 20 (1999), pp. 98–104; Archer, 'Horizons and Hermeneutics of Doctrine: A Review Essay', *JPT* 18 (2009), pp. 150–56; and John W. Wyckoff, *Pneuma and Logos: The Role of the Spirit in Biblical Hermeneutics* (Eugene, OR: Wipf and Stock, 2010). For discussion informed by these concerns outside strictly Pentecostal circles, see Clark Pinnock, 'The Work of the Holy Spirit in Hermeneutics', *JPT* 2 (1993), pp. 3–23; Clark Pinnock, 'The Work of the Spirit in the Interpretation of Holy Scripture from the Perspective of a Charismatic Biblical Theologian', *JPT* 18 (2009), pp. 157–71; Daniel Fuller, 'The Holy Spirit's Role in Biblical Interpretation', *IJFM* 16 (1997), pp. 91–95; Veli-Matti Kärkkäinen, 'Authority, Revelation, and Interpretation in the Roman Catholic-Pentecostal Dialogue', *Pneuma* 21 (1999), pp. 89–114; Amos Yong, 'The Word and the Spirit, or the Spirit and the Word? Exploring the Boundaries of Evangelicalism in Relationship to Modern Pentecostalism', *TJ* 23 (2002), pp. 235–52; and Yong, *Spirit-Word-Community*.

4. The most recent and most thorough effort to combine a concern for Pentecostal identity with the recovery of the initial Pentecostal hermeneutic has been the work of Kenneth Archer. See his recent monograph, *A Pentecostal Hermeneutic*; now reformatted and reprinted as *A Pentecostal Hermeneutic: Scripture, Spirit and Community* (Cleveland, TN: CPT Press, 2009).

5. In this context the terms charisma and charismatic are used in the Weberian sense to be explored later in this chapter.

was also different in significant ways that smoothed the rougher edges of the latter. But underlying the domesticated hermeneutic of the denomination was a similar tendency to triumphalism. While immediacy continued to characterize Pentecostal triumphalism, it became an attenuated immediacy, and one more easily manipulated by institutional rhetoric. I argue that the early Pentecostal hermeneutic is beyond reproduction by contemporary Pentecostals because it was conditioned by a sense of immediacy derived from the Latter Rain narrative which can no longer be held due to the extended delay of the *parousia*.

By charting various contemporary proposals about the key facets of the interpretive grid of the earliest Pentecostals, it will be possible to suggest a model that can be evaluated against later developments in Pentecostal thought. In order to limit the scope of this chapter, I will concentrate discussion of the institutional hermeneutic to the stage of institutional formation, roughly from 1919 to 1940, to determine in what way the earlier hermeneutic was transformed. I will consider the process of institutionalization in Canada in continuity with the American scene. Virtually every major leader of the Pentecostal Assemblies of Canada (PAOC) in its earliest years had either been to Azusa Street, or had been exposed to its message by both Canadians and Americans who were a part of the initial 1906 revival.[6] Crosscurrents were regular between Azusa Street and its uniquely Canadian counterpart, the Hebden Mission at 651 Queen Street East, Toronto where Ellen Hebden received the baptism in the Holy Spirit on 17 November 1906.[7] These facts point to an underlying unity of thought and purpose, and thus of hermeneutic, at the earliest level of Pentecostal development. Most of these same leaders were part of the formation of the denomination in 1919, and their writings, particularly in the *Pentecostal Testimony* over the next 20 years reflect their maturing theology, as it developed over 30 years after the initial revival. *The Pentecostal Testimony* forms an excellent source for this study because it consciously styled itself 'the official organ', the voice of the institution. Like the *Pentecostal Evangel* in America, it offers a helpful perspective from which to evaluate changes from the revivalist hermeneutic of Azusa to the institutional hermeneutic we are proposing.

II. *Defining a Revivalist Hermeneutic*

The process of identifying a 'Pentecostal hermeneutic' that captures the *mentalité* of the earliest Pentecostals is complicated by several factors. First the project is challenged by separating the thought-world of *fin de siècle* Radical Holiness from that of emerging Pentecostalism. Often they involved the same people, and their

6. Thomas Miller, *Canadian Pentecostals: A History of the Pentecostal Assemblies of Canada* (Mississauga: Full Gospel Publishing House, 1994) see especially chapters 2 and 3, pp. 62 and 75.

7. Miller, *Canadian Pentecostals*, pp. 40–41; and William Sloos, 'The Story of James and Ellen Hebden: The First Family of Pentecost in Canada', *Pneuma* 32 (2010), pp. 181–202. Mrs Hebden was arguably the first Canadian to receive the Pentecostal experience.

Pentecostal experience was an outgrowth of the Holiness passion for 'Latter Rain'.[8] One might properly ask if there was anything distinctly Pentecostal in the hermeneutic of Azusa that was not true of the healing movement, the holiness revivals or the pre-Fundamentalist millenarianism of the 'gilded age'.[9] Second, any effort to define this elusive hermeneutic must deal with the multiple interpretations offered, no one of which has won the day. This diversity of opinion, at times even diametrically opposed opinions, calls the entire project into question. Finally, the purpose behind the search for the earliest hermeneutic may betray its objectivity. At first the investigation was primarily historical. In asking how to account for the phenomenon of Pentecostalism, one might properly pursue the historical sources of the movement.[10] The search for a 'Pentecostal hermeneutic' to fund a historically rooted Pentecostal contribution to postmodern theology is more suspect, however.[11] Such teleologically driven quests are usually frowned upon by historians, and often involve unjustifiably anachronistic leaps.

8. As Donald Dayton comments, 'Pentecostalism is to be understood as a radical wing of the Wesleyan/holiness movement of the late nineteenth-century'; 'The Limits of Evangelicalism: The Pentecostal Tradition', in *The Variety of American Evangelicalism* (ed. D. W. Dayton and R. K. Johnston; Downers Grove: InterVarsity, 1991), pp. 36–56 (p. 49). Grant Wacker makes this point cogently in 'Travail of a Broken Family: Radical Evangelical Responses to the Emergence of Pentecostalism in America, 1906–1916', in *Pentecostal Currents in American Protestantism* (ed. Edith L. Blumhofer, Russell P. Spittler and Grant A. Wacker; Urbana and Chicago: University of Illinois Press, 1999), pp. 23–49, where he indicates the essential unity of two diverging groups, Pentecostals and radical evangelicals (holiness and more Keswick-oriented groups), and how this similarity fuelled significant antipathy from Holiness adherents against nascent Pentecostalism, see especially pp. 24–25.

9. See Charles E. Jones, 'Reclaiming the Text in Methodist-Holiness and Pentecostal Spirituality', *WTJ* 30 (1995), pp. 164–81, who claims that a significant difference in approaching the text was that Holiness interpretation abounded in metaphor (Exodus=justification, Crossing into Canaan=sanctification), while Pentecostals saw themselves as actually fulfilling prophecy.

10. In *Vision of the Disinherited*, Robert Mapes Anderson attempts to recreate the *mentalité* of early Pentecostals by discovering the underlying sources of Pentecostalism in economic and social dislocation, suggesting that an uneducated ministry could only have had recourse to a pre-critical hermeneutic. Donald W. Dayton approaches the question from a theological perspective and still manages to discover a Pentecostal hermeneutic, the sources of which he finds in the 'subjectivizing hermeneutic' of the pietists; a restorationism that overturns all talk of cessation of the charismata, and an 'assertion of direct access to the experience of Pentecost'; Dayton, *Theological Roots of Pentecostalism*, pp. 23–26.

11. In addition to Archer's work, consider efforts such as those by Thomas to root a postmodern hermeneutic in early Pentecostal uses of Scripture in 'Women, Pentecostals and the Bible', and Thomas and Alexander, '"And the Signs Are Following"'. For more theoretical papers on the interface between postmodern and Pentecostal hermeneutics see Richard Israel, Daniel Albrecht and Randall McNally, 'Pentecostals and Hermeneutics: Texts, Rituals and Community', *Pneuma* 15 (1993), pp. 137–61; Hannah K. Harrington and

Still, some fascinating proposals have emerged from Pentecostal scholars attempting to excavate this early Pentecostal hermeneutic. Stephen Parker charts four distinct approaches to the question of whether there is indeed a distinctively Pentecostal hermeneutic. These responses appear to form two diametrically opposed poles between those who advocate the refinement of evangelical models, and who hail the Pentecostal contribution to Evangelical theology, on the one hand, and those who fear that the 'evangelicalization' of Pentecostalism will mark its demise and who pursue the recovery of an authentically Pentecostal hermeneutic, on the other.[12] For the latter to come about will mean returning to the days before Pentecostals deliberately modified their more spontaneous revivalistic approach to the Bible by taking on a more rationalist (read Fundamentalist) method. Assuming, for the moment, that this dichotomy between Pentecostal revivalism and Fundamentalist rationalism holds true, just what were the elements of such a hermeneutic?

A significant amount of scholarship has addressed this question, often suggesting one integrating principle or another for defining the approach of the earliest Pentecostals to the Scriptures.[13] The consensus of opinion tends towards Robert Mapes Anderson's contention that 'the outstanding characteristics of the holiness movement – literal-minded Biblicism, emotional fervor, puritanical mores, enmity toward ecclesiaticism, and above all belief in a "Second Blessing" in Christian experience – were inherited and perpetuated by the Pentecostals.'[14] Kenneth Archer proposes that this constellation of ideas formed around a 'pre-critical . . . inductive and deductive Bible reading method' that was shared by holiness, Pentecostal and Fundamentalist believers alike.[15] What, then, made the early Pentecostal interpretive paradigm unique? The difference may have been quantitative. Pentecostals took their Bible 'neat'. As Grant Wacker noted 'the really

Rebecca Patten, 'Pentecostal Hermeneutics and Postmodern Literary Theory', *Pneuma* 16 (1994), pp. 109–14; and Gerald Sheppard, 'Biblical Interpretation After Gadamer', *Pneuma* 16 (1994), pp. 121–41.

12. Stephen E. Parker, *Led by the Spirit: Toward a Practical Theology of Pentecostal Discernment* (Sheffield: Sheffield Academic Press, 1996), pp. 24–26. Parker considers Howard M. Ervin, and William and Robert Menzies as exemplars who seek to enhance Evangelical hermeneutics through the application of a pneumatic sensitivity. At the other extreme he places Mark D. Mclean; and the participants of a two-issue discussion of the matter in the pages of *Pneuma* (see n. 3) as promoters of the recovery of a primitive Pentecostal hermeneutic to assist in Pentecostal contributions to the postmodern discussion.

13. Archer surveys the efforts of Russell Spittler, Grant Wacker, David Reed and Donald Dayton to come to terms with the essence of the early Pentecostal hermeneutic; Archer, *Pentecostal Hermeneutic*, pp. 89–99.

14. Anderson, *Vision*, p. 28; See also, Synan, *The Holiness-Pentecostal Tradition*; Dayton, 'Limits of Evangelicalism' and *Theological Roots*.

15. Archer, *Pentecostal Hermeneutic*, p. 91.

operative principle of interpretation was the conviction that exegesis is best when it is as rigidly literal as credibility can stand.'[16]

The cumulative result of this excessively literal interpretive schema created a peculiarly Pentecostal sense of immediacy that led Pentecostals to extreme interpretations that even their Radical Holiness brethren could not accept. The concept of immediacy permeated early Pentecostal thought and occasionally resurfaces today in Pentecostal churches, especially in times of renewal. Its pervasiveness in the *mentalité* of the original participants and its elusiveness within the institutional entity demonstrate its usefulness in creating a model that accounts for the inconsistencies between pioneering Pentecostalism and its denominational expression, while at the same time explaining the perpetuation of the Pentecostal experience and its supporting theology. This immediacy represents the form that triumphalism took in early Pentecostalism and in modified ways, throughout the larger Pentecostal penumbra including the charismatic movement and the Third Wave. Immediacy affected the worldview of early Pentecostals and thus their interpretation of Scripture in at least three interlocking ways: in matters of narrative, perspective and praxis.

a. Pentecostal Narrative: A Hermeneutic of Eschatological Immediacy

> The Lord has poured out the Holy Ghost as He promised He would in the last days with 'signs and wonders' following. He said He would give the latter rains of the Spirit before the notable Day of the Lord came. This was to be given to gather in the last harvest of souls before Jesus comes in the clouds.[17]

These words, uttered by healing-evangelist-turned-Pentecostal Maria Woodworth-Etter, offer typical elaboration of the *mentalité* of early Pentecostals. They were a people living in the last days. The ends of the world were coming upon them, time was short, and the mission was urgent. What else could account for the unprecedented appearance of Pentecostal gifts with which to 'get the job done'? Historian Grant Wacker tells of a letter left at her home by a delegate to the Assemblies of God General Conference of 1917 detailing special instructions to be followed if she were 'raptured' while on the journey. 'While people expect the Lord's return at any moment, frivolousness is not merely imprudent,' concludes Wacker, 'it is immoral.'[18] The eschatological immediacy that informed the Pentecostal hermeneutic became a central dimension of Pentecostal worldview.[19]

16. Wacker, 'The Functions of Faith in Primitive Pentecostalism', *HTR* 77 (1984), pp. 353–75 (p. 365).

17. Woodworth-Etter, *Signs and Wonders*, p. 37.

18. Wacker, 'The Functions of Faith', p. 371.

19. 'The Latter Rain motif presents the broad framework for the movement's world-view'; Faupel, *Everlasting Gospel*, p. 32.

Kenneth Archer locates the uniqueness of the Pentecostal *mentalité* not in its hermeneutical methodology, which he sees as a shared entity with other radical Evangelicals; nor in the theological concept of Spirit-baptism that was held in one form or another, especially in Holiness circles, but in the peculiarly Pentecostal metanarrative proposed by Azusa and its adherents.[20] The very term 'Pentecostal' had a prehistory within the holiness movement, which carried with it eschatological connotations.[21] The key to the narrative was the concept of 'Latter Rain' rooted in texts such as Joel 2.23: 'Be glad then, ye children of Zion, and rejoice in the LORD your God: for he hath given you the former rain moderately, and he will cause to come down for you the rain, the former rain, and the latter rain in the first month.' The notion of extreme literalism expressed here does not preclude the heavily typological interpretation of such concepts as 'Latter Rain', rather it promotes them, provided the fulfilment is literal, and immediate. The earliest telling of the story was D. Wesley Myland's *The Latter Rain Covenant*, which provided an early interpretive (and hence theological) basis for Pentecostal understanding. Myland, a major leader and teacher in the Christian and Missionary Alliance fully endorsed the Pentecostal experience and in a series of lectures given in Chicago's Stone Church in 1909 provided the outline of a Pentecostal hermeneutic.[22] 'There are many scriptures that are not only double-barreled, but triple-barreled; they are literal, typical and prophetical, or putting it in other words historical, spiritual, and dispensational.'[23] The Latter Rain Covenant is one of these triple-barreled texts, applying literally to the two rainy seasons of Palestinian meteorology; spiritually to

20. 'The Pentecostal story is the primary hermeneutical context for the reading of Scripture . . . The Pentecostal narrative tradition is an eschatological Christian story . . .' Archer, *Pentecostal Hermeneutic*, p. 134. Indeed, Archer, in agreement with Faupel, also sees the 'Latter Rain' story as the key lens through which to understand the Pentecostal experience; Faupel, *Everlasting Gospel*, pp. 30–41. I am in substantial agreement with both; however I wish to add the concept of immediacy as a key dimension of the Pentecostal *mentalité*, as it developed around the Latter Rain narrative.

21. According to Donald W. Dayton, 'By the turn of the century everything had become "Pentecostal." Sermons are published in the column "Pentecostal Pulpit"; women's reports are entitled "Pentecostal Womanhood"; testimonies are "Pentecostal Testimonies"; and devotions are held in the "Pentecostal closet". This is but an extreme illustration of what had become generally true in most strands of the holiness movement by 1900.' Dayton traces the emphasis on 'Latter Rain' to distinctions Asa Mahan made in exegeting phrases like 'in that day'; 'Asa Mahan', p. 64.

22. The fulfilment of the 'Latter Rain' for Pentecostals involved the physical sign of glossolalia, which spelled the distinction between Holiness and Pentecostal interpretations. 'This disparity', Jones argues, 'lay at the root of the Holiness rejection of signs and of the Pentecostal focus on healing and tongues. Methodist-Holiness people reclaimed the text by means of metaphor'; Jones, 'Reclaiming the Text', pp. 165–66.

23. Myland, *Latter Rain*, p. 32. Elizabeth Robinson claims his book was 'the first definitive Pentecostal theology'; E. B Robinson, 'Myland, David Wesley', in *NIDPCM*, pp. 920–21 (p. 921).

the contemporary outpouring of the Spirit, and prophetically to the eschatological climax, which culminates with the return of the Jews to Israel, and the coming of the Lord.[24] 'The early rain started it and the latter rain shall complete it, just as it does the crop in Palestine, just as it did the Jewish nation, so it is going to complete the body of Christ.'[25]

This narrative provided an urgent, eschatological immediacy to Pentecostal practice. It functioned in at least three ways. First, as I will explore later, the 'Latter Rain' motif envisioned a form of dispensational parenthesis, which allowed the rest of church history to be lumped together as 'the great apostasy' with early birth pangs felt during the Reformation and Great Awakening; and intensifying during the nineteenth century.[26] Second, it facilitated the ahistoricism that allowed Pentecostals to feel the immediacy of apostolic continuity. This, too, will be developed in the next section. In Archer's words, 'the Pentecostal story was teleological in that it brought the beginning and end of the church age together.'[27] However, eschatological immediacy must have a pragmatic dimension as well. Workers were needed for the great endtime harvest and within months of the Azusa outpouring, the response of Pentecostals with a sense of apocalyptic urgency in their evangelistic and missionary efforts was nothing short of stunning. This will be pursued in the third section, but here the emphasis is on the sense of divine destiny that possessed early Pentecostals. As their evangelistic and missionary efforts were met with success around the globe, countless papers headlined the glorious reports of Pentecostal triumph.[28] Myland was encouraged that in the Latter Rain 'God was making workers and landing them in the uttermost parts of the earth in about the same length of time that it requires an ordinary bible-school to examine them and enter them as students.' While not wishing to deprecate proper training, nor 'putting a premium on the short cut', he could not resist adding, 'I do love to see the Lord cut the thing short in righteousness.'[29] Thus, Maria Woodworth-Etter's words cited earlier, hold true as a programmatic expression of the Pentecostal narrative.

The underlying eschatological immediacy that fuelled the Pentecostal vision provided an existentially unfolding framework of ultimate triumph that reinterpreted the set-backs and successes of the fledgling Pentecostal movement against a backdrop of cosmic proportions. Was there a price to pay for the Apostolic witness? Pentecostals expected as much, for Jesus himself had warned persecution would come in the last days (Mt. 24.9–13). In August 1913 Woodworth-Etter was arrested in Framingham, Massachusetts, and tried over four days on charges of obtaining money under false pretenses. Her later

24. Myland, *Latter Rain*, pp. 1, 100–1.

25. Myland, *Latter Rain*, p. 116.

26. Archer, *Pentecostal Hermeneutic*, pp. 139–40.

27. Archer, *Pentecostal Hermeneutic*, p. 160.

28. Wacker, *Heaven Below*, pp. 263–65. The line between rhetoric and reality was not always clear in such optimistic statements.

29. Myland, *Latter Rain*, p. 85.

reflection on the matter was that 'Apostolic faith, producing results such as the healing of the sick and other demonstrations of God's mighty power, naturally results in Apostolic persecutions.'[30] But in spite of the devil's last hurrah, there would also be revival, a latter day revival to parallel and maybe outstrip Pentecost itself. When Pentecostals read, 'in the last days, saith God, I will pour out of my Spirit upon all flesh (Acts 2:17),' they recognized two frontiers of fulfilment: the former rain that empowered the early church; and this current latter rain, which was empowering the end time church and marked the promised coming of the Lord. Early Pentecostal Holiness leader George Floyd Taylor believed he was witnessing the fulfilment of prophecy.

> The Scriptures seem to teach that the Latter Rain will be far greater than the former. The most of Old Testament prophecy is two-fold, *i.e.*, it has two fulfillments, the first being the shadow of the second. Joel's prophecy quoted by Peter (Joel 2:28–32 and Acts 2:17–20) was partially fulfilled on the day of Pentecost, but that its greater fulfillment is still future appears from Joel 2:30–32. So we may expect the latter rain to be greater and more powerful than the apostolic revivals.[31]

In this way, eschatological immediacy nurtured a motivational assurance of success. While the world might oppose or scorn, the certainty of ultimate victory was enough for many to commit to the cause.

By 1908, only two years into the Azusa revival, it is estimated that missionaries from various centres of Pentecostal fervor had reached at least 25 nations. Myland anticipated they would be of a heartier stock and superior effectiveness than others. 'I would rather see one person baptized in the Holy Ghost and fire, dead in love with God's Word, reading it day and night, and praying the heathen through to salvation than a score of missionaries go out with only an intellectual equipment.' Some might seek to educate, others might bring medical help but under the Latter Rain,

30. Etter claims to have been acquitted as the 'charges proved to be false'; Woodworth-Etter, *Signs and Wonders*, pp. 309–10.

31. George F. Taylor, 'The Spirit and the Bride: A Scriptural Presentation of the Operations, Manifestation, Gifts and Fruit of the Holy Spirit in His Relation to the Bride with Special Reference to the "Latter Rain" Revival', in *Three Early Pentecostal Tracts* (vol. 14 of The Higher Christian Life; ed. Donald W. Dayton; New York: Garland, [1907] 1985), p. 91. Taylor understood the Day of Pentecost as the Early Rain, a shower to nourish the crop as it germinated, and the Latter Rain 'not to bring up seed, but to ripen fruit'. As a result, he did not expect a great harvest of salvation in places where the gospel had been proclaimed for years, but 'it is the *Baptism* of the Holy Spirit upon the church at large that was typified by the annual rains in Canaan'. Thus, 'a great revival is upon us and is sweeping the world. This is the latter rain . . . lands upon which the early rain has never fallen, *i. e.*, the heathen fields will receive both the early and the latter rain during this revival. So I am expecting to see millions of souls saved, sanctified, and filled with the Holy Spirit on foreign fields' (Taylor, 'The Spirit and the Bride', pp. 92 and 96).

'God is giving us another class; God is giving us another kind.'[32] These preachers would experience signs and wonders confirming their proclamation. Prompted by eschatological urgency, the missionary rhetoric of early Pentecostalism painted a romantic story of triumph, even as missionaries succumbed to sickness and death, and many were reduced to poverty, having 'gone out on the faith line'.[33] Nevertheless, as Allan Anderson claims, the Pentecostal passion for missionary endeavour propelled an enterprise that was 'arguably the most significant global expansion of a Christian movement in the history of Christianity'.[34] Eschatological immediacy proved a potent source of Pentecostal triumphalism.

b. Pentecostal Perspective: A Hermeneutic of Ontological Immediacy[35]

Early Pentecostals were unabashedly ahistorical in their approach to Scripture. Their *mentalité* was built on the assumption that their experience was continuous with that of the apostles. This ahistoricism was evidenced in a disdain for the history of the past (church history in particular); a rejection of the assumptions of the present (predominantly the acutely modernist positivism of the day); and a preoccupation with the history of the future (in all its apocalyptic splendor).[36] In the words of Edith Blumhofer, 'historylessness was a badge of honor'.[37] Ontological immediacy created a sense of existential proximity to the apostolic age. Wacker defined primitivism generally, and applied it to Pentecostals, as an 'effort to deny history . . . by returning to the time before time, to the golden age that preceded the corruptions of life in history'.[38] As a function of their restorationist perspective, they saw no distance between themselves and the text, or the events it proclaimed.

32. Myland, *Latter Rain*, pp. 85–86. While some missionary accounts were rife with miraculous healings, some that were later proved to be exaggerated, Anderson notes that 'occasionally, missionaries reported cases of failed healings . . . There is little evidence that they were any different from those missionaries who were not Pentecostal'; Alan Anderson, *Spreading Fires: The Missionary Nature of Early Pentecostalism* (Maryknoll, NY: Orbis Books, 2007), p. 217.

33. The story of Aimee Semple McPherson and the loss of her first husband Robert Semple in China was not uncommon. Anderson recounts a number of tales of hardship and suffering, as well as indomitable spirit and passion; ibid., pp. 55–57.

34. Ibid., p. 68.

35. I use the word 'ontological' in the same sense as Mark D. McLean in his essay 'Toward a Pentecostal Hermeneutic', as stronger than an existential sense of union, but an essential unity of being with the apostolic church. As Mclean says, 'God speaks and acts today on behalf of his creation, as he did then, with no ontological distinction between the mode of God's presence in and among his people'; McLean, 'Toward a Pentecostal Hermeneutic', p. 47.

36. Wacker, 'Functions of Faith', p. 364.

37. Blumhofer, *Restoring the Faith*, p. 13.

38. Grant Wacker 'Playing for Keeps: The Primitivist Impulse in Early Pentecostalism', in *The American Quest for the Primitive Church* (ed. Richard T. Hughes; Urbana: University of Illinois Press, 1985), pp. 196–219 (p. 197).

Proximity to the text admitted of no need for historical or cultural sensitivity in appropriating its message, while proximity to its miraculous events implied their accessibility to all Pentecostal seekers. As B. F. Lawrence, early chronicler of the revival, declared, charging historic denominations with bondage to their tradition, 'The Pentecostal Movement has no such history. It leaps the intervening years crying "*Back to Pentecost.*"'[39] Even among restorationists these Pentecosals were unique. They experienced an ontological immediacy with the New Testament church that others may have claimed, but proved theirs with the crowning experience of the supernatural gifts of the Spirit, and the restoration of Pentecost itself.

Ontological immediacy also marked the Pentecostal encounter of the border between the concrete and the spiritual, with no discontinuity between the physical and the supernatural realm. Pentecostals dwelt in a spiritual world. Standard distinctions between the otherworldly and this-worldly ceased to apply. Alongside vivid encounters with Jesus and the Holy Spirit, Pentecostals inhabited a world populated by angels and demons, and indeed, conceived of the physical universe as the battlefield for an intensely fought cosmic warfare. Frank Bartleman, unofficial historian of Azusa Street, protested that in spite of crowds flocking to the rundown warehouse, 'the devil overdid himself again. Outside persecution never hurt the work. We had most to fear from the working of evil spirits within . . . Many were afraid to seek God for fear the devil might get them'.[40] With such a broad horizon of reality, the Pentecostal vision demanded spiritualized interpretations of this-worldly events, both large and small. Bartleman, preparing to preach in the wake of the San Francisco earthquake of 1906, was clearly told by God that in spite of what more moderate voices might say, this was 'His judgment on sin' in that 'terribly wicked city'. He was 'to argue the question with no man, but simply give them the message'. Still, when Bartleman went to have the sermon printed, Satan tried to hinder its printing by creating problems in the press, problems of which Bartleman, 'not being ignorant of his devices', had warned the printer beforehand.[41]

This ontological immediacy led to what Donald Dayton termed 'a subjectivizing hermeneutic' that perceived a community of thought and experience between the first-century church and the pockets of revivalist sects in twentieth-century North America.[42] The Scriptures were addressed to these particular disciples 'upon whom the ends of the earth had come'. Thus Charles Fox Parham could announce with absolute certitude, 'All we claim is that if you get the baptism in the Holy Ghost it will correspond to the experience in the Second chapter of Acts . . . We believe in having the Bible evidence, and the chief evidence if you get the same experience is, that "they spake in tongues."'[43] No other interpretive methods were needed.

39. Lawrence, *Apostolic Faith Restored*, p. 12.

40. Bartleman, *Azusa Street*, p. 48.

41. Ibid., pp. 49–50.

42. Dayton, *Theological Roots*, p. 23.

43. Robert Parham, *Selected Sermons of Charles F. Parham, Sarah E. Parham: Co-Founders of the Original Apostolic Faith Movement* (Baxter Springs, KS: Apostolic Faith Bible College, 1941), pp. 66 and 70; cited in; Archer, *Pentecostal Hermeneutic*, p. 108.

Another early writer called it 'The Pentecostal Standard': 'Demons must be cast out, those of all tongues must be addressed in their own language, sick must be healed, the unbelieving must see signs and know of a truth "this is that."'[44] Parham's reference to Peter's sermon on the day of Pentecost included with ontological immediacy the twentieth century 'this' with the prophetic 'that' of Joel, chapter 2. This feature of Pentecostal interpretation gave rise to the 'Latter Rain theology' discussed earlier.

The value of ontological immediacy, was, of course, that it made the supernatural world, the New Testament church, and the activity of the divine, something that could be, rather, should be experienced in the here and now. After all this was the Pentecostal promise that was 'unto you, and to your children, and to all that are afar off, even as many as the Lord our God shall call' (Acts 2.39). An unexpected, and thus, unintended effect of ontological immediacy was its ahistorical hubris. Between New Testament Christianity and its recovery at Azusa, or Topeka, or Appalachia, the 'intervening years', as B. F. Lawrence called them, were no more than an intercalation. The original Pentecostals were companions with Peter and Paul, and when they sought a name for themselves, the term 'Apostolic' was quick at hand. Along with this ahistoricism, came the additional arrogance of 'the initiated' – that God-has-spoken certainty that, as Bartleman put it, 'argues with no man'. Embattled as early Pentecostals were, their absolute confidence in the Pentecostal experience was a necessity. Nevertheless, their sheer conceit, and overweening self-importance as individuals to whom the Almighty had revealed himself, led, not only to a lack of humility, but to a divisiveness that both separated Pentecostals from others, and spoiled the internal beauty of the earliest movement.[45] Such attitudes would inevitably draw criticism from outsiders, and as Wacker details in an insightful essay, the worst critics were other Radical Evangelicals who were perhaps incensed that their former brethren dared claim to have bested their experience.[46]

The variety of triumphalism that marked early Pentecostalism was shaped by a sense of immediate access to the divine and involved a kind of dislocation of time and place that situated Pentecostals in the same symbolic universe as the

44. J. E. Sawders of Toronto wrote in to G. B. Cashwell's *The Bridegroom's Messenger*, published in Atlanta Georgia, to comment on 'The Pentecostal Standard'; *BM* 1 (1907), p. 4; cited in Alexander, *Pentecostal Healing*, p. 90.

45. The very first issue of the Azusa Street publication, *The Apostolic Faith*, 1 (September, 1906) proclaimed, '"Love, Faith, Unity" are our watchwords', p. 2. Even Parham, who eventually brought division, appealed to all to 'keep together in unity till I come', p. 1. But the reality was not so clear. Jacobsen suggests that the early movement was so differentiated as to make claims of unity at Azusa suspect; Jacobsen, *Thinking in the Spirit*, pp. 9–11. Blumhofer noted that 'Azusa Street could not hold the allegiance of its own enthusiasts, who broke away to form numerous rival congregations nearby, none of which was known to replicate the racial mix of the mother congregation'; Blumhofer, 'For Pentecostals, a Move toward Racial Reconciliation', *CC* 111 (1994), pp. 444–46 (p. 445).

46. Wacker, 'Travail of a Broken Family'.

primitive church. Such was the power of ontological immediacy that this perceived community of meaning with the apostolic age and 'the same Spirit that raised Christ from the dead' gave early Pentecostals the sense that even their most banal actions might have cosmic significance in the eschatological endgame of which they were a part. Thus, ontological immediacy was marked by the zeal of those who believed they had encountered the divine. While we must take their experience seriously, we must also examine it critically. To do both is to reckon with the triumphalism this immediacy created.

c. Pentecostal Praxis: A Hermeneutic of Pragmatic Immediacy

Grant Wacker has suggested part of the genius of Pentecostalism has been its ability to balance primitivism and pragmatism. The two stood in an unavoidable dialectic, 'partly because the logic of the primitive excluded the pragmatic, and partly because pentecostals almost always denied that the pragmatic existed at all'.[47] This pragmatic immediacy manifested itself on at least three levels and brought into play a functional and activist priority that tempered the mystical, and ecstatic dimensions of early Pentecostalism. First, it created an entrepreneurial approach to the business of ministry that accommodated the realities of the modern world; second, it fuelled a 'whatever-it-takes' attitude to the accomplishment of ministry that refused to be intimidated or cowed by circumstance or persecution; and finally, it forced Pentecostals to the border of the mystical and the mundane in their interpretation of Scripture.

Taking the last of these first, the blurring of natural and supernatural worlds created by ontological immediacy was abetted by a pragmatism that demanded a certain approach to biblical interpretation. The Pentecostal hermeneutic that fuelled Parham's Topeka Bible School, Seymour's Azusa revival, and Tomlinson's southern snake-handling was marked by a strict, even excessive literalism that demanded radical practice not just pious platitude. If the Azusa Pentecostals were the extremists of biblical literalism, the 'Jesus Only' 'come-outers' of 1913 became the revolutionaries of Pentecostal interpretation. Their restorationist logic forced them to apply a hermeneutic that transcended Christian tradition, thus, finding no trace of the word 'Trinity' in their Bibles, Oneness Pentecostals reinterpreted the Holy Spirit in modalist fashion as the Spirit of Jesus, and salvation as coincident with the baptism in the Holy Spirit.[48] Pragmatic immediacy meant that these doctrinal novelties were not the source but the result of baptism in Jesus' name. First came a revelation at the Arroyo Seco Worldwide Camp Meeting of baptism in

47. Wacker, *Heaven Below*, p. 14; This interplay of the two forms the argument of Wacker's book. See also Wacker, 'Searching for Eden with a Satellite Dish: Primitivism, Pragmatism, and the Pentecostal Character', in *The Primitive Church in the Modern World* (ed. Richard T. Hughes; Urbana: University of Illinois Press, 1985), pp. 139–66, where he develops this thesis at length.

48. Stephen R. Graham, '"Thus Saith the Lord": Biblical Hermeneutics in the Early Pentecostal Movement', *EA* 12 (1996), pp. 121–35 (pp. 128–29).

Jesus' name, then came the doctrinal elaboration. Once received as authentic, the revelation of this baptismal formula must certainly be acted upon.[49]

Today the most extreme of these Oneness groups are the independent snake-handling churches of Appalachia such as The Church of Jesus with Signs Following, described in Dennis Covington's *Salvation on Sand Mountain*.[50] For most early Pentecostals the 'signs following' of Mark 16 became a 'litmus test' for the true movement of God, though not necessarily extending to the poison and serpents clause.[51] From Azusa to Appalachia the pragmatic application of the text grew from its insistence on healing, tongues and exorcism until the irresistible logic of Pentecostal exegesis forced the question of 'taking up serpents' and drinking 'deadly things', at least for A. J. Tomlinson's followers. While the Church of God did not make these signs tests of salvation, Tomlinson reproved other Pentecostals for neither quoting nor practising the entire verse, and clearly saw them as signs commanded by Jesus.[52] The pragmatic immediacy of the text was apparent to Tomlinson, if not to others, and the boundary between the mystical and the mundane seemed erased as the Spirit fell and the snakes came out of the boxes that stored them to test the promise of Scripture.

The further implications of Pentecostal praxis led in the direction of evangelistic ministry. Russell Spittler recognized that the primary use of Scripture in Pentecostal heritage is in setting the agenda for evangelism and missions.[53] The earliest

49. Frank Ewart and Glenn Cook baptized one another in Jesus' name a year later at the first public baptism to be carried out with a 'theologically consistent rationale' arising from the Arroyo Seco revelation; Reed, *'In Jesus' Name': The History and Beliefs of Oneness Pentecostals*. [Journal of Pentecostal Theology Supplement Series Number 31] (Blandford Forum, UK: Deo, 2008), p. 937.

50. Dennis Covington, *Salvation on Sand Mountain: Snake-Handling and Redemption in Southern Appalachia* (New York: Penguin, 1995), pp. 17 and 87.

51. Thomas and Alexander, '"And the Signs . . ."', pp. 150–51 and 155.

52. Robins, *A. J. Tomlinson*, pp. 189–90, 287, n. 7; Thomas and Alexander, '"And the Signs . . ."', pp. 153–54. Snake-handling in Pentecostal circles originated in the Church of God in 1909 or 1910, when introduced by George Hensley, who claimed a revelatory experience while meditating on Mark 16; Synan, *Holiness Pentecostal Tradition*, pp. 188–90; and H. D. Hunter, 'Serpent Handling', in *NIDPCM*, pp. 1052–53. The uniqueness of the practice to the southeastern states and pathway by which snake-handling moved between a Trinitarian Holiness-Pentecostal church such as the Church of God to Oneness Holiness churches such as those mentioned by Covington and others do not yet seem to have been elaborated. Though snake-handling seems to be primarily a twentieth-century phenomenon, Ralph Hood's editing of Jimmy Morrow's oral history dates it as far back as the 1890s and maybe 1880s in the Appalachian mountains; Jimmy Morrow, *Handling Serpents: Pastor Jimmy Morrow's Narrative History of His Appalachian Jesus' Name Tradition* (ed. Ralph W. Hood; Macon: Mercer University Press, 2005).

53. Russell Spittler, 'Scripture and the Theological Enterprise: View from a Big Canoe', in *The Use of the Bible in Theology: Evangelical Options* (ed. R. K. Johnston; Atlanta: John Knox Press, 1985), pp. 56–77 (p. 75).

Pentecostals understood tongues primarily as a missionary gift and anticipated that the 'foreign heathen' to whom they were sent would recognize the untaught languages they spoke. As a tactic to complete the task of world evangelization quickly before the return of Christ, 'it is hard to imagine a strategy more clearly born of pragmatic inclinations'.[54] A. G. Garr and his wife Lillian were among the first missionaries to leave Azusa, arriving in Calcutta in early 1907, only to find that they were unable to speak Bengali as they had anticipated.[55] Such episodes establish the clear link between Pentecostal experience, Pentecostal interpretation and Pentecostal praxis. The reception of the Bible promise coupled with Bible evidence, and the Bible command to go could only mean one thing.[56]

The emphasis on practical ministry, however, included a stubborn 'stick-to-it-iveness' that accounted in large part for the success of Pentecostal mission in spite of opposition. The passion of these early leaders led them to overwhelming efforts to receive all they could from God and to proclaim all they could of God. When R. E. McAlister, that doughty pioneer of Canadian Pentecostalism, first heard of Azusa he was engaged in evangelism in the West. The pragmatic response was to drop everything, and go directly to Los Angeles. Arriving there on 11 December 1906, he sought the baptism, soon receiving it and was on his way home a few hours later.[57] The same attitude was apparent in A. H. Argue, the Winnipeg realtor who made the journey to Chicago where at the end of 21 days 'waiting on God' he was 'filled with the Holy Ghost as the Spirit gave utterance'. On his return to Winnipeg he began to hold 'tarrying meetings' and three days later three were filled with the Spirit.[58] Argue went on to be a tireless worker, commenting in 1908 that he had held nine weekly services over a nine-month period.[59] Both Argue and McAlister also demonstrated that pragmatic business savvy typical of many early Pentecostal entrepreneurs that enabled them to be effective in the promotion and administration of the revival. Both began publishing ventures to promulgate the Pentecostal experience around the world. McAlister's *The Good Report* begun in 1911 had press runs of 45,000 copies distributed free of charge, while another paper, *The Morning Star* was sent to Egypt for publication. Argue's vision was

54. Wacker, *Heaven Below*, p. 48.

55. Gary McGee, 'Garr, Alfred Goodrich, Sr.', in *NIDPCM*, pp. 660–61; and Gary McGee, 'Missions, Overseas (N. American Pentecostal)', in *NIDPCM*, pp. 885–901 (pp. 887–88). Parham and his followers claimed tongues to be xenolalia (foreign languages). Garr was among the first to contradict this and to focus on tongues as prayer.

56. Fuelled by Parham's teaching on xenolalia, Anderson indicates that 'by 1906 . . . the first Pentecostals almost universally believed that by this means they would preach the gospel "abroad" to the ends of the earth in the last days'. Still, he points out, 'there was no shortage of the report of missionary tongues'; Anderson, *Spreading Fires*, pp. 41, 53 and 58–59.

57. Miller, *Canadian Pentecostals*, p. 62.

58. A. H. Argue, 'Azusa Street Revival Reaches Winnipeg', *PT* 37 (May, 1956), p. 8.

59. *Apostolic Messenger* (March–April, 1908) cited in Wacker, 'Searching for Eden', p. 151.

equally broad. His *The Apostolic Messenger*, some early numbers of which ran at 40,000 copies, purported to report on the progress of the outpouring in 40 different nations.[60] Pentecostal doctrine simply did not exist without corresponding Pentecostal practice. The pragmatic impulse began with the Bible but ended in a hermeneutic of praxis.

Radical Evangelicalism was already possessed of an elevated awareness of the supernatural.[61] But the pragmatic immediacy of early Pentecostals was fuelled by a sense of calling and empowerment arising from an even more extremely literal interpretation of Scripture. It raised still higher the expectation of supernatural intervention that existed in Radical Evangelicalism. They took God at his word, and believed they were led by his Spirit. They journeyed to far-flung corners of the world assuming they had miraculously received the language of the inhabitants, trusting that God would provide for their financial need. And for some it happened, just as they expected. The marvelous story of Sophia Hanson, missionary to China, was uncommon to be sure, but according to a letter signed by 14 Chinese witnesses, she preached the gospel in Mandarin without ever having learned it.[62] For many, though, such as the Brelsfords, the experience was harsh. They left their children behind in America as they travelled to Egypt, arriving in Alexandria with $2 in their pocket, left to depend on Egyptian Christians until funds came from home.[63]

The same held true in terms of entrepreneurial praxis. Pragmatic immediacy carried with it a little social Darwinism. In the atmosphere of confident faith, divine promise and untold opportunity, it was little wonder that risk-taking leadership would thrive. Some of the most colourful characters of early Pentecostalism were its leaders. Many of them were rugged individualists who exhibited a strong bent to independence of thought and action.[64] Particularly so was A. J. Tomlinson who combined entrepreneurial flair and prophetic authority to establish not one, but two denominations, The Church of God (Cleveland TN) and the Church of God of Prophecy. But for each story of heroic success lay strewn multiplied victims of defeat. Tomlinson himself, who had successfully managed to manipulate charismatic leadership and political prowess so as to be nominated 'General Overseer for Life',

60. Miller, *Canadian Pentecostals*, pp. 63–64, 78.

61. Wacker notes that the differences between early Pentecostals and the Radical Evangelicalism from which they derived were hardly noticed by outsiders, so common was their worldview; Wacker, 'Travail of a Broken Family'.

62. Anderson, *Spreading Fires*, p. 63; and Wacker, *Heaven Below*, pp. 46–47. Hansen made the claim first in 1908, and continued to experience the gift until as late as 1921. Wacker offers this as the only example he has discovered of a first-generation Pentecostal claiming a permanent gift of missionary tongues, though she made it clear the gift only functioned when the topic was the gospel.

63. Anderson, *Spreading Fires*, p. 56.

64. 'Radical holiness prospered . . . in a . . . culture where militancy and nonconformity, under the right circumstances, were not just allowed. They were positively encouraged'; Robins, *A. J. Tomlinson*, p. 29.

fell victim to even better maneuvering in 1922, when he was ousted, in spite of organizational success, largely due to questions of mismanagement arising from his authoritarian control of the entire denomination.[65] Triumphalism, it appears, even in its pneumatic variety, is a two-edged sword where the victors write the history.

Early Pentecostalism, then, exhibited a hermeneutic that was impelled by immediacy. It provided direct access to apostolic authority (in its ahistorical, pre-critical literalism); apostolic mission (in its renewed commitment to follow the mandates of the early church); and apostolic power (through the Pentecostal visitation and renewal of the gifts implied by the Latter Rain). The hermeneutic of ontological immediacy created a uniquely Pentecostal perspective that in turn demanded a supernaturally driven praxis fuelled by a hermeneutic of Pentecostal pragmatism. It remained, however, for the eschatological immediacy of the 'Latter Rain' motif to provide the metanarrative necessary to give prophetic cohesion to a distinctly Pentecostal identity. Within this worldview, however, some were victorious and others weren't. The natural selection of those who could wield charismatic power effectively, and surf the treacherous waves of harsh experience favoured the savvy, the rugged; those who could spiritually reinterpret life's vagaries on the run. For some it came naturally, for others the supernatural supply apparently ran dry. Thus arose the typical story arc of Pentecostal triumphalism: high expectation, substantiating tales of victory, but precious little to speak to the frustrated experience of those for whom the promise failed.

III. The Shift to an Institutional Hermeneutic

Immediacy was the key to unfolding the *mentalité* of the earliest Pentecostals. It created an experience of the numinous so enthralling that participants were drawn to make substantial sacrifices, and to go to uncommon extremes for its propagation. With time, however this immediacy was necessarily blunted. On the one hand, as the *parousia* delayed, Pentecostals had to find more nuanced expressions of their 'latter rain' faith.[66] On the other, as Pentecostals experienced success, less provisional ecclesiastical forms than the so-called store-front mission were needed to provide stability and direction. The result was predictable. A steady process of institutionalization began that, while ensuring continued growth, also made substantial though subtle changes to the Pentecostal hermeneutic that had given rise to the movement in the first place.

65. Robins tells the story of Tomlinson's rise to leadership, and rejection from the Church of God most compellingly against a meticulously detailed background he calls 'plainfolk modernism'; ibid.

66. Opinions differ as to how soon the shift began. Faupel, following Robert Mapes Anderson, places it as early as the end of 1908. He marks three changes that were afoot by that time: (1) the generally acknowledged failure of missionary tongues, (2) the failure of Pentecost to unify the church and (3) the delayed return of the Lord; Faupel, *Everlasting Gospel*, p. 228.

Long ago, sociologist of religion Max Weber, claimed that charismatic movements arise under shaman-like leaders with magical properties. He contended that 'if this is not to remain a purely transitory phenomenon, but to take on the character of a permanent relationship forming a stable community of disciples . . . it is necessary for the character of charismatic authority to become radically changed'.[67] Margaret Poloma suggested that this Weberian model of the routinization of the charisma applies remarkably well to Pentecostalism as a charismatic movement.[68] Indeed Poloma once credited the growth of the Assemblies of God (AG), the largest white Pentecostal denomination to arise out of Azusa, to the fact that it successfully encouraged 'personal participation in charisma without jeopardizing its organizational structure'.[69]

That such a process took place at all is the more remarkable considering the attitudes of early Pentecostals towards denominationalism.[70] Founding General Superintendent of the PAOC, George A. Chambers, recalled as he was retiring in 1934 that before 1917 'we took the position that God was forever through with organization . . .' However, 'after years of battling along, each man for himself (some calling it the faith life), seeing and doing some quite foolish things, we finally woke up to the fact that some order and system was needed and right.'[71] Institutionalization had begun, and the immediacy that marked early Pentecostal interpretation would have to undergo some alteration to accommodate it. Sociologist Thomas O'Dea defined the process as follows: 'The *routinization* of charisma is . . . a process that involves *containment* of the charisma.'[72] I will argue that this containment occurred through the subtle but definite attenuation of immediacy. O'Dea held that routinization of a charismatic community takes place

67. Weber, *The Theory of Social and Economic Organization* (trans. A. M. Henderson and Talcott Parsons; New York: Free Press, 1947), p. 364. In this section the terms charismatic and charisma are used in the Weberian sense.

68. Margaret M. Poloma, *The Assemblies of God at the Crossroads: Charisma and Institutional Dilemmas* (Knoxville: University of Tennessee Press, 1989), pp. 4–11.

69. Ibid., p. 11. Later observation of denominational change has forced Poloma to modify this position somewhat; Margaret Poloma, 'The Symbolic Dilemma and the Future of Pentecostalism: Mysticism, Ritual, and Revival', in *The Future of Pentecostalism in the United States* (ed. Eric Patterson and Edmund Rybarczyk; Lanham, MD: Lexington, 2007), pp. 105–21 (pp. 111–14); and Margaret Poloma, 'The Future of American Pentecostal Identity: The Assemblies of God at a Crossroad', in *The Work of the Spirit: Pneumatology and Pentecostalism* (ed. Michael Welker; Grand Rapids: Eerdmans, 2006), pp. 147–65. Poloma considers the 'Toronto Blessing' in terms of a revitalization of the American Pentecostal/Charismatic movement; Margaret Poloma, *Main Street Mystics: The Toronto Blessing and Reviving Pentecostalism* (Walnut Creek, CA: Alta Mira, 2003), pp. 15–16 and 237.

70. Hollenweger, *The Pentecostals*, pp. 29–30. Poloma noted the subtle transition from the first decade to the second; Margaret Poloma, 'The "Toronto Blessing": Charisma, Institutionalization, and Revival', *JSSR* 36 (1997), pp. 257–71 (p. 257).

71. George A. Chambers, 'In Retrospect . . .', *PT* 15 (November, 1934), p. 7.

72. O'Dea and Aviad, *The Sociology of Religion, Second Edition* (Englewood Cliffs: Prentice-Hall, [1966] 1986), p. 41, italics O'Dea's.

on three levels: the intellectual, the cultic and the organizational. An examination of each will demonstrate the shift in Pentecostal self-definition that took place as institutionalization continued apace. It will also reveal that Pentecostal triumphalism went through a subtle transformation, adding, as already hinted in the discussion of Tomlinson, an institutional dimension unthought-of in its early days.

a. Intellectual Containment of the Charisma

Intellectual changes among Pentecostals were inevitable once the first blush of revivalism had passed. These occurred as a response to the lengthening gap between the 'Latter Rain' and the coming of the Lord. While the 'Latter Rain Covenant' began to unravel as an organizing principle for Pentecostal theology, it continued as a rhetorical device at least until the renewal movement of that name arose to challenge the established institutional hegemony of the late 1940s. The nature of these changes to the interpretive grid may be seen as a return to the flow of proto-Fundamentalist reaction to the incipient modernism of mainline denominations. Much of Radical Evangelicalism had followed in this Fundamentalist path – particularly the Keswick or 'deeper life' stream, which had a distinct appeal to Baptists, Presbyterians and Anglicans. But for the Holiness radicals who could appreciate it, early Pentecostalism afforded a brief revivalist hiatus from the doctrinal rigors of the Fundamentalist-Modernist controversy.[73] With the ebbing of revival, however, ultimately, and uncomfortably, since it was never a welcome participant, Pentecostalism fell into the essential contours of Fundamentalism.[74] This intellectual transition is observed in the growing dispensationalism of Pentecostal eschatology, the increasingly Fundamentalist tone of Pentecostal theology, and, particularly in Canadian Pentecostalism, a growing affirmation of historic Christianity.

While the 'Latter Rain Covenant' involved clearly dispensational implications, early Pentecostalism, birthed in the fire of revival, had not had the leisure to develop a sophisticated eschatology. The restorationist impulse of Azusa Street, no doubt reflecting the premillennial consensus of the Gilded Age, saw the Pentecostal outpouring as the ultimate fulfilment of New Testament expectation in the latter days. But eventually restorationism itself faded against the institutional vision of growth, development and acceptance by the broader Christian establishment.[75] In an insightful paper, Gerald Sheppard questioned the assumption that early Pentecostalism was strictly dispensational. He shows persuasively that standard dispensational categories such as the exclusive separation of Israel and the

73. Joel Carpenter, *Revive Us Again: The Reawakening of American Fundamentalism* (New York: Oxford University Press, 1997), p. 81; and Marsden, *Fundamentalism and American Culture*, pp. 93–95.

74. Ibid., p. 94.

75. Wacker, while not suggesting the reasons for it, notes the eventual regression of restorationism; Wacker, 'The Functions of Faith . . .', p. 365.

church, the parenthetical character of the church age and the secret rapture of the church were absent from the earliest writing of Pentecostals.[76] Indeed, in a 1926 article in the Canadian *Pentecostal Testimony*, British Bible teacher Donald Gee offered a relatively negative assessment of the disposal of the supernatural 'along ingenious "dispensational" lines', asking 'why such things were quite necessary then, but are quite UNneccessary now; and the hunger of the believer who reads the New Testament longing to participate in its experiences is lulled to sleep with the oft-repeated label – "NOT FOR TO-DAY"'.[77] By the 1930s, however, the *Pentecostal Testimony* was advertising Clarence Larkin's *Dispensational Truth*, a classic exposition of the system, and the March, 1936 edition carried a centre-page spread of A. E. Booth's famous 'Chart of the Course of Time from Eternity to Eternity', complete with the offer of a full-colour, 15-foot, hand-made edition for 20 dollars, and the possibility of ordering extra copies of that particular issue for teaching purposes.[78] In an editorial in the *Testimony*, Canadian pioneer R. E. McAlister offered what appeared to be a more careful dividing of the Word than Myland had performed in the early days. McAlister provided a fully dispensational approach to 'three distinct classes of people'; Jews, Gentiles and the church, and perhaps consciously extending Myland, suggested that the Latter Rain, and healing are indeed Jewish realities, the spiritual benefits of which are available to the church.[79] The full-blown treatment, however, awaited Frank M. Boyd's *Ages and Dispensations*, which according to William Menzies 'turned dispensationalism on its head, making the Church Age the age of the Spirit, rather than the hiatus advocated by Scofieldian dispensationalism'.[80] Against the relatively inchoate eschatology of early Pentecostalism, Boyd represented those who 'sought to bring Pentecostal views into a full harmony with Fundamentalist-Dispensationalist orthodoxy'.[81]

The incipient Fundamentalism of institutional Pentecostalism was in no way a surprising, or unexpected development. After all, the Holiness and Keswick cousins of Pentecostals all imbibed the same elixir, and shared the same dispensational assumptions as Fundamentalists. But such a transition implied two accommodations that were impossible at Azusa. First was the adoption of a more reflective theology that took account of the possibility that 'the end

76. Gerald T. Sheppard, 'Pentecostals and Dispensationalism: The Anatomy of an Uneasy Relationship', *Pneuma* 6 (1984), pp. 5–33 (pp. 7–13).

77. Gee, 'The Baptism of the Holy Ghost', *PT* 7 (July, 1926), p. 5.

78. A brief ad offering Larkin's book for $5, postpaid appears in the February, 1931 issue of the *Testimony*, Booth's chart appears in the March 1936 issue, 8–9.

79. R. E. McAlister, 'The Jew-The Gentile . . . and the Church of God', *PT* 18 (November, 1937), pp. 3, 8–9.

80. Frank M. Boyd, *Ages and Dispensations* (Springfield, MO: Gospel Publishing House, n.d.); and William Menzies, 'The Reformed Roots of Pentecostalism', *PentecoStudies* 6 (2007), pp. 78–99 (p. 85). Menzies claims Boyd entered Pentecostal ranks in 1908 with a clearly defined eschatology; Menzies, 'Non-Wesleyan Origins', p. 85.

81. Sheppard, 'Pentecostals and Dispensationalism . . .', p. 21.

was not yet'. Such adjustments to the 'Latter Rain' theology of Myland, itself a relatively sophisticated expression of the 'Jesus-is-coming-soon' preaching of the early revival, allowed the rhetoric of 'Latter Rain' to continue within a widened temporal context. But, secondly and perhaps even more crucially for the institutional hermeneutic, these modifications represented an inevitable attenuation of the eschatological immediacy of the earlier *mentalité*. On this modified view, the Azusa outpouring, rather than signalling the end, fell into the unexpected parenthetical church age of dispensationalism. The more the baptism in the Holy Spirit now belonged more properly to this period of undetermined length, punctuated finally by the rapture itself, the more it could be seen as yet another element of the recovery of New Testament truth leading to the consummation. While this move saved Spirit-baptism from the demise of the Latter Rain narrative, it could not rescue its concomitant immediacy. Thus, the more dispensationalism shaped Latter Rain rhetoric, the more difficulty existed in existentially experiencing the immediacy so essential to the revivalist worldview. Today, with its Latter Rain theology substantially discarded, Pentecostalism faces the same theoretical problems dispensationalism does in its eschatology, but with the further challenge of creating, in the same way Myland did, a sense of immediacy in its eschatological expectancy, immediacy verified by the end time recovery of the supernatural. As revival faded into institutionalization, the last days timetable made a subtle but distinct shift. In 1923, evangelist W. T. Gaston could write, 'Verily we are living in a wonderful epoch of the world's history – a time for which many have prayed. The latter rain is falling.'[82] Yet, in 1939, amid articles asking 'Have We Lost Divine Healing?' and lamenting the 'cooling down of revival fires' due to the scarcity of 'soul travail', a full page piece on home missions invites us to pray, 'May we be enabled to prepare the way of the Lord, so that we may witness the greatest outpouring of spiritual blessing since the day of Pentecost.'[83] Of course, this outpouring would be seen as an extension of Azusa's Latter Rain, but it might still be the greatest since Pentecost itself. Eventually, anticipation of the rapture, and a final outpouring of the Sprit, of which Azusa was simply the harbinger replaced the earlier Latter Rain paradigm that anticipated the end momentarily. Occasionally purists lament that Pentecostals have sold their souls to Evangelicalism. The irony remains that it is perhaps the dispensational paradigm, as modified by Pentecostals that saved the Latter Rain metaphor. This adjustment facilitated the sustained rhetoric of Pentecostal discourse through the period of its institutionalization, and contained the charisma without extinguishing it altogether.

While dispensational eschatology is the most easily discernible influence of Fundamentalism on Pentecostal thought, the two streams flowed together as, at length, Pentecostals had to fashion a more complete theology for the training

82. W. T. Gaston, 'The Latter Rain', *PT* 2 (September 1923), p. 6.

83. Leslie W. Smith, 'Have We Lost Divine Healing?', *PT* 20 (15 August 1939), pp. 6–7; D. N. Buntain, 'Soul Travail', *PT* 20 (1 March 1939), pp. 2–3; and Frank Harford, 'A Home Missions Opportunity', *PT* 20 (1 May 1939), p. 13.

of a second generation of pastors and leaders.[84] Far from refining a specifically Pentecostal response to the Christian tradition, doctrinal development among Pentecostals was framed more as an apologetic for the acceptance of Pentecostalism as an expression of historic Christianity.[85] Two examples of this, one Canadian and the other American demonstrate how institutional Pentecostalism endeavoured to identify itself with mainstream Christianity.

The writings of Jewish convert Myer Pearlman have been known to generations of Pentecostal students. Pearlman taught at the Assemblies of God's Central Bible College in Springfield, Missouri until his untimely death in 1943. He penned the Assemblies' adult Sunday School curriculum for a number of years while he taught classes there.[86] Two of Pearlman's works are especially significant for our purposes. *Through the Bible Book by Book*, an effort at Bible introduction, published in 1935, does exactly what the title implies. Pearlman's notes are a brief, literalist guide through the Scriptural text, with very little comment on historical issues and none at all on critical matters. The survey assumes that one may approach the Bible just as it is, with few barriers to impede the modern reader. Pearlman perpetuates the ahistoricism, not only of early Pentecostals, but of Fundamentalism generally. On the other hand, the text lacks any sense of the polemical tone one might have expected from Fundamentalists of the time. Pearlman was writing simply to inform, not to defend.[87]

In the more complex *Knowing the Doctrines of the Bible*, however, Pearlman spells out a larger aim. 'We confidently expect that theology or doctrine will find its deserved place in religious thought and education. Whatever has been said, in recent years derogatory to this branch of study, has been ill-timed in view of the world's great need of sobering and satisfying truth.'[88] Pearlman's approach is not experiential, but decidedly doctrinal. He quotes from a wide variety of authors both fundamentalist conservatives and moderate liberals, but in all, his purpose is to show the fully orthodox nature of Pentecostal doctrine.[89] Pearlman's concern for the place of doctrine, and his goal to provide 'sober and satisfying truth' reflect the defensiveness of the theological enterprise in the face of the established Pentecostal *mentalité*. This hat-in-hand request for a place at the Pentecostal table will continue for years to come. Often it is assumed that the anti-intellectual nature of Pentecostalism reflects the social status of its early adherents, but instead, one

84. Douglas Jacobsen, 'Knowing the Doctrines of Pentecostals: The Scholastic Theology of the Assemblies of God, 1930–55', in *Pentecostal Currents in American Protestantism* (ed. Edith L. Blumhofer, Russell P. Spittler and Grant A. Wacker; Urbana: University of Illinois Press, 1999), pp. 90–107 (p. 90).

85. Ibid., p. 91.

86. Gohr, G. W. 'Pearlman, Myer', in *NIDPCM*, p. 959.

87. Myer Pearlman, *Through the Bible Book by Book, 4 Volumes* (Springfield, MO: Gospel Publishing House, 1935).

88. Myer Pearlman, *Knowing the Doctrines of the Bible* (Springfield, MO: Gospel Publishing House, 1937), p. 7.

89. Jacobsen, 'Knowing the Doctrines of Pentecostals', pp. 94–96.

may perceive the growing demand for a theological rationale as exemplifying, once more, the subtle attenuation of revivalist immediacy.

In Canada, there is little doubt that Pentecostal theology was marked indelibly by J. Eustace Purdie, Anglican vicar turned Pentecostal educator.[90] Purdie is a fascinating character, not only because he was the founder of the first Pentecostal Bible College in Canada in 1925, but also because in spite of joining the Pentecostal movement, he remained a convinced and lifelong Anglican in heart.[91] This set him in a unique position among those who had left behind the 'dead formalism' of denominational Christendom. It also shaped the theology of the 600 students who passed through his classes between 1925 and 1950 many of whom went on to pastor the churches and shape the *mentalité* of institutional Pentecostalism.[92] In the booklet *What We Believe*, Purdie established a remarkably broad creedal basis for Pentecostal faith. He asserted that Pentecostals held to 'the three Ancient Creeds of the early Church known as the Apostles', the Nicene, and the Athanasian; and also the Confessions of Faith drawn up at the time of the Reformation by the Reformed churches of the sixteenth and seventeenth centuries.'[93] Purdie's teaching was clearly shaped by his own education at Wycliffe College and by the Keswick atmosphere there.[94] Considering his towering influence in Pentecostal education, one can hardly doubt Purdie's influence towards an expanded view of Christian theology and experience among Canadian Pentecostals. While broadening their sectarianism, however, Purdie's passionate sense of continuity with historic Christianity and emphasis on the catholicity of the church had the further influence of taming the wild ontological immediacy that allowed early Pentecostals to traverse 2,000 years of church history with the utterance of an unknown tongue.

As institutionalization progressed and Pentecostalism faced its second generation of leaders, efforts to define itself in historic continuity with what the earlier generation may have seen as the 'apostate church' indicate the continual blunting of the sharp edge of immediacy on which the revivalist hermeneutic

90. For an elaboration of Purdie's significance, see James Craig's '"Out and Out for the Lord" – James Eustace Purdie: An Early Anglican Pentecostal', [Unpublished MA thesis] Online: https://paoc.org/docs/default-source/paoc-family-docs/Archives/Academic-Resources/j-craig---purdie-thesis.pdf (Accessed 14 August 2014).

91. Ibid., pp. 34–39. Indeed, Purdie sought at least twice to return to the Anglican church; ibid., pp. 37–39.

92. Ibid., p. 28.

93. J. Eustace Purdie, *What We Believe* (Toronto: Full Gospel Publishing House, 1954), p. 2. Purdie later endeavoured to encourage catechetical instruction through a booklet entitled; *Concerning the Faith* (Toronto: Full Gospel Publishing House, 1951).

94. Peter Althouse, 'The Influence of Dr. J. E. Purdie's Reformed Anglican Theology on the Formation and Development of the Pentecostal Assemblies of Canada', *Pneuma* 19 (1996), pp. 3–28 (pp. 19–20); Althouse shows persuasively that Purdie's teaching was clearly modelled after his Anglican mentors, among whom was Keswick leader W. H. Griffith Thomas.

turned. 'Latter Rain' either marks a break from the slumber of Christendom and an immediate reconnection with the New Testament church; or it loses its force entirely. While other theological constructs may account for the present-day experience of the miraculous, they are incapable of recovering the immediacy of the early Pentecostal hermeneutic. The intellectual containment of the charisma by appeal to dispensational, Fundamentalist, and historic presuppositions, though not consciously intended to catalyze transformation, actually allowed the charisma to survive in the rhetoric of institutional Pentecostalism. In the process, though, the ontological blurring of the frontier between the physical and the spiritual, the eschatological urgency, and the pragmatic drive that had birthed Pentecostalism began a subtle process of transmutation consistent with denominational success.

While attenuating the immediacy of early Pentecostalism, the intellectual containment of the charisma enabled Pentecostal triumphalism to moderate its shrillness without completely losing its edge. No longer the final Holy Ghost visitation preceding the end, Pentecostalism could look for yet more prodigious rain in the future, though some measure of declension had set in for a season. Founding General Superintendent George Chambers lamented in 1941

> If solemn assemblies were called, to wait on God for His next move and downpour of the Latter Rain and the restoration to the church the things that have been lost or let slip, worldliness would again take wings from our midst; substitutions for power and anointings would find no place.[95]

The dispensational broadening of 'Latter Rain' language allowed it to continue as a powerful tool of motivational rhetoric, even as its immediacy was attenuated. Its Janus-like effectiveness was double-edged. By calling Pentecostals back to an Azusa that the younger generation could only know as 'myth', the 'Latter Rain' paradigm could still offer a passionately future-oriented impetus for triumphalism.[96] Meanwhile, the elaboration of a more secure doctrinal footing, and one that situated Pentecostalism in the mainstream of Fundamentalist, and even historic Christianity could only create the sense that Pentecostals had been raised up to offer their gift as the crowning jewel of the doctrinal and experiential restoration of

95. G. A. Chambers, 'Worldward or Godward, Which?', *PT* 22 (15 July 1941), p. 13.

96. I use the word 'myth' here much as Joe Creech does in his assessment of Azusa Street: as 'a sacred Narrative that explains the origins or meaning of a particular religious group'; Joe Creech, 'Visions of Glory: The Place of the Azusa Street Revival in Pentecostal History', *CH* 65 (1996), pp. 405–24 (406, n. 2). As Rogerson suggests, the category of myth does not determine issues of historicity; J. W. Rogerson, 'Slippery Words: Myth', in *Sacred Narrative: Readings in the Theory of Myth* (ed. Allen Dundes; Los Angeles: University of California Press, 1984), pp. 62–71 (p. 68). One definition, useful in this particular context, sees myth as '*any presentation of the actual in terms of the ideal*'; Theodor Gaster, 'Myth and Story', in *Sacred Narrative: Readings in the Theory of Myth* (ed. Allen Dundes; Los Angeles: University of California Press, 1984), pp. 110–36 (p. 112).

the church age.[97] Now the story could be told like this: The theologically marginal, racially diverse and socially varied collection that found Pentecost in the least likely of places, the Azusa Street warehouse, were indeed rising above their humble origins to lead the Church into its end-time destiny.

b. Cultic Containment of the Charisma

Like the blowing of the wind, revival is an uncertain quantity, and one cannot tell whence it came or whither it goes. So it was with the Pentecostal renewal and its sense of revivalist immediacy. As early as 1929 R. E. McAlister, editor of the *Pentecostal Testimony* was lamenting its passing. 'How many have looked back to those days with wonder! Such things are not so prevalent now in the great Movement.'[98] But the denomination-building McAlister was no misty-eyed sentimentalist longing for the past. He brought a critical eye to the matter as well. The 'heavenly scenes' of Azusa and its kin 'were marred by a lack of wisdom, a lack of Spiritual and Scriptural understanding of the nature of them. We recognized them as of God, but how to have them continue and yet to have a service that would appeal to the intelligence of those who come in and look on, was the problem and that is the crucial point where we make or break'. The containment of the charisma in the cultus of institutional Pentecostalism presented the most challenging dimension of perpetuating a form of ontological immediacy without allowing it to overwhelm organizational priorities. McAlister went on to give clear

97. In a sermon reprinted in the *Pentecostal Testimony*, editor R. E. McAlister offers the classic statement, employing a dispensational model. Explaining the rather sudden appearance of the Pentecostal manifestations, McAlister states the solution is clear 'when you understand God's dispensational plan and the dispensational setting of the Holy Spirit in the Scriptures'. He claims that 'practically all the fundamental truths of the Word of God were lost in the dark ages', not just Spirit Baptism. After chronicling the restoration of the gospel through Luther, Wesley, The Salvation Army and the Christian and Missionary Alliance, McAlister declares, 'now following in its logical place is the Pentecostal Movement, restoring the truths of the Baptism of the Holy Spirit with its initial evidence, followed by the manifestation of the nine gifts of the Spirit. What shall the next great, glorious drama be? Christ and His Kingdom in eternity'; McAlister, 'Our Distinctive Testimony: Replying to Rev. James McGinlay', *PT* 13 (March, 1932), p. 18. This notion was not absent from the revivalist elaboration of the Pentecostal experience. In an unsigned article in *The Apostolic Faith*, the writer (ostensibly Seymour himself) claims, 'All along the ages men have been preaching a partial Gospel. A part of the Gospel remained when the world went into the dark ages. God has from time to time raised up men to bring back the truth to the church.' The article mentions Luther, Wesley, and Dr Cullis as great reformers, and then proceeds to give a synopsis of the ministry of Charles Parham, 'who was surely raised up of God to be an apostle of the doctrine of Pentecost'; 'The Pentecostal Baptism Restored', *AF* 1 (October, 1906), p. 1.

98. R. E. McAlister, 'Spiritual Leadership', *PT* 10 (May, 1929), p. 6.

instruction in the quest for proper spiritual leadership rather than carnal control in the leading of 'the song service'.

Discovering this balance remains the 'holy grail' of Pentecostal worship. Mrs J. E. Purdie, wife of the redoubtable college administrator, stated the problem in classically Pentecostal terms: 'Some magnify the Word at the expense of the Spirit and develop dead orthodoxy – a mere head knowledge. Others magnify the Spirit at the expense of the Word and this often produces fanaticism and wild-fire.'[99] The balance, in the late 1930s, at least, seemed decidedly in favour of decency and order. The tale is a fascinating exploration of the routinization of the charisma.

A curious piece in the December 1937 *Pentecostal Testimony* ran under the heading 'Oswald Smith Testifies'. The leader of the non-Pentecostal People's Church in Toronto had visited Stockholm, and witnessed 'the most aggressive evangelical work' in the country, the Philadelphia Pentecostal Church. Smith's report, reprinted from his own publication, was the more stunning for appearing in a Canadian Pentecostal periodical. 'Pentecostalism in Sweden is very different from Pentecostalism in America. It is conservative and sane. There is no wild fire in it at all', Smith concluded.[100] The term 'testifies' in the article's title is perhaps deliberately ambiguous having both legal and spiritual registers. The uncertainty arises from the larger context of this particular issue of the *Testimony*. Smith's article may have been part of an effort to suppress the enthusiasm of Pentecostal worship within the 'official organ of the Pentecostal Assemblies of Canada'. This was occasioned by the loss of an appeal before the Ontario Supreme Court by the Reverend E. N. O. Kulbeck of Woodstock, who had been indicted for disturbing the peace with noisy services. The contrast is heightened by noting that both the Smith report and two editorials reprinted from the *Peterborough Examiner* extolling the salutary example of Kulbeck's congregation on sleepier churches occur in the same issue.[101] The tension between the institutional and the charismatic is clearest in an article by denominational leader A. G. Ward, placed immediately adjacent to the *Examiner* articles. Ward indicates his concern that 'our Organization' seemed 'anything but popular' to the Supreme Court, due to a 'lack of intelligent understanding of who we are and what we believe'. Ward's prescription is that Pentecostals demonstrate that they are 'law-abiding people, that our religious views are not different in the main from those held by other Evangelical Bodies', and that they do everything possible to comply with the Magistrates. 'I would suggest to my brethren in the Ministry that in all our Assemblies we seek to avoid unnecessary noise and that we do not continue our services beyond a reasonable hour, *unless we are confident to do otherwise would grieve the Holy Spirit and bring our people into bondage*

99. Mrs J. E. Purdie, 'The Same Jesus Christ-A Meditation on Hebrews 13:8', *PT* 19 (September, 1938), p. 7.

100. 'Oswald Smith Testifies', *PT* 18 (December, 1937), p. 7.

101. 'Note and Comment: Why Send Him to Jail?', *PT* 18 (December, 1937), pp. 3 and 14; 'Note and Comment: A Preacher in Jail?', *PT* 18 (December, 1937), pp. 14 and 23; and A. G. Ward, 'The E.N.O. Kulbeck Case', *PT* 18 (December, 1937), p. 3.

[italics mine].'[102] The last phrase says it all. Ward finds himself caught between the containment of the charisma on the one hand and its release on the other.

Pentecostalism had been facing this dilemma from the beginning. At Azusa Street there was a constant concern about fanaticism.[103] And even the earliest Pentecostals had divided on the matter of snake-handling. In his study of serpent-handling sects, Ralph W. Hood claims that it was their 'control and constraint on emotion as much as its expression that facilitated the Pentecostal and Holiness movements to move from small sects to major denominations'.[104] Far from being expressions of revolt against modernity, Pentecostal churches have leveraged their experience with a delicately balanced institutional order. The true protest against modernity lies in those groups, which, through their refusal to contain the charisma in its cultic dimensions, perpetuated extravagant claims of pragmatic immediacy. Hood finds this experience of the numinous among the adherents of snake-handling churches, who by their rejection of institutional success have somehow managed to retain the immediacy of early Pentecostalism.

The attenuation of immediacy brought about by the cultic containment of the charisma represents the development of an institutional triumphalism that was antithetic to the ethos of the early revival. A novel awareness of 'the uninitiated' arises in McAlister's concern for the orderliness of services that will 'appeal to the intelligence of those who come in and look on'. The creative tension between the charisma and its containment maintains the attenuated immediacy on which institutional Pentecostalism depends. The same McAlister published, in 1941, former General Superintendent George Chambers' diatribe against worldliness in the church. Chambers registered large apprehension about what was happening to Pentecostal worship. Unspiritual choirs and orchestras, and 'especially non-consecrated talent' were spoiling the purity of Pentecostal worship. The church is not dependent upon these for power. 'God does not choose to tickle our fancies and have His house for a place to entertain the mind, with an empty form of a religious program, and then have us console ourselves that because hymns and solos and poetry of a religious nature were in the program, that it became sacred.'[105] It is the dialectic between these two trajectories within the institutional psyche that perpetuates the attenuated immediacy that sustains denominational Pentecostalism.

This embedded ambiguity creates its own triumphalism within Pentecostalism: the triumphalism of rhetoric. This manifests itself most clearly in A. G. Ward's carefully crafted advice. Once more, the perception of outsiders is deemed significant, and the court's opinion of Pentecostals is based on misinformation

102. Ibid.

103. Frank Bartleman gives voice to his concerns, and also laments what had been lost from the days of the revival; Bartleman, *Azusa Street*, pp. 80–82.

104. Ralph W. Hood, Jr, 'When the Spirit Maims and Kills: Social Psychological Considerations of the History of Serpent Handling Sects and the Narrative of Handlers', *IJPR* 8 (1998), pp. 71–96 (p. 73).

105. Chambers, 'Worldward or Godward, Which?', *PT* 22 (15 July 1941), p. 13.

and ignorance. Yet nothing is more precious to Pentecostal worship than freedom; the liberty of the individual worshipper to give open expression in the exaltation of God. Still, pastors are urged to consider how they might contain the charisma in the cultus. In this context arises the rhetorical ambiguity: for the sake of appearances, avoid unnecessary noise, end services at a sensible hour, officialdom says, but do not grieve the Spirit, and at all costs, keep your people from spiritual bondage. The idealistic young pastor who sought to follow these admonishments would be understandably confused. It has never been a simple matter to say 'giddy-up' and 'whoa' at the same time. The subtle effect of such rhetoric is to shift Pentecostal triumphalism from its personal and existential expression to the institutional and denominational level. What begins to matter now is the institutional profile and not simply the individual experience.

c. Organizational Containment of the Charisma

Perhaps it is at the organizational level that one comes to the heart of the tension between the revivalistic hermeneutic of immediacy and the attenuated hermeneutic of institutional Pentecostalism. As mentioned earlier, the first Pentecostals decried any involvement with institutional organization. Ellen Hebden, famed mother of Canadian Pentecostalism entirely eschewed the very idea of denomination.[106] While A. G. Ward, R. E. McAlister and A. H. Argue were among the first in Canada to see value in some measure of organization, their efforts were largely rejected.[107] But experience is a harsh teacher, and it took the challenge of doctrinal unity to force early Pentecostals to acknowledge the necessity of banding together. The nascent movement faced three major doctrinal controversies that threatened its very continuation. These involved a crisis over the nature of the Godhead, issues related to sanctification and the central role of tongues as initial evidence of the baptism in the Holy Spirit. Regarding the organizational containment of the charisma, the oneness controversy is paramount.

Mention has already been made of the Arroyo Seco Worldwide Camp Meeting of 1913 from which arose the oneness crisis. The question over the nature of the Godhead would ultimately split the first generation of Pentecostals into two camps. R. E. McAlister had preached a sermon in which he suggested that the reason the apostles baptized in the name of Lord Jesus Christ rather than in the triune formula Jesus commanded in Matthew 28 was that they understood the title Lord-Jesus-Christ to be equivalent to Father-Son-Holy Ghost. That night one of McAllister's listeners, John Schaepe, received a 'revelation' from God concerning 'the name of Jesus'.[108] Pentecostal enthusiasm for apostolic practice, and Full Gospel openness to 'new light' on old truths led some to embrace a modalistic concept of

106. Miller, *Canadian Pentecostals*, p. 44.

107. Ibid., pp. 104–7 and 113.

108. Reed, 'Oneness Pentecostalism', in *NIDPCM*, pp. 936–44; and Reed, *'In Jesus' Name'*, pp. 138–41; Cecil Robeck, 'Schaepe, John G.', in *NIDPCM*, p. 1042.

the Trinity and demand rebaptism in Jesus' name.[109] By 1915 both R. E. McAlister and Franklin Small of Winnipeg were among the leaders of a growing 'oneness' movement.[110] Though the earliest Canadian Pentecostals were primarily 'Jesus only', it wasn't long before leaders saw the danger to Christian orthodoxy in this 'unitarianism of the Son'. By 1920, Gordon Atter claimed, Canadian Pentecostal leaders were following their American brothers in returning to a more confessional view of the Trinity.[111]

But how could such alleged movements of the Spirit be tamed? Within a purely charismatic environment, the leader, as the most spiritually endued, would be the ultimate judge of such guidance, but this matter was too critical to be left to dissenting leaders. When the Assemblies of God adopted a 'Statement of Fundamental Truths' in 1916, it included a lengthy affirmation of Trinitarianism. The Pentecostal Assemblies of Canada, chartered in 1919, did not adopt its own statement until 1928, and when it finally did, 'The Statement of Fundamental and Essential Truths' looked a lot like the American one they had already been using.[112] Faced with a split in the ranks, and the emergence of new 'oneness' organizations like Franklin Small's Apostolic Church of Pentecost, and the United Pentecostal Church, it remained a necessity, even 15 years later, to underscore Trinitarian orthodoxy. On this point, Canadians adopted almost verbatim, the lengthy American wording of 1916 in a declaration that carefully bridged tradition and restorationism.

> The terms 'Trinity' and 'Persons' as related to the Godhead, while not found in the Scriptures, yet are in harmony with Scripture . . . We, therefore, may speak with propriety of the Lord our God, who is One Lord, as a Trinity or as one being of Three Persons, and still be absolutely scriptural.[113]

Occupying a full three pages, the doctrine of 'The One True God' appearing immediately after the first of the Fundamentals on 'The Holy Scriptures', is by far the most fully elaborated of the truths in the original Statement. It contains creedal language, including repetition of the *filioque* clause. And in its own crude way, it attempts to regain the transcendence of Nicene language: 'this distinction and relationship [of the Father, Son and Holy Ghost] as to its existence, is an eternal fact, but as to its mode it is inscrutable and incomprehensible, because unexplained'.[114] Talk of mystery notwithstanding, the Scriptural basis of this

109. 'The movement's self-identity has continued to be one of divine origin in which the pure Apostolic doctrine and practice were divinely restored. This may explain why the story of 1913 as told by the bearers of the Oneness tradition depends more upon Schaepe's "revelation" in the night than McAlister's exegesis'; Reed, *'In Jesus' Name'*, p. 141.

110. Reed, 'Oneness Pentecostalism', pp. 936–38; and Reed, *'In Jesus' Name'*, pp. 143–46.

111. Gordon F. Atter, *The Third Force. 3rd Edition* (Caledonia, ON: Acts, 1970), pp. 131–32; and Miller, *Canadian Pentecostals*, pp. 65–66.

112. Ibid., 120.

113. 'Statement of Fundamental and Essential Truths, 1928', p. 12.

114. Ibid., p. 12.

doctrine was considered essential, and 'transgression of the Doctrine of Christ' was now to be seen as a 'denial of the Father and the Son; and a displacement of the truth that Jesus Christ is come in the flesh (2 John 9; John 1:1, 2, 14, 18, 29, 49; 8:57, 58; 1 John 2:22,23; 4:1–5; Heb. 12:3,4)'.[115] Having turned decisively from 'oneness' Pentecostalism, it appears the early leaders may have had a tendency to protest too much their orthodoxy.

Organization in this instance forced a very literal containment of the charisma. It became clear that in denominational Pentecostalism, the spirit of prophecy, whether human or otherwise would not go unchecked. This can be compared with the legacy of A. J. Tomlinson, first General Overseer of the Church of God (Cleveland, Tennessee), and indeed 'Overseer for Life' as of 1914, who was ousted from office in 1923. After his establishment of the rival Church of God of Prophecy later that year, Tomlinson began a series of doctrinal departures that were surely incipient in his early claim that the Church of God represented the 'Latter Day' restoration of theocracy. These innovations included the 'Great Speckled Bird' emphasis on racial integration, and the 'Mountain Theology', which sacralized the spot where Tomlinson had received the revelation of the one true church of God.[116] In many ways Tomlinson appears as the shaman-like leader of Weber's unroutinized charismatic movement. While a gifted organizer and administrator, Tomlinson managed to maintain the edge of early Pentecostal immediacy with occasional outbursts of highly 'prophetic' revelation. With Tomlinson's death in 1943, however, the mantle passed to his sons, Milton who administrated the denomination with institutional excellence until 1990, and Homer, who began his own denomination and in charismatic excess, crowned himself 'King of All the Nations of Men, Sitting on the Throne of David'.[117]

Clearly some institutional means of curbing such extremes was necessary. But as institutional structures become the channels through which the charisma flows, the danger arises that the institution will lose its power. One may catch the wind, only to discover, on examination, nothing but dead air. However, the genius of denominational Pentecostalism, as Poloma has shown, has been its ability to negotiate a structure embodying 'simultaneous loose-tight properties'.[118] The democratization of the charisma in the Spirit-filled community ensures some continued immediacy of the Pentecostal gift, but this immediacy is attenuated by the significant control structures in Pentecostal congregations. Peter Wagner long

115. Ibid., pp. 13–14.

116. Robins, *A. J. Tomlinson*, pp. 171–72 and 227–28.

117. Ibid., p. 230 and H. D Hunter, 'Tomlinson, Milton Ambrose', in *NIDPCM*, p. 1147.

118. The phrase originates in Tom Peters and Robert Waterman's classic management primer *In Search of Excellence: Lessons from America's Best-Run Companies* (New York: Warner Books, 1982). Simultaneous loose-tight properties are demonstrated in an institution that nurtures high dedication to its core values and maximally empowers all who accept those values. Such organizations are, 'on the one hand, rigidly controlled, yet at the same time allow (indeed, insist on) autonomy, entrepreneurship, and innovation from the rank and file'; ibid., p. 318.

ago noted the relative autonomy of Pentecostal pastors within their leadership role. Nevertheless the checks and balances of denominational hierarchy impose limits even on pastoral license. Still, the simultaneous loose–tight properties of charismatic communities at least admit the possibility, and at their best, encourage the likelihood that any member of the body might have something significant to contribute to the life and mission of the church. This empowers the individual within charismatic communities, raising aspirations at the personal level. Yet, with the development of organizational containment, the process of institutional triumphalism comes into its own. At this stage emphasis on personal revival is subtly exchanged for participation in the revivalist movement. The institution, which thrives in increasingly contrived continuity with the original outpouring, becomes as significant as the individual. As the wind of the Spirit finds gradual enshrinement in buildings and structure, policies and doctrines, the triumph of the institution is, at least for a time, assured, and participation in it is perceived as a mark of renewal.

In an insightful, if incendiary, essay Mel Robeck suggests that in the Assemblies of God, institutionalization itself may have become a primary activity. Robeck charges that executive officers, the General Presbytery, and the Doctrinal Purity Commission have taken on the role of gatekeepers of 'the Tradition' and in order to preserve the fresh wind of the Spirit intact, have formed a sort of magisterium that determines 'the only authentic or official interpretation of that Tradition'.[119] Similarly in Canada, when financial considerations forced changes at Eastern Pentecostal Bible College, the Pentecostal Assemblies of Canada's only training institution east of Saskatoon, its successor, the redesigned and renamed Masters College and Seminary, was charged with providing 'closure' for students 'on Pentecostal issues in Scripture'.[120] The wind, it appeared, could be caught, formalized and laid down in ways that would ensure the perpetuation of the initial revival.[121]

Poloma noted that Weber's concept of charisma was limited to the charismatic leader but her model proposed that in a charismatic community such as the Assemblies, the charisma was diffused between leaders and congregants alike.

119. Robeck develops the concept of magisterium as the authoritative teaching office of the Roman Catholic Church that acts as the appointed guardian of apostolic tradition. Cecil Robeck, 'An Emerging Magisterium? The Case of the Assemblies of God', *Pneuma* 25 (2003), pp. 164–215 (pp. 170–71).

120. The phrase is found in a key document entitled 'Education for the Next Generation', (N.p.: N.p., 1999). It was written as a summary of agreements reached in April, 1999 by 'The Eastern Canada Superintendents' (the four District Superintendents of Western Ontario, Eastern Ontario, Quebec, and the Maritimes, and the General Superintendent of the separate denomination, the Pentecostal Assemblies of Newfoundland). The document captures their determination to recast the Bible College in the institutional mould.

121. Poloma notes the tension within the AG between a resistance to renewal movements both within and outside its boundaries, and 'attempts to control ministers through doctrinal edicts in hopes of making them more "Pentecostal"'; Poloma, 'Charisma and Structure', p. 90.

Among the traits of charismatic authority, Weber indicated a sharp opposition to both rational and bureaucratic authority.[122] The symbiotic balance between charisma and organization depends on the ability of Pentecostal institutions to perpetuate the values of the revival, while providing the infrastructure for governance and growth; and as Poloma shows persuasively through the application of O'Dea's five institutional dilemmas, the tension between the two is essential to the health of the denomination, and the continued viability of the charisma.

When adversity strikes, though, or when corporate identity is in question, charisma is the first casualty. The delicate equilibrium between institution and charisma that Poloma applauded in her 1989 work *The Assemblies of God at the Crossroads* has come under pressure with the current realities these institutions are facing. When institutional ascendancy is challenged by demographic shifts, or financial pressure, or when identity and values are in question, the two most likely institutional reactions are the invocation of rhetoric and the reassertion of corporate values writ large. This is the current state of institutional triumphalism. In questions of identity and values, the magisterium speaks with an authority 'tantamount to the Word of God', Robeck says. Meanwhile the organization reaffirms its culture with institutional rhetoric. Poloma observed in 1989 the insistence of Pentecostal leaders on referring to their organization as a *movement* rather than a *denomination*.[123] The rhetoric continues over 20 years later. The following promotional blurb for PAOC discipleship curriculum reveals some of the institutional concerns about the charisma along with rhetoric about being 'Pentecostal enough' and growth of 'the entire Pentecostal movement'.

> If you are like me, you have asked yourself how your church can be strengthened in the vital areas of discipleship, fruitfulness, missions and genuine Pentecost. We wonder if the people we serve are living out the Christian disciplines? Are our ministries fruitful (i.e. are there real kingdom results)? Are people coming to Christ? Are our churches missions-minded? Are we Pentecostal enough? Or have we neglected the New Testament emphases that contributed to the vitality and growth of the early church and the entire Pentecostal movement?[124]

These questions neatly package the ambiguities of the routinization of the charisma. In defence of the piece, it must be noted how true these questions are

122. Poloma, *Assemblies of God at the Crossroads*, p. 6; Weber, *Theory of Social and Economic Organization*, pp. 361–62.

123. Poloma, *Assemblies of God at the Crossroads*, p. 9. 'Leaders such as Thomas F. Zimmerman [AG General Superintendent, 1959–1985] and Thomas Trask [AG General Superintendent, 1993–2007] have been reluctant to surrender the term "movement", likely because it seems to convey the idea of vitality and growth more than does the term "denomination". The truth, however, is the AG became a denomination within fifteen years of its birth', William Menzies argues, at the time of its adoption of a constitution in 1927; 'Organization and Spirit', pp. 105–6.

124. 'Discipleship Series'.

to the concerns of long-term Pentecostals, that is, persons largely invested in the institution, and possibly cognizant of institutional woes. Conversely, one might also note how inconsequential they are to the average congregant whose roots are not within the denomination. Institutional routinization of the charisma is an organizational and sociological necessity. The challenge of organizational containment of the charisma resides in the questions of whether and how wind may be channelled or harnessed if not contained.

IV. Immediacy, Containment and the Revision of Pentecostal Triumphalism

The containment of the charisma had ramifications for Pentecostal triumphalism as it emerged from the revivalist period to the era of institutional development. In one sense it assimilated the latent triumphalism of nascent Fundamentalism, and in another, it rediscovered the inherent triumphalism of American Protestantism. Along with Fundamentalists generally, Pentecostals could share in the defense of orthodox Christianity in the last days. Yet, running at cross-purposes with the provisional nature of Latter Rain urgency was the growing denominational structure of classical Pentecostalism. Like Douglas John Hall's officially optimistic church, the more Pentecostals invested in buildings and institutions, the more they betrayed their prophetic role as critics of the status quo, and became fellow boosters of 'the (North) American dream'. Therein lays the intrinsic tension between the revivalist and the institutional hermeneutic. The very success of the revival assured its demise, particularly in light of the delayed *parousia*, while the triumph of the institutional entity put it in perpetual opposition with the very dynamic that created it.

The attenuation of immediacy caused by the containment of the charisma created its own ambiguity. A domesticated immediacy was not only more viable in a world where eschatological expectation had been shorn of its Latter Rain urgency, but also proved more pliable to the goals and aspirations of institutional triumphalism. But such a tamed immediacy was of limited value in raising Pentecostal expectation to the levels known in the early revivalist years. Individuals who discovered how to develop their charismatic potential within the vision and mission of the organization, be it the local church, or the denomination, experienced the least attenuation of their sense of immediacy.[125] Those who had tasted the unbridled passion of the revival, but could only seem to recapture bits of it in the period of institutionalization experienced a large moderation of their sense of Pentecostal immediacy. But others, who sensed an ontological immediacy with the apostolic age, or a pragmatic immediacy that urged them to independent action, or an eschatological immediacy that displaced the comfort or materialism of emerging Pentecostalism, felt increasingly marginalized. In short, the more one is in alignment with the revivalist *mentalité* of

125. Hollenweger captures this sentiment as follows: 'Participation, vision, and dreams are welcome as long as they do not jeopardize established theological and ecclesiological values, which is of course a normal behavioural pattern in any organization, secular or religious'; 'The Pentecostals . . .', p. 552.

early Pentecostalism, the more one will sense that the Spirit has departed from the 'Great Movement' and be inclined to write 'Ichabod' upon it. In spite of momentary revitalizations such as the Toronto Blessing, such individuals will be forced to drift to the periphery in order to discover anything similar to Azusa Street.

These responses may be seen in the writings of the institutionalizing era mourning the passing of a bygone day. As already shown, concerns of this kind began with the very first stirrings of organization, and in fact reach back to the days of Azusa. Frank Bartleman, having returned to Los Angeles after an extended tour of several months, sensed a 'deadness . . . had crept in there'. Eventually, however, Bartleman came under 'the spirit of prayer', and 'the power ran all through the building'. But Seymour was out of town and the leaders remaining 'did not understand it'. Bartleman complained, 'The Spirit could not work.'[126] There emerged a new genre of literature that might be termed 'the Pentecostal jeremiad'. It consisted of laments of having lost the reality of Pentecost, and how to regain it; and warnings of the dismal danger of failure.

By the late 1930s and early 1940s matters had reached the point of alarm for those who had witnessed the early revival. One of these, W. A. Hines pointed the way back to the lost Pentecost of the previous generation. Youth 'today' have never known the power of the 'latter rain outpouring', but 'some of us' older folk have. However, if 'Christians everywhere' would 'pay the price' and seek God, 'signs and wonders' would reappear would 'move the hearts of the coldest'.[127] Bartleman was already blaming institutionalizing factors for the loss of Pentecost at Azusa in 1907. Even there, 'they had organized now fast and hard, and I had not joined their organization'. The situation continued in 1925, as he penned his account. 'We affiliate with only those who carrying our papers. "Pentecost" took that thing out of us. Why go back to it?'[128] In 1941, founding Superintendent of the PAOC George Chambers echoed similar concerns. 'Committees, conventions, conferences, [and] camp meetings' can only accomplish so much, but spiritual effectiveness would be achieved '*if we would take God into consideration in a way that we have never done*' [emphasis mine].

> If solemn assemblies were called, to wait on God for His next move and downpour of the Latter Rain and the restoration to the church the things that have been lost or let slip, worldliness would again take wings from our midst; substitutions for power and anointings would find no place. Fewer Pentecostal people would be such frequent patients in hospitals. Less carnal and worldly methods would be resorted to, to get crowds. Preachers would get a new message for their people. Less money would be spent at a loss, both at home and abroad.[129]

Chambers remained a member of the General Executive, but resisted the allure of 'business-as-usual'. His appeal, like much of the Latter Rain rhetoric of the

126. Bartleman, *Azusa Street*, p. 115.
127. W. A. Hines, 'To Bring Back the King', *PT* 21 (15 July 1940), p. 4.
128. Bartleman, *Azusa Street*, p. 115.
129. Chambers, 'Worldward or Godward, Which?', *PT* 22 (15 July 1941), p. 13.

period looked both backward and forward. Something has been 'lost or let slip'. 'Worldliness', Chambers claims, was at one time absent from the Pentecostal fold, and Holy Spirit power and healing were common. But what is needed is something greater than Azusa: 'God's next move and downpour of the Latter Rain and the restoration to the church' of Pentecostal power were assured, '*if we would take God into consideration in a way that we have never done*'.

The attenuated immediacy of the institutional period was never intended to be 'enough' ,it was simply the sociological necessity that allowed Pentecostalism to thrive as it developed the organizational, cultic and intellectual stability so necessary to its marketability to the larger mass of North Americans who might balk at the extremes of revivalist immediacy. But, and the adversative here is significant, the Pentecostal jeremiad was an equally necessary component of Pentecostal success, for it kept the charisma of Pentecost always in the background, and occasionally with undomesticated boldness, at centre stage.[130]

It appears, through organizational, cultic and intellectual means that the Pentecostalism that survived the original revival was in some ways similar but in some very significant ways different than that which gave rise to it. This was to be expected. The immediacy of the Pentecostal revival was an unstable compound, with a limited shelf life that could only be prolonged with sustained rhetoric. Pentecostalism successfully shaped that rhetoric so as to allow for the continued use of the categories of Azusa Street while subtly shifting their content. 'Latter Rain' continued for some time as a useful device. Currently, the spontaneity of worship (though limited), occasional prayer for healing, Spirit baptism (particularly at camp meetings), and a moderate openness to the prophetic still offer contemporary Pentecostalism an attenuated sense of immediacy. Yet the world has changed, the church has transformed, and Pentecostal sophistication, both organizationally, and theologically has come of age. And somehow the delicate immediacy that created Azusa Street is gone forever.

The associated effects of this shift in immediacy on Pentecostal triumphalism were subtle but significant. The heightened level of expectation inherent in the revivalist hermeneutic could simply not be sustained, and the delayed *parousia* was only the most obvious indicator of this. As Faupel pointed out, the disappointing failure of missionary tongues (xenolalia), and the amazingly rapid disintegration of Pentecostal unity were further factors that predicted the demise of revivalist idealism.[131] Unfulfilled prophecies, the inescapable rise of charlatans and the shameful disappearance of Parham from the scene were symptomatic of larger problems with revivalist immediacy.[132] The attenuated immediacy of the institutional era polished the rough edges of the earlier version, and put Pentecostalism within

130. In time this jeremiad would lead to the first major crisis of institutional Pentecostalism, the 'New Order of the Latter Rain'.

131. Faupel, *Everlasting Gospel*, p. 268.

132. Unsubstantiated allegations of 'sodomy' against Parham hastened his fall from leadership of the midwestern Apostolic Faith churches, and from the Pentecostal movement as a whole. This was accelerated by accounts in the religious press that were far worse than

increasing reach of those not so accustomed to the raucous spirituality of Radical Evangelicalism. But, it still existed in direct continuity with the immediacy of the revivalist period, and with its historic antecedents. This pentecostalized version of the larger Evangelical triumphalism of the nineteenth century was similar in kind, but more insistent, more demanding and more determined to experience existentially the fulfilment of its rhetoric. It combined the perfectionist currents of antebellum revivalism with American pragmatic know-how, and a progressive-era positivism along with the restorationism of populist appeal as a religion of the people. And it was accompanied by an emerging institutional triumphalism, the visionary breadth of which combined supernatural possibility with savvy practicality.

V. Triumphalism and the Crisis of Pentecostal Identity

A contemporary Pentecostal identity crisis is the issue that began this chapter. The remedy suggested by several scholars has been to somehow return to the hermeneutic that informed Azusa. An early Pentecostal hermeneutic, we have discovered, is irrecoverable since it is dependent on the kinds of immediacy that tease out of a highly literal, and typological reading of the Latter Rain covenant. Charles E. Jones suggests that this is the distinguishing characteristic of the Pentecostal hermeneutic from that of Radical Holiness: it abolishes metaphors, and literalizes all things.[133] The kind of restorationism currently *de rigueur* in Pentecostal scholarship is not so much a quest for the primitive church as it is a longing for the romantic 'founding age' of Azusa.[134] Of course none of the Pentecostal sophisticates imagine returning to the wild, raw revivalism of Azusa. Instead they recommend a Ricouerian 'second naiveté', a return to the primordial experience with enlightened eyes.[135] 'The initial impulse which gave rise to the Movement', says Faupel, 'must be recovered'.[136] But what that impetus was, much less how to recover it, is not so clear. Pentecostal scholarship is advocating in place of the literalistic hermeneutic of early Pentecostals, one that reproduces its narrative concern, its existential voice and its potentially multivalent interpretation. In the

what was reported in the secular press, possibly indicating a vendetta on Parham, perhaps for his authoritarian approach; Goff, *Fields White*, pp. 135–41.

133. Jones, 'Reclaiming the Text', pp. 164–67.

134. The 'founding age', Hughes indicates, is the 'normative' age for restorationists. It 'exercises an exclusive claim on their allegiance, a claim they are unwilling to give to any other period in Christian history'. Hughes, of course, is speaking of the primitive church (Richard T. Hughes, 'Preface: The Meaning of the Restoration Vision', in *The Primitive Church in the Modern World*, edited by Richard T. Hughes, pp. ix–xviii. Urbana and Chicago: University of Illinois Press, 1995), p. xi.

135. Faupel, 'Whither Pentecostalism?', p. 26; see Archer, *Pentecostal Hermeneutic*, pp. 7–10 for an autobiographical insight into his personal journey to a 'second naiveté'.

136. Faupel, 'Whither Pentecostalism?', p. 26.

hands of many Pentecostal scholars the answer appears to involve the formation of a postmodern hermeneutic based on early Pentecostals' narrative readings of Scripture. At the most basic level, the hermeneutical principles of Archer's proposed 'tridactic negotiation for meaning between the biblical text, the Holy Spirit, and the Pentecostal community', or Yong's trialectic hermeneutic, seem not unlike the Wesleyan Quadrilateral.[137] All three methods seem to be invoking a wider interpretation of Scripture than the strict reading of the text with the tools of the historical-critical method. Whatever the value of such a hermeneutic, and it is by no means clear that all Pentecostal scholars wish to follow this trajectory, it should not be based on the historical foundations of early Pentecostalism, as though their interpretive paradigm was unique and antithetical to that of their Fundamentalist contemporaries.[138] Nor is it fair to compare the literalism and allegorism of early Pentecostals with the better developed hermeneutics of mid-twentieth-century Evangelicalism. The quest for a truly Pentecostal identity is not to be found in recovering a hermeneutic that cannot, in any event be reproduced. Restorationists that we are, our natural tendency is to go back to the golden founding age to recover something we have lost. But perhaps the problem is not what we have lost, but something we have retained: the triumphalism that has become endemic to contemporary Pentecostalism.

Immediacy is the driving dynamic of Pentecostal triumphalism. The types of immediacy detailed in this chapter (ontological, eschatological and pragmatic) combined with the prospective and retrospective triumphalism described in the last chapter were combined to synthesize a unique form of Pentecostal triumphalism. While the institutional hermeneutic attenuated the raw immediacy of early Pentecostalism, it did not eradicate it. The implication for the Spirit-filled believer that there is an existential immediacy of God, along with the corollary of an access to divine power for the miraculous, that is, an immediacy of the supernatural; all predicated on the immediacy of human perfectibility, conspire together in an exceptional synthesis of Pentecostal triumphalism. This triumphalism is the underlying issue facing Pentecostalism today. It fuels the crisis of expectancy and experience by constantly promising the immediate and often providing the indeterminate. It privileges power, success and moralism; and neglects to come to terms with suffering, failure and the on-going struggle with sin. Distinguishing this condition from the essence of Pentecostalism and proposing a better approach forms the burden of this book. In what follows, Martin Luther's theology of the cross will be examined as a resource for resolving this central crisis.

137. Archer, *Pentecostal Hermeneutic*, p. 213 and Yong, *Spirit-Word-Community*. The Quadrilateral was a model developed by Albert Outler to describe Wesley's theological method that sought to provide a truly Christian epistemology by evaluating the world through the lens of Scripture, reason, tradition and experience. See Albert Outler, 'The Wesleyan Quadrilateral in John Wesley', *WTJ* 20 (1985), pp. 7–18. See also Winfield Bevins, 'A Pentecostal Appropriation of the Wesleyan Quadrilateral', *JPS* 14 (2006), pp. 229–46.

138. For dissenting voices see, R. Menzies, 'Jumping Off the Postmodern Bandwagon'; and Poirier and Lewis, 'Pentecostals and Postmodernist Hermeneutics'.

Conclusion

The quest for Pentecostal identity seems a perennial topic of Pentecostal scholarship. A significant quorum of the scholarly community has sought the answer to this question in the first ten years of the movement's history, and in the search for a Pentecostal hermeneutic. Often the result has been to claim parallels between the narrative literalism shared by radical Evangelicals, and other proto-Fundamentalists and contemporary narrative theology and postmodern interpretative paradigms.

The hermeneutic of the earliest Pentecostals was dominated by Latter Rain theology, which, by definition, had a limited shelf-life. While robust, it created a sense of immediacy that drove early Pentecostal mission and growth. As the *parousia* delayed, the Latter Rain narrative ran out of the steam of immediacy. Pentecostalism became a victim of its own success. Storefront missions gave way to church buildings, and the spirit of non-conformity gave way to denominations. The combination of institutionalizing forces and the loss of eschatological urgency caused the sense of Pentecostal immediacy to be attenuated. This attenuated immediacy, though similar to its forebear, was a much more stable compound, and was responsible for the phenomenal growth of Pentecostalism during the institutional period.

The containment of the charisma, through the process of institutionalization had significant consequences for the nature of Pentecostal triumphalism. While immediacy predicated its own kind of triumphalism – the unhindered rise of the charismatically endowed believer – the new attenuated immediacy was more palatable to the masses, and allowed an ambiguity that tempered the expectancy/experience dialectic intrinsic to triumphalism. Institutional Pentecostalism could cultivate high expectations, but not so high, nor as liable to failure as those of early Pentecostalism. On the other hand, before the maelstrom of harsh experience, it could point to the institutional symbols of its success to mollify personal disappointment. In this way the new Pentecostalism was better qualified to compete for the role of the officially optimistic religion of America. Along the way, it lost the voice of protest that animated the old Pentecostalism, and became increasingly a part of 'the establishment'.

Part II

Luther and the Theology of the Cross: Synthesizing a Resource for Pentecostal Theology

Chapter 3

'THE SPIRIT AND THE GIFTS ARE OURS': LUTHER'S THEOLOGY AS RESOURCE FOR PENTECOSTALISM

And though this world, with devils filled,
Should threaten to undo us,
We will not fear, for God hath willed
His truth to triumph through us:
The Prince of Darkness grim,
We tremble not for him;
His rage we can endure,
For lo, his doom is sure,
One little word shall fell him.

That word above all earthly powers,
No thanks to them, abideth;
The Spirit and the gifts are ours
Through Him who with us sideth:
Let goods and kindred go,
This mortal life also;
The body they may kill:
God's truth abideth still,
His kingdom is forever.

—Martin Luther (1483–1546), 'A Mighty Fortress Is Our God'

[A]n honest investigation of Church history reveals that all through the Church age wherever there has been a great revival of religious fervour in any denomination or group of people there has always been an accompanying manifestation of gifts of the spirit [*sic*] – speaking in other tongues, divine healing, etc. . . .

In a German Church history, Sauer's 'History of the Christian Church' vol. 3 page 406, the following words are found: 'DOCTOR MARTIN LUTHER was a prophet, evangelist, speaker in tongues, interpreter, and in one person, endowed with all the gifts of the Spirit.'

Gordon Atter, *The Third Force*, 11, 12

What has Azusa to do with Wittenberg? – a legitimate question, judging what has been said regarding the antecedents and emergence of Pentecostalism and comparing it with general knowledge about Luther and the Reformation. On the surface one might easily cast Pentecostals in the role of the *Schwärmer* pitted against Luther's outright rejection of enthusiasm and social autonomy.[1] And in many ways there are stunning parallels between the two groups to sustain such an approach. Early Pentecostalism may, in fact, represent a twentieth-century version of the left wing of the Reformation, proposing, as the enthusiasts did, a rejection of tradition in favour of a more democratized experience of Spirit-inspired apocalyptic community.[2] But the burden of this dissertation is to find the continuities between Pentecostals and Luther. And the project may not require as severe a deconstruction as might at first appear. The epigenetic connections between Pentecostalism and Luther can best be seen by tracing resonances between Luther's concerns and those of Pentecostals. These can be found in four primary areas: the supernatural, the priesthood of all believers, eschatology and spiritual experience. Once these links are uncovered, Luther has much to say to the current condition of Pentecostalism.

In 1983 Carter Lindberg published a significant volume addressing what was then a contentious issue in Lutheran circles. 'Can the Pentecostal experience be harmonized with Lutheran theology?' was the question Lindberg sought to answer. He titled his book *The Third Reformation?* – the question mark cautioning his readers of the doubtful value of the assertion. Lindberg chooses a historical and theological approach to the question. He explores the interaction between Luther and the 'enthusiasts' looking for clues to address the issue. He follows this with a briefer examination of Pietism, and then with a discussion of the charismatic renewal, particularly among Lutherans. In each section he surveys representative voices, and returns to Luther and the Lutheran tradition for analysis. He is careful never to claim historical connections where they do not exist. Lindberg is not arguing for a direct relationship between Pentecostals, charismatics and these

1. The term '*Schwärmer*' (best translated 'enthusiasts') was first applied to the radical wing of the Reformation, such as the Zwickau prophets, Thomas Müntzer and Andreas Karlstadt. The term was extended to apply to all manner of Anabaptists, as though they all shared the same essence, though more recent scholarship has made clear that while the Reformers assumed this, Anabaptist writings show it was not so. Anabaptism, was, in fact, a geographically and theologically diverse movement; John S. Oyer, *Lutheran Reformers against Anabaptists: Luther, Melanchthon, and Menius, and the Anabaptists of Central Germany* (The Dissent and Nonconformity Series, No. 13; Paris, AR: Baptist Standard Bearer, 2000), pp. 1–5. See also Harry Loewen, *Luther and the Radicals: Another Look at Some Aspects of the Struggle between Luther and the Radical Reformers* (Waterloo: Wilfrid Laurier University, 1974), pp. 21–24 for a variety of taxonomies offered by scholars for determining interrelationships between different groups.

2. As distinguished a Mennonite scholar as John Howard Yoder declared that Pentecostalism, 'is in our century the closest parallel to what Anabaptism was in the sixteenth'; 'Marginalia', *Concern* 15 (1967), pp. 77–80 (p. 78).

earlier movements. His method is more thematic and comparative.[3] In the end, however, Lindberg sees more discontinuity than continuity between Luther and Pentecostals.

I wish to show that the theology of the cross is more than a damning bludgeon with which to decimate the entire Pentecostal project as a *theologia gloriae*. Instead, the cross may be seen as a constructive corrective that affirms some of the basic impulses of Pentecostalism. Ultimately, though, Lindberg challenges the underlying assumption of this chapter that there are continuities between Luther and Pentecostals. No doubt some will see the present project as a substantial deconstruction of Luther, but I believe a rapprochement can be made that includes a general acquiescence to Luther's concerns about experiential subjectivism, and the triumphalism that it so often funds. While Lindberg, as I do, notes the excessive sense of immediacy in contemporary Pentecostalism. Yet, I do not find the subjective triumphalism to which Lindberg objects to be an essential feature of Pentecostal experience. Neither do I hope to make a Pentecostal of Luther, or Lutherans of Pentecostals.[4] The goal here is to notice the resonance between a few categories not normally pursued at length in Luther scholarship and some of the primary emphases of Pentecostals. What emerges, I suggest, is a picture of Luther as an untapped resource for Pentecostal contemplation.

I. Luther's Pentecostal Resonances

It is a rare thing indeed to find Luther referenced in Pentecostal scholarship. He is much more likely to appear in popular treatments of the doctrine of salvation

3. Stll, Lindberg regularly refers to the enthusiasts as 'sixteenth century charismatics', an objectionable designation given some of their extremes. He sees the 'lines of continuity' as 'leitmotivs reaching back to the Reformation and Pietism'; *The Third Reformation? Charismatic Movements and the Lutheran Tradition* (Macon: Mercer University Press, 1983), p. 187.

4. Lindberg's treatments of Luther as well as those of the Lutheran denominations in the face of charismatic incursions, reflect a larger concern with the sensibilities of contemporary and historic Lutheranism. Official statements from the Lutheran Church-Missouri Synod such as 1972s 'The Charismatic Movement and Lutheran Theology' are relatively pessimistic as to a charismatic/Lutheran synthesis, though they do not close the door completely. The same is true of the 'Conference Report on the Holy Spirit in the Life of the Church' published by the Division of Theological Studies of the Lutheran Council in the USA; Paul Opsahl, *The Holy Spirit in the Life of the Church: From Biblical Times to the Present* (Minneapolis: Augsburg, 1978). But see the recent *Lutherans and Pentecostals in Dialogue* Online: http://strasbourginstitute.org/wp-content/uploads/2012/08/Lutherans-and-Pentecostals-in-Dialogue-Text-FINAL.pdf (Accessed 16 August 2014) which opens new vistas for constructive encounter and suggests the value of the *theologia crucis* for Lutheran apprehension of the *charismata*.

or in sermon illustrations under the rubric 'justification by faith' with a vivid account of his Tower experience, or the heading 'spiritual courage' with his nailing of the Ninety-Five Theses on the castle church door, or his bold stand at the Diet of Worms. All of these tales are, of course, told less with concern for historical accuracy, than as legend, or myth. Indeed the historical basis of each is in some doubt. But, to look to Luther as theological resource, and particularly to inquire as to the usefulness of his theology of the cross as a basis for Pentecostal theology has been essentially a null set. In 2004, Veli-Matti Kärkäinnen published an article with a preliminary exploration of the challenge the theology of the cross offers to Pentecostal theologies of glory.[5] But until now no further discussion has ensued, and Luther remains fallow ground in Pentecostal discussion. In light of this I wish to propose four potentially fruitful intersections between Luther and Pentecostalism, one of which I will develop at length.

a. Luther and the Supernatural

Probably the most obvious place to begin is with an area that has generally been seen as inessential to the marrow of Luther's theology, and therefore easily jettisoned, since it could be disposed of as an artefact of medieval worldview, rather than a significant spiritual reality with which Luther constantly reckoned. I refer to the supernatural world: the habitat of angels and demons; the domain of signs, wonders and the miraculous; and *terra incognita* for the modern rational mind.[6] The scholar who most boldly demanded that Luther studies take seriously the supernatural bent of Luther's thought was Heiko Oberman.

Oberman's Luther is neither fully medieval nor fully modern. He is, however, fully aware of the supernatural realm and this becomes clearest in his struggle with the devil. Oberman points out that Luther's world of thought is wholly distorted and apologetically misconstrued if his conception of the Devil is dismissed as a medieval phenomenon and only his faith in Christ retained as relevant or as the only decisive factor. Christ and the Devil were equally real to him . . . There is no way to grasp Luther's milieu of experience and faith unless one has an acute sense of his view of Christian existence between God and the Devil.[7]

5. Kärkkäinen does not 'recommend' that Pentecostals 'neglect[ ] talk about faith, power, healing and miracles' but wishes to challenge them with the theology of the cross 'as they face the dark side of life'; Veli-Matti Kärkkäinen, 'Theology of the Cross: A Stumbling-Block to Pentecostal-Charismatic Spirituality?' in *The Spirit and Spirituality: Essays in Honor of Russell P. Spittler* (ed. Wonsuk Ma and Robert P. Menzies; London and New York: T&T Clark International, 2004), pp. 150–63 (p. 151).

6. Brengt R. Hoffman, *Luther and the Mystics: A Re-examination of Luther's Spiritual Experience and His Relationship to the Mystics* (Minneapolis: Augsburg, 1976), p. 18.

7. Heiko Oberman, *Luther: Man between God and the Devil* (trans. Eileen Walliser-Schwarzhart; New York: Image Books, 1992), p. 104.

Luther was not simply a victim of the superstitions of his time. Indeed in several ways his biblical theology of the devil went against common misapprehensions.[8] For Luther, at least according to Oberman, Satan held a central position theologically. Not that Oberman was posing a dualism, but Satan as 'god *of* this world' seems to have existed for Luther in a sort of dialectical tension with Christ, God *in* this world. We want power that overcomes the power of Satan, but Oberman claims such power is not immediately available to us. He asserts, '[T]he *omnipotent* God is indeed real, but *as such* hidden from us. Faith reaches not for God hidden but for God revealed, who, incarnate in Christ, laid himself open to the Devil's fury.'[9] This is how Jesus came at Christmas, and it is how he met the Devil at his temptation: with reliance on power mediated through the external Word.

Commenting on the temptation of Eve by the serpent, Luther compared Eve's response to Jesus'. 'Satan wanted to persuade Christ to attempt something without the Word', Luther claims. 'But he could not deceive Christ as he deceived Eve, for He held to the Word and did not allow Himself to be led away from the true God to the false, new god.'[10] For Luther, then, the Devil and his power are essential to the theology of the cross, for he is a prime source of *Anfechtung*.[11] The reality of Satan is as essential to Luther as the notions of sin and temptation or incarnation and cross. Otherwise, the whole Christian project is a matter of mere myth or imagination.[12]

8. Hamm lists three ways Oberman has showed that Luther championed what Oberman termed 'a *new* belief in the Devil'; ibid., p. 104. First, 'Luther no longer believes that the Devil is put to flight where there is holiness and sanctity . . . Jesus Christ does not banish the Devil but attracts him.' Second, 'for Luther the Devil becomes *Magister conscientiae*, Master of Piety and Inner Life. He attempts to tie a person down to his religiosity.' Third, 'nothing suits [the Devil] better than that people, in their striving for holiness, should retire from the world and seek their salvation where they wrongly imagine themselves to be safe from Devil', since he desires to be free to destroy the world and plunge it into chaos; Berndt Hamm, 'An Opponent of the Devil and the Modern Age: Oberman's View of the Luther', in *The Work of Heiko A. Oberman: Papers from the Symposium on His Seventieth Birthday* (Kirkhistoriche Bijdragen, vol. 20; ed. Thomas A. Brady, Katherine G. Brady, Susan Karant Nunn and James D Tracy; Leiden: Brill, 2003), pp. 31–49 (pp. 34–35).

9. Oberman, *Luther*, p. 104.

10. 'Lectures on Genesis, Gen. 3:2' (1535), *LW* 1:148.

11. The complex nature of *Anfechtungen*, those potent trials, tribulations, and attacks of doubt and despair, is such that the Devil, the world and death are potentially proximate sources, but as McGrath indicates, 'God himself must be recognized as the ultimate source of *Anfechtung*: it is his *opus alienum*, which is intended to destroy man's self-confidence, and complacency, and reduce him to a state of utter despair, in order that he may finally turn to God . . .'; Alister McGrath, *Luther's Theology of the Cross: Martin Luther's Theological Breakthrough* (Oxford: Basil Blackwell, 1985), pp. 170; see pp. 169–71.

12. Oberman, *Luther*, p. 105.

The role of the supernatural, though, was also a pastoral category for Luther, not simply one developed at theological length. Warnings and practical advice about how to handle satanic attack punctuate his letters of spiritual council. Whether in matters of internal turmoil, or outward attack, Luther saw the devil as the chief enemy of believers. To the depressed and despondent, such as Matthias Weller, an organist and court official, Luther wrote

> When you are sad, therefore, and when melancholy threatens, to get the upper hand, say: 'Arise! I must play a song on my regal' [a portable organ] . . . Then begin striking the keys and singing in accompaniment, as David and Elisha did, until your sad thoughts vanish. If the devil returns and plants worries and sad thoughts in your mind, resist him manfully and say, 'Begone. Devil! I must now play and sing unto my Lord Christ.'
>
> In such fashion you must learn to oppose him and not permit him to put thoughts in your mind. . . . Therefore the best thing you can do is to rap the devil on the nose from the very start.[13]

And lest someone attempt to psychologize Luther's advice, to say it is a simple matter of joy banishing sadness, the Reformer goes on to advise, 'If you are convinced that such thoughts come from the devil, you have already gained the victory.' For Luther, what charismatics call 'spiritual warfare' was serious business.[14]

This connection between spiritual warfare and praise parallels Pentecostal experiences. African-American preacher Myles Munroe reiterates a similar concern.

> . . . when God's presence comes, the devil must leave. Truly, a praising saint is the devil's worst nightmare. This is why perseverance is called for in such times. You must make the conscious choice to ignore whatever distractions satan [sic] sends . . . By doing this you render satan powerless . . .
>
> Praise in your everyday life protects you by disarming satan before his assault gains momentum.[15]

In the same way, Luther appears to advise praise as a powerful means of overcoming demonic onslaughts.

In his 'Sermon on Preparing to Die', Luther deals with an inevitability that was particularly close to those who dwelt in that ruthless, unremitting world. He pointed

13. 'To Matthias Weller' (1534), *LSC*, p. 97. Examples could be multiplied. See, for example, Luther's letter to Matthias' brother Jerome; ibid., pp. 84–87; and in other places; ibid., pp. 87, 154–55, 202–3 and 206–7.

14. Bengt Hoffman lists a few of Luther's physical encounters with the demonic, and suggests that they be taken as 'impingement[s] of paranormal reality' rather than 'hallucinations'; Hoffman, *Luther and the Mystics*, pp. 188–89.

15. Myles Munroe, *The Purpose and Power of Praise and Worship* (Shippensburg, PA: Destiny Image, 2000), p. 159.

to the Devil as the source of the triple terrors of death, sin and hell.[16] Luther sees the battle as a supernatural one in which the Devil wishes to inundate Christians with *Anfechtungen*. He attacks at three levels: first, regarding the wrath of the God who consigns to death; second, the depth of our sin compared with others who were condemned to hell for less; and ultimately with the question of election. The remedy for Luther is a fuller vision of the cross where Christ 'takes your sin from you, bears it for you, and destroys it'.[17] But, Luther is not only concerned with psychological, or spiritual attacks, he is also capable of perceiving physical ailment as demonic attack. While Melanchthon gave leadership to the Reformation position at the Diet of Augsburg in the summer of 1530, Luther had fallen ill during his sojourn at the Coburg castle. In a letter of encouragement, Luther urges Melanchthon not to worry about his ill-health. 'To be sure, I do not know what is the matter. But because I feel that I am not suffering from any natural disease, I bear my condition more easily and scoff at the messenger of Satan who buffets my flesh.'[18]

After surveying Luther's attitude to the demonic, one might have expected him to embrace the full expression of the spiritual gifts, after all, these, too are supernatural manifestations. This is not the case. Luther's primary interest is not in the manifold variety of *charismata* but in the *charis* that saves.[19] Nevertheless, Luther does admit their possibility and validity. Preaching on Mark 16.17–18 on Ascension Day, 1522, Luther raises the possibility of signs following believers. 'If a Christian has the faith, he shall have power to do these signs. . . . For a Christian has equal power with Christ, is one cake with him . . . Where there is a Christian, there is therefore the power to do such signs even now if it is necessary.' Luther imagines that the day of necessity may have passed, but 'if they should threaten and oppress the Gospel' or 'should God send me elsewhere where they do not understand my language', God may yet bestow these gifts. [20] One may note in

16. 'Sermon on Preparing to Die' (1519), *LW* 42:99–115.

17. 'Sermon on Preparing to Die' (1519), *LW* 42:104. See also Dennis Ngien's treatment of this sermon in 'The Art of Dying'; *Luther as a Spiritual Adviser: The Interface of Theology and Piety in Luther's Devotional Writings* (Studies in Christian Thought and History; Milton Keynes, UK: Paternoster, 2007), pp. 29–47.

18. 'To Philip Melanchthon' (1530), *LSC*, pp. 154–55. In writing to the widow of a suicide, Luther discerned demonic activity: 'That your husband inflicted injury upon himself may be explained by the devil's power over our members. He may have directed your husband's hand, even against his will . . . How often the devil breaks arms, legs, backs, and all members! He can be master of the body and its members against our will'; 'To Widow Margaret' (1528), *LSC*, p. 59.

19. Oskar Föller, 'Martin Luther on Miracles, Healing, Prophecy and Tongues', *SHE* 31 (2005), pp. 333–51 (p. 349).

20. *WA* 10:3, 145 cited in Karlfried Froelich, 'Charismatic Manifestation and the Lutheran Incarnational Stance', in *The Holy Spirit in the Life of the Church: From Biblical Times to the Present* (ed. Paul D. Opsahl; Minneapolis: Augsburg, 1978), pp. 136–57 (p. 151).

passing Luther's awareness that he writes in the context of a state-protected church within the framework of Christendom.

Any discussion of Luther's view regarding charismatic gifts should be couched in the broader context of his involvement with the enthusiasts and their claims of unmediated divine revelation. That discussion will take place under the heading of 'spiritual experience'. Suffice to say here that Luther is generally sceptical of extra-biblical revelation, though he is not completely closed to the concept. Still, he prefers the certainty of the Scriptures.

> For I am content with this gift which I have, Holy Scripture, which abundantly teaches and supplies all things necessary both for this life and also for the life to come . . . However, I do not detract from the gifts of others, if God by chance reveals something to someone beyond Scripture through dreams, through visions, and through angels. They may be gifts, to be sure, but I am not concerned about them and do not desire them. For I am influenced by that infinite multitude of illusions, deceptions, and impostures by which the world was horribly deceived for a long time through Satan under the papacy. I am also influenced by the sufficiency of Scripture, and if I do not put my faith in this, I shall not easily believe an angel, a vision, or a dream.[21]

This reflects Luther's view generally as it concerns the gifts of the Spirit. He does not forbid the exercise of *charismata*, nor does he claim that they are no longer possible. Rather he acknowledges that 'now until the end of the world He gives the Holy Spirit and the gifts secretly and invisibly to his Christians', and he urges caution.[22] In keeping with the theology of the cross, he is aware of an ambiguity in all human experience. 'Among Christians there have been many who had fine charismatic gifts (Gnadengaben). Some were able to do miracles, and yet this served the devil.'[23]

For Luther the *charismata* are incidental, and while not a part of his regular experience, they are secondary issues and quite possibly distractions from what is essential.[24] Christ and his cross are the primary matters. Commenting on John 16.14 where Jesus tells us that the Holy Spirit, when he comes, 'will not speak on His own authority, but whatever He hears He will speak', Luther points out the role of the Spirit in relation to the Word.

> Here Christ makes the Holy Spirit a Preacher. He does so to prevent one from gaping toward heaven in search of Him, as the fluttering spirits and enthusiasts do, and from divorcing Him from the oral Word or the ministry. One should know and learn that He will be in and with the Word, that it will guide us into all

21. 'Lectures on Genesis: Chapters 31–37', Genesis 37:9 (1543), *LW* 6:329.

22. *WA* 18:304, cited in Föller, 'Luther on Miracles', p. 343.

23. Cited in Froelich, 'Charismatic Manifestations', p. 154.

24. Later in this chapter I will take up the categories of 'ultimate' and 'penultimate' to make this point more forcefully.

> truth, in order that we may believe it, use it as a weapon, be preserved by it against all the lies and deception of the devil, and prevail in all trials and temptations.[25]

Thus Luther may be said to have a fairly ambiguous relationship with the *charismata*. Still, he certainly anticipates that a sovereign God may intervene in the natural state of affairs and he did experience healings and miracles in answer to prayer.

Bengt Hoffman records a number of these episodes in his *Luther and the Mystics*. What is apparent from a review of these is that Luther at no time imagined himself master of the healing gift, but always its servant. In a letter he comments on an illness he is undergoing, claiming 'Christ has triumphed so far. I commend myself to the prayers of yourself and the brethren. I have healed others, I cannot heal myself.' Nevertheless he was healed, and by his prayers Melanchthon, too, was healed though at death's doorstep.[26]

In spite of Luther's tepid attitude towards the *charismata*, it must be acknowledged that endeavouring to apply a Pentecostal grid to the sixteenth-century Reformer is anachronistic folly. One should not expect to find Luther speaking directly to matters of Pentecostal theology. Yet he is far from an Enlightenment rationalist, as some nineteenth- and twentieth-century scholarship has painted him.[27] And while Luther is not a charismatic, his apprehension of the unseen world, and its role in his thought call for a reassessment of Luther's theology, particularly in light of the contemporary Lutheran encounter with the burgeoning Pentecostal movement in the majority world. Within the present discussion, it suffices to point out the vitality of Luther's supernaturalism. This awareness of the supernatural world and its interface with life and ministry is a common concern of Luther and Pentecostals, and underscores a genuine barrier for most Luther scholarship.

b. Luther and the Priesthood of All Believers as Charismatic Locus?

One of the most revolutionary aspects of Luther's theology in its historic context was his concept of the priesthood of all believers, often termed 'the universal priesthood of the baptized'. While the exact verbiage never occurs in Luther's works, the concept is clearly there.[28] It arose as a natural consequence of his struggle

25. 'Sermons on the Gospel of St. John: Chapters 14–16', John 16:14 (1538), *LW* 24:362.

26. Hoffman, *Luther and the Mystics*, pp. 195–201.

27. Hoffman devotes a chapter to liberal and neo-orthodox approaches to Luther, demonstrating, 'despite their polemical relationship', their rationalizing tendency to subvert an adequate evaluation of the non-rational contribution to the rational in Luther's thought; Hoffman, *Luther and the Mystics*, p. 37; pp. 37–100.

28. Wengert traces the development of the term in Lutheran theology through Jacob Spener, to Georg Rietschel, who called it 'the most important result of the doctrine of justification'; Wengert 'The Priesthood of All Believers and Other Pious Myths', pp. 1–36 (pp. 2–5). Online: http://www.valpo.edu/ils/assets/pdfs/05_wengert.pdf (Accessed 14 August 2014).

with the Catholic church, and medieval notions of vocation. But this paradigm has become the axis on which much Protestant 'Free Church' ecclesiology has turned. And, certainly taking it beyond Luther's use of the idea, Pentecostals have been at the forefront of teasing out its implications.[29] Charismatic concepts of body life, every-member giftedness and lay leadership all play on the premise of the priesthood of all believers.

The Middle Ages had enshrined two levels of Christian faith. It was no accident that western monasticism arose in the wake of the post-Constantinian shift. Once Christianity became the state religion, those who sought a more profound experience responded to a higher calling and became monks.[30] By Luther's time this had become institutionalized in a formal process of admission to the monastery. Those who were deeply concerned about their souls were counselled to go there, for the rigours of monastic discipline were the surest road to salvation.[31] By 1521 the implications of justification by faith had dispensed with this two-tiered spirituality, and the first monks were leaving their cloisters and marrying. Luther, still in the seclusion of the Wartburg Castle, penned his advice regarding monastic vows. The making of vows was a serious matter, Luther claimed, but some vows are not worth making, and are nullified by their inconsistency with the faith. If the vows of monks are the gospel, as some Franciscans said, then what else could it mean than that only Franciscans are Christians? On this basis, 'the gospel is not common to all, but is divided into counsels and precepts': precepts for ordinary Christians, but counsels for the truly devoted who had vowed to live the narrower life of monks or nuns.[32] This was clearly a contradiction of the *sola fide* on which the Reformation was built, and Luther was incensed. Indeed Luther dedicated his pamphlet on monastic vows to his father in a letter containing an apology for having broken the fourth commandment by disobeying him and entering the monastery.[33] Luther's Reformation discovery set aside all distinction between the monastic and the mundane.

But another dualism divided the medieval world: that between secular and spiritual power, and their respective realms. In a more adversarial tone, Luther wrote the treatise *To the Christian Nobility*, in which he proposed to dismantle three walls behind which the papists had 'ensconced themselves' as a means of rebuffing any attempt at reform.

> In the first place, when pressed by the temporal power they have made decrees and declared that the temporal power had no jurisdiction over them, but that,

29. Veli-Matti Kärkkäinen, *An Introduction to Ecclesiology: Ecumenical, Historical, & Global Perspectives* (Downers Grove: InterVarsity, 2002), pp. 65–66 and 70–72.

30. Karlfeild Froelich, 'Luther on Vocation', in *Harvesting Martin Luther's Reflections on Theology, Ethics, and the Church* (Lutheran Quarterly Books, ed. Timothy Wengert; Grand Rapids: Eerdmans, 2004), pp. 121–33 (p. 124).

31. Oberman, *Luther*, pp. 127 and 139.

32. 'The Judgment of Martin Luther on Taking Monastic Vows' (1521), *LW* 44:256.

33. 'To Hans Luther, Wartburg' (1521), *LW* 48:333.

> on the contrary, the spiritual power is above the temporal. In the second place, when the attempt is made to reprove them with the Scriptures, they raise the objection that only the pope may interpret the Scriptures. In the third place, if threatened with a council, their story is that no one may summon a council but the pope.[34]

The most significant implication of the paper was captured in its title: *To the Christian Nobility of the German Nation Concerning the Reform of the Christian Estate*. There were not several estates, as medieval polity suggested, but only one Christian Estate which represented the nation. Luther appealed to Paul's reasoning in 1 Corinthians 12 to show that all Christians form part of one body. 'This is because we all have one baptism, one gospel, one faith, and are all Christians alike; for baptism, gospel, and faith alone make us spiritual and a Christian people.'[35] The corollary of this is that all Christians are gifted and called, and have a specific vocation to live out wherever Christ has placed them. Whether the secular sphere or sacred, all belong to one priesthood. Baptized Christians are all equally part of the body of Christ, extensions of his ministry whether they serve as garbage collectors or governors. Thus the Christian priesthood flows directly from Christ's priesthood.[36] As Luther puts it elsewhere, 'Christ is a priest, therefore Christians are priests.'[37]

The bit of theological wrangling which separated Pope from Emperor, Bishop from Prince, and priest from peasant allowed the church to maintain a spiritual trump card over all temporal power relations.[38] Rather than making the spiritual function of the priesthood available to all and any laity, as the Free Church tradition has advanced, the purpose of the priesthood of all believers was to put the temporal sphere of political authority on equal footing with the clerical powers. Some effort was made by Lutheran scholars to develop the order of ministry from the priesthood of all believers, but as both Timothy Wengert and Bernhard Lohse show, the two were not related in Luther's thought. Though all are priests, there must still be an order of ministry for the proclamation of the word, the administration of the sacraments.[39]

34. 'To the Christian Nobility' (1520), *LW* 44:126.

35. Ibid., p. 127.

36. Paul Althaus, *The Theology of Martin Luther* (trans. Robert C. Schultz; Philadelphia: Fortress, 1966), p. 314.

37. 'Concerning the Ministry' (1523), *LW* 40:20.

38. 'To the Christian Nobility' (1520), *LW* 44:127.

39. The current notion of the priesthood of all believers was never developed by Luther. 'It is not clear what ecclesiological consequences he intended to draw from his view of the universal priesthood . . . At no time did he draw consequences for congregations from his doctrine'; Bernhard Lohse, *Martin Luther's Theology: Its Historical and Systematic Development* (trans. Roy A. Harrisville; Minneapolis: Fortress, 1999), p. 291. Wengert, 'The Priesthood of All Believers', pp. 6–20.

While Pentecostals have followed the Free Church tradition in developing Luther's priesthood of all believers as an ecclesiological paradigm, they have not done so well at appropriating its ramifications for a unified view of secular and spiritual reality, and the notion of vocation in the secular world. On the one hand Pentecostals have always considered the priesthood of all believers as the primary locus of charismatic activity. Pentecostals, charismatics and neo-charismatics have each elaborated more democratized models of church governance and ministry, to the place where the necessity of trained clergy is an open question among some.[40] But while Pentecostal notions of the *charismata* have been generally applied to the church, little interest has been shown at developing a doctrine of vocation that would equip Christians for service in the world. Indeed the world is often conceived in its most biblically dark tones, as an inhospitable place for Christian witness and work. Still, Luther's ideals about the universal priesthood of the baptized represented a dynamically democratizing move in a static world of established boundaries. In this way, it may be seen as an area of seminal interaction with Pentecostal thought.

c. Luther, the Apocalypse and Pentecostal Anticipation

A third dimension of overlap between Luther and Pentecostals is apocalyptic expectation. Suffice to say one of the distinguishing features of the Middle Ages was its curious mixture of apprehension and anticipation about the end of all things.[41] The mood hung over the late Middle Ages like an ominous cloud, informing not only Luther, and his radical opponents, but much medieval spirituality.[42] Carole Bynum and Paul Freedman suggest that medieval eschatology played in three keys: an eschatology of resurrection, an eschatology of immortality and an eschatology of apocalypse. The three are related, as follows:

> Sharing with the eschatology of resurrection an emphasis on the end of time, a sense of the person as embodied, and a focus on humanity as collective, the

40. One example among many from charismatic sources is James Rutz, *The Open Church: How to Bring Back the Exciting Life of the First Century Church* (Auburn, ME: Seedsowers, 1992).

41. Bynum and Freedman offer an overview of recent scholarship on apocalyptic expectation during the middle ages; Carole W. Bynum and Paul Freedman, 'Introduction', in *Last Things: Death and the Apocalypse in the Middle Ages* (ed. Carole Walker Bynum and Paul Freedman; Philadelphia: University of Pennsylvania Press, 2000), pp. 1–17 (pp. 2–5).

42. Lohse comments, 'The late medieval period was marked partly by an extraordinarily strong apocalyptic'; Lohse, *Luther's Theology*, p. 332. In a seminal work, Robin Barnes traces the sense of the impending return of Christ in Lutheran thought for the century following Luther. He points out that Lutheranism was the only branch of confessional Reformation Protestantism to promote eschatological expectancy; Robin Barnes, *Prophecy and Gnosis: Apocalypticism in the Wake of the Lutheran Reformation* (Stanford: Stanford University Press, 1988), p. 3.

> eschatology of apocalypse shares with the eschatology of immortality a sense that what matters is the here and now, an end that looms as immediate or very soon. Apocalyptic eschatology contrasts, however, with both the eschatology of resurrection and that of immortality in implying a political payoff. It faces toward society and coerces the here and now, although it can be reformist as well as radical and does not necessarily . . . recruit the disadvantaged or the discontent.[43]

While not always consistent with one another, all three eschatologies usually feature together in any given treatment.[44] This was true in Luther's case as well.

Both as a man of his times; and as a theological innovator, Luther gave eschatology a central place.[45] He was committed to all three eschatologies mentioned above. Luther understood that the Christian lives with both Law and Gospel. The Law reminds us that in the midst of life, death surrounds us; the Gospel, that in the midst of death, life surrounds us.[46] Generally, Luther holds that the soul sleeps until the resurrection; but he is also capable of promoting an eschatology of immortality, saying that the dead have even *now* learned, heard and seen all that they were taught in the church.[47] 'Each of us has his own Last Day when he dies.'[48] This apparent inconsistency he resolves by claiming that 'in that world there is neither time nor measurement of time, but everything is one eternal moment'.[49] But Luther's eschatology focuses on the resurrection, as well. His eschatology of resurrection is closely tied to his doctrine of sacrament, particularly of baptism. The daily dying and rising which baptism anticipates is not simply a spiritual discipline, but the promise of eternal life.[50] Luther advises those who question their predestination to focus on Word and Sacrament: 'I have been baptized. I believe in Jesus Christ. I have received the Sacrament.'[51] The eschatological dimension of the

43. Bynum and Freedman, 'Introduction', p. 8; see pp. 5–10.

44. Ibid., p. 9.

45. Althaus comments on the significance of eschatology for Luther: '[Luther's] thoughts about the eschaton are not a conventional appendix but a section of his theology which is rooted in, indispensable to, and a decisive part of the substance of his theology'; *Theology of Martin Luther*, p. 404.

46. 'Psalm 90' (1534), *LW* 13:83.

47. *WA* 53:400, cited in Althaus, *Theology of Martin Luther*, p. 415.

48. *WA* 14:71, cited in Althaus, *Theology of Martin Luther*, p. 416.

49. 'Sermon' (1522) *WA* 10 (III):194, cited in Althaus, *Theology of Martin Luther*, p. 416.

50. 'The Small Catechism' inculcates this daily discipline: 'What does such baptizing with water signify? Answer: It signifies that the old Adam in us, together with all sins and evil lusts, should be drowned by daily sorrow and repentance and be put to death, and that the new man should come forth daily and rise up, cleansed and righteous, to live forever in God's presence'; 'The Small Catechism' (1529), BC, p. 349.

51. 'Table Talk Recorded by Conrad Cordatus' (1532), *LSC*, p. 122. Luther often resorted to the declaration that he had been baptized.

sacraments is not immediately clear to the untrained observer. 'In baptism we here and now undergo the death and resurrection that we will go through when Christ returns.' In the body and blood of Christ we hear the promise 'for the forgiveness of sins', and know that we are now participants 'in the eschatological banquet in the age to come'. Thus in the cup and in the water of baptism is 'God's eschatological word, his final word, spoken in the present'.[52]

These two eschatologies, of immortality and resurrection, represent the consensus of Protestant thought historically. With the erosion of supernaturalism through the Enlightenment, however, Protestantism has lost its general accord regarding an eschatology of apocalypse. But Luther cannot be fully understood without reference to this category. Paul Althaus insists that 'Luther's theology is thoroughly eschatological in the strict sense of expecting the end of the world.'[53] The consummation is a necessary corollary of a salvation which admits that the redeemed are *simul justus et peccator*. One aspect of Luther's formula reminds the Christian that he is *peccator in re* (a sinner in fact) but *justus* only *in spe* (righteous in hope).[54] The full manifestation of this takes place at the end of history.

Luther's apocalyptic vision was populated by the coming Last Day, the Antichrist (the Pope) and Satan raging against the church.[55] Here we come full circle to the supernaturalism that animated Luther's basic worldview. He interpreted the historical events of his time as fulfilments of the visions of Daniel and the Revelation, and was persuaded that he was living through the very signs of the end.[56] Internally he battled the Pope, externally he felt the encroaching pressures

52. Robert Kolb and Charles Arand, *The Genius of Luther's Theology: A Wittenberg Way of Thinking for the Contemporary Church* (Grand Rapids: Baker Academic, 2008), p. 44.

53. Althaus, *Theology of Martin Luther*, p. 404. James Nestingen claimed that 'Luther's way of thinking theologically cannot be understood without it. His recovery of the eschatology of the New Testament, in its apocalyptic form, has to be counted with the theology of the cross as constitutive of his theology'; 'The End of the End: The Role of Apocalyptic in the Lutheran Reform', *W&W* 15 (1995), p. 204. Contra, see Lohse, *Luther's Theology*, pp. 332–35.

54. 'Lectures on Romans' Romans 4:2 (1515–16), *LW* 25:358.

55. Argument regarding Luther's apocalyptic vision has been ongoing. Michael Parsons, however, provides extensive bibliography arguing the centrality of apocalyptic thought for Luther, claiming this represented the scholarly consensus in 2001; Michael Parsons, 'The Apocalyptic Luther: His Noahic Self-Understanding', *JETS* 44 (2001), pp. 627–45 (pp. 628–35). Lohse is particularly sceptical about questions of imminence rather than the significance of apocalyptic; Lohse, *Luther's Theology*, pp. 332–35. But Eric Gritsch portrays Luther as persuaded of the imminence of the world's end; Gritsch, *Martin – God's Court Jester: Luther in Retrospect* (Philadelphia: Fortress, 1983), pp. 39 and 127–28; and Edwards perceived Luther as the end of his life approached, as a man 'gripped by apocalyptic hopes and fears'; Mark Edwards, *Luther's Last Battles: Politics and Polemics, 1531–46* (Leiden: E. J. Brill, 1985), p. 208.

56. Ibid., p. 97. See 'Table Talk No. 1297: Signs on Every Hand' (1 January 1532), *LW* 54:134.

of the Turks. 'The pope is the spirit of the antichrist, and the Turk is the flesh of the antichrist', Luther commented. 'The two help each other to strangle us, the latter with body and sword, the former with doctrine and spirit.'[57]

The very acuteness of this eschatological awareness brings Luther in remarkably close proximity to the early Pentecostals. There is a sense in which Luther, like the early Pentecostals, experiences an eschatological immediacy that prompts the viciousness of his attacks, and the ferocity of his rhetoric. Indeed, Oberman stresses, 'we will fail to grasp his self-understanding if we do not see him as emerging from the beginning of his public career onward as the apocalyptic prophet at the end of time, placed in the increasing power struggle between God and the Devil.'[58] While distancing himself from the chiliasm of the radical Reformation, which took on more violent and destabilizing tones the more extreme it became, Luther knew something of the sense of imminence that coloured Azusa and its kin. Robin Barnes claims that '[m]ore effectively than any previous interpreter, [Luther] gave a world-historical, indeed a world-transforming significance to contemporary events by placing them in an eschatological framework.'[59] So Luther, like the early Pentecostals, emerges as one 'upon whom the end of the ages is come' (1 Cor. 10.11, KJV). This parallel, perhaps, enables Pentecostals to appreciate Luther more fully, and to appropriate him more easily as a forebear, and resource for Pentecostal theologizing. But there is one more area where Luther may inform Pentecostals. His vivid supernaturalism, and stunning apocalypticism were matched, and in important ways, moderated by his approach to spiritual experience.

d. Luther, Enthusiasm and Spiritual Experience

The religion of Martin Luther was a religion of experience – mediated experience, perhaps, but experience no less.[60] As Jürgen Moltmann said, commenting on a passage from the Large Catechism, Luther 'set the standard for modern times by assigning the religious category largely to the subjectivity of "the heart"'.[61] The Reformer proposed a synthesis of Word and experience at the centre of his

57. *WA* Tr 1:135, No. 330, cited in Lohse, *Luther's Theology*, p. 334.

58. Heiko Oberman, 'Teufelsdreck: Eschatology and Scatology in the "Old" Luther', *SCJ* 19 (1988), pp. 435–50 (p. 446).

59. Barnes, *Prophecy and Gnosis*, p. 4.

60. Experience is one of those difficult concepts to define precisely. Discussing experiential language in the New Testament, Luke Timothy Johnson arrives at the following definition derived from Joachim Wach: 'Religious experience is a response to that which is perceived as ultimate, involving the whole person, characterized by a peculiar intensity and issuing in action'; Luke Timothy Johnson, *Religious Experience in Earliest Christianity: A Missing Dimension in New Testament Studies* (Minneapolis: Fortress, 1998), pp. 4–6, 60.

61. Jürgen Moltmann, *The Spirit of Life: A Universal Affirmation* (trans. Margaret Kohl; Minneapolis: Fortress, 1992), pp. 27–28.

Reformation discovery. For Luther, faith arose *ex auditu*, by hearing, and was based on the proclamation of a Word that must come *extra nos*, from beyond the individual. The irreducible core of Luther's Gospel is that God is the author of salvation. But this external Word mediates for Luther some sort of internal experience which both decimates human confidence in self and elevates salvation in the Crucified. The existential dimension of this encounter is undeniable. Whether one reads the Tower experience as a crisis moment in the castle privy, or the result of a long process of discernment; whether one dates it early or late; all accounts of Luther's 'Reformation breakthrough' must come to terms with Luther's rapturous description of his liberating discovery:

> . . . I began to understand that the righteousness of God is that by which the righteous lives by a gift of God, namely by faith . . . the passive righteousness with which merciful God justifies us by faith, as it is written, 'He who through faith is righteous shall live.' Here I felt that I was altogether born again and had entered paradise itself through open gates.[62]

It is impossible to imagine Luther as anything but a theologian of experience. But as Luther also said, 'God is not to be known through feeling but faith.'[63] This kind of dialectic is typical of the Reformer.

1. Luther and the Enthusiasts Luther's mature views regarding experiential spirituality were most often expressed as a result of his controversies with the 'enthusiasts'.[64] The progressively radical nature of dissent, from his dispute with Andreas Bodenstein von Karlstadt beginning in 1521, through the violence of Thomas Müntzer, and culminating with the tragedy of Münster in 1535, had made Luther suspicious about subjective religious experience. While it is clear both Luther and the radicals had roots in the German mystical tradition, it is

62. 'Preface to the Complete Edition of Luther's Latin Writings'; *LW* 34 (1545), p. 337. Lewis Spitz gives a useful, though somewhat dated, digest of various views on the dating of the experience in his introduction to this text; ibid., p. 326. Lohse, *Luther's Theology*, offers a helpful chapter summarizing scholarly discussion on the dating and content of Luther's experience. See also Brecht, *Luther: His Road*, pp. 221–37 where he gives a vigorous defence of a date between spring and fall of 1518.

63. *WA* 15:536, cited in Karl Holl, *What Did Luther Understand by Religion?* (ed. James Luther Adams and Walter F. Bense; trans. Fred W. Meuser and Walter R. Weitzke; Philadelphia: Fortress, 1977), p. 82.

64. William Hordern points out that Luther`s battle with the radicals was fought on several fronts: baptism, and the Eucharist, relationship with the state, liturgical issues, and the use of art in the church. But at the centre of all these controversies was the role of experience, and its limits; William Hordern, *Experience and Faith: The Significance of Luther for Understanding Today's Experiential Religion* (Minneapolis: Augsburg, 1983), p. 51.

equally obvious they took different elements from that encounter. Müntzer, for instance, drank deeply of Johann Tauler and emphasized the subjective aspects of spiritual preparation for experiencing God, especially *Gelassenheit*, a state of perfect submission essential to hearing the voice of God.[65] The radical reformation, including even the moderate evangelical Anabaptists, certainly contained its share of charismatic phenomena.[66] The enthusiasts' claims of revelation through the Spirit unmediated by the Word sound like some of the more extreme forms of Pentecostalism.[67] Luther, on the other hand, rejected the profound subjectivism of the German mystics, but managed to find in them some of the building blocks of his theology of the cross. These included an emphasis on God's hiddenness, and the role of suffering in Christian experience.[68] The more radical the enthusiast, however, the more likely there would be calls to moral perfection, sometimes as a prerequisite for acceptance with God.[69] In dispensing of the traditions of medieval Catholicism for the simplicity of New Testament worship, a definite restorationism

65. Loewen, *Luther and the Radicals*, p. 54. Müntzer developed a radicalism not unlike the apocalyptic fifteenth-century Taborites. From Tauler he derived a concept of Christian suffering as a necessary precursor to communion with God. He held that true salvation should lead to unmediated communication with God in the Spirit; ibid., pp. 52–53.

66. Kenneth Davis finds evidence of charismatic manifestations across a wide spectrum of the radical Reformation from the most moderate to the most extreme. He draws a parallel with Montanism between the heterodox followers of Montanus, and the more moderate wing represented by Tertullian; Davis, 'Anabaptism as a Charismatic Movement', *MQR* (1979), pp. 219–34 (pp. 221–24).

67. Sebastian Frank railed against the Reformers because 'they retch out the Word solely according to the letter, soiled with human filth, not according to the divine sense. For they also don't know another word to say but what is Scriptural, and of no other teachers except their evangelists'. He called them 'learned divines, who have learned, not from God, but only Scripture, and from men who themselves have not learned from God'. Frank's counsel is to 'interpret the Scripture as a confirmation of thy conscience, so that it testifies to the heart and not against it. Again thou shouldst not believe and accept something [merely] reported by Scripture – and feel that the God in thy heart must yield to Scripture. It were better that Scripture should remain Antichrist's!' Frank, 'Letter to Campanus, 1531'; George H. Williams, *The Radical Reformation: Third Edition* (Sixteenth Century Essays and Studies, vol. XV; Kirksville, MO: Truman University Press, 2000), pp. 158 and 159.

68. Lindberg, *The Third Reformation?*, p. 29. Bengt Hoffman has argued that Luther was by far more experientially oriented than scholars have given him credit for. Hoffman's book, *Luther and the Mystics*, though endorsed by Heiko Obermann, was received with significant criticism by the historical guild. Criticism and the question of Luther's relationship to mysticism aside, Hoffman does manage to marshal a significant amount of textual evidence to speak of Luther's profound, and vivid spiritual experience.

69. Melchior Hoffman proposed a charismatic ecclesiology headed by sinless 'apostolic shepherds' who led the prophets, who in turn gave direction to 'the entire multitude of pastors' who guide the simple members of the community. These latter are barred from

coloured much Anabaptist thought.[70] Among the most strident enthusiasts, restorationism took an increasingly militant tone. Müntzer and later, the Münster debacle, confused the violent implementation of Old Testament kingship, complete with plural marriage, for the establishment of Christ's kingdom.[71]

At times, therefore, Luther`s response to enthusiasm, and its embrace of mystical ascent, seems like a complete repudiation of experiential Christianity in favour of an external and sacramental credo.

> They come from heaven, and hear God himself speaking to them as to angels. What is taught at Wittenberg concerning faith and love and the cross of Christ is an unimportant thing. 'You yourself must hear the voice of God,' they say, 'and experience the work of God in you and feel how much your talents weigh. The Bible means nothing. It is Bible – Booble – Babel,' etc.[72]

This is an experience of divine immediacy far more extreme than even early Pentecostalism asserted; for early Pentecostals were nothing, if not devotees of the written Word, which in effect mediated their experience of the divine. But

unmediated contact with the 'apostolic messengers'; Klaus Depperman, *Melchior Hoffman: Social Unrest and Apocalyptic Visions in the Age of Reformation* (ed. Benjamin Drewery; trans. Malcolm Wren; Edinburgh: T&T Clark, 1989), pp. 264–67; and Lindberg, *The Third Reformation?*, p. 93. Deppermann, Packull and Stayer discover in Hoffman as early as 1526 a notion of the 'deified man' and the doctrine that sins committed after illumination cannot be forgiven; Klaus Deppermann, Werner O. Packull and James Stayer, 'From Monogenesis to *Polygenesis*: The Historical Discussion of Anabaptist Origins', *MQR* 49 (1975), pp. 83–121 (pp. 120–21). See also Lindberg on Schwenckfeld, *The Third Reformation?*, pp. 104 and 128.

70. John Howard Yoder, 'Primitivism in the Radical Reformation: Strengths and Weaknesses', in *The Primitive Church in the Modern World* (ed. Richard T. Hughes; Urbana: University of Illinois Press, 1985), pp. 74–97, rejects primitivism as a construct for understanding the sixteenth century. He wishes to rephrase the question and generalize it. 'Everyone in the sixteenth century wanted to renew original Christianity; what problems were inherent in that vision?'; ibid., pp. 75–76.

71. For instance, this motivated Bernhard Rothmann in Münster who anticipated the restitution of all things with the restoration of David's throne. Only after that would be the 'time of reviving and deliverance of the true Israelites from the violent and murdering Babylon and the retribution of the same, then shall the Lord come'; Rothmann, 'Van Verborgenheit der Schrifft des Rykes Christi vnde van dem Daghe des Heren durch de Gemeinte Christi tho Münster', p. 340, in Robert Stupperich, ed., *Die Schriften Bernhard Rothmanns* (Münster: Aschendorffsche Verlagsbuchhandlung, 1970), cited in Gary Waite, 'David Joris' Thought in the Context of the Early Melchiorite and Münsterite Movements in the Low Countries, 1534–1536', *MQR* 62 (1988), pp. 296–317 (p. 307). Such rhetoric incited revolutionary activity.

72. 'Letter to the Princes of Saxony Concerning the Rebellious Spirit' (1524), *LW* 40:50.

Luther is not simply a critic of experiential spirituality. He is similarly capable of extolling the value of spiritual experience, particularly as mediated by the external Word. 'You must experience unshakably that it is God's Word, even though the whole world should dispute it. As long as you do not have this feeling, just so long you have certainly not yet tasted of God's Word.'[73] Such expressions become more guarded after his encounters with the enthusiasts, but they remain nonetheless. As late as 1539, as he outlined David's threefold approach to theology (*oratio, meditatio, tentatio*), Luther described *Anfechtung* as 'the touchstone which teaches you not only to know and understand, but also to experience how right, how true, how sweet, how lovely, how mighty, how comforting God's Word is, wisdom beyond all wisdom.'[74] This experiential wonder, this sensitivity to the numinous is consistent throughout the Reformer's career.

2. Luther and the Pietists The years following the Reformation and the passing of Luther's generation were marked by the emergence of Lutheran orthodoxy.[75] A series of intramural controversies within Lutheranism and doctrinal debates with the Calvinists were generally resolved by the adoption of the Book of Concord in 1580, which encompassed the confessions that Luther himself had ratified, and the Form of Concord (1577), which resolved the later debates. Confessional Lutheranism brought a season of unity to the German Protestants that led to a period of doctrinal development. Taking its cue from the more negative of Luther's appraisals concerning spiritual excesses, the orthodoxy of the seventeenth century led to a sterile rationalism which stifled existential encounter.[76] The context was ripe for the rise of a more experiential Christianity. Johann Arndt had begun calling for a programme of spiritual renewal as early as 1605 in his manifesto, *True Christianity*.[77] With the publication, in 1675, of *Pia Desideria*, Philipp Spener's introduction to a volume of Arndt's sermons, Pietism, as a movement of personal spirituality within confessional Lutheranism began to gather momentum.[78] The result was a long and

73. 'Receiving Both Kinds in the Sacrament', *LW* 36 (1522), p. 248.

74. 'Preface to the Wittenberg Edition of Luther's German Writings' (1539), *LW* 34:287.

75. This era of Lutheran Orthodoxy or Scholasticism was marked by 'the reintroduction of Aristotelian concepts and methods of argumentation'; Lindberg, *The Third Reformation?*, p. 137.

76. The cold rationalist nature of Lutheran scholasticism has been open to debate. See Ernest Stoeffler, *The Rise of Evangelical Piety* (Leiden: Brill, 1965), p. 183, for a critique of the orthodox period. But consider also Kolb, *contra*, who calls attention to 'the rich tradition of piety and preaching in the period'; *The Genius of Luther's Theology*, p. 11.

77. 'Many think that theology is mere science, or rhetoric, whereas it is a living experience and practice'; *Johann Arndt: True Christianity* (The Classics of Western Spirituality, trans. Peter Erb; New York: Paulist, 1979), p. 21.

78. Pietism should be set in the context of a number of other European renewal movements including 'Jansenism, Precisianism, Puritanism, and a widespread chiliastic

acrimonious struggle for the soul of Lutheranism. Lohse characterizes the division as a rending of the internal balance of Luther's theology into an objectivism rooted in the doctrine of Scripture (the Lutheran scholastics) and a spirituality increasingly measured by the criterion of subjective experience (the Pietists).[79] This unravelled the synthesis of Word and experience that stood at the core of Luther's project.

At the heart of the Pietist vision was a thorough-going conversionism that called for spiritual rebirth, and focused attention on the capacities of 'the New Man'.[80] Against the perceived moral laxity of the confessional Lutheranism of the time, the notion of individual rebirth implied a restructuring of personal morality. But the new birth had social implications as well, as illustrated in August Francke's institution of orphanages, schools and colleges. In many ways Francke's institutionalization of his mentor, Spener's, theology coincided with the love of neighbour Luther had envisioned in *Two Kinds of Righteousness* (1519) and *On the Freedom of a Christian* (1520).[81] Constantly charged by the scholastics with enthusiasm, and challenged over their concept of conventicles where the true believers met (*ecclesiola in ecclesia*), the Pietists defended their commitment to Luther by citing his invitation to the new birth and its ethical imperative in the preface to his lectures on Romans:

> Faith, however, is a divine work in us which changes us and makes us to be born anew of God, John 1[:12–13]. It kills the old Adam and makes us altogether different men, in heart and spirit and mind and powers; and it brings with it the Holy Spirit. O it is a living, busy, active, mighty thing, this faith. It is impossible for it not to be doing good works incessantly. It does not ask whether good works are to be done, but before the question is asked, it has already done them, and is constantly doing them. Whoever does not do such works, however, is an unbeliever.[82]

Spener's piety, then, was not so much a means of mystical ascent, as it was an encouragement to practical godliness.[83]

spiritualism', all 'eliciting impressive forms of personal piety and communal revival'; Peter Erb, 'Introduction', *Johann Arndt: True Christianity*, pp. xiii–xiv.

79. Bernhard Lohse, *A Short History of Christian Doctrine: From the First Century to the Present-Revised American Edition* (trans. Ernest F. Stoeffler; Minneapolis: Fortress, 1985), pp. 224–25.

80. Christian Hoburg (1607–75) who stated that 'Justification is fiction, rebirth is fact' illustrates how radical the emphasis on rebirth and its ethical dimension could become; Lindberg, 'Introduction', in *The Pietist Theologians: An Introduction to the Theology of the Seventeenth and Eighteenth Centuries* (ed. Carter Lindberg; Oxford: Blackwell, 2005), pp. 1–20 (p. 6).

81. 'Two Kinds of Righteousness' (1519), *LW* 31:292–306; and 'The Freedom of a Christian' (1520), *LW* 31:327–56.

82. 'Preface to the Epistle of Saint Paul to the Romans', *LW* 35 (1522, 1546), p. 370.

83. Stoeffler, *The Rise of Evangelical Piety*, p. 238.

At times, however, not unlike the earlier enthusiasts, Pietism demonstrated an inclination to perfectionism, and restorationism. Among Spener's recommendations in *Pia Desideria* was the reintroduction of 'the ancient and apostolic kind of church meetings . . . held in the manner in which Paul describes them in 1 Corinthians 14:26–40'. Rather than a commotion of ecstatic utterances, he proceeds to describe an orderly sharing of pious observations by various members of a gathering. Still, Spener clearly believed this would represent a restoration of New Testament order. In support of his argument he marshalled Luther's call for the reading of Scripture by all Christians.[84] Indeed, Spener never saw himself as anything but a devout Lutheran.[85] But even in his careful efforts to reiterate commitment to Luther's spirituality, there was a measure of ambiguity regarding the perfectibility of the reborn.[86]

While he denied any absolute perfection, Spener's concept of salvation distinguished between a new birth that was wholly divine, and renewal, which required human cooperation, and left the door open to Pelagianizing influences that others took much farther than Spener would have allowed. This occurred primarily among the radical Pietists who manifested increasingly separatist tendencies. Embattled on the right with the scholastics, Spener fought running border skirmishes on the left with these separatist radicals who often claimed visionary experiences, prophetic revelations, unique conceptions of imminent apocalypse and heterodox soteriologies. The multifarious nature of their separatism made a virtue out of novelty, and their escalating emphasis on spiritual experience made fresh revelation a necessity.[87] At the extreme, were the Inspirationists, who arose in Germany in 1714. Convulsive states of involuntary agitation, followed by cataleptic stupor, ultimately leading to revelatory utterance were taken, no doubt, as a sign of the restoration of prophetic activity. And the persecution they encountered, first in France, then in England, and later in the German states was interpreted as a sign of

84. Philip Jacob Spener, *Pia Desideria* (trans. and ed. Theodore G. Tappert; N.p.: Fortress, 1964), pp. 89 and 91–92.

85. Stoeffler, *The Rise of Evangelical Piety*, pp. 238–39.

86. Spener's dialectic concerning perfection is well illustrated in the following passage from *Pia Desideria*. 'If one seeks perfection one must leave this world and enter the world to come. Only there will one encounter something perfect; one cannot hope for it before then.' His rejection of perfection seems clear, nevertheless he goes on: 'we are not forbidden to seek perfection, but we are urged on toward it. And how desirable it would be if we were to achieve it!' The possibility seems palpable, yet he 'cheerfully concede[s] that here in this life we shall not manage that'; ibid., p. 80.

87. In his 2007 monograph; Hans Schneider, *German Radical Pietism* (Pietist and Wesleyan Studies, No. 22; trans. Gerald MacDonald; Lanham, MD: Scarecrow, 2007), opens up the Byzantine world of Radical Pietism and introduces readers to a field that is only beginning to be investigated. He asserts that a full history cannot yet be written but gives a summary of the current state of studies.

their apocalyptic role as the church in the desert (Rev. 12.6).[88] Once more, excessive subjectivity and claims of divine immediacy combined with perfectionism and restorationism to spoil a movement which in its original inception was committed to the furthering of Luther's Reformation.[89]

3. *Luther and Wesley* The historical link between Luther, Pietism and Pentecostalism is forged in the relationship between Count Nikolaus Ludwig von Zinzendorf's Moravians and John Wesley. The Wesleyan legacy in Pentecostalism has been traced at length, but the connection between Pietism and Methodism is a significant factor in the emergence of experiential Christianity through the Great Awakening. In fact, in a monograph tracing *The Genesis of Methodism*, Frederick Dreyer claims:

> Methodism as a finished and developed system owes little to its background in England. Deriving from German Pietism, it originated in Saxony and came to England by way of Georgia . . . In its pedigree it owes nothing to High Anglican tradition; its ecclesiastical antecedents lie in Lutheran Pietism.[90]

Bold assertions, indeed, and open to considerable debate. But whether they can be fully defended, there is no doubt of the immense impact of Wesley's encounter with Moravian missionary Peter Böhler, and his subsequent involvement in Böhler's Fetter Lane Society. Wesley had first come across Moravians on his ill-fated mission to Georgia, and had there even applied for membership in the Moravian Church.[91] The shaping of what eventually became Methodism, following his break with the Moravians in 1740, owed much to the severed connection.[92]

After his Aldersgate Street conversion, in the summer of 1738 Wesley made a pilgrimage to Herrnhutt to visit the home of Moravianism, and meet its leader, Count Zinzendorf. As a Pietist, Zinzendorf's credentials were impeccable. Raised

88. John says, 'The woman fled into the wilderness to a place prepared for her by God, where she might be taken care of for 1,260 days'; ibid., pp. 118–24. The Inspirationists were attacked, predictably, by Lutheran Orthodoxy, but also by the moderate evangelical Pietists centred at Halle, and other 'similarly minded' radicals as well; ibid., p. 124.

89. James K. Stein, 'Philipp Jakob Spener', in *The Pietist Theologians: An Introduction to the Theology of the Seventeenth and Eighteenth Centuries* (ed. Carter Lindberg; Oxford: Blackwell, 2005), pp. 84–98 (p. 96).

90. Frederick Dreyer, *The Genesis of Methodism* (Cranbury, NJ: Lehigh University Press, 1999), pp. 110 and 113.

91. Colin Podmore, *The Moravian Church in England, 1728–1760* (New York: Oxford University Press, 1998), pp. 32–33.

92. Dreyer, *The Genesis of Methodism*, pp. 13–29. Colin Podmore takes a similar, though more measured approach; Podmore, *The Moravian Church in England*, pp. 29–71. Podmore analyses Wesley's famous 'heart strangely warmed' account of conversion for its clear allusions to Moravian piety; ibid., p. 42.

by his godly grandmother, a leading Pietist, herself; Zinzendorf's godfather was Philipp Spener. Following the journey, Wesley's assessment of the Moravian movement was mixed: among other criticisms, he was taken aback by the centrality of Zinzendorf. But Zinzendorf was not simply a follower of his forebears. His encounter with the Moravians who came to live on his estates blended fresh emphases with his Lutheran Pietism to form something new.

After Wesley seceded from the Moravians, Zinzendorf invited him to discuss the matter when he was in London in September, 1741.[93] Two matters separated them. Wesley's insistence on Christian perfection and an activist approach to sanctification, as opposed to the affective Christology of the Moravians which recommended a quietist sanctification through meditation on the 'blood and wounds' of the Lamb.[94] For Wesley sanctification was a distinct and actual possibility in the believer. For Zinzendorf, perfection was in Christ. Nevertheless Wesley took at least three foundational concepts from his encounter with Zinzendorf and Pietism: the replacement of justification with regeneration as the key to Christian experience; the use of small groups for discipleship and discipline; and a Christocentric emphasis in sanctification.[95]

While Wesley was no doubt committed to perfectionism, it is unclear how far one may go in labelling him a restorationist. The epitaph inscribed in Wesley's City Road Chapel invites all to remember him as one who arose to 'revive, enforce, and defend The Pure, Apostolical Doctrines and Practices of The PRIMITIVE CHURCH'[96] And there is much to warrant this concern with early Christianity. Wesley was an ardent student of the church Fathers, and even those who would call Wesley a restorationist admit that the golden age to which Wesley appealed extended to the time of Constantine, and was abridged from an earlier dating he held that included the ecumenical councils.[97] But as David Hempton indicates, '[t]

93. Campbell asserts that the split was not with Moravian movement generally, but specifically with the English community, and certainly not with the whole of Pietism; Ted Campbell, 'Close Encounters of the Pietist Kind: The Moravian-Methodist Connection', *CV* 45 (2003), pp. 67–80 (p. 73).

94. 'The quarrel at Fetter Lane is not between Lutheran Evangelicals and Anglican Sacramentalists, but between pietists of two different kinds arguing over the techniques of conversion'; Dreyer, *The Genesis of Methodism*, pp. 40–42 and 114.

95. Campbell, 'Close Encounters', p. 70. Dreyer sees multiple parallels, which he summarizes in chapter 5 of *The Genesis of Methodism*, pp. 106–16.

96. Cited in Luke Keefer, 'John Wesley: Disciple of Early Christianity', *WJT* 19 (1984), pp. 23–32 (p. 21).

97. Keefer explains Wesley's idea of a 'golden age'. 'For Wesley the golden age of the church extended from Christ's incarnation to the coronation of Constantine. His golden age, however, was arranged hierarchically in a series of concentric circles. An analogy to the biblical temple might illustrate his understanding. The subapostolic age was the temple courtyard. The New Testament era was the holy place and thus qualitatively distinct from the second and third centuries. Within the New Testament era, the church

he range of theological influences on the young Wesley is legion.'[98] Wesley certainly did not incline to an ahistorical leap across the centuries. His restorationism, if it may be called that, was a broader, more informed search for Scriptural patterns.[99] Still, like other restorationists, Wesley was capable of blunt appeals to the apostolic church and the Word.[100] But unlike later restorationists who looked only to the Bible, Wesley's theology was informed by Albert Outler's famous quadrilateral, made up of 'Scripture (guided by the Holy Spirit), experience (not longevity but rather personal experimental religion), reason (not rationalism, but reasonableness), and tradition (not as a straitjacket, but as a spiritual electricity cable extending from the past to the present)'.[101] The quadrilateral kept Wesley from falling into enthusiasm, on the one hand, but allowed him to explore experimental Christianity on the other. Shaped, in part by the emerging Enlightenment, Wesley was an empiricist: reason unaided was not the source of knowledge, but rather experience.[102] Still,

of the first four chapters of Acts constituted the holy of holies. The Jerusalem Church was Wesley's supreme model of primitive Christianity; ibid., pp. 24 and 29. Howard Snyder also affirms a restorationist view of Wesley; Howard Snyder, 'Spirit and Form in Wesley's Theology: A Response to Keefer's "John Wesley: Disciple of Early Christianity"', *WJT* 19 (1984), pp. 33–35.

98. Hempton traces the influences on Wesley. 'He was well read in the church fathers and was intrigued by early monastic piety and ancient liturgies. He was influenced by Macarius, Gregory of Nyssa and other Byzantine traditions of spirituality. Although he later repudiated the French mystics for their tendencies towards illuminism, spiritual indiscipline and weak intellectual content, he read voraciously in the works of Madame Guyon, Fenelon, Fleury, De Renty, Brother Lawrence and Antoinette Bourignon. His mother Susanna, an important influence in her own right, introduced him to Pascal and some of the classics of Anglican spirituality of the seventeenth and eighteenth centuries. But perhaps his most obvious debts were to Thomas a Kempis, Jeremy Taylor, and William Law on the one hand and to the Moravians on the other'; David Hempton, 'John Wesley (1703–1791)', in *The Pietist Theologians: An Introduction to the Theology of the Seventeenth and Eighteenth Centuries* (ed. Carter Lindberg; Oxford: Blackwell, 2005), pp. 256–72 (p. 257).

99. Clarence Bence argues that Wesley's use of restorationist rhetoric tends to be defensive, and opportunistic. He prefers to root Wesley's impetus for church renewal in the eschatological vision of the kingdom; Clarence Bence, 'A Response to Luke Keefer', *WJT* 19 (1984), pp. 36–38 (pp. 37–38).

100. 'As our American brethren are now totally disentangled both from the state, and from the English hierarchy . . . They are now at full liberty, simply to follow the Scriptures and the primitive Church. And we judge it best that they should stand fast in that liberty, wherewith God has so strangely made them free'; Wesley, 'To "Our Brethren in America"', in Albert Outler ed., *John Wesley* (New York: Oxford University Press, 1964), p. 84.

101. Outler, 'The Wesleyan Quadrilateral'. The description presented here is Hempton's and not Outler's; Hempton, 'Wesley', p. 257.

102. Randy Maddox, *Responsible Grace: John Wesley's Practical Theology* (Nashville: Abingdon, 1994), p. 40.

raw experience, even enhanced by rational reflection was not enough. And while tradition offered a path, only Scripture could present authoritative direction. As Wesley's brother Charles put it, 'Whate'er his Spirit speaks in me, must with the written Word agree.'[103] Thus the Wesleyan quadrilateral provided an epistemological basis for faith and the interpretation of experience.

Luther, then, touched Wesley through the Pietism of Zinzendorf. Moravian spirituality had a clear influence on Wesley's development of Methodism, its evidence seen in the class meeting, and its Christocentrism. While shades of perfectionism and restorationism colour Wesley's theology, he manages to mitigate their extremes with his appeal to Scripture, tradition and reason. Such elements appear to be foreign to Luther's thought, as seen in his violent reaction to their abuse by Radical Reformers. Both Luther and Wesley had to deal with the vexing problem of spiritual experience, and its assessment, and while both maintained a vital place for experience, they also appealed to external standards to adjudicate the matter.

4. Luther and the New World Pietism made further contribution to the historical linkage of Pentecostalism with Luther in the New World, as well. This occurred chiefly through the importation of German Pietist devotional writings and hymns, and through immigration. The spirit of Pietism came to North America in the writings of leading Pietists such as Gerhard Tersteegen, who while he died in 1769, exercised enormous influence in the German-American revivalism of the nineteenth century. A recurring motif in Tersteegen's hymns and sermons was the theme of a coming Pentecost that would presage the final judgement.[104] This 'baptism with the Spirit' was a typically perfectionist experience, the goal of which was sanctification of the whole heart.[105] But Pietism was also disseminated

103. Charles Wesley's words in their context speak directly to the issue at hand: 'Doctrines, experiences to try,/ We to the sacred standard fly/ Assured the Spirit of our Lord/ Can never contradict His word:/ Whate'er His Spirit speaks in me/ Must with the written word agree;/ If not – I cast it all aside,/ As Satan's voice, or nature's pride'; Wesley, 'Scripture Hymns: On Isaiah 8:20', *PW* 9, p. 380.

104. In Tersteegen's typology, the first Pentecost was 50 days after the Exodus, on Mount Sinai, the second was the outpouring of Pentecostal glory 50 days after Easter, and the final manifestation will culminate with the appearance of the Son of Man in great glory at the last day; O'Malley, 'The Influence of Gerhard Tersteegen in the Documents of Early German American Evangelicalism', in *Pietism, Revivalism and Modernity, 1650–1850* (ed. Fred van Lieburg and Daniel Lindmark; Newcastle-upon-Tyne: Cambridge Scholars Publishing, 2008), pp. 232–55 (p. 234).

105. O'Malley claims the German-American 'Evangelical Association', was eventually the first denomination to publish a declaration on 'Entire Sanctification and Christian Perfection' in their Book of Discipline (1807); ibid., p. 245.

through the early Methodists. Wesley's *Standard Sermons* and his *Notes Upon the New Testament* were a significant and foundational part of American Methodism's doctrinal standards.[106] Both bore the marks of Pietism. The *Notes Upon the New Testament*, in particular, owe a clear debt to the work of Johann Albrecht Bengel, the Swabian New Testament scholar, whose work Wesley borrowed and simplified for his unlettered preachers.[107] But at the more popular level Pietism was no more completely experienced than in its influence on Charles Wesley's hymnody. The Pietist and Moravian tropes in Wesley's hymns were particularly apparent to those familiar with Continental Pietism.[108]

Pietism also had direct impact through the arrival of Moravians en masse. The founding of Bethlehem, on the Pennsylvania frontier, in June 1742, involved all 120 Moravians then in America.[109] While Moravian influence far outpaced its numbers, Pietist groups influenced Continental Protestants of every stripe from Lutherans, to the Reformed and the Mennonites. Pietism was a crucial contributor to the establishment of American Lutheranism, in particular, as its leading founders were steeped in the Halle spirituality.[110] Samuel Schmucker, perhaps the pre-eminent Lutheran leader of the nineteenth century represents the synthesis of Pietist spirituality, moderate Lutheran confessionalism and a temperate revivalism. Schmucker, who died in 1873, was clearly both an American Evangelical and a Lutheran Pietist.[111] So significant was the Pietist encounter in America that Stoeffler contends that the traditional view of American Protestantism being defined by the Puritan experience requires significant revision, in terms of Pietist impact. He argues that Pietism shaped the intensely biblical and ethical emphases of American theology; the broadly democratizing forces of voluntaryism and lay participation in the church; and, particularly, the especially experiential nature of American Christianity.[112] As such, it forms an interesting precursor to Pentecostalism.

106. Stoeffler, 'Pietism, the Wesleys, and Methodist Beginnings in America', in *Continental Pietism and Early American Christianity* (ed. F. Ernest Steoffler; Grand Rapids: Eerdmans, 1976), pp. 184–221 (pp. 197–98).

107. Ibid., pp. 198–201.

108. Ibid., p. 208.

109. John Weinlick, 'Moravianism in the American Colonies', in *Continental Pietism and Early American Christianity* (ed. F. Ernest Stoeffler; Grand Rapids: Eerdmans, 1976), pp. 123–63 (p. 145).

110. Mark Granquist, 'Between Pietism, Revivalism and Modernity: Samuel Simon Schmucker and American Lutheranism in the Early Nineteenth Century', in *Pietism, Revivalism and Modernity, 1650–1850* (ed. Fred van Lieburg and Daniel Lindmark; Newcastle-upon-Tyne: Cambridge Scholars Publishing, 2008), pp. 256–73 (p. 256).

111. Ibid., pp. 264–69.

112. Ernest Stoeffler, 'Epilogue', in *Continental Pietism and Early American Christianity* (ed. Ernest Stoeffler; Grand Rapids: Eerdmans, 1976), pp. 266–71.

5. Luther, the Ultimate and the Penultimate At this point a summary of findings is in order. While Luther, left to his own devices had worked out a synthesis of Word and experience to account for justifying faith, his interactions with the enthusiasts caused him to rephrase his position polemically against their claims of divine immediacy. It appears that the more pronounced the assertion of divine immediacy, the more extreme the accompanying perfectionism and restorationism. In both the Thomas Müntzer matter and the later Münster tragedy, along with the increasing relativization of Scripture, perfectionist and restorationist propensities reached especially dangerous proportions. Similar conditions obtained among the Pietists, whose assertion of subjective experience arose in response to the emphasis on objectivity in Lutheran Orthodoxy. Along with the stress on the existential, perfectionism and restorationism also emerged in Pietist spirituality. It was particularly the radical Pietists who, once more, relativized the role of Scripture, and thus professed ever grander experiences of divine immediacy. Similarly, the perfectionism and restorationism of these groups became progressively more pronounced. The Pietist heritage was handed through the Moravians to John Wesley, who in his turn manifested moderate tendencies of perfectionism, and maybe even restorationism. But Wesley kept experience in its place, through the application of his quadrilateral of Scripture, experience, tradition and reason; not allowing experience to become the defining factor of his spirituality. In so doing he avoided the kind of claim to divine immediacy that raised Luther's concern with the enthusiasts. As shown in the previous chapters, however, Wesley's offspring, much like Luther's stepchildren did not maintain the synthesis of objective Word and subjective experience their forebears recommended. Indeed one may discern the progressive displacement of divine initiative, and the expanding domain of humanity as active subject from Luther through Wesley down to contemporary Evangelicalism and its quintessential expression in the broader Pentecostal movements. With this observation, some conclusions may be drawn about the nature of religious experience, and particularly Luther's ideas about it. This may be done, first with a brief comparison of Wesley and Luther.

Interestingly, it is Wesley's measured appeal to reason and tradition and their limitation of the realm of experience that bring him in theological proximity to Luther, part of whose struggle was to overcome scholastic speculation and the tradition of the Roman church. Even Wesley's perfectionism was tempered by the quadrilateral, for while he taught the possibility of perfection he admitted that he had never achieved it himself. Luther's hedge against enthusiasm was the external and objective categories of Word and sacrament. Methodist Luther scholar Philip Watson goes so far as to suggest that Wesley and Luther were not as distant as a superficial reading would suggest. Both acknowledged the principles of *sola gratia* and *sola fide*, both anticipated that salvation involved not only the removal of guilt, but the transformation of life, and that it was not complete until the age to come. Within this framework, Wesley and Luther disagree on the possibility of perfection in this life, Luther flatly refusing it, and Wesley seeking, though never having experienced it, but both expecting true believers to live and grow in the love of Christ.[113] With regard to the primacy of Scripture, Wesley resembles Luther more than the Reformation enthusiasts or the radical Pietists. Like Wesley whose prior pastoral failures impelled him, the journey for Luther also begins with painful experience: *Anfechtung* was Luther's preliminary experience with God, but it needed to be interpreted and transcended by Scripture, for as raw experience it was devastating.

Thus Luther appeals to Scripture and existential encounter with the Holy Spirit to create and inform Christian faith.[114]

> The Holy Spirit wants this truth which He is to impress into our hearts to be so firmly fixed that reason and all one's own thoughts and feelings are relegated to the background. He wants us to adhere solely to the Word and to regard it as the only truth. And through this Word alone He governs the Christian Church to the end.[115]

For Luther there was little doubt that it was the objective, *extra nos* nature of Scripture that the enthusiasts were ignoring in their zeal for unmediated encounter with the divine. But it was this very objectivity and externality that provided the necessary rubric by which to interpret and limit experience.

Much is written by Lutheran commentators to underscore this ultimacy of both Scripture, and Sacrament. But little is said about the penultimacy of experience. Given the extremes against which Wittenberg was battling, the emphasis is anticipated. But deconstructing Luther in a non-polemical milieu should yield a more balanced dialectic between Word and experience. Indeed, even in the heat of debate, Luther posits a twofold process by which faith is created.

113. Philip Watson suggests a rapprochement between Wesley and Luther. '[I]f Wesley has much to say of Christian Perfection, or perfect love as the sole conscious motivation of the entirely sanctified, while Luther flatly denies the possibility of perfection in this life, we cannot too often remind ourselves that the two men mean quite different things by perfection. Luther means absolute perfection: Wesley means a "relative" perfection – relative to the possibilities of a fallen world by the grace of God. In fact, we might be tempted to say that Luther means perfection "properly so called", Wesley perfection "improperly so called", We should do better, however, to remember that Wesley, who was steeped in the Ante-Nicene Fathers, thinks along the more dynamic lines of the Greek [teleiosis], while Luther has the more static concept of the Latin *perfectio* in mind'; Philip Watson, 'Wesley and Luther on Christian Perfection', *ER* 15 (1963), pp. 291–302 (p. 301).

114. Simeon Zahl imagines that Luther calls all experience into question when in fact he is suspicious of fallen experience, experience without the Word; Zahl, *Pneumatology and Theology of the Cross in the Preaching of Christoph Friedrich Blumhardt: The Holy Spirit between Wittenberg and Azusa Street* (London: T&T Clark, 2010), pp. 9–10.

115. 'Sermons on the Gospel of St. John: Chapters 14–16', John 16.13 (1538), *LW* 24:362.

> Now when God sends forth his holy gospel he deals with us in a twofold manner, first outwardly, then inwardly. Outwardly he deals with us through the oral word of the gospel and through material signs, that is, baptism and the sacrament of the altar. Inwardly he deals with us through the Holy Spirit, faith, and other gifts. But whatever their measure or order the outward factors should and must precede. The inward experience follows and is effected by the outward. God has determined to give the inward to no one except through the outward. For he wants to give no one the Spirit or faith outside of the outward Word and sign instituted by him[116]

The outward/inward dialectic is an unavoidable concomitant of human existence. Luther's genius is in acknowledging, rather than denying it, even while disputing with the 'heavenly prophets'.

Once more he upholds the ultimacy of the Divine Subject. It is God who speaks; God who saves; God who offers objective and tangible signs that may be held, tasted, felt, and heard; and God who promises. But this same God also deals with us inwardly, existentially, experientially. And Luther anticipates these encounters may be abundant ('whatever their measure'), and ('whatever . . . their order') they may even precede the objective encounter chronologically (as indeed *Anfechtungen* do). This is not the received understanding among Luther scholars. It is typical to follow interpretations like Regin Prenter's, who contends that the chronological order is significant: 'the outward "parts" must come first and the inward afterwards and dependent on the outward'.[117] My revision of standard interpretations is to suggest the relationship is not merely one of temporal primacy, but, rather, as I will demonstrate, ultimacy. Generally Luther scholars are in agreement about the essential centrality of the external Word. They are either more sceptical, or at best, more silent about the inner subjective reality.

In order to properly assess the relationship of the Word of grace; inner experience, whether charismatic, spiritual or merely human; and the emergence of faith; I wish to develop Dietrich Bonhoeffer's concept of the ultimate and the penultimate. These categories, to be sure, differ from Luther's inner/outer dichotomy, but they present a fresh perspective from which to unpack his meaning.[118] Bonhoeffer's concern was not to explicate the role of experience, but applied to this issue, his

116. 'Against the Heavenly Prophets' (1525), *LW* 40:146.

117. Regin Prenter, *Spiritus Creator* (trans. John M. Jensen; Philadelphia: Muhlenberg Press, 1953), p. 249. Prenter makes clear that Luther's views are set against the enthusiasts. Where they imagined that mortification of the sinful nature was the essential preparation for receiving the Spirit, Luther contended that the outward Word created faith as the Spirit worked by overcoming the internal hatred of the world and the old man. The essential dimension to grasp is Luther's rejection of any human ascent to God in favour of the divine initiative 'from heaven to earth'; ibid., p. 251.

118. 'Inner' and 'outer' are geographical designators. They point to the locus of divine activity, and suggest that all subjective 'inner' experience must be mediated by objective 'outer' realities (i.e. Word and Sacrament). Bonhoeffer's categories, while not positional,

paradigm produces some useful insights. First I will summarize the salient points from Bonhoeffer's chapter on 'Ultimate and Penultimate Things' in his *Ethics*. Then I will expand these ideas to facilitate a dialogue with Luther's concept of spiritual experience.

For Bonhoeffer, the ultimate is both God's most significant word and his final word. 'God's mercy to a sinner must and can be heard only as God's final word, or it will not be heard at all . . . it is a *qualitatively* ultimate word', Bonhoeffer explains. 'There is no word of God that goes beyond God's grace.'[119] Still, '[t]he justifying word of God is also, however, the *temporally* ultimate word. Something penultimate always precedes it.'[120] Behind the temporal dimension of the ultimate is the idea of eschatological judgement, and the final justification of the individual.[121] The only possible source for such a word is the Divine Subject, the Author and Finisher of our salvation.

If the ultimate is God's boundary, beyond which nothing more can be said, if it is the eschatological last word, then what is the value of the penultimate? Is the penultimate meaningless in the face of the ultimate? For Bonhoeffer penultimate things matter a great deal, for they 'prepare the way' for the coming of the Lord (Isa. 40.3; Lk. 3.4–6).[122] God has chosen to use penultimate things to shape hearts, create circumstances, and demonstrate his care and compassion, so that people will be prepared to receive his word. And all of this is grace! 'The penultimate, therefore, does not negate the freedom of the ultimate; instead the freedom of the ultimate empowers the penultimate.'[123] It is the role of Christians to enhance the penultimate experience of others so that they may be prepared to receive the Word of the Lord.[124] Ultimately, though, it is Christ, himself, who prepares his own way. Humanly devised

order the significance of divine activities and human experience. I believe this paradigm yields useful insights for understanding the role of experience, and whether it accurately interprets Luther's position, it modifies it in a way consistent with his underlying concern. Simeon Zahl, to the contrary, proposes an absolute disjunction between Word and Spirit: 'For Luther the Spirit cannot precede the external Word, and neither can the two work together in a mutual way'; Zahl, *Pneumatology and Theology of the Cross*, p. 5.

119. Dietrich Bonhoeffer, *Ethics* (German Edition, 1949, Dietich Bonhoeffer Works, vol. 6; Minneapolis: Fortress, 2005), p. 149.

120. Ibid., p. 150, see also 159, 'What is the penultimate? It is all that precedes the ultimate – the justification of the sinner by grace alone – and that is addressed as penultimate after finding the ultimate.'

121. Ibid., p. 149, n. 10.

122. Ibid., pp. 159–67.

123. Ibid., p. 160.

124. Bonhoeffer expands this thought: 'None of this excludes the task of preparing the way. It is, instead, a commission of immeasurable responsibility given to all who know about the coming of Jesus Christ'; ibid., p. 163; and particularly for preachers, 'Those who proclaim the word yet do not do everything possible so that this word may be heard are not true to the word's claim for free passage, for a smooth road'; ibid., p. 160.

programmes cannot accomplish the task. 'Method is the path from the penultimate to the ultimate. Preparing the way is the path from the ultimate to the penultimate.'[125] Salvation, as much for Bonhoeffer as for Luther 'is of the Lord'.

Within this concept of the ultimate and the penultimate are clues which illumine Pentecostalism's difficult impasse at the beginning of the twenty-first century, as well as Luther's concerns about the enthusiasts. The first item to note is the need for a saving Word, *extra nos*. For Bonhoeffer this is the ultimate, the justifying word of grace, for Luther it is 'the oral word of the gospel' and the 'material signs' of the sacraments. Luther perceived correctly the goal of the enthusiasts. They were persuaded of the possibility of mystical ascent, of preparing themselves, often through multiple steps, and ascetic practice to attain communion with God. 'Instead of the outward order of God in the material sign of baptism and the oral proclamation of the Word of God [the enthusiast] wants to teach you, not how the Spirit comes to you but how you come to the Spirit.'[126] Luther, like Bonhoeffer, saw the gospel as ultimate, both temporally, in the sense that it qualifies all that has gone before, and qualitatively, as boundary, beyond which no other word could go. For Luther, Word circumscribes experience, defines it, qualifies and limits it.

But this does not put an end to penultimate things. Indeed, Bonhoeffer warns that the disparagement of the penultimate 'leads to strengthened disregard for, and devaluation of, the ultimate . . . From this perspective the task is to strengthen the penultimate through stronger proclamation of the ultimate, and to protect the ultimate by preserving the penultimate'.[127] In the area of religious experience, these penultimate things may be thought of as the 'inward' means by which God deals with us, namely, 'the Holy Spirit, faith, and other gifts', as Luther had indicated, presumably the very means by which the enthusiasts claimed to experience divine immediacy.[128] But Luther and Bonhoeffer (by extension) deny ultimacy to any of these things. They may be valuable, but they are to be tested by the Word.

> Inasmuch as the office of preaching the gospel is the greatest of all and certainly is apostolic, it becomes the foundation for all other functions, which are built upon it, such as the offices of teachers, prophets, governing [the church], speaking with tongues, the gifts of healing and helping, as Paul directs in I Cor. 12[:28].[129]

125. Ibid., p. 167.

126. The actual subject of the sentence, to whom the missing pronoun 'he' refers is Karlstadt; 'Against the Heavenly Prophets' (1525), *LW* 40:147.

127. Bonhoeffer, *Ethics*, p. 169.

128. I take it that Luther does not refer here to the person of the Holy Spirit, but to the internal experience of the Spirit, similarly he refers to faith here as the growing experience of trust in a gracious God.

129. 'Concerning the Ministry' (1523), *LW* 40:36. Luther thinks of tongues differently in 'Against the Heavenly Prophets' (1525). There, Luther refers to the use of Latin in the mass as 'speaking in tongues', and the translation of Latin into German as the 'interpretation.'; 'Against the Heavenly Prophets' (1525), *LW* 40:142.

Thus spiritual experiences are valid, important, and inasmuch as they are granted by God, and not created by fancy, they are essential. But they are not ultimate, they are penultimate.[130]

The penultimate, however, is the place in God's economy that humanity currently occupies. This is a crucial matter insofar as spiritual experience is concerned. The vital issue is in differentiating between ultimate and penultimate, and Bonhoeffer points out the two dangers he perceives. The seriousness of the penultimate 'consists, to be sure, precisely in never confusing the penultimate with the ultimate, and never making light of the penultimate over against the ultimate'.[131] As such all experience of the ultimate here in the penultimate must be mediated experience, and yet must be taken with utter seriousness. Luther criticized the enthusiasts, in essence, for confusing the two. But Lutheran Orthodoxy, it might be said, was guilty of making light of penultimate spiritual experience. The key to properly appreciating spiritual experience is the 'already-and-not-yet' dialectic of inaugurated eschatology. 'Christian life is the dawn of the ultimate in me, the life of Jesus Christ in me. But it is also always life in the penultimate, waiting for the ultimate.'[132] As Paul puts it, 'where there are prophecies, they will cease; where there are tongues, they will be stilled; where there is knowledge, it will pass away. For we know in part and we prophesy in part', but when the ultimate comes, what is in penultimate disappears (1 Cor. 13:8b–10). Thus spiritual experience is limited, bounded, and must be determined by the external, objective Word in this penultimate world. But experience remains an essential dimension of Christian existence. 'The penultimate will be swallowed up by the ultimate, yet it retains its necessity as long as the earth endures.'[133]

6. Luther and the Question of Priority The preceding discussion has proposed a fundamental reconstruction of the common interpretation of Luther's thought. It is generally agreed by Lutheran theologians that there can be no experience of the Holy Spirit before, or apart from the *externum verbum* of Scripture. The very words of Luther seem conclusive: 'God gives no one his Spirit or grace

130. Steven Land asks the inevitable Pentecostal question and answers it, 'Does this . . . mean that Pentecostals place the Spirit above the Word and thus elevate experience from the category of source for theology to that of norm? The answer is "Yes" and "No."' His response is expectedly ambiguous, acknowledging a significant place for the Spirit in the inspiration of Scripture and its illumination; and yet arguing for a freedom of the Spirit that does not relegate him to being a servant of Scripture. Ultimately Land claims that 'the Word as living Word of God in Jesus is, of course, equal with the Spirit.' Luther's concern, however is not to tame the Holy Spirit or limit him, but rather to place personal subjective experience as penultimate and the external 'Spirit-Word' as ultimate; Land, *Pentecostal Spirituality*, p. 39.

131. Bonhoeffer, *Ethics*, p. 168.

132. Ibid., p. 168.

133. Ibid.

except through or with the external Word.'[134] Certainly this is the consensus of confessional Lutheranism, not only in its doctrinal standards but as expressed by its theologians. One Lutheran theologian, Francis Pieper, asserted that God 'builds up, maintains, and governs His church exclusively through His Word and the Sacraments, by which He creates and preserves faith in the Gospel through the Holy Ghost, and for the administration of which He gives His gifts to the church.'[135] The same position is taken by the Lutheran Church-Missouri Synod:

> The emphasis of our Lutheran heritage on the external Word as the instrument of the Holy Spirit helps prevent a subjectivism that seeks divine comfort and strength through an interior experience rather than in the objective word of the Gospel. To accent the former rather than the latter as the basis of Christian certainty can easily lead either to pride or despair instead of humble trust in the Gospel promises.[136]

This interpretation appears to undermine the proposal that Luther is arguing for the ultimacy of the Word, rather than its temporal primacy.

Simeon Zahl's *Pneumatology and Theology of the Cross in the Preaching of Christoph Friedrich Blumhardt* offers a different approach to the issues I raise. Zahl argues that Luther was mistaken in assuming that the enthusiasts' claims of unmediated experience must all founder on the self-deception of fallen human nature. He presents Christoph Blumhardt as an example of a theologian who successfully held the possibility of both unmediated experience of God and a pessimistic view of humanity within the framework of a theology of the cross. The goal of Zahl's project is to find a means of bridging the pneumatological impasse between Pentecostal theologies, which he claims are open to immediate experiences of God and Reformational theologies which are closed to such experiences, proposing, as they do, a completely mediated encounter involving Scripture as the medium of revelation. His book provides a thoughtful evaluation of Blumhardt in order to explore this quandary. Zahl's creative synthesis, however, is based on two assumptions that I question: first, the value of unmediated experience; and second, the matter whether Luther is sceptical of all such experience.

What is 'unmediated experience'? Zahl does not imagine that there is any such thing as experience that is not mediated psychologically or culturally. He offers the following definition.

> 'Unmediated' for Pietists and their interpreters means first and foremost 'not mediated by the Word.' [H]owever, that for Blumhardt and for most Pietists

134. 'Smalcald Articles' (1537): III, art. viii, par. 3–4, BC 312.

135. Pieper, *Christian Dogmatics* (4 vols; St. Louis: Concordia Publishing House, 1950–53), vol. 2, p. 388.

136. Lutheran Church-Missouri Synod, 'The Charismatic Movement and Lutheran Theology', pp. 34–35.

> and Pentecostals this nonmediation by the Word is not to be understood as against the Word, or as never involving the Word. Rather, it means simply that the experience is not *necessarily* or *exclusively* Word dependent. . . . It signifies personal communication from God, and a 'felt' directness unlike any other form of divine–human relationship.[137]

Thus, Zahl's definition envisions the possibility that God may communicate with individuals in a deeply existential way, both with and without Scripture.

Furthermore, Zahl posits a radical disjunction between this kind of immediate experience and Luther's view. As Zahl assesses it, Luther offers a sweeping rejection of experience unmediated by the proclaimed Word. 'For Luther, the testimony of personal inner experience is not only unreliable but also often testifies to precisely the opposite of what is in fact true *coram deo*.'[138] Instead, Luther anticipates the Spirit to work through mediation of the preached word, Law and Gospel, first to convict, then to comfort.[139] 'For Luther', Zahl concludes, 'an unmediated understanding of the Spirit equates directly to erroneously high anthropology, and the price of the error is the Gospel'.[140] Zahl offers Blumhardt as an example of the possibility of holding to both unmediated experiences of the Spirit and a pessimistic anthropology, and thus a model for Pentecostal and Lutheran discussion.

With a few reservations, I generally concur with Zahl's summary concerning Luther. To the extent that charismatic experience claims to be an immediate communion with God, it appears to also espouse a perfectionist triumphalism, Blumhardt notwithstanding. But I do not believe that charismatic experience must necessarily be construed as unmediated, or that Luther's concern that 'God gives no one his Spirit or grace except through or with the external Word' must be applied as strictly as Zahl and conventional Lutheran scholarship suggest.[141]

Zahl's definition of 'unmediated encounter' is much tamer than the legacy he traces from Pietism, which includes two types of revelatory experience. The first or 'weak' kind equates to the type of guidance that believers may sense comes from God in day-to-day life and ministry. It is generally acknowledged in Pentecostal spirituality that such guidance is valid but tentative, and must be subjected to the judgement of Scripture.[142] In its more extreme forms, it may include 'strong'

137. Zahl, *Pneumatology and Theology of the Cross*, pp. 92–93.

138. Ibid., p. 10.

139. Ibid., pp. 171–78. Zahl understands Luther to be exclusively interested in the preached Word.

140. Ibid., p. 179.

141. 'Smalcald Articles' (1537): III, art. viii, par. 3–4, BC 312.

142. See the classic treatment by noted charismatic teacher; Bob Mumford, *Take Another Look at Guidance: A Study of Divine Guidance* (ed. Jorunn Oftedal Ricketts; Plainfield, NJ: Logos International, 1971), who offers Scripture as the objective standard, the Holy Spirit as the subjective standard and circumstances as the providential standard of guidance; ibid., pp. 65–74.

revelatory experiences that provide new divine revelation that implies 'that God's revelation in Jesus Christ and scripture is inadequate or incomplete'.[143] This dimension of revelation is generally disavowed in Pentecostal circles.[144] In essence, this is the form of 'enthusiasm' against which Luther inveighs so vehemently in his rhetoric. For instance, Luther insists that 'we should and must constantly maintain that God will not deal with us except through his external Word and sacrament. Whatever is attributed to the Spirit apart from such Word and sacrament is of the devil.'[145]

Luther's comments about the Spirit must be interpreted in the context of his dispute with the enthusiasts. Often he mentions them explicitly in the context of statements that God will not give his Spirit apart from the external Word and sacrament. The disputes with Karlstadt, Müntzer and Rothmann became, in the emergence of Luther's Reformation, formative crises that threatened the entire enterprise, and called for a hard-line approach. Similar to the New Issue which divided early Pentecostals, and is evidenced by the lengthy article on the Trinity in the AG's Statement of Fundamental Truths, the Radical Reformation posed a traumatic cleavage which left a legacy in the Lutheran Confessions. Thus, Luther's teaching regarding the Holy Spirit and charismatic experience must be read against this specific background. One must avoid assuming Luther is addressing twenty-first-century Pentecostals, just as one must properly reckon with the nature of sixteenth-century enthusiasm.

There is a larger question answered by my reconstruction of Luther. What is the underlying theological freight in Luther's insight, after one accounts for the vehemence of his statements? Is Luther really denying that God is at work in the human heart except as it is exposed to Word and sacrament? Or, like his rejection of natural theology, is his primary concern that human fallenness cannot make a proper and full assessment of God's work apart from these? The enthusiasts, from Karlstadt's more modest statements, to the increasingly radical claims of Sebastian

143. Zahl, *Pneumatology and Theology of the Cross*, p. 90.

144. Consider the furor over Benny Hinn's revelation that the Trinity consists of three persons each of whom is a triune being. On the one hand, that such statements could be made publically over the airwaves is a commentary on the state of the charismatic church, but that they were repudiated generally and eventually recanted (although, affirmed again, two years later) says something more; Hank Hanegraaf, *Christianity in Crisis: 21st Century* (Nashville: Thomas Nelson, 2009), pp. 145–46. See also Pentecostal Assemblies of Canada, 'Contemporary Prophets and Prophecy', [Position Paper] (Mississauga: PAOC, 2007), pp. 6 and 8. Online: https://paoc.org/docs/default-source/Fellowship-Services-Docs/credential-resources/Forms-Documents/contemporary-prophets-and-prophecy.pdf (Accessed 14 August 2014); and the Assemblies of God, 'Apostles and Prophets', (Position Paper, AG, 2001), pp. 9–10, especially 1 and 3. Online: http://ag.org/top/Beliefs/Position_Papers/pp_downloads/pp_4195_apostles_prophets.pdf (Accessed 14 August 2014).

145. 'Smalcald Articles' (1537): III, art. viii, par. 10, BC p. 313.

Frank and Melchior Hoffman, asserted the Spirit's revelation apart from and above Scripture. Luther was incensed.

> [S]hould you ask how one gains access to this same lofty spirit they do not refer you to the outward gospel but to some imaginary realm, saying: Remain in 'self abstraction' [one of the seven stages of the mystic apprehension of God] where I now am and you will have the same experience. A heavenly voice will come, and God himself will speak to you . . . Do you not see here the devil, the enemy of God's order? With all his mouthing of the words, 'Spirit, Spirit, Spirit', he tears down the bridge, the path, the way, the ladder, and all the means by which the Spirit might come to you.[146]

In this context, Luther's cautions are powerful, incisive and essential. They raise a corrective to which contemporary Pentecostal triumphalism must respond. But that corrective is not about temporal dimensions of the Spirit's ministry, whether he was at work before or after Word and sacrament, but rather about what is ultimate and what is penultimate. An over-concern with the temporal serves only to place Luther in a corner he may not have anticipated entering. Rather Luther complains that separating the two destroys the very means by which spiritual experience becomes effective.

Even Luther acknowledges the work of *Anfechtung* as preparatory for the gospel, and he acknowledges it as a work of God. Furthermore, Zahl mentions miracles and healings as a type of unmediated experience, and observes that Luther may not have rejected them out of hand as enthusiasm. Another type of experience that Zahl indicates is the punctiliar encounter: the moment of profound feeling that may surround the conversion experience, or the moment of Spirit baptism. Luther, as has been noted, was certainly a theologian of experience, yet, it must be admitted, he was also suspicious of it. For Luther, human experience might be fickle, uncertain, fallen – and human interpretation of experience, even more prone to error. Both experience and its interpretation exist *in nobis*, in the realm of the penultimate. But God's Word, his gift of justification, the sacraments, these were stable, objective, dependable. In essence, they were ultimate, accomplished *pro nobis*, but *extra nos*. An experience may be from God, but what is its meaning? One may encounter the divine in prophecy, healing or in a deep sense of divine love, or divine displeasure, but by what canon are such encounters to be interpreted? On what basis is an experience to be embraced or rejected? These, I suggest, are more germane to Luther's underlying concern with the enthusiasts.

When the Lutheran Council addressed the matter of charismatic experience, the non-charismatic majority noted the 'existential ambiguity of the Christian life' and the consequent ambiguity of spiritual experience and asked if charismatics saw their experience as self-validating.[147] Both the observation and the question

146. 'Against the Heavenly Prophets' (1525), *LW* 40:147.

147. 'Conference Report on the Holy Spirit in the Life of the Church', p. 238.

are pertinent. As I have argued, experiences are penultimate, God's Word is ultimate. The approach advocated here, I believe, follows Luther's prescription. All spiritual experiences must be assessed, indeed, find their meaning, signification, and significance, only in the context of the external Word. However, and I believe this would follow Luther in spirit if not necessarily in letter, spiritual experience itself is a valid, even necessary category if moderated, limited and circumscribed by the Word. If the model of ultimate and penultimate things is appropriate to the discussion of spiritual experience, and if it illumines Luther's thought on the matter, it also raises major questions about how it is possible for the two domains to interact. This is a question of great magnitude, and for Bonhoeffer, it is finally a Christological question. It is Christ, his incarnation, cross and resurrection, who gives meaning to the penultimate.[148] But with this question the entire issue of Luther's theology of the cross comes to the fore.

Conclusion

On the surface, Luther appears to be a strange interlocutor for Pentecostals. In the conventional narrative, he is pitted against the enthusiasts of the Radical Reformation, and pictured as the implacable enemy of all things Pentecostal. But this is a caricature of both Pentecostals and Luther himself. Indeed there are resonances between Luther and Pentecostals that make him a fascinating conversation partner, and one whose insights may contribute to shifting the foundations of Pentecostal theology. These include his emphases on the supernatural, the priesthood of all believers and the apocalyptic. But it is his thought about the nature and limitation of spiritual experience that invites Pentecostals to a potentially fruitful dialogue.

Luther's struggles with *Anfechtungen*, and the relief he experienced in his discovery of the gospel cannot be understood, except in existential terms. Yet Luther found himself embattled by radical forces, who based on their appeal to spiritual experience, threatened to undermine the Reformation, and even the social order. His response to the enthusiasts, who set their own immediate experience of the divine above Scripture, tempered his developing understanding of spiritual experience. His basic stance appears to be an affirmation of experience as something that may find meaning only in the context of the external and objective elements of the Word and Sacrament.

Luther's approach to qualifying spiritual experience in response to the threat of the radical Reformation, was to subsume the experiential under the objective in temporal terms: first come the objective Word and Sacrament, then the subjective experience. Bonhoeffer's treatment of ultimacy and penultimacy provides a useful device for understanding Luther, and for appropriating his understanding in the context of Pentecostal triumphalism. Luther perceives outward things such

148. Bonhoeffer, *Ethics*, pp. 157–59.

as Word, Sacrament, justification as ultimate categories. They form a boundary and circumscription of all spiritual experience. But it is the penultimate which prepares the way for the ultimate. The experience of 'the Holy Spirit, faith and other gifts' as inward means by which God deals with us, is nevertheless essential, if not ultimate. There is a fixed boundary between the work of God *extra nos*, and *pro nobis*, and his work *in nobis*. This is the essential distinction for Pentecostals in the current debate.

The theology of the cross, however is where the matter of ultimate and penultimate finds significance. The cross decimates human experience apart from God, and places boundaries on human expectation in this age. The *theologia crucis* was thus a useful device in Luther's battle with enthusiasm, and with appropriate adjustments may prove to be a corrective paradigm for application against Pentecostal triumphalism. The following chapter examines this very dimension of Luther's thought.

Chapter 4

'WHERE I FIRST SAW THE LIGHT': LUTHER'S THEOLOGY OF THE CROSS AS PENTECOSTAL RESOURCE

At the cross, at the cross where I first saw the light,
And the burden of my heart rolled away,
It was there by faith I received my sight,
And now I am happy all the day!

—Isaac Watts (1674–1748)

There is a crucial hour in every man's and every woman's life. Someone now may be facing their cross, their Gethsemane. Will you say, 'Father save me from this hour?' You know the blessing that came when Jesus endured the cross, despising the shame. Face the hour of your opportunity. Some are drawing back. Let us pray, 'Lord, save me from drawing back.' Our Christ, who went every step of the way, says, 'I will never leave thee nor forsake thee.' When we get on the resurrection side of the cross, the glory and victory will be unspeakable.

Unsigned, 'Victory Follows Crucifixion',
The Apostolic Faith 1 (September 1906), 4

Pentecostalism has always rejoiced at the cross. Indeed, so has all Evangelicalism, which is, in part, defined by its crucicentrism. This delight in the cross has been celebrated in its hymnody, and few hymn writers have had as unblemished evangelical credentials as Isaac Watts. His poem 'At the Cross' has found acceptance in all evangelical circles, even Pentecostal ones. After all, since coming to the cross Watts claims, 'Now I am happy all the day.' Surely this is the ultimate goal of coming to the cross in the first place. At least this is what the best-sellers tell us. Isn't the cross at the core of *The Christian's Secret of a Happy Life*?[1] Isn't it

1. Hannah Whitall Smith imagines it to be so. 'Everywhere and always His work is said to be, to deliver us from our sins, from our bondage, from our defilement; and not a hint is given anywhere, that this deliverance was to be only the limited and partial one with which the Church so continually tries to be satisfied'; *The Christian's Secret of a Happy Life: New and Enlarged Edition* (Chicago, New York and Toronto: Fleming H. Revell, 1888), p. 17.

the source of the *Power Thoughts* that will lead to success as we 'win the battle of the mind'?[2]

But as they have celebrated the cross, have Pentecostals, or Evangelicals generally, plumbed the depths of its meaning? The second chapter of Jürgen Moltmann's *The Crucified God* is provocatively titled 'The Resistance of the Cross against its Interpretations'. In it Moltmann demythologizes the Christian interpretation of the cross. He reminds his readers that the cross is horror and scandal, repugnance and devastation before it is anything else. It may become the place from which I derive joy and hope, but from the moment I first see the light, from the moment I receive my sight, it must be the place of desolation and godforsakenness. The cross will eventually give way to the resurrection, but it will never be the locus of 'now I am happy all the day'. Instead Moltmann asserts what Luther does about the nature of the cross: 'It destroys the destruction of man. It alienates alienated man. And in this way it restores the humanity of dehumanized man.'[3]

The following chapter unfolds the meaning of the theology of the cross in terms of *katabasis* and *anabasis*, its downward and upward dynamics. The theology of the cross becomes an essential category for discussing the experience of God for it deals with the interface between the divine and the human, the sacred and the secular, the ultimate and the penultimate. Particularly, a consideration of the theology of the cross is essential to grasping the dialectic of expectation and experience that troubles all forms of triumphalism. By exploring the limits of human understanding in Luther's notion of hiddenness, and then the potential of divine encounter through an examination of the resurrection side of the *theologia crucis*, Luther will be seen to provide a uniquely useful probe for examining Pentecostalism.

I. Luther's Theology of the Cross: The Critique of Experience

Appropriations of Luther's central motif have become fashionable since Jürgen Moltmann's ground-breaking *The Crucified God* first appeared in its German edition in 1972. Liberation theologians have appealed to it, feminists have

2. Joyce Meyer indicates that '[w]e need to *learn* to think and then behave according to the new nature we have rather than the old nature that officially went to the cross. It's so important to realize at the beginning of our journey that success will require time and effort– probably more than we would like!' Meyer refers here to success in the domain of discipline and self-control; Meyer, *Power Thoughts: 12 Strategies to Win the Battle of the Mind* (New York: FaithWords, 2010), p. 239.

3. Jürgen Moltmann, *The Crucified God: The Cross of Christ as the Foundation and Criticism of Christian Theology* (trans. R. A. Wilson and John Bowden; New York: Harper & Row, 1974), p. 71. This is not to say that Moltmann and Luther are in complete agreement on the meaning of the *theologia crucis*, as will be seen in this chapter. In fact in this very

found it useful, it has been at the centre of theodicies and it has funded social criticism. And while all these functions are legitimate applications of Luther's paradigm, they often take shortcuts around its core soteriological concern rather than apprehending the theology of the cross at its most basic and incisive level. Luther's *theologia crucis* does indeed provide a matrix for theological reflection, but it is essential to remember that as he initially employed it, the cross primarily addressed a central epistemological question for Luther: how can I know God? And for Luther, this question is not merely philosophical, or theological, but existential as well. The theology of the cross is concerned with the nature of spiritual experience.

Historically, misunderstanding, misuse and, in fact, ignorance of the theology of the cross have been its lot. It became what Douglas John Hall has called a 'thin tradition'. He traces its slim progress through Søren Kierkegaard, and Karl Barth down to the present.[4] Yet it is particularly suited to our day. A world that has witnessed the horrors of the Great War, the Holocaust, Hiroshima and 9–11, like the late medieval world that Luther faced, is equally in need of a theological revolution. The twin threats of totalizing systems and secularism parallel, in our world, the papal machinery of the institutional church of Luther's time and the scholasticism that gave it ideological underpinning.[5] While profoundly different from each other, our age may be as much in need of the radical remedy of the *theologia crucis* as was the late medieval period which produced it. And, similarly to Luther, we, too, may be theologizing in the interstices of two eras. This, in itself, is a significant motivator for a Pentecostal recovery of the theology of the cross, since the transition between modern and postmodern frameworks only exacerbates the quandary of expectation and experience from which it suffers.

Indeed, a recovery, of sorts, is precisely what we find. As already noted, Luther's methodology has been revived and applied in assorted contexts and with varying degrees of faithfulness to his original aims. The general features of Luther's *theologia crucis* are important to keep in mind. In his definitive work, Walther von

context Moltmann charges Luther with failing to develop the political implications of the cross during the Peasant's Revolt.

4. Hall, *Lighten Our Darkness*, pp. 114, 115–37.

5. McGrath credits the recovery of the theology of the cross in the period following the Great War to the fact that it was a theology that faced the pressing question 'is God *really* there amidst the devastation and dereliction of civilisation? Luther's proclamation of the hidden presence of God in the dereliction of Calvary, and of the Christ who was forsaken in the cross, struck a deep chord of sympathy in those who felt themselves abandoned by God and unable to discern his presence anywhere'; McGrath, *Luther's Theology of the Cross*, p. 179. See also Jürgen Moltmann's account of his coming to faith and his search for hope in the aftermath of the Second World War in; Jürgen Moltmann, *A Broad Place: A Biography* (trans. Margaret Kohl; Minneapolis: Fortress, 2008), pp. 29–31; and *Crucified God*, p. 1.

Loewenich, the scholar who in the 1920s was the first to highlight the theology of the cross as the central motif of the Reformer's thought, spells out five essential aspects of Luther's paradigm.[6]

- 'The theology of the cross as a theology of revelation, stands in sharp antithesis to speculation.' The theology of the cross is always a negation. It exists as a refutation of what Luther calls *theologia gloriae*, a theology of glory. Every theology of glory presumes to ascend to the divine by human work and ingenuity. In Luther's day the pre-eminent theology of glory was the speculative thought of the scholastics, but as the Reformation unfolded, he had the enthusiasts to reckon with as well.
- 'God's revelation is an indirect, concealed revelation.' All conclusions about the reality of God drawn from human reason or natural theology are misleading. We do not actually find God where reason would expect him because God has chosen to be *deus absconditus*, the hidden God, always at work *sub contrario*, under the contrary of human speculation.
- 'Hence God's revelation is recognized not in works but in suffering, and the double meaning of these terms is to be noted.' This is what Luther means when he says in the explanation of thesis 21 of the Heidelberg Disputation, 'He who does not know Christ does not know God hidden in suffering. Therefore he prefers works to suffering, glow to the cross, strength to weakness, wisdom to folly, and, in general, good to evil.'[7] The 'double meaning' von Loewenich notes refers to the words 'works' and 'cross'. By works, Luther means both 'created works' and ethical achievements. The ambiguity implies the interchangeability of moralism and rationalism as useless means to the knowledge of God. The ambiguity of 'cross' will be taken up presently.
- 'The knowledge of the God who is hidden in his revelation is a matter of faith.' Since God can only be known in his humanity, weakness, and foolishness, only faith will be able to apprehend him as he has hidden himself in the suffering of the cross, and such faith can only be the gift of God.
- 'The manner in which God is known is reflected in the practical thought of suffering.' Von Loewenich suggests that Luther entertains an ambiguity in his use of the words 'works' and 'cross'. The 'double meaning' of 'cross' includes both the suffering of humanity and that of the Lord. Our personal suffering which brings us to an end of self, also brings us to the revelation of God in suffering and cross.

It is apparent that Luther's concerns in the theology of the cross, though honed originally against the scaffolding of the speculative theology of the Scholastics, form an equally sharp critique of notions of divine immediacy, and the subjective experience of the enthusiasts. The 'indirect, concealed revelation' of God

6. These points are developed in von Loewenich, *Theology of the Cross*, pp. 19–22.

7. Luther, 'Heidelberg Disputation' (1518), *LW* 31:58.

entertained by the *theologia crucis* is the means by which the ultimate makes its claim upon the penultimate known.

In 1959 there appeared an English version of Danish theologian Regin Prenter's assessment of the state of this 'thin tradition'. In it he lamented that modern approaches to the theology of the cross had fallen into one of two errors. Either they offered a 'theology of the cross without the word' or a 'theology of the word without the cross'. The former represented an existential approach, in practice not unlike the medieval *imitatio dei* and was represented by Bultmann.[8] The latter he illustrates with Karl Barth, whom he sees as having created a sacred/secular split and for whom the cross is not so much insignificant as indecipherable unless the word brings it into a sacred realm of sterile orthodoxy.[9] At issue for Prenter is the significance of a literal suffering on the cross for the sins of humankind, and a personal appropriation of that suffering by the individual's embracing her own cross.[10] The soteriological aspect of the cross is central.

a. The Cross and Personal Glory

Crux probat omnia, Luther says.[11] Gerhard Forde worries that too many have romanticized Luther's theology of the cross, and fallen into the shortcut of circumnavigating this painful but stubborn dimension of the cross. We have too quickly made Jesus into 'the one who "identifies with us in our suffering", or the one who enters into solidarity with us "in our misery"'.[12] Forde is concerned about the 'serious erosion' or 'slippage' of theological language. 'Sentimentality leads to a shift in focus', he says, 'and the language slips out of place'.

> We apparently are no longer sinners, but rather victims, oppressed by sinister victimizers . . . We no longer live in a guilt culture but have been thrown into meaninglessness – so we are told. Then the language slips out of place. Guilt puts the blame on us as sinners, but who is responsible for meaninglessness? . . . As Alan Jones, Dean of the Episcopal Cathedral of San Francisco put it once, 'We are living in an age in which everything is permitted and nothing is forgiven.'[13]

The theology of the cross has reference first to sin. 'A theologian of glory calls evil good and good evil. A theologian of the cross calls the thing what it actually is.'[14] And while Dorothee Soelle applied it to suffering, the theology of the cross

8. Regin Prenter, *Luther's Theology of the Cross* (Philadelphia: Fortress, 1971), pp. 7–11.

9. Ibid., pp. 12–17.

10. Ibid., pp. 3–4 and 17–18.

11. 'The cross tests all things' or 'The cross is the criterion of all things'; 'Labours in Psalms' (1519–21), *WA* 5:279; 'CRUX sola est nostra theologia' or 'The cross alone is our theology' found in 'Labours in Psalms' (1519–21), *WA* 5:176; capitals in the original.

12. Forde, *On Being a Theologian of the Cross*, p. viii.

13. Ibid., pp. ix–x.

14. 'Heidelberg Disputation: Thesis 21' (1518), *LW* 31:40.

will not brook any dissimulation. It 'says what the situation is'.[15] The fundamental issue with the human condition is called 'sin'. Without an acknowledgement of this there can be no progress.

This may not be clear from a preliminary, or modern reading of the 'Heidelberg Disputation', the *locus classicus* for any discussion of the theology of the cross. On first blush, the theses set forth seem more occupied with matters of medieval philosophy and only obliquely with the very heart of theology. To crack the code, though, one must recall that Martin Luther was a product of the late Middle Ages.[16] He was steeped in the scholastic system of speculative theology, a method that had developed after Anselm of Canterbury (1033–1109), and found its stride in Peter Lombard (*ca.* 1100–60), and Thomas Aquinas (1225–74). Scholasticism was a sophisticated process of argumentation based on classical authorities (particularly Aristotle, but also the church fathers) and detailed reasoning. By Luther's time it had provided definitions of key concepts such as sin, grace and righteousness that were derived from debate, rather than empirical encounter with the Bible.[17] The further removed from Scripture these premises became, the more convoluted and unwieldy the system of theology that supported the outward praxis of the church.

Luther studied under professors who had been shaped by one of the last and most influential theologians of late medieval scholasticism, Gabriel Biel (*ca.* 1420–95).[18] Much of the debate in Biel's day surrounded the role of grace in acknowledging the small motions of the soul towards God.[19] Following the consensus of speculative

15. Dorothee Soelle, *Suffering* (trans. Everett R. Kalin; Philadelphia: Fortress, 1975), p. 70.

16. Alister McGrath claims this as a key premise for understanding both Luther and his *theologia crucis*; *Luther's Theology of the Cross*, pp. 25–26.

17. I do not mean to suggest that Scholastic discussion did not interact with Scripture, but that Luther wished to give Scripture a sort of empirical primacy. The *via moderna* demanded that all theological assertion appeal to an objective standard, just as philosophy and later natural science must ultimately be based on the empirical rather than the speculative. Oberman claims that 'only Luther's quest for God's reliable and certain word in the Scriptures put an end to the supremacy of speculative philosophy' by providing that objective criterion in the holy canon; Oberman, *Luther*, p. 119.

18. Biel was a leading exponent of the *via moderna* a nominalist approach to philosophy arising in the fourteenth century, and influenced by the writings of William of Ockham (*ca.* 1280–1349). It proposed a more empirical methodology and logic over the speculative abstraction of the realism which marked the *via antiqua* of the twelfth and thirteenth centuries, as exemplified by Thomas Aquinas and Duns Scotus (1266–1308); *BDWP*, p. 725. The system of justification theology which led to Biel and his contribution is discussed in Dennis Ngien, *The Suffering of God According to Martin Luther's 'Theologia Crucis'* (New York: Peter Lang, 1995), pp. 20–24; and McGrath, *Luther's Theology of the Cross*, pp. 55–57.

19. Luther's reformation breakthrough was not so much a shift from 'earning' salvation to God 'granting' it. Rather, his insight was more about the *basis* on which God grants salvation; Anna M. Madsen, *The Theology of the Cross in Historical Perspective. Distinguished*

thought, Biel, held that there remained within fallen humanity some vestige of divine goodness called the *synteresis*. God has chosen in his mercy to bestow grace when one 'does one's best' or more literally 'does what is within one to do' (*facere quod in se est*). In themselves, ontologically, such acts are not meritorious, but by God's grace they become so. Thus for Biel, the Christian who acts in agreement with the *synteresis* in order to perform even the smallest work, receives the fitting reward of grace. Once in a state of grace, a person may receive salvation as a reward for works that are done in grace.[20]

But how could one remain in a state of grace? And what and how many works done in that state would merit salvation? And what might one do, having received salvation, if one fell out of the state of grace? Luther's well-known over-productive conscience was responsive to the profound attacks of *Anfechtung*, that assault of despair and doubt, helplessness and hopelessness that led him time and again to the confessional.[21] There he probably was confronted by two differing approaches to penitence prevalent in his day. The first set great store by the depth and quality of the penitent's contrition, the second placed confidence in the sacrament of penance itself, and the authority of priestly absolution.[22] Neither provided Luther with the needed relief. Thankfully, he also received council in the confessional from Johannes Staupitz the vicar general of his order, confessor, mentor and friend. David Steinmetz suggests Staupitz offered Luther two kinds of counsel, spiritual and theological, which consequently impacted his formation both as pastor and theologian. Staupitz confronted Luther's scholastic theology with judicious application of Augustine and Paul.[23] Steinmetz indicates three observations Staupitz made that Luther took hold of as helpful. With Augustinian insight, he helped Luther grasp that love of God was the beginning of repentance, and not the final step of self-discipline. He cautioned him of the risk of trusting in his own moral

Dissertations in Christian Theology (Eugene, OR: Pickwick, 2007), p. 79; and McGrath, *Luther's Theology of the Cross*, pp. 59–60.

20. Ngien, *The Suffering of God*, p. 25. Considerable debate has been occasioned over the question of whether Biel's model of justification represents a form of Pelagianism; McGrath, *Luther's Theology of the Cross*, pp. 57–62; Heiko Oberman, *The Harvest of Medieval Theology: Gabriel Biel and Late Medieval Nominalism* (Cambridge: Harvard University Press, 1963), pp. 176–77; and Michael G. Baylor, *Action and Person: Conscience in Late Scholasticism and the Young Luther* (Leiden: Brill, 1977), pp. 113–15.

21. McGrath provides an insightful discussion of *Anfechtungen* with ample bibliography in *Luther's Theology of the Cross*, pp. 169–74.

22. For a discussion of these two penitential traditions, and Luther's exposure to them, see; David Steinmetz, 'Luther against Luther', in *Luther in Context, Second Edition* (Grand Rapids: Baker, 1996), pp. 1–11 (pp. 2–7).

23. While the mechanisms by which Luther was influenced by Augustine and humanism are matters of intense debate among Luther specialists, the fact of their influence is not. See 'Preface to the Wittenberg Edition of Luther's German Writings' (1539), *LW* 34:285.

fortitude to earn divine favour. And perhaps most importantly, he gave Luther a litmus test for true theology: genuine doctrine gives glory to God whereas the false gives it to man.[24] This last, clearly foreshadows Luther's dialectically opposed categories, the theology of glory and the theology of the cross.

Staupitz's pastoral wisdom might have come from any medieval confessor. Perhaps due to their apparent relationship, however, this counsel struck Luther with powerful intensity. When anxious over election, Staupitz pointed to the cross of Christ; when troubled by guilt, Staupitz warned him that unbelief in God's mercy was a possibly fatal sin; when plagued by thoughts, he was told 'if our thoughts condemn us, our thoughts are not Christ'; when concerned about the wrath of God, he was admonished that the wrath of God never falls on the feeblest of penitents who cling to the cross.[25] Devotion to the cross was a venerable tradition of medieval popular piety. Within monastic circles, it arose from the study of mystics such as Bernard of Clairvaux and particularly German mysticism as represented by Johannes Tauler and the *Theologia Germana*.[26] Thus Luther was directed to find solace in the cross alone. He concluded

> What others have learned from Scholastic theology is their own affair. As for me, I know and confess that I learned there nothing but ignorance of sin, righteousness, baptism, and of the whole Christian life. I certainly did not learn there what the power of God is, and the work of God, the grace of God, the righteousness of God, and what faith, hope and love are . . . Indeed, I lost Christ there, but now I have found him in Paul.[27]

24. David Steinmetz, *Luther and Staupitz: An Essay in the Intellectual Origins of the Protestant Reformation* (Duke Monographs in Medieval and Renaissance Studies, Durham: Duke University Press, 1980), pp. 32–33.

25. Ibid., pp. 32–33.

26. Graham Tomlin, 'The Medieval Origins of Luther's Theology of the Cross', *AR* 89 (1998), pp. 22–40 (pp. 32–37); and Graham Tomlin, *The Power of the Cross: Theology and the Death of Christ in Paul, Luther and Pascal* (Paternoster Theological Monographs, Milton Keynes, UK: Paternoster, 1999), p. 133; Steven Ozment, 'Eckhart and Luther: German Mysticism and Protestantism', *The Thomist* 42 (1978), pp. 258–80 (p. 262). The German mystics vividly depicted passivity, suffering and self-denial as indispensable facets of any relationship with God. Luther echoes these concerns in his application of humility, temptation and self-accusation in his first lectures on the Psalms, between 1513 and 1515. 'One becomes a theologian by dying and being damned', Luther protested, 'not by understanding, reading, and speculating'. As Steven Ozment observes, 'German mysticism here contributed to the formation of what came to be known as Luther's theology of the cross'; ibid., p. 267.

27. 'Sermon on the Sunday After Epiphany' (1523), *WA* 12:414, cited in Ngien, *The Suffering of God*, p. 27; from Wilhelm Pauck, ed., trans., *Luther: Lectures on Romans* (The Library of Christian Classics; Louisville: Westminster John Knox, 1961), pp. xxxviii–xxxix.

According to the canons of humanism and the *via moderna*, the Scriptures became, for Luther, a field of objective study that could yield empirical data about God. By the power of God's Spirit such data became life-transformative.[28]

Crux probat omnia. The cross tested scholasticism and found it wanting. It also tested Luther himself and found there, what he had already discovered: the ubiquity of sin. Luther's movement from scholastic notions of original sin as 'absence of divine righteousness' to a more profound concept of *peccatum radicale*, made sin, as Bernahrd Lohse comments, 'like a root (*radix*) affecting everything growing from it'. [29] The dreadful result 'is that our nature has been so deeply curved in upon itself because of the viciousness of original sin'.[30] Eberhard Bethge notes that Luther's concept of *cor curvum in se* ('the heart turned in on itself') became a primary category in Dietrich Bonhoeffer's thought.[31] The incisive nature of Luther's critique of the self, and Bonhoeffer's penetrating elaboration of it underscore the profound anguish and solitude of life in Adam. 'Who shall deliver me from this body of death (Rom. 7.24b)?' The sharpness of Luther's dialectic is not that he castigates our most heinous works, but our highest and best. This is particularly spelled out in Thesis 13 of the Heidelberg Disputation, 'Free will, after the fall, exists in name only, and as long as it does what it is able to do [that is, *facere quod in se est*, 'to do one's best'], it commits a mortal sin.'[32]

28. 'To put it briefly, there are two kinds of clarity in Scripture, just as there are also two kinds of obscurity: one external and pertaining to the ministry of the Word, the other located in the understanding of the heart. If you speak of the internal clarity, no man perceives one iota of what is in the Scriptures unless he has the Spirit of God. All men have a darkened heart, so that even if they can recite everything in Scripture, and know how to quote it, yet they apprehend and truly understand nothing of it . . . For the Spirit is required for the understanding of Scripture, both as a whole and in any part of it. If, on the other hand, you speak of the external clarity, nothing at all is left obscure or ambiguous, but everything there is in the Scriptures has been brought out by the Word into the most definite light, and published to all the world'; 'The Bondage of the Will' (1525), *LW* 33:28, for a lengthier elaboration see pp. 89–99.

29. Lohse, *Martin Luther's Theology*, p. 71; cf. 46, and 70 for comment on original sin as absence of divine righteousness.

30. 'Lectures on Romans' Romans 5:1 (1515–16), *LW* 5:1 and 25:291–292, for more on the concept of '*cor curvum in se*', see pp. 313, 345, 351 and 513.

31. Eberhard Bethge, *Dietrich Bonhoeffer: Theologian, Christian, Man for His Times* (ed. Edwin Robertson; trans. Eric Mosbacher et al. Second revised and unabridged version. ed. Victoria Barnett; Minneapolis: Fortress, 1999), p. 68. 'For "in Adam" means to be in untruth, in culpable perversion of the will, that is, of human essence. It means to be turned inward into one's self, *cor curvum in se*. Human beings have torn themselves loose from continuity with God, and, therefore, also from that with other human beings, and now, they stand alone . . .'; Bonhoeffer, *Act and Being*, p. 137.

32. 'Heidelberg Disputation: Thesis 13' (1518), *LW* 31:40; Forde, *On Being a Theologian of the Cross*, pp. 52–54.

The central dialectic at the heart of the theology of the cross, then, is this distance between God-as-He-is and humanity-as-it-is; the gap between the ultimate and the penultimate. The *theologia crucis* is sceptical about human efforts to grasp the divine. In Theses 19 and 22 of the Heidelberg Disputation, Luther raises a profound critique of the limits of four commonly used means for apprehending divinity: ethical behaviour (morality); existential experience (mystical ascent); empirical experience (creation, and natural theology) and human reason.[33] Humanity-as-it-is remains shut off from any meaningful knowledge of God, not because it is not available, but because of the perversity of human nature.[34]

Clearly Luther's assessment is at variance with the evaluations of New School Presbyterianism, and the Oberlin Theology of Charles Finney. Both systems were based on a conception of moral government that anticipated human ability to know and obey God. Nathaniel Taylor had argued that while 'the natural man, the man enthralled by groveling appetite and passion, discerneth not the things of the Spirit, neither can he know them', still, it was by the 'healthful and earnest use of the mental powers, influenced indeed *in some cases* by the Spirit of truth, but employed with honest intention on the materials of discovery, and directed by sober well-known laws of interpretation [italics supplied]' that men and women could grasp divine revelation.[35] The 'New Divinity' applied this to the question of volition, and simply asserted that the sinner 'can' obey God if only he 'will'.[36] Finney took such arguments to their logical conclusion by asserting a perfectionism that

33. Thesis 19: 'That person does not deserve to be called a theologian who looks upon the invisible things of God as though they were clearly perceptible in those things which have actually happened [Rom. 1:20]' and Thesis 22: 'That wisdom which sees the invisible things of God in works as perceived by man is completely puffed up, blinded, and hardened'; 'Heidelberg Disputation' (1518), *LW* 31:52 and 3–54.

34. 'Because men misused the knowledge of God through works [read "creation" here], God wished again to be recognized in suffering, and to condemn wisdom concerning invisible things by means of wisdom concerning visible things, so that those who did not honor God as manifested in his works should honor him as he is hidden in his suffering'; 'Heidelberg Disputation: Proof of Thesis 20' (1518), *LW* 31:52. Few discussions of the Heidelberg Disputation point out that it concludes with 12 'Philosophical Theses' which clearly aim at demolishing all Aristotelian presuppositions in scholastic theology.

35. Nathaniel W. Taylor, *Lectures on the Moral Government of God, Vol. II* (New York: Clark, Austin & Smith, 1859), pp. 216–17 (published posthumously). Taylor and his followers were not uncritical of the limits of natural theology, but they did affirm its value, even to the extent that for Taylor, theology must operate on a rational inductive basis and 'must be common-sense-philosophy, such as all the world can understand if we would defend orthodox theology'; Taylor, 'Review of Butler's Analogy of Natural and Revealed Religion', *Quarterly Christian Spectator* 2 (December, 1830), pp. 694–719, quotation from 703; cited in Sweeney, *Nathaniel Taylor*, p. 109, see also n. 43.

36. Ibid., p. 32.

flowed naturally from the premise of human ability.[37] Luther would categorize these approaches as aberrations. He would call them theologies of glory.

The tension between Luther's interpretation of reality and Finney's creates the dynamic for the discussion in Chapters 5 and 6. These perfectionist currents, as demonstrated in previous chapters, influenced the antecedents of the Pentecostal movement, and will raise crucial questions as to the viability of Pentecostalism as a theology of glory. The issues that are highlighted by this tension call on Hall's paradigm of expectation and experience in critical ways that probe the very essence of Pentecostal experience. How does salvation function? What about perennial problems with sin? What are the implications for a theology of healing? In each of these circumstances Pentecostalism presents the possibility, rather, the expectancy of a 'full gospel': not simply salvation, but sanctification; not only power for service, but healing and the miraculous; not only an end time schema but an existential awareness of its nearness and an urgency to 'go into all the world'. While they vary in some ways from the divine immediacy proposed by the enthusiasts of Luther's time, and the Radical Pietists that followed them, they have their root in a similar overleveraging of the penultimate into the domain of the ultimate. But often the experience of Pentecostals is to live with the disappointment of these expectations, and to develop rhetorical strategies to dodge the impact of reality. Can a Pentecostal appropriation of the theology of the cross retain Pentecostal hope and accommodate reality at the same time, or must Pentecostalism be dispensed with as a theology of glory?

b. The Cross and Institutional Glory

Luther's use of the theology of the cross not only indicts humans as individuals, but it calls all human systems to accountability. At the heart of Luther's Reformation was not simply justification by faith, but a notion of justification grounded in and driven by the theology of the cross.[38] Luther penned three significant treatises in 1520 that touch on the social ramifications of Reformation spirituality. They

37. Yet Finney agreed with the Calvinists that individuals, left to themselves, never do obey God, rather they 'universally and voluntarily consecrate their powers to the gratification of self, and . . . therefore they will not, unless they are divinely persuaded, by the gracious influence of the Holy Spirit . . .' Finney, *Systematic Theology*, pp. 325, 342, 358–63 and 405. See also; Allen C. Guelzo, 'Oberlin Perfectionism and Its Edwardsian Origins, 1835–1870', in *Jonathan Edwards' Writings: Text, Context, and Interpretation* (ed. Stephen J. Stein; Bloomington, IN: Indiana University Press, 1996), pp. 159–73 (p. 174).

38. The centrality of the theology of the cross to Luther's thought is open to some debate. McGrath makes clear that while the fully worked out concept of the *theologia crucis* does not emerge until the Heidelberg Disputation (1518) or Luther's second lectures on the Psalms; *Operationes in Psalmos*, 'Labours in Psalms', 1519–21, all the ingredients appear as early as 1515, in his first lectures on the Psalms; *Dictata super Psalterium*, 'Lectures on the Psalter', 1513–15. McGrath, *Luther's Theology of the Cross*, pp. 141–47 and 153–61. It seems that the

are infused with the implications of the theology of the cross as it impinges on institutions. In *The Freedom of a Christian* Luther makes the famous paradoxical assertions: 'A Christian is a perfectly free lord of all, subject to none. A Christian is a perfectly dutiful servant of all, subject to all.'[39] This, Luther bases on a central premise of the *theologia crucis*, that before the law 'a man' is 'truly humbled and reduced to nothing in his own eyes' but the promises of God provide precisely 'what the commandments of God demand and fulfil what the law prescribes so that all things may be God's alone, both the commandments and the fulfilling of the commandments'.[40] Two consequences of this are the priesthood of all believers, and the limits of spiritual and secular authority. The spadework for this bold declaration of liberty had already been done in two other tracts. In an open letter *To the Christian Nobility*, Luther addressed the crisis of Rome's encroachment on secular authority, and called on the secular princes to assert their proper power. *The Babylonian Captivity of the Church*, on the other hand, attacked Rome's corruption of the sacraments. The salient point, however, is that Luther's social critique was, itself, an extension of the *theologia crucis*.

theology of the cross may have been required to create a matrix for the insight regarding the righteousness of God. Dating of Luther's 'Reformation breakthrough' is problematic. While debate surrounding dating is inconclusive, it impinges on the *theologia crucis* with regard to its centrality. The term 'theology of the cross' is relatively rare in Luther's writings, and beyond the time of the Heidelberg Disputation (1518) remained an almost unused category; Lohse, *Luther's Theology*, pp. 37–38, n.12. In spite of this, Von Loewenich demonstrated that Luther's theology of the cross was not a minor part of his thought, but the central thesis from which arose many of his other insights such as the hiddenness of God, and the uniqueness of faith as externally conditioned experience; ibid., pp. 12–13, 29–30, 93–94 and 101. If Luther's spiritual discovery was late (between 1518 and 1520), it would seem that he had only accidentally stumbled upon the theology of the cross, and discarded it as one step towards his later conclusions. But if von Loewenich is correct, the Heidelberg Disputation must be the result of a carefully thought out process, the corollaries of which are not yet fully developed in 1518. It represents a conscious synthesis of his earlier musings, and as a dialectical tool the *theologia crucis* must intentionally form the rational basis for many of the tensions that colour Luther's emerging theology. Jared Wicks contends that Luther developed his theology of the cross between 1513 and 1518 as he lectured on Psalms, Romans, Galatians and Hebrews. Thus it was a developed theology which was 'portrayed succinctly' in his Heidelberg Disputation; Jared Wicks, *Luther and His Spiritual Legacy* (Wilmington: Michael Glazier, 1983), pp. 62 and 61–79. As a result, one should expect to see its concerns reverberated in Luther's later work.

39. 'The Freedom of a Christian' (1520), *LW* 31:344.

40. Ibid., 31:348–9; see Luther`s use of the phrase 'reduced to nothing' in 'The Heidelberg Disputation' (1518): 'he who has not been brought low, reduced to nothing through the cross and suffering, takes credit for works and wisdom and does not give credit to God'; *LW* 31:55.

Perhaps no one has shown the contemporary social implications of the theology of the cross better than Douglas John Hall. The cross has been the centre of Hall's thinking since his 1976 book *Lighten Our Darkness* – and from the start he was interested in a contextualized theology, subtitling his study 'toward an indigenous theology of the cross'.[41] Hall's *theologia crucis* is primarily social criticism of the prevailing theologies of glory in North American society. He writes from the perspective of a crumbling Constantinian Christendom, and as a theologian of the cross, finds this an appropriately humble position for Christian theologizing.[42]

Hall diagnoses the specific theology of glory that besets our culture. He calls North America 'the officially optimistic society' and sees it dominated by modern men made in the new *imago hominis*: anthropocentric, autonomous, and in Henley's phrase, captain of his soul.[43] Not that this image of man is inferior to the more theocentric image of medieval times. Both represent theologies of glory, this one, however, trumps any concept of divine providence with a doctrine of human progress.[44] And both, have been aided and abetted by the 'the official religion of the officially optimistic society' – Christianity. The transition from theocentric to anthropocentric man was encouraged by a Christianized vision of man as the steward entrusted with the dominion of God's earth which in turn has allowed its objectification, and commodification, and, ultimately, its exploitation.[45]

This transition was accelerated by the growing positivism of the nineteenth century. This positivism reflected the perfectionism that permeated the Evangelical consensus, from its Wesleyan extremes to its calmer Higher Life expressions. It was further extended by perfectionism's more secular parallels of pragmatism, and progressivism. Pentecostalism, through the confluence of these social and theological forces, was inevitably concerned with anthropocentric man. At first it envisioned the empowerment and enlistment of anthropocentric persons on the periphery of society for a spiritual revolution, but eventually it became more domesticated, more complicit with the status quo, until finally it became yet another expression of the 'officially optimistic religion'. From the first, though, it seized upon the possibilities of human progress, a potential, of course, fuelled by the Holy Spirit, but still a potential that was certain to raise expectation, and just as certain to crash on the shoals of experience.

The failure of Christianity as 'official religion' has been its resistance to draw on the dialectic of the cross to critique humanity's direction. In the Western world the combination of official optimism and ecological irresponsibility has put humankind into a kind of schizophrenia where the inconsistency between a continued expectation of progress and the ongoing experience of the demise of the environment (and the

41. David J. Monge discusses Hall's thoroughgoing sense of context in 'Contextuality in the Theology of Douglas John Hall', *dialog* 41 (2002), pp. 210–20.

42. Hall, *The Cross in Our Context*, pp. 88–89.

43. Hall, *Lighten Our Darkness*, pp. 43–47.

44. Ibid., pp. 44–45.

45. Ibid., pp. 79–98.

soul!) has simply not registered.[46] The challenge to Christians, and this is particularly pertinent for Pentecostals, is to find 'a theology of expectation which is not in essence, and *a priori*, a denial of contemporary experience'. For Hall the answer is in the 'thin tradition' of the *theologia crucis*.[47] And it is the church's reluctance to apply it that is its most profound betrayal of its calling. Instead, Hall complains that 'the most popular churches on this continent are those that present Jesus and the divine kingdom as the most desirable sort of "product" that one could ever want to acquire'. The fundamental assumptions of this commodified 'megachurchianity' are at radical divergence with a profoundly unpopular theology of the cross.[48]

Hall's appropriation of the *theologia crucis* forms a devastating critique of North American values and rightly analyses the ennui of the Western soul so obvious within our culture, and yet to which we are so oblivious.[49] Worse, though, in Luther's terms, is the ugly reality that 'the desire for glory is not satisfied by the acquisition of glory, nor is the desire to rule satisfied by power and authority, nor is the desire for praise satisfied by praise, and so on, as Christ shows in John 4[:13], where he says, "Everyone who drinks of this water will thirst again"'.[50] The gaping question Luther raises is whether one can ever be free of the cycle of exploitation and sin with which we are implicated. Is it possible even to exist in North America and not be complicit in the wholesale rape of the world? – And not only in North America, but in any web of self-serving human relation whether personal, social or societal. Does anyone anywhere escape the temptation of glory; even the most oppressed who yearn for the day of vindication? *Crux probat omnia*!

II. The Mechanics of the Theologia Crucis*: The Boundaries of Expectation*

Having contemplated the cross as critique of experience, whether personal or institutional, the question naturally arises as to its corrective regarding expectation. A general criticism of the theology of the cross has been its unremitting pessimism.[51] Not only does it lower expectation, it may decimate

46. Ibid., pp. 63–69.

47. 'Can Christian faith really enter the darkness of the world today without succumbing to it, on the one hand, or on the other, without carrying with it all sorts of ersatz light . . .?'; Hall, *Lighten Our Darkness*, pp. 113–14.

48. Hall, *The Cross in Our Context*, p. 101.

49. Popular culture, Hall claims, is beginning to dissect this ennui. 'When people see films like *American Beauty, In the Bedroom, Midnight in the Garden of Good and Evil, About Schmidt, The Hours*, or so many of the other films that emerge from the Hollywood that used to be the chief factory for our high estimate of ourselves, they are at least slightly unsettled by the mirror that is being held up to their way of life'; ibid., p. 102.

50. 'Heidelberg Disputation: Proof of Thesis 22' (1518), *LW* 31:54.

51. Cousar is aware of the problem. 'The theology of the cross, with its demand for honesty and realism, is very likely to conjure up images of pessimism and despair, what

hope of anything good in this world altogether. A closer look at the mechanics of the *theologia crucis* will reveal that far from being the case, this thin tradition addresses unrealistic expectation by undercutting human presumption and provides genuine this-worldly hope that comes from beyond humanity, from God. Luther does this by the novel use of the ancient art of dialectic.

Luther delights in nothing more than dialectic. James Arne Nestingen points out the distinctly pre-Enlightenment nature of Luther's dialectic. The most common understanding of dialectical thought picks up on its Hegelian form of thesis-antithesis-synthesis. Luther's approach, however, was in the tradition of late scholasticism. The key was to hold two opposites in tension without endeavouring to resolve the strain. We see this over and over again in Luther's thought: law and gospel, faith and reason, the two kingdoms. The legacy of dialectic in the theology of the cross is the notion of the Hidden and Revealed God captured in the cross and suffering of Christ and the *simul justus et peccator* which arises from it.[52] Once more, the imponderable of how the ultimate relates to the penultimate is a central driver of Luther's thought. The mystery of Christianity is located here in the incarnation, cross, and resurrection of Jesus Christ, and in the dialectic between *deus absconditus* and *deus revelatus*

a. The Two Hiddennesses

According to von Loewenich, the cross has a double function as the locus of both God's revelation and God's hiddenness. Confusion arises, von Loewenich points out, because Luther uses the term 'the hidden God' differently in various contexts.[53] Scholars have observed two hiddennesses in Luther's theology. Hiddenness I, as Brian Gerrish calls it, is the hiddenness that is revealed in the cross. Roland Bainton gives eloquent expression to the human quandary: 'Nature is indeed very wonderful, and every particle of creation reveals the handiwork of God, if one has

Barth referred to as "Nordic morbidity"'; Charles B. Cousar, *A Theology of the Cross: The Death of Jesus in the Pauline Letters* (Minneapolis: Fortress, 1990), p. 186.

52. Luther's doctrine of the Hidden and Revealed God is a highly nuanced and abstract concept developed in a number of places within the Luther corpus. Walther Von Loewenich offers the classic treatment of this issue with respect to the theology of the cross; Von Loewenich, *Luther's Theology of the Cross*, pp. 27–49. David Steinmetz calls it '[t]he center of Luther's understanding of Christianity'; David C. Steinmetz, 'Luther and the Hidden God', in *Luther in Context, Second Edition* (Grand Rapids: Baker, 1996), pp. 23–31 (p. 23).

53. Von Loewenich, *Luther's Theology*, p. 28. Brian Gerrish surveyed the field as it stood in 1973 and summarized it thus: 'It is not difficult to group Luther interpreters, despite differences within each group, according as they stress that the Hidden and Revealed Gods are antithetical (Theodosius Harnack, the two Ritschls, Reinhold Seeberg, Hirsch, Elert, Holl), or identical (Kattenbusch, Erich Seeberg), or both (Althaus, Heim, von Loewenich)'; Brian Gerrish, '"To the Unknown God": Luther and Calvin on the Hiddenness of God', *JR* 53 (1973), pp. 263–92 (p. 267).

the eyes to see. But that is precisely the problem.'[54] While creation should have unveiled to us the truth about God, human corruption has perverted its message, and caused it to be fruitless in terms of accessing the essence of the divine nature.[55] God has chosen, instead, to reveal himself where people would least expect to find him. 'God can only be found only in suffering and the cross', Luther claims, and this means one thing that is starkly clear to him, 'He who does not know Christ does not know God hidden in suffering.'[56] He did this 'so that those who did not honor God as manifested in his works should honor him as he is hidden in his suffering.'[57] As von Loewenich contends, the theology of the cross is essentially a theology of revelation. The cross is the core of Christian epistemology, that is, it answers the question 'how can a person know God'; and, at its heart, the cross is existential encounter – in short, spiritual experience. 'The essence of the ultimate character of reality has become clear at this point' (i.e. the cross). Indeed, this is what it means to say that a theologian of the cross calls a thing 'what it actually is.' Such understanding is inevitably existential.

> The cross of the Christian corresponds to the cross of Christ. To know God through 'suffering and the cross' means that the knowledge of God comes into being at the cross of Christ, the significance of which becomes evident only to one who himself stands in cross and suffering.[58]

Not only is Christ's cross the place of divine hiddenness, but our own cross becomes the place of divine revelation. This is the nature of Hiddenness I.

54. Roland H. Bainton, *Here I Stand: A Life of Martin Luther* (New York: Abingdon-Cokesbury Press, 1950), p. 216. As Steimetz expresses Luther's view of the human predicament, '[r]ather than modifying their notions of what God is like to conform to God's self-disclosure, they construct for themselves a tame and gracious God who conforms to their expectations'; Steimetz 'Luther and the Hidden God', p. 24.

55. This is the burden of Thesis 19 of the Heidelberg Disputation. 'That person does not deserve to be called a theologian who looks upon the invisible things of God as though they were clearly perceptible in those things which have actually happened [Rom. 1:20]'; 'Heidelberg Disputation' (1518), *LW* 31:40.

56. Ibid., 31:53.

57. Ibid., 31:52. Luther elaborates on the nature of this hiddenness in several places. His comments from his lectures on Romans are illuminating: 'For the work of God must be hidden and never understood, even when it happens. But it is never hidden in any other way than under that which appears contrary to our conceptions and ideas.' Or even more strikingly, 'For what is good for us is hidden, and that so deeply that it is hidden under its opposite. Thus our life is hidden under death, love for ourselves under hate for ourselves, glory under ignominy, salvation under damnation, our kingship under exile, heaven under hell, wisdom under foolishness, righteousness under sin, power under weakness'; 'Lectures on Romans', (1515–16) *LW* 25:366, 382–83.

58. von Loewenich, *Luther's Theology*, p. 20.

The hiddenness of God as it is spoken of in *The Bondage of the Will*, however, is a twofold hiddenness. Luther refers, not only to the hiddenness of God revealed in the suffering of the cross, but he contemplates a more profound hiddenness behind cross and Word. This, Gerrish calls Hiddenness II, the hiddenness of God beyond revelation. The God of Hiddenness I is *deus indutus* (God clothed in the Word); he is 'God incarnate, crucified, hidden in suffering (*deus incarnatus, deus crucifixus, deus absconditus in passionibus*)'.[59] And, in a most troubling aspect of Luther's theology, he is set in contrast with God behind this veiled *deus revelatus*, as *deus nudus* (the naked God), *deus absolutus* (God out of relation with the world) and ultimately *deus absconditus* (the hidden God). While the God of Hiddenness I has proved to be a useful device, and therefore a welcome construct in the theological toolbox, Gerrish points out that Protestant theology has been embarrassed by the fearful specter of Hiddenness II. For Luther there is a necessary distinction between 'the Word of God and God himself'. Here we are dealing with the ultimately ultimate God. While the Word offers us what Francis Schaeffer called 'true truth' about God, it does not claim to present 'exhaustive truth'. Thus 'God does many things that he does not disclose to us in his word; he also wills many things which he does not disclose himself as willing in his word.' This creates an inevitable discontinuity between 'God or the will of God as preached, revealed, offered, and worshiped', and 'God as he is not preached, not revealed, not offered, not worshiped'.[60]

The context of this development of Hiddenness II is Luther's debate with Erasmus, particularly, in this instance, over the interpretation of Ezekiel 18.23: 'I do not desire the death of the sinner, but rather that he should be converted and live.' Erasmus held that the verse proved human free will, since it made clear that God, whose desire was for life and not death, was plainly not the cause of the sinner's judgement. Luther saw this as a confusion of law and gospel. He contended that Ezekiel 18 was a gracious offer of life, and not a statement about essential nature of God.

> But why some are touched by the law and others are not, so that the former accept and the latter despise the offered grace, is another question and one not dealt with by Ezekiel in this passage. For he is here speaking of the preached and offered mercy of God, not of that hidden and awful will of God whereby he ordains by his own counsel which and what sort of persons he wills to be recipients and partakers of his preached and offered mercy.[61]

About this hidden God, Luther advises that beyond what he has revealed to us in the cross and the Word, 'God *hides himself* and *wills to be unknown* to us, it is no

59. Gerrish, '"To the Unknown God"', p. 268.

60. All of the above Luther citations from 'The Bondage of the Will' (1525), *LW* 33: 139–40.

61. Ibid., 33:138.

business of ours. For here the saying truly applies, "Things above us are no business of ours".'[62] Indeed, 'This will is not to be inquired into, but reverently adored, as by far the most awe-inspiring secret of the Divine Majesty, reserved for himself alone and forbidden to us much more religiously than any number of Corycian caverns.'[63] Such intimations conjure the image of the deep impenetrable darkness which veils *deus absconditus*: they bring to mind Rudolf Otto's concept of the numinous, the *mysterium tremendum*.[64] Surely such a God is hidden, terrible and inscrutable. If one were even slightly aware of his existence, such a God could become the stuff of severe inner trials, deep torments of the soul, fearful insecurities about the future. Indeed, without some place of refuge this is the kind of God who could give rise to *Anfechtungen*.

Luther has been criticized for introducing a dualism in the Godhead. Jürgen Moltmann, for instance, castigates Karl Barth for falling into the same trap of setting up a distinction between the work of God-in-Christ-on-the-cross and the God-who-is-in-himself. For Moltmann the answer to both Luther and Barth is found in their insufficiently Trinitarian understanding of the cross. As long as the cross remains an event in God only insofar as God is in Christ, the duality must remain, but once it is also seen as an event in God-in-himself, once it is recognized as implicating the *deus absconditus*, the God of Hiddenness II, the fearfulness of Luther's dialectic dissolves.[65] I contend that this is a category error in Moltmann's assessment of Luther. Moltmann wishes to apply Hegelian dialectic to what is intended within the *theologia crucis* model as an irresolvable antinomy in accordance with the medieval method. In doing so, Moltmann not only dispenses with the radical hiddenness of God but also with his free and absolute sovereignty. Indeed Richard Bauckham claims that this was, in part, Moltmann's goal in *The Crucified God*. 'The God who, omnipotent and unaffected, remains simply sovereign over the horrors of twentieth-century history' is the target of Moltmann's critique.[66] In the teeth of the God of classical theism, Moltmann both asserts divine passibility and absolves divine responsibility. Christian faith provides, Moltmann declares, 'liberation from the childish projections of human needs for the riches of God; liberation from human impotence for the omnipotence of God; from human helplessness for the omnipotence of God; from human helplessness for the responsibility of God'.[67] Nevertheless, the crucial question becomes one of

62. Ibid., 33:139; italics mine.

63. Ibid., 33:138.

64. Rudolf Otto, *The Idea of the Holy: An Inquiry into the Non-rational Factor in the Idea of the Divine and Its Relation to the Rational* (trans. John W Harvey; London: Oxford University Press, 2nd edn, 1950).

65. Moltmann, *Crucified God*, p. 203 (see especially note 16).

66. Richard Bauckham, 'Preface', in Jürgen Moltmann, *The Crucified God: The Cross of Christ as the Foundation and Criticism of Christian Theology* (trans. R. A. Wilson and John Bowden; London: SCM, 2001), pp. ix–xvi (p. xi).

67. Moltmann, *Crucified God*, p. 222.

unremitting dialectic: is it possible to affirm the passible Trinitarian God who is 'in-himself' involved with suffering and the cross, while maintaining the absolute sovereignty of God in the universe, including the world of suffering and crosses? This, it seems to me, is both the mystery and the power of the theology of the cross.

Hiddenness I (the hidden God revealed in the cross) generates the critique inherent in the *theologia crucis* of all theologies of glory. The astonishing awareness that God in his essence is unavailable to us whether through personal introspection and ethical effort; or through empirical or existential encounter, underscores the bankruptcy of life in Adam. Neither the Babel Tower of human aspiration and endeavour, nor the making of many books of human philosophy and psychology will liberate us from the pain, sorrow and brokenness of a world in defiance of its Creator. Such is the function of Hiddenness I that it discloses its treasure to us only in 'suffering and the cross'. However, it is Hiddenness II (God hidden behind Word and cross), which is the source of the *Anfechtung* that creates the condition of human incommensurability with the divine. David Tracy captures the profound distress engendered by the divine incomprehensibility.

> . . . this literally awful, ambivalent sense of God's hiddenness can be so overwhelming that God is sometimes experienced as purely frightening, not tender, sometimes even as an impersonal reality – 'it' – of sheer power and energy signified by such metaphors, such *fragmentary* metaphors as abyss, chasm, chaos, horror.[68]

Given that the above situation is a direct consequence of the theology of the cross, what possible comfort can be found there?

Von Loewenich locates the only achievable resolution of the relentless dialectic in the concept of faith, and yet faith itself resolves nothing, it simply draws the trembling soul away from the terrors of *deus absconditus* to the comfort of *deus revelatus*. As von Loewenich explains, revelation is only possible where there is something hidden, and faith can only be faith in what is unseen, according to Hebrews 11.1, the defining text for Luther's notion of faith.[69] The revelation of God

68. David Tracy, 'Form & Fragment: The Recovery of the Hidden and Incomprehensible God', in *The Concept of God in Global Dialogue* (ed. Werner G. Jeanrond and Aasuly Lande; Faith Meets Faith Series; Maryknoll, NY: Orbis Books, 2005), pp. 98–114 (p. 110).

69. Luther explains the dynamic of faith in these terms: '. . . faith has to do with things not seen [Heb. 11:1]. Hence in order that there may be room for faith, it is necessary that everything which is believed should be hidden. It cannot, however, be more deeply hidden than under an object, perception, or experience which is contrary to it. Thus when God makes alive he does it by killing, when he justifies he does it by making men guilty, when he exalts to heaven he does it by bringing down to hell, as Scripture says: "The Lord kills and brings to life; he brings down to Sheol and raises up" (I Sam. 2[:6])'; 'The Bondage of the Will' (1525), *LW* 33:62.

in the cross is revealed to faith, then, not to sight, nor to reason; for only faith can apprehend the God hidden in suffering and the cross.[70]

Faced with the twin realities of Hiddenness I and II, Luther can only cast himself on faith in the revealed God whose wounds beckon him from the terrors of God's wrath. Luther is emphatic that relief from the pressure of *Anfechtung* comes only when we cling to the Word of God and look to the cross of Christ, when we 'firmly believe that his wounds and sufferings are your sins, to be borne and paid for by him', and 'stake everything' on the promises of Scripture for 'the more your conscience torments you, the more tenaciously must you cling to them. If you do not do that, but presume to still your conscience with your contrition and penance [i.e. your experience], you will never obtain peace of mind, but will have to despair in the end'.[71] And yet, living in the tension of the two Hiddennesses makes large demands of faith.

> This is the highest degree of faith, to believe him merciful when he saves so few and damns so many, and to believe him righteous when by his own will he makes us necessarily damnable, so that he seems, according to Erasmus, to delight in the torments of the wretched and to be worthy of hatred rather than of love. If, then, I could by any means comprehend how this God can be merciful and just who displays so much wrath and iniquity, there would be no need of faith.[72]

Much discussion has ensued around this paradigm of redemption that seems to pit God against God.[73] Indeed we find here the building blocks of Moltmann's divine passibility.

Japanese theologian Kazo Kitamori contemplates the tension between the Hidden and Revealed God as the very locus of divine pain. 'An absolute being without wrath can have no pain', Kitamori asserts. But it is the very wrath of Hiddenness II that gives meaning to the love of God revealed in the cross! 'The pain of God is his love – this love is based on the premise of his wrath, which is absolute, inflexible reality.'[74] The problem of the two Hiddenesses is not primarily a rational, or logical one, but rather a theological one. Its solution lies within the

70. 'Reason can only establish a dualism. Faith presses through the revealed God to the hidden God, yet does not meet a second hidden God behind or beside the former. But this is something only faith can achieve.' Von Loewenich, *Luther's Theology*, pp. 35–37.

71. 'A Meditation on Christ's Passion' (1519), *LW* 42:12.

72. 'The Bondage of the Will' (1525), *LW* 33:62.

73. 'Here we have an invitation to face with hope, but a hope against all hope, the terrible void, the *horror vacui* of a God that, according to our perception, cannot be but the One who is against God. In Luther's words: *ad deum contra deum confungere*, "to flee from and find refuge in God against God." Such is the impossibility that makes theology possible'; Vitor Westhelle, *The Scandalous God: The Use and Abuse of the Cross* (Minneapolis: Fortress, 2006), p. 58; citing 'Labours in Psalms' (1519–21), *WA* 5:204, 26f.

74. Kazo Kitamori, *Theology of the Pain of God* (Richmond: John Knox, 1965), p. 27.

interpersonal relations of the Trinity. Commenting on this passage from Kitamori, Paul Fiddes argues that such an understanding limits divine pain to an internal matter within the Godhead, and while ascribing to God a certain pathos unique to his Trinitarian nature, it does not bring about involvement with our pain and suffering.[75] Fiddes prefers to deal with the tension between wrath and love by turning wrath into a passive 'giving up' of people to the consequences of their wrong choices, and sees the divine pain as empathy with the condition of humans under those consequences.[76]

The difficulty which Fiddes and Moltmann resolve by removing divine initiative in judgement or sovereignty is central to the debate. Such critiques imagine the two Hiddennesses to represent a dualism, a kind of divine schizophrenia, rather than seeing them as mere constructs that enable us to recapture the dynamic of the cross within the Trinitarian mind. The God of which Luther speaks retains absolute sovereignty while exhibiting a Trinitarian passibility, allowing him to be 'in-himself' involved with suffering and the cross, while entering into the suffering and crosses of a world of tormented humans.

Whatever one makes of the intra-Trinitarian puzzle of sovereignty and suffering, it is clear that it is only once we have affirmed our sense of incommensurability with the divine (Hiddenness II) that we can find the true comfort of Christ's cross (Hiddenness I).

> The godly who are burdened with a cross and in various ways are hard pressed and sigh have need of promises in order to be buoyed up by them. On the other hand, those who are callous, obdurate and smug should be frightened by the examples of wrath, to the end that . . . they may learn to fear God.[77]

Most contemporary approaches to the theology of the cross wish to take up the concept of divine passibility without facing the challenge of the second Hiddenness. We have already noted this in Moltmann, but there are other theologians from a diversity of fields who share his point of view. Dorothee Soelle, for instance, is horrified by the notion, calling it 'theological sadism' and comparing it to Himmler. 'The ultimate conclusion of theological sadism', she protests, 'is worshiping the executioner'.[78] Feminist complaints of divine child abuse follow a similar trajectory, and call for significant revisions of the biblical interpretation of the atonement.[79] Such models find themselves surrendering the sovereignty

75. Fiddes, *The Creative Suffering of God* (Oxford: Clarendon Press, 1988), p. 22.

76. Ibid., pp. 23–25.

77. 'Lectures on Genesis: Gen. 18:20' (1535–39), *LW* 3:221; see also the proof of Thesis 18, 'Heidelberg Disputation' (1518), *LW* 31:40, 51.

78. Soelle, *Suffering*, pp. 27–28.

79. See Rita Nakashima Brock, *Journeys by Heart: A Christology of Erotic Power* (New York: Crossroad, 1988); and Joanne Carlson Brown and Rebecca Parker, 'For God So Loved the World?', in *Christianity Patriarchy and Abuse: A Feminist Critique* (ed. Joanne Carlson

of God, and producing theodicies that absolve God of any responsibility for or complicity with the pain and suffering of the fallen world. They demand some kind of theological shortcut that undermines the full integration of the biblical data into a well-formed orthopraxy. Ultimately these paradigms must find the cross itself to be an awful tragedy that God, in his infinite wisdom, and perhaps even in his foreknowledge, if he retains such 'super powers', has managed to put to good use. Luther, on the other hand, dares to do the unthinkable. He claims the God of Hiddenness II is responsible, that God performs an alien work (suffering, wrath, *Anfechtungen*) to accomplish his proper work (grace, justification). He affirms the divine freedom of the incomprehensible Majesty to do as he wishes and sees fit, and challenges us to believe that the will of this God is still 'good, perfect and acceptable'.

If we should balk at this, as indeed, he himself has done, Luther urges us to the cross. There, whatever else God may have hidden from us, he has disclosed his loving solidarity with us. There he has taken up our own suffering and cross, and there he has affirmed our revulsion, and our revolt against all that is unjust, oppressive and injurious. Indeed even Moltmann cannot do without this tension in some form or other. 'The cross stands between the Father and the Son in all the harshness of its forsakenness.' Yet here Moltmann affirms, and Luther affirms, and here I endorse both, and I do so because, and not in spite, of the irresolvable dialectic of the two Hiddennesses: 'There is no suffering which in this history of God is not God's suffering; no death which has not been God's death on Golgotha.'[80] Moltmann has more to say about the life, fortune and joy that have become a part of God's history as well, but that awaits further development momentarily. For now, it is sufficient to note that the two Hiddennesses provide the necessary dialectic to sustain both divine sovereignty and divine pathos; divine election and the free offer of grace; divine wrath and divine love. If one should ask whether this is divine schizophrenia, Luther replies that the inevitable dialectic cannot be resolved until the *eschaton*, that human reason cannot comprehend what the

Brown and Carole R. Bohm; New York: Pilgrim, 1989), pp. 1–30; and Rita Nakashima Brock, 'And a Little Child Will Lead Us: Christology and Child Abuse', in *Christianity Patriarchy and Abuse: A Feminist Critique* (ed. Joanne Carlson Brown and Carole R. Bohm; New York: Pilgrim, 1989), pp. 42–61.

80. Moltmann, *Crucified God*, p. 246. Moltmann is not without recognition of the intense polarity that the cross creates within the Godhead. Indeed this is the centre of his theology of the cross. 'We must not allow ourselves to overlook this "enmity" between God and God by failing to take seriously either the rejection of Jesus by God, the gospel of God which he lived out, or his last cry to God upon the cross. As a "blasphemer", Jesus was rejected by the guardians of his people's law . . . As a "rebel", he was crucified by the Romans. But finally and most profoundly, he died as one rejected by his God and his Father.' Not only did Christ know what it was to be forsaken by his Father, but in Moltmann's striking phrase, 'the Fatherlessness of the Son is matched by the Sonlessness of the Father'; ibid., pp. 152 and 243.

light of glory will reveal, that in the end the hidden God and the revealed God are one and the same.[81] Wolfhart Pannenberg captures the final resolution of Luther's dialectic well: 'Only at the end of history will the God who is hidden in his overruling of history and in individual destinies finally be universally known to be the same as the God who is revealed in Jesus Christ.'[82]

b. Resurrection as Necessary Corollary of the Theology of the Cross

But where does the theology of the cross leave us with regard to an assessment of Pentecostal expectation? How does it bridge the gap between ultimate and penultimate? On the surface it seems to revel in dereliction, defeat and death, though Luther promises that 'God hidden in his majesty neither deplores nor takes away death, but works life, death, and all in all.'[83] Yet in the cross we find nothing but frailty and anguish: 'For just as divinity was veiled under the flesh of weakness, so His works were veiled in the weakness of suffering.'[84] The critic of the theology of the cross would be justified in asking what victory is to be found in such an approach, or is all talk of victory itself to be touted as mere triumphalism, and yet another theology of glory? Are we to be shut up to this cloying dismal gospel of defeat forever? Is there no relief, but the psychological solace of looking to the cross to find the solidarity of Christ's sufferings with ours? These are fair and necessary questions, and they deserve a response consistent with the *theologia crucis* Luther has proposed.

It is at this point that *katabasis* gives way to *anabasis*. As he spoke of 'divinity veiled under the flesh of weakness' and 'works veiled in the weakness of suffering', Luther went on to describe just what it was that was veiled, what was hidden in ignominy. 'These works were especially the casting down of the devil, victory over the world, destruction of hell, the gaining of heaven, the sanctification of the church, and the killing of the flesh, which are utterly divine works.' And then he asks the question that liberates: 'Who would believe that the cross and suffering would achieve such incalculable results?'[85] In the Heidelberg Disputation, Luther

81. See Luther's classic explanation of the lights of nature, grace and glory. Only the light of glory will demonstrate incontrovertibly 'that the God whose judgement here is one of incomprehensible righteousness is a God of most perfect and manifest righteousness. In the meantime, we can only *believe* this, being admonished and confirmed by the example of the light of grace . . .'; 'The Bondage of the Will' (1525), *LW* 33:292 (but see also the longer passage starting at p. 289).

82. 'Precisely for this reason theology must hold fast to both aspects of the divine reality, even if their unity is not immediately apparent and the tension makes itself felt in the tension between philosophical and theological talk about God'; Wolfhart Pannenberg, *Systematic Theology, Volume I* (trans. Geoffrey Bromiley; Grand Rapids: Eerdmans, 1991), p. 340.

83. 'The Bondage of the Will' (1525), *LW* 33:140.

84. 'First Lectures on the Psalms: Psalm 78:2' (1513–15), *LW* 11:32.

85. Ibid., 11:32.

gives a hint as to the ultimate disposition of the theology of the cross. 'Now you ask, "What then shall we do? Shall we go our way with indifference because we can do nothing but sin?" I would reply, By no means. But, having heard this, fall down and pray for grace and place your hope in Christ in whom is our salvation, life, and resurrection.'[86] It is because of the resurrection that Moltmann can add to his statement that there is no suffering or death which is not God's, that, also, 'there is no life, no fortune and no joy which have not been integrated by his history into eternal life, the eternal joy of God'.[87]

The resurrection is a necessary corollary of the theology of the cross. Without it, desperation is alleviated only by the cold comfort that human misery has divine company. Such comfort gains blazing heat with the power of the resurrection. Here, Moltmann properly apprehends the relation of the two. He makes a profound insight at the outset of *The Crucified God*, which is borne out by the fact that it was the second book of a trilogy that began with *Theology of Hope*.[88] He states that the theology of hope was worked out as an *eschatologia crucis*; that 'it began with the *resurrection* of the crucified Christ' but that *The Crucified God* is a 'turning to look at the *cross* of the risen Christ'.

> I was concerned then with the remembrance of Christ in the form of the *hope* of his future, and now I am concerned with hope in the form of the *remembrance* of his death. The dominant theme then was that of *anticipations* of the future of God in the form of promises and hopes; here it is the understanding of the *incarnation* of that future, by way of the sufferings of Christ, in the world's sufferings.[89]

This paradigm for the theology of the cross makes explicit what Luther and his interpreters claim is implicit in the *theologia crucis*. While Luther's forceful and passionate style sometimes testifies to the resurrection side of the cross, it seems, more often, that his interpreters lose sight of it in their zeal for the cruciform dialectic. Moltmann's success in adapting Luther must be measured in terms of this programmatic statement regarding hope and remembrance, anticipation and incarnation.

It is impossible to divide the one from the other. The relation between cross and resurrection is well described by Robert Kolb as he rehearses their effect on the human condition.

> The cross and the Word that delivers it have created a new reality within God's fallen creation: a new reality for Satan (since God nailed the law's accusations to

86. 'Heidelberg Disputation: Thesis 16' (1518), *LW* 31:50.

87. Moltmann, *Crucified God*, p. 246.

88. Jürgen Moltmann, *Theology of Hope: On the Ground and the Implications of a Christian Eschatology* (trans. James W. Leitch; New York: Harper & Row, 1967).

89. Moltmann, *Crucified God*, p. 5.

> the cross and rendered them illegible by soaking them in Christ's blood); a new reality for death (since it was laid to eternal rest in Christ's grave); a new reality for sinners (since they were buried, too, in Christ's tomb and raised to new life through the death and resurrection of the Crucified One).[90]

The entire dynamic is predicated on the basis of a unified cross-and-resurrection motif, for without the cross, the law has merely been defaced, death remains triumphant and there is no new life for sinners. Yet without the resurrection we remain in our sins, sorrow and death. Moltmann concurs. The strength of Moltmann's theology of the cross is its dialectic between Easter and Good Friday. 'The cross and the resurrection are mutually related and they have to be interpreted in such a way that the one event appears in the light of the other.'[91] Though he raises questions as to the historicity of the resurrection, Moltmann is clear that the resurrection is an apocalyptic event and brings the end of all things near.[92] 'The attested resurrection of Jesus before all other men is in fact meant proleptically.' This means that the believer is no longer a subject of the realm of death but already tastes the powers of the coming age.[93] This is a substantial corrective to what may be perceived as an overarching pessimism in some approaches to the *theologia crucis*.

90. Robert Kolb, 'Luther on the Theology of the Cross', *Lutheran Quarterly* XVI (2002), pp. 443–67 (p. 449).

91. Jürgen Moltmann, *The Way of Jesus Christ: Christology in Messianic Dimensions* (trans. Margaret Kohl; Minneapolis: Fortress Press, 1993), p. 213.

92. The question of the historicity of the resurrection is more complicated than it seems on the surface. 'The resurrection of Jesus from the dead by God does not speak the "language of facts", but only the language of faith and hope, that is the "language of promise"'; Moltmann, *Crucified God*, p. 173. See also Moltmann, *Way of Jesus Christ*, pp. 214–15, indeed, the whole of Ch. 5. *Contra*, see Ryan Neal, *Theology as Hope: On the Ground and Implications of Jürgen Moltmann's Doctrine of Hope* (Princeton Theological Monograph Series 99; Eugene, OR: Pickwick, 2008), pp. 8–12, who suggests that Moltmann 'makes central both the truth of the resurrection and God's promises, while also maintaining that the resurrection is beyond the scope of historical investigation and analogy'; ibid., p. 9. Interestingly, Luther is similarly uninterested in the historical evidence of Jesus' resurrection in his discussion of 1 Cor. 15. He seems more impressed that Christ rose according to the Scriptures; David P. Scaer, 'Luther's Concept of the Resurrection in His Commentary on 1 Corinthians 15', *CTQ* 47 (1983), pp. 209–24 (pp. 210–13). Gerhard Sauter points out Luther's insistence on the proclamation of the resurrection, rather than proving it, because faith in it can only come from God, just as all faith comes from proclamation of the Word; Gerhard Sauter, 'Luther on the Resurrection', in *Harvesting Martin Luther's Reflections on Theology, Ethics, and the Church* (Lutheran Quarterly Books; ed. Timothy Wengert; Grand Rapids: Eerdmans, 2004), pp. 99–118 (pp. 100–1).

93. Moltmann, *Way of Jesus Christ*, p. 214; and *Crucified God*, p. 171.

What, then does the theology of the cross have to say to the suffering and broken in the world? At times it seems that Luther exults in suffering, that he glorifies it. Certainly he sees it as a necessary part of the Christian journey.

> He [who has been emptied by suffering] knows that it is sufficient if he suffers and is brought low by the cross in order to be annihilated all the more . . . To be born anew, one must consequently first die and then be raised up with the Son of Man. To die, I say, means to feel death at hand.[94]

Luther's rhetoric, it must be recalled, was originally drawn as a sabre in the death battle with an entire system of thought antithetic to biblical theology. It expresses with great ardour, one movement in Scripture. There is, however, another dimension in God's scheme. The emergence of Pentecostalism on the world stage in the twentieth century bears eloquent testimony to this. The Pentecostal is convinced that this downward movement is not the only motion in Scripture. She perceives that *katabasis* must be balanced by *anabasis* just as it is in the Christological hymn of Philippians 2. Kitamori observed these opposing movements when he pointed out that, '*God in pain is the God who resolves our human pain by his own. Jesus Christ is the Lord who heals our human wound by his own (1 Peter 2:24).*'[95] The corrective brought to Pentecostalism by the theology of the cross, and to the triumphalism of western Evangelicalism, is something North Americans must constantly remember: there can be no ascent without first descent. But the corollary is just as potent: when the descent is true, and deep, the ascent is assured and increasingly present. This may be a contribution Pentecostalism makes to Lutheran orthodoxy, and to the broader appropriation of the theology of the cross.

It was this great insight that Moltmann restored to the *theologia crucis*. His early trilogy began with the dialectic of Easter (theology of hope) and Good Friday (theology of the cross). The obvious synthesis to this dialectic was Pentecost and *The Church in the Power of the Spirit*.[96] But already I have too quickly resolved the tension. I have rushed too quickly past Good Friday and Easter, neither of which can be understood without the other, without pausing at Holy Saturday.[97] Douglas

94. 'Heidelberg Disputation: Proof of Thesis 24' (1518), *LW* 31:55.

95. Kitamori, *Pain of God*, p. 20.

96. Moltmann expresses the synthesis in this way: 'It looks as if I have now arrived theologically at Pentecost and the sending of the Spirit, having started from Easter and the foundation of the Christian hope and travelled by way of Good Friday and the exploration of God's suffering . . . Both perspectives would be incomplete if "the sending of the Spirit", its messianic history and the charismatic power of its church were not added'; Jürgen Moltmann, *The Church in the Power of the Spirit: A Contribution to Messianic Christology* (trans. Margaret Kohl; New York: Harper & Row, 1977), pp. xx–xxi.

97. See Alan Lewis' profound theology of Holy Saturday, Lewis reminds us that Holy Saturday 'prevents at once both rank despair and cheap triumphalism'; Alan Lewis, *Between Cross and Resurrection: A Theology of Holy Saturday* (Grand Rapids: Eerdmans, 2001), p. 324.

John Hall notes that many critics of the theology of the cross have bemoaned its lack of emphasis on the resurrection.[98] Hall demurs, seeing the *theologia crucis* as an incisive attack on what he terms 'resurrectionism': 'a blend of cultic-folkloric heroism, New World optimism, and religious triumphalism' to which he finds North Americans peculiarly vulnerable.[99] Resurrectionism rushes quickly from the cross to gather all its Easter benefits in the here and now. It shares a sense of immediacy with the early Pentecostals, who were so full of the 'already' they had forgotten there might be a 'not yet'. Instead, a proper perspective of resurrection reaffirms the work of the cross. It recalls where God has chosen to reveal himself, and to redeem human suffering, before it makes its resurrection prescription. Vitor Westhelle captures this concept memorably, when improving on Tillich, he offers four, rather than three 'theories of the resurrection': first, the *physical*, the raising back to life of a dead body; second the *spiritual*; by which Jesus the proclaimer becomes *kerygma*, Jesus the Proclaimed; then the *psychological*, which transforms the mind of the one in whom it occurs; and finally the *social*, involving the overthrowing of oppressive structures. Westhelle retains the connection between resurrection and cross. He urges us to the 'practice' of resurrection, 'a practice of labor, of mourning, and of love, that moves beyond and across the limits of the régimes of truth to which we are beholden'.[100] In this way we recover a praxis of resurrection that is intimately consistent with the theology of the cross.

Our interpretation of the resurrection should, as Hall asserts, turn us back to the cross with insight, courage and power to pursue its mission. Once more, it seems that quick and easy equations of the cross with God's solidarity with human suffering seem to be a kind of spiritual shortcut that evades the cross' significance, and the proper integration of all aspects of Christian theology into an ethic of transformation. As Gerhard Forde states, 'Penultimate cures are mistaken for ultimate redemption.'[101] The chapters to follow will catalogue the unfortunate instances of this in Pentecostal spirituality, but will also revise the Pentecostal paradigm with resurrection motifs as mediated by the theology of the cross.

Does this mean that Christians should seek to suffer, whether in pursuit of justice, or simply in the harsh realities of life this side of the resurrection? Is this what Hall might mean by a return to the cross? Timothy Wengert writes as one who

98. Douglas J. Hall, 'The Theology of the Cross: A Usable Past', n.p., n.d., p. 7. Online: http://www.bradschrum.com/wp-content/uploads/2011/10/TheTheologyoftheCross_pdf.pdf (Accessed 14 August 2014).

99. Hall, *Professing the Faith*, p. 96, see especially footnote 3.

100. Westhelle, *The Scandalous God*, pp. 163–64.

101. Forde, *On Being a Theologian of the Cross*, p. xi; Forde continues 'When that happens the church becomes predominantly a support group rather than the gathering of the body of Christ where the word of the cross and resurrection is proclaimed and heard.'

watched his wife of 26 years succumb to terminal cancer. He addresses a carefully worded question: 'does a theology of the cross bless suffering?' – a question he finds preposterous. With Luther, he claims that 'the inexperienced have no clue.'[102] They imagine that one might devise a theology to rationalize pain. 'The world needs something stronger, or rather, weaker', Wengert contends.[103] The key to answering whether suffering is something to be gloried in or an end to be pursued is in a simple but significant distinction that Wengert makes. The theology of the cross, he demonstrates, is not *pre*scriptive, but *de*scriptive.

> The cross does not bless suffering, punishment and the rest; rather, it forces us to tell the truth that such things are curses. Suffering is not some great salvific act in and of itself. On the contrary, it is God's alien work, opposed to God's very nature. . . . The cross reveals that the senseless suffering of this sorry existence has a point in God and that this point is penultimate – God's first alien work clears the way in us for God's proper work of salvation.[104]

Thus the ministry of Jesus shows that he is implacably opposed to suffering and sickness. He 'went about doing good and healing all who were under the power of the devil, because God was with him' (Acts 10.38). This opposition took him to the cross where he suffered, and where we, broken by life's suffering, discover him.

Nuanced by the theology of the cross, this statement in Acts may be seen as programmatic for Christian life and ministry. In fact, here in Acts 10 is a suitable paradigm for Pentecostal ministry. Appeals such as Soelle's recitation of Marx must be heard again. The Christian call to justice is in fact a '"categorical imperative to overthrow all those conditions" in which man is an abased, enslaved, abandoned, contemptible being' in a spiritual revolution that ministers to spirit, soul and body.[105] Indeed, this call must be heard by Christians only when they have established it soundly on biblical and theological foundations that carry its burden and impress it with an imprimatur weightier than Marx's. The pervasive evil of all human structures, what Walter Wink called 'the powers that be', must be unmasked, engaged, and hastened to their fall, in the sure hope of the *parousia*. This has both individual and institutional dimensions. There is a biblical call here to charismatic ministry, coupled with compassionate social action. The pervasive results of sin and human rebellion have affected, and continue to affect, every element of creaturely existence. Thus salvation must be a reconstitutive process that encompasses spirit, soul and body; the culmination of which is tied to the *eschaton*. But the church's mission must include social transformation as well. The reality that all social systems, even Christian ones, are inevitably corrupt, that they are rife

102. Timothy J. Wengert, '"Peace, Peace . . . Cross, Cross": Reflections on How Martin Luther Relates the Theology of the Cross to Suffering', *TT* 59 (2002), pp. 190–205 (p. 192).

103. Ibid., p. 194.

104. Ibid., p. 200.

105. Soelle, *Suffering*, p. 2.

with human sin and limitation must not deter us. The utter incommensurability of both personal and societal realities with divine mandate, divine justice, and divine holiness should push us back to the cross, where all incommensurabilities are transcended in the crucifixion of the Resurrected, and the resurrection of the Crucified.

c. Pentecost: Living between Incommensurability and Consummation

Luther's theology of the cross leaves us here, in our present reality. Luther is nothing if not real, earthy, authentic. There's no gilding the lily, no pretense or positive confession with Luther. Humanity is encompassed with sin and sorrow. But there is something more that arouses the hope of expectation. It is summarized in two Luther maxims, one well known, the other less so. The first is *simul justus et peccator* (at the same time righteous and a sinner). The theology of the cross can never be divorced from its soteriological roots. 'A theologian of the cross calls the thing what it actually is.'[106] And for Luther the essential issue was sin. This is ultimately the seed from which the human predicament sprouts until, *coram deo*, it becomes a great tree that blocks the heavens. The concept of '*simul justus et peccator*', is Luther's dialectical solution to the sinner's quandary, uniting him with Christ, and linking him directly to the theology of the cross. In his Lectures to the Galatians, Luther makes the connection.

> But faith must be taught correctly, namely, that by it you are so cemented to Christ that He and you are as one person, which cannot be separated but remains attached to Him forever and declares: 'I am as Christ.' And Christ, in turn, says: 'I am as that sinner who is attached to Me, and I to him. For by faith we are joined together into one flesh and one bone.'[107]

This ontological union is core to the theology of the cross. The Christian is '*simul justus et peccator*' because that is what Christ has become. The Father said to him

> Be Peter the denier; Paul the persecutor, blasphemer and assaulter; David the adulterer; the sinner who ate the apple in Paradise; the thief on the cross. In short, be the person of all men, the one who has committed the sins of all men. And see to it that You pay and make satisfaction for them.' Now the Law comes and says: 'I find Him a sinner, who takes upon Himself the sins of all men. I do not see any other sins than those in Him. Therefore let Him die on the cross!'[108]

In this way incommensurability retains some of its existential angst in the long wait for the *eschaton*, and yet it is transcended in the overflowing mercy of the

106. 'Heidelberg Disputation: Thesis 21' (1518), *LW* 31:40.
107. 'Lectures on Galatians' (1535), *LW* 26:168.
108. Ibid., 26:280.

cross and surpassing victory of the resurrection. *Simul justus et peccator* is an effective formula for expressing one way in which Christians remain suspended in the 'already' and 'not yet'.

Another aspect of living in that tension is the phrase '*simul gemitus et raptus*' (at the same time groaning and rapturous).[109] *Raptus* in the medieval tradition referred to the ultimate goal of the mystical life, union with God. *Gemitus*, is the first sorrowful step of separation from the world the mystical pilgrim must take. Luther, on the other hand, reinterprets *raptus* as the complete ontological union of the believer with Christ on the basis of the righteousness of Christ *extra nos*. He fixes this rapture in dialectical tension with *gemitus*, not as a preparatory stage, but as a mark of absolute dependence on God. Thus *gemitus* overcomes any notion of a theology of glory in *raptus*; and *raptus* dissipates any possibility of human works in *gemitus*.[110] The Christian finds herself stranded in a world of suffering and sorrow, injustice and oppression, in short, in a world of groaning. For the true believer, there is no escaping the call of the world's pain, no escaping the crushing load of one's own anguish, except that even as the call to respond comes, it returns us to the outstretched arms of Christ, whose nail-pierced hand extended through us will bring healing. 'The Christian does not turn away from the bitterness of this world but is in that very valley of tears identified with the cross of Christ.'[111]

But how does the Christian engage this broken, sorry world? If the theology of the cross has no answer to this question besides tears and identification, it has no useful orthopraxy, and as a result remains a questionable orthodoxy. But Luther offers a counterpoise to the groaning of the cross: the *raptus* of the resurrection victory! The same theology of the cross that results in *katabasis* also produces *anabasis*. Only the Christian who is *peccator* can be *simul justus*. In the same way, only the one who is *gemitus* can be truly *raptus*. The *logos* of Christian theology is precisely this. The necessary corollary of the cross is the resurrection, and it is that reality which brings the in-breaking of the *eschaton*.

> We must not let death and other misfortune, distress and misery, terrify us so. Nor must we regard what the world has and can do, but balance this against what we are and have in Christ. For our confidence is built entirely on the fact that He has arisen and that we have life with Him already and are no longer in the power of death. Therefore let the world be mad and foolish, boasting of and relying on its money and goods; and let the devil rage with his poisonous darts in our conscience; and let him afflict us with all sorts of trouble – against all of this our

109. Oberman claims *simul gemitus et raptus* is a formula that summarizes the same truth as *simul justus et peccator* in terms of mystical spirituality; Oberman, '*Simul Gemitus et Raptus*: Luther and Mysticism', in *The Reformation in Medieval Perspective* (ed. Steven Ozment; Chicago: Quadrangle Books, 1971), pp. 219–51 (p. 239).

110. Oberman, *Luther: Man between God and the Devil*, p. 184 and Oberman, 'Luther and Mysticism', pp. 236–39.

111. Ibid., p. 232.

> one defiant boast shall be that Christ is our Firstfruits, that He has initiated the resurrection, that He has burst through the devil's kingdom, through hell and death, that He no longer dies or sleeps but rules and reigns up above eternally, in order to rescue us, too, from this prison and death.[112]

Here Luther anticipates Moltmann, whose programmatic statement in *Theology of Hope*, demonstrates the proleptic nature of the resurrection that colours his entire opus.[113] Moltmann distinguishes Christian hope from Jewish apocalyptic in this way: whereas the Jewish imperative was to wait for the resurrection of the dead, the Christian's is to participate in the resurrection of Christ in whom 'the process of the raising of the dead is set in motion' and in whom we 'already live in the midst of the transitory world of death from the powers of the new world of life that have dawned in him'.[114]

Thus Luther's theology of the cross, properly understood as encompassing death and resurrection, provides an abundantly fruitful resource for Pentecostal contemplation. This process of reflection may be catalyzed by Moltmann's appropriation of Luther, for Moltmann dichotomizes the resurrection of the Crucified and the death of the Resurrected at length, offering Pentecostals the opportunity to ponder their experience more profoundly. Pentecostalism may be described as an extreme example of looking back to the apostolic church in order to restore the dynamic of its experience. It may also be portrayed as an extreme example of reaching forward to the eschaton to realize that age's perfection of human potential. Rather than taking its impetus from these retrospective and prospective forms of triumphalism, Luther offers another approach. The *theologia crucis* acknowledges the value of the backward, and the forward look, but proposes a more objective basis for both. Let the historical perspective entail the cross, for there the truth is told about God and humanity. And let the futurist perspective entail the resurrection, for there the possibilities of eternity break in upon the present. Popular Pentecostal spirituality has historically been nurtured by romantic notions of the 'early church' that always seem beyond our grasp, or perfectionist tales of victorious faith that constantly obtains miraculous results. But 'a theologian of the cross calls the thing what it actually is'.[115] Rather than establishing Pentecostal identity on these subjective experiences of immediacy, Luther offers the cross and the resurrection as objective bases for identity. In the theology of the cross the believer receives a Word that comes *extra nos*, from beyond us, and a work that is done *pro nobis*, something that is done for us. This may be the source of a genuine

112. 'Commentary on 1 Corinthians 15' (1534), 1 Cor. 15.20–21, *LW* 28:111.

113. '[I]n the medium of hope our theological concepts become not judgments which nail reality down to what it is, but anticipations which show reality its prospects and future possibilities'; Moltmann, *Theology of Hope*, p. 36. For the centrality of hope as the key to opening Moltmann's entire oeuvre, see Neal, *Theology as Hope*.

114. Moltmann, *Crucified God*, p. 171.

115. 'Heidelberg Disputation: Thesis 21' (1518), *LW* 31:40.

Pentecostal expectation, one that reckons with the limitations of the frustrated experience of the present age, while anticipating the powers of the age to come. And for the Pentecostal who fears the loss of personal subjective experience, there remains *after* Good Friday and Easter Sunday and their *extra nos* realities, a Day of Pentecost, which of necessity takes place *in nobis*, within us.

Conclusion

Luther's theology of the cross proves to be a fertile resource for Pentecostal theology, particularly in terms of the question of triumphalism. It does so by giving the lie to disappointed experience and decimates all human aspirations of self-deification. Regarding the nature of spiritual experience, the cross calls into question all theologies of ascent, citing them as variations of the heart turned in on itself. This places it in opposition to optimistic notions of human ability that imagine that the sinner 'can' obey God, if only she 'will'. At the organizational level, the cross indicts all projects of achievement that seek to mollify personal disenchantment by appeal to institutional glory.

The mechanics of the theology of the cross are complex, playing on two notions of the Hiddenness of God that bring humanity to the nadir of its ability to access and comprehend the divine. Humans desire a kind, compassionate and gentle God, and preferably one who will do their bidding. The god of human expectation is an idol, but there is a God who is hidden in the suffering of the cross and this God is only accessible by faith. Behind Word and cross, though, there is hidden an inscrutable God who is completely inaccessible, at least in space and time. The God of the second hiddenness assumes responsibility for the alien works of suffering and struggle through which humanity travails. But faith believes, in spite of the dashed expectations of human experience that this inscrutable God is somehow the same God who has revealed himself in the cross.

Moltmann, Fiddes, Soelle and many others have resisted this dimension of the *theologia crucis*, but the genius of Luther is that he pushes the dialectic to the extreme, and in the process retains a God who is not only sovereign and free, but also passible and compassionate. The cross is not merely a veil of tears, but once it has descended to the deepest hell, it must ascend to the highest heaven. This leads to Pentecost, the place where what Christ has done *pro nobis* begins to take place *in nobis*. And here are the possibilities of charismatic ministry, both spiritual and social. For the same dialectic that Christ lives also becomes ours. The church, too, enters into the pain of this broken world, takes it on, experiences it, and in the power of the Spirit, drives back the darkness, in the remembrance of Christ's death and the anticipation of his future.

Part III

A PENTECOSTAL THEOLOGY OF THE CROSS: LISTENING TO LUTHER WITH PENTECOSTAL EARS

Chapter 5

'VICTORY IN JESUS': A PENTECOSTAL THEOLOGY OF THE CROSS

I heard about His healing,
Of His cleansing pow'r revealing.
How He made the lame to walk again
And caused the blind to see;
And then I cried, 'Dear Jesus,
Come and heal my broken spirit,'
And somehow Jesus came and bro't
To me the victory.

O victory in Jesus, my Saviour forever!
He sought me and he bought me with his redeeming love
He loved me ere I knew him
And all my love is due him
He plunged me to victory
Beneath the cleansing flood

—Eugene M. Bartlett (1885–1941), 'Victory in Jesus'

That is the victory by which death is to be swallowed up, so that we need fear death no longer or remain in it . . . For although he is not yet entirely swallowed up in us, the victory gained by Christ is already present, and through Gospel, Baptism, and faith it has become our victory.

Martin Luther, 'Commentary on 1 Corinthians 15' 15.54–55 (1527–28), *LW*, 28.206

Thus if I am to gain comfort in a struggle of conscience or in the agony of death, I must take hold of nothing except Christ alone by faith, and I must say: 'I believe in Jesus Christ, the Son of God, who suffered, was crucified, and died for me. In His wounds and death I see my sin; and in His resurrection I see victory over sin, death, and the devil, and my righteousness and life. I neither hear nor see anything but Him.'

Martin Luther 'Lectures on Galatians' Galatians 3.28 (1535), *LW*, 26.357

'Victory in Jesus' is certainly the recurring motif of most Pentecostal spirituality, whether classical, charismatic or neo-charismatic. While emphases vary, the key signature remains the same. To live the Spirit-filled life is to live in victory![1] Early Pentecostal formation was driven by two forms of triumphalism, one retrospective, the other prospective. These two dynamics, the one reaching back in history, the other reaching forward to the *eschaton*, indeed represent broader tendencies intrinsic to Christian theology. I have contended that Pentecostalism's historical foundation of restorationism and perfectionism has been wrong-headed, and has created no end of problems in its development and future viability. In their place, I propose, in this chapter, an application of Luther's *theologia crucis*, which replaces these dynamics in terms of a *pneumatologia crucis* and an *eschatologia crucis*. These categories honour the historical intent of Pentecostalism, while repositioning it theologically, and rephrasing it in terms that answer the essential triumphalism that drives not only Pentecostalism, but Evangelicalism as well. The result will be the integration of Pentecostal experience with the theology of the cross.

Pentecostalism is not marked so much by its theology at the popular level, as by its spirituality. This dimension is supported by an underlying doctrinal infrastructure, which in turn interacts with the growing apparatus of contemporary Pentecostal theology. In this chapter, I wish to apply the theology of the cross to the basic 'depositum' of Pentecostalism: the baptism of the Holy Spirit. Arguing the eschatological orientation of Spirit baptism, the emerging *pneumatologia crucis* and *eschatologia crucis* provide a lens for the consideration of a series of problems in Pentecostalism as they are experienced at the popular level of spirituality, the more sophisticated level of doctrine, and where possible, the level of theology. Any true evaluation of Pentecostalism will have to reckon with all three dimensions. This chapter, then, creates a Pentecostal *theologia crucis* as the basis for the analysis that will take place in the next chapter.

I. Pentecostal Spirituality, Doctrine and Theology

World Pentecostalism exists today as a multifaceted collection of believers, churches and movements within Christianity. Some years ago Walter Hollenweger noted that several features characterize these various expressions of Pentecostal/charismatic experience:

- An emphasis on the oral aspect of liturgy;
- Theology and witness cast in narrative form;

1. According to Kärkkäinen, 'Pentecostal-Charismatic Christianity has reintroduced to Christian spirituality an ideal of victorious Christian living, an intensive faith expectation, and an emphasis on spiritual power to overcome problems in one's life. The attitude of "overcoming" is characteristic to Pentecostal and Charismatic preaching'; Kärkkäinen, 'Theology of the Cross', p. 150.

- Maximum participation at the levels of reflection, prayer and decision-making and therefore a form of community which is reconciling;
- Inclusion of dream and vision into personal and public forms of spirituality, so that the dreams function as kinds of icons of the individual and collective; and
- An understanding of the body/mind relationship which is informed by experiences of correspondence between body and mind.[2]

These features imply that Pentecostalism is primarily a kind of spirituality rather than a doctrinally or theologically driven movement.

a. Pentecostal Spirituality

To begin by approaching Pentecostalism as spirituality is fraught with problems of definition. Christian interest in the term 'spirituality' began in the wake of Vatican II and particularly with the emergence of the Catholic charismatic movement. Eventually Protestants yielded their suspicions of the 'mystical' and 'enthusiastic' connotations of the word, and applied it to the kinds of interior experience they had once termed as 'piety', and 'devotion'.[3] The domain of spirituality as an academic discipline, however, has been notoriously difficult to pin down.[4] Commentators as early as Sandra Schneiders (1986) and as recent as Peter Holmes (2007) note that the question is complicated by growing interdisciplinary interest.[5] Indeed Holmes

2. Hollenweger adds, 'If one measures by this list the experiences of present day [1986] American/European pentecostal and charismatic groups, one still discovers a fair amount of the original elements. However, they are limited by the fact that in certain instances the authority which is based on speech, narrative and communication, enters into conflict with the authority which is based on status, education, money, and juridical power'; Hollenweger, 'Pentecostals and the Charismatic Movement', in *The Study of Spirituality* (ed. Cheslyn Jones, Geoffrey Wainwright and Edward Yarnold; London: SPCK, 1986), pp. 549–54 (pp. 551–52).

3. Sandra M. Schneiders, 'Theology and Spirituality: Strangers, Rivals, or Partners?', *Horizon* 13 (1986), pp. 253–74 (pp. 254–55).

4. Defining 'spirituality' is challenging. See ibid.; Carlos M. N. Eire, 'Major Problems in the Definition of Spirituality as an Academic Discipline', in *Modern Christian Spirituality: Methodological and Historical Essays* (ed. Bradley C. Hanson; Atlanta: Scholars, 1990), pp. 53–61; Bradley C. Hanson, 'Spirituality or Spiritual Theology', in *Modern Christian Spirituality: Methodological and Historical Essays* (ed. Bradley C. Hanson; Atlanta: Scholars, 1990), pp. 45–51; Ewert H. Cousins, 'What Is Christian Spirituality?', in *Modern Christian Spirituality: Methodological and Historical Essays* (ed. Bradley C. Hanson; Atlanta: Scholars Press, 1990), pp. 39–44; and Peter R. Holmes, 'Spirituality: Some Disciplinary Perspectives', in *A Sociology of Spirituality* (ed. Kieran Flanagan and Peter C. Jupp; Theology and Religion in Interdisciplinary Perspective; Farnham, UK: Ashgate, 2007), pp. 23–42.

5. Schneiders, 'Theology and Spirituality', pp. 267–68; and pp. 23–24.

doubts whether any mutually agreed upon definition will emerge.[6] One dimension of the problem for Christian thought is the dramatic emergence, in recent years, of non-religious spiritualities, which force reappraisals of traditional categories.[7]

Still, some common denominators that are helpful to the trajectory of this chapter reappear in efforts to define spirituality. Bernard McGinn set the emphasis on the experiential dimensions of spirituality. Endeavouring to arrive at a working definition for a publishing project, McGinn and a team of editors agreed that 'Christian spirituality is the lived experience of Christian belief.' They distinguished it from doctrine 'in that [spirituality] concentrates not on the faith itself, but on the reaction faith arouses in religious consciousness and practice'.[8] In his definition of 'spiritual theology', Bradley Hanson concurs with the role of experience, but wishes to take it further, including the experience of the student. Spiritual theology for Hanson is unabashedly existential, involving the 'stance of the subject toward the subject matter' and combining 'hard reflection with a strong existential concern to grow in faith'.[9]

That existential concern with spiritual experience makes spiritual theology a formidable posture from which to discuss Pentecostalism, but it also underscores some of the concerns that arise from the theology of the cross. The subject matter of spirituality is a concern with 'ultimate reality' and the means of achieving a sense of union with the ultimate is 'self-transcendence'.[10] These categories are helpful for the discussion of Pentecostal experience in terms of ultimacy and penultimacy. But the subjectivity of 'self' that spiritual theology entails and its experiential bias may limit spirituality as a category for analysing Pentecostal experience.

The construal of Pentecostalism as spirituality is the basis of two significant works of Pentecostal theology: Steven J. Land's *Pentecostal Spirituality* and Simon Chan's *Pentecostal Theology and the Christian Spiritual Tradition*. Both Land and Chan follow Hollenweger in viewing the first ten years of Pentecostal history as the heart rather than the infancy of the movement.[11] And both recognize the danger of conscripting an overly narrow rational theology to communicate the Pentecostal

6. Ibid., pp. 24–25, 36–37.

7. Ibid., p. 23.

8. Bernard McGinn, 'Introduction', in *Christian Spirituality: Origins to the Twelfth Century* (ed. Bernard McGinn, John Meyendorff and Jean Lelerq; World Spirituality, vol. 16; London: Routledge and Kegan Paul, 1986), pp. xv–xxiii (pp. xv–xvi). Cousins shows the persistence of this notion in other religions; 'What Is Christian Spirituality?', pp. 41–43. See also Schneiders, 'Theology and Spirituality', pp. 266–67; and Eire, 'Problems in the Definition', pp. 57–58 and 61. Correspondingly, Steven Land notes that '[t]he Pentecostal concern is . . . to emphasize the lived reality of the faith'; Land, *Pentecostal Spirituality*, p. 33.

9. Hanson, 'Spirituality as Spiritual Theology', p. 50.

10. Schneiders, 'Theology and Spirituality', pp. 266–67; and Cousins, 'What Is Christian Spirituality?', pp. 42–43.

11. Land, *Pentecostal Spirituality*, p. 26; and Simon Chan, *Pentecostal Theology and the Christian Spiritual Tradition* (London: Sheffield Academic Press, 2000), p. 7. Others

vision. Chan points out the failure of Pentecostalism to find a vocabulary for communicating the Pentecostal reality. 'The central doctrine called "baptism in the Spirit" is far richer in Pentecostal *experience* than in Pentecostal *explanation*', says Chan.[12] He acknowledges the dualism of letter and spirit in modern theology, and advises the recovery of 'the ancient art of spiritual theology' as a remedy.[13] His proposal is to find resources in the broader spiritual tradition to nourish Pentecostal traditioning.

Land has a similar concern for rationalist notions of theology and spirituality.[14] The burden of his project is to recapture affective categories for rephrasing Pentecostal spirituality in terms of orthodoxy, orthopraxy and orthopathy.[15] This pattern of eschewing modern theological categories as incapable of communicating the existential dynamic of Pentecostalism is a commonplace of Pentecostal scholarship. Pentecostal ritual, as Daniel Albrecht notes, 'is both a conscious and intuitive and effort to construct a sphere in which together a congregation most likely will *encounter* their God'. This intentionality, both intellectually, and ritually, underscores 'the centrality of the mystical element in Pentecostal spirituality, the strong desire and claim to experience God directly and intimately'.[16] The lived experience of Pentecostals forms a compelling category for understanding Pentecostalism.

It will be essential, then, to encounter Pentecostalism as a species of spirituality. The benefits of this approach are that it puts the nature of spiritual experience, immediacy and the question of ultimacy at the centre. The downside, though, is that if the trend of Pentecostal scholarship is to acknowledge this intense subjectivity as intrinsic to Pentecostal identity, then any criticism on this point will be tantamount to an out and out rejection of Pentecostalism. Spirituality, however, is not the only category by which to evaluate Pentecostalism.

At the 'lived-out' level, contemporary Pentecostalism is also formed by a loose doctrinal matrix inherited from the institutionalizing period. Shortly after the initial passion of the early revival was displaced by the failure of the Latter Rain paradigm, Pentecostals faced the challenge of establishing more permanent structures, physically, administratively and doctrinally. Douglas Jacobsen has

who define Pentecostalism in terms of spirituality and not theology include; Veli-Matti Kärkkäinen, *Introduction to Ecclesiology*, p. 70; and *Pneumatology: The Holy Spirit in Ecumenical, International, and Contextual Perspectives* (Grand Rapids: Baker Academic, 2002), pp. 89–92; and Anderson, *Introduction*, pp. 14 and 195–99.

12. Chan, *Pentecostal Theology*, p. 10.

13. Ibid., p. 12.

14. Land, *Pentecostal Spirituality*, pp. 26–27.

15. Land seeks to elevate spirituality beyond 'the outdated and fruitless antinomy of reason and feelings'. In this regard, though he appears critical of Lutheran theology; ibid., pp. 27, 29–30, 46 and 221. Land and Luther share a similar concern for the dialectic of reason and experience; ibid., p. 13.

16. Albrecht, *Rites in the Spirit*, p. 149.

performed an invaluable service by uncovering the diversity of theological trajectories displayed in the first generation of Pentecostal leadership.[17] However for the present discussion I wish to distinguish between the doctrinal period of Pentecostal thought (what Jacobsen in another place has called 'Pentecostal scholasticism') and the season of more mature theological reflection marked by the emergence of self-conscious scholarship embracing dialogue with the larger academic enterprise.[18] Thus, I differentiate doctrinal formation from theological reflection, and suggest that both of these dimensions receive separate consideration.

b. Pentecostal Doctrine

Early Pentecostals had been understandably uncomfortable with doctrine. An article from a 1914 *Evangel* warned

> We may be established in our doctrine, steadfast and unmoveable, stubborn, like a balking horse on a mountain road: so rooted and grounded in our own theories and traditions handed down that neither the Word of God nor His Spirit can move us on from our dogmatic position.[19]

The burden was not so much *against* doctrine as *for* the Spirit. Spirit-filled teaching will point 'toward the cross of Christ [what the author calls the 'death-to-self route'] and life in the Holy Ghost'. The article claimed, 'The spirit behind the discourse will penetrate farther than the word he utters.'[20] That is, it will lead to experiential Christianity, or Pentecostal pietism, in short. However, as the process of institutionalization advanced, the necessity of setting forth a doctrinal framework for Pentecostal experience became increasingly apparent.

Jacobsen marks the heyday of Pentecostal scholasticism between the publications of two classic texts: Myer Pearlman's *Knowing the Doctrines of the Bible* (1937) and Ernest Swing Williams' *Systematic Theology* (1953). Pearlman recognized that he was writing in a somewhat polarized environment: 'There is a tendency *in some quarters* not only to minimize the value of doctrine, but to dismiss it as outgrown and useless.'[21] He offers a fairly pedestrian approach to cataloguing biblical data

17. Jacobsen, *Thinking in the Spirit*.

18. Jacobsen discusses 'Pentecostal scholasticism' without making the distinction I propose. 'Knowing the Doctrines of Pentecostals: The Scholastic Theology of the Assemblies of God, 1930–55', in *Pentecostal Currents in American Protestantism* (ed. Edith L. Blumhofer, Russell P. Spittler and Grant A. Wacker; Urbana: University of Illinois Press, 1999), pp. 90–107.

19. 'Overzealous for Doctrine', *CE* 2 (28 March 1914), p. 6.

20. Ibid., p. 6.

21. Pearlman, *Knowing the Doctrines*, p. 9 (emphasis added). This kind of repartee is a recurring motif in Pearlman's work.

into 'compartments (topics) and in smaller receptacles (sub-topics)'.[22] Along the way Pearlman embraces the modified Wesleyan perfectionism, and moderate Arminianism that have marked the doctrinal underpinnings of most contemporary Pentecostalism.[23] In many ways Williams follows a similar approach. This style of 'doctrinal' writing became a peripheral necessity in Pentecostal circles, usually encountered in Bible College, and by the occasional lay Bible teacher, and not changing significantly until the 1990s. A well-known volume written by Four-Square Bible School teachers Guy Duffield and Nathaniel Van Cleave was *Foundations of Pentecostal Theology*, first published in 1983. Their goal, not unlike Pearlman's, is to 'compile the Scriptural teachings concerning the great doctrines of our faith'.[24] Thus, the doctrinal era lasted well into the 1980s.

One can scarcely overestimate the impact of such doctrinal writings in shaping the ethos of institutional Pentecostalism. They were elemental in the formation of Pentecostal pastors in the Bible Colleges that prepared them for the ministry. These works went on to be the first line of reference for pastors when they encountered theological issues in the course of ministry, and as a result became the grist for the more doctrinal moments of Pentecostal teaching in the local church. The moderate perfectionism of books like these ensured the triumphalist motif of Pentecostal doctrine would be reproduced in the spirituality of the churches. The restorationist impulse was well-represented in ministerial training, too, in denominational histories like Charles W. Conn's *Like a Mighty Army*, Stanley Frodsham's *With Signs Following* or Carl Brumback's *Suddenly from Heaven*. Canadian students had the benefit of Gordon Atter's *The Third Force* and Gloria Kulbeck's *What God Hath Wrought*. All of these saw the Pentecostal revival as the restoration of apostolic Christianity, and as Atter discerned, 'It seems clearly to be the great END-TIME REVIVAL PROPHESIED IN THE WORD OF GOD'.[25] Pentecostal spirituality was shaped in significant ways both by the perfectionism and restorationism of these doctrinal and historical works.

c. Pentecostal Theology

Theology, as reflective, scholarly dialogue did not emerge among Pentecostals until the 1970s. Amos Yong provides a useful model for charting the progress of

22. Ibid., p. 11.

23. Having repudiated any notion of eradication; ibid., p. 257, Pearlman sets forth the 'possibilities of perfection' culminating in '**entire sanctification**' and acknowledging that 'progress in sanctification often involves a crisis experience almost as definite as that of conversion'; ibid., pp. 265–66. With regard to the Calvinist/Arminian question, Pearlman avoids a final pronouncement, but his sympathies clearly lie with the moderate Arminianism of Wesley; see his discussion of a Scriptural balance, ibid., pp. 267–76.

24. Guy P. Duffield and Nathaniel M. Van Cleave, *Foundations of Pentecostal Theology* (Los Angeles: L.I.F.E. Bible College, 1983), p. xv.

25. Atter, *Third Force*, p. 22.

nascent Pentecostal scholarship. He demonstrates that the process began among historians in the 1960s. Indeed, Pentecostal history continues to make important contributions to the new social history that was taking shape at that time. With the 1970s came the appearance of Pentecostal contributions in the field of biblical studies.[26] The escalating debate in Lucan theology, and postmodern hermeneutics has been advanced by Pentecostal scholarship. Yong suggests theological reflection came into its own among Pentecostals in the 1990s. A growing reconsideration of the role of the Holy Spirit has led to truly Trinitarian reappraisals in all of theology, and Pentecostals appear to be at the vanguard.[27]

At the theological level, Pentecostal thought becomes far divorced from Pentecostal spirituality 'on the ground'. This both complicates and simplifies the analysis attempted here applying Luther's theology of the cross. The task is complicated by some of the goals of Pentecostal scholarship. Much current scholarly thought appears to be dedicated to a two-fold task: the recapturing of early Pentecostal ethos, and the reformulation of Pentecostal theology in a broader theological paradigm.[28] This agenda seems to be driven by the need to arrive at a definable Pentecostal identity, particularly one that sees it as distinct from Evangelicalism. Often, the search for an early Pentecostal ethos drifts dangerously towards anachronism, especially when it seeks to reinterpret similarities to contemporary concerns in present-day terms. For instance one is constantly treated to an overinflated view of the racial diversity of early Pentecostalism, without the necessary reminders of the inherent racism which formed a counterpoise to what was perhaps incidental at Azusa Street.[29] In the event, race played its ugly card, particularly at Azusa Street, itself, with the October 1906 arrival of Charles Parham and his damning condemnation of the 'darky camp meeting'. Later Clara Lum and Florence Crawford who helped publish the *Apostolic Faith* broadsheet fled Los Angeles for Portland after opposing Seymour's marriage to Jennie Moore. They absconded with the 50,000 address mailing list, crippling the ministry.[30]

26. Cecil M. Robeck, 'Spotlight on The Society for Pentecostal Studies', *ET* 14 (1985), pp. 28–30, offers a brief history of the formation and development of the Society for Pentecostal Studies.

27. Amos Yong, 'Pentecostalism and the Theological Academy', *TT* 64 (2007), pp. 244–50 (pp. 245–48).

28. Faupel, 'Whither Pentecostalism?'; and Veli-Matti Kärkkäinen, 'Identity and Plurality: A Pentecostal-Charismatic Perspective', *IRM* 91 (2002), pp. 500–3, are two cases in point.

29. See Kärkkäinen's comments: ibid., p. 501. *Contra*, see Joe Newman, *Race and the Assemblies of God Church: The Journey from Azusa Street to the 'Miracle of Memphis'* (Youngstown, NY: Cambria Press, 2007).

30. Cheryl Sanders, *Saints in Exile: The Holiness-Pentecostal Experience in African American* (Religion in America; New York: Oxford University Press, 1996), pp. 29–30. Mel Robeck takes a less strident tone, but after analysing the situation, comes to a similar conclusion; Robeck, *Azusa Street*, pp. 299–310. See also Edith Blumhofer, 'Revisiting

We hear all too often of the ecumenicity of the early movement, and its resistance to denominationalizing as though these were expressions of Spirit-led transcendence of rigid categorizations of propositional truth. Calls for return to a Pentecostal hermeneutic sound as though early Pentecostals had more in common with contemporary postmodern paradigms, than with dispensational charts. Often these efforts fail to take adequate account of the essential unity of the thought world of early Pentecostals and their proto-Fundamentalist and Radical Evangelical kin.[31] It was their closeness, rather than the distance between them, that exacerbated the pitched tensions between Pentecostals and their Holiness cousins.[32] The same might be said about the rejection of Pentecostals by Fundamentalists. The depth of the pain was a measure of their similarities rather than their differences.[33] One function of this dissertation is to question the historical validity of this sort of revisionism, and to call for a return to a more values-free approach to Pentecostal history.

On the other hand, the current recognition of Pentecostalism's contribution to the recent resurgence of pneumatological inquiry is to be duly celebrated. In two volumes charting the Pentecostal-Roman Catholic dialogue, which began in 1972, Veli-Matti Kärkkäinen pointed out the ecumenical challenge of theologically defining a Pentecostal position.[34] Yet, D. Lyle Dabney finds it incredulous that Pentecostals themselves failed to see the significance of their own potential trajectory, what he calls a theology of the third article![35] As the broader Pentecostal movement has come of age, and begun critical reflection on its theological underpinnings, there has been a happy shift from merely apologetic writing in defence of traditional Pentecostal dogma and experience, to a more constructive approach to the creation of a distinctively Pentecostal theology, and an appreciation of the properly existential value of Pentecostal reflection on pneumatology.

Azusa Street: A Centennial Retrospect', *IBMR* 30 (2006), pp. 59–64; and Blumhofer, 'For Pentecostals . . . Racial Reconciliation'.

31. Yong, 'Pentecostalism and the Theological Academy', pp. 244–45.

32. Wacker, 'Travail of a Broken Family'.

33. Blumhofer, *Restoring the Faith*, pp. 159–60.

34. Veli-Matti Kärkkäinen, *Spiritus Ubi Vult Spirat: Pneumatology in Roman Catholic-Pentecostal Dialogue (1972–1989)* (Schriften der Luther-Agricola-Gesellschaft 42; Helsinki: Luther-Agricola-Society, 1998); and *Ad Ultimum Terrae: Evangelization, Proselytism and Common Witness in the Roman Catholic Pentecostal Dialogue (1990–1997)* (Studies in the Intellectual History of Christianity, vol. 117; Frankfurt-am-Main: Peter Lang, 1999).

35. See Lyle D. Dabney's, 'Saul's Armor: The Problem and the Promise of Pentecostal Theology Today', *Pneuma* 23 (2001), pp. 115–46 (p. 125), in which he charges Kärkkäinen with missing the boat theologically; and Veli-Matti Kärkkäinen, 'David's Sling: The Promise and the Problem of Pentecostal Theology Today: A Response to D. Lyle Dabney', *Pneuma* 23 (2001), pp. 147–52, where Kärkkäinen responds that his goal was not to point out the potential, but to simply lay out objectively the state of Pentecostal self-understanding at the time of the dialogue; Dabney, 'Saul's Armor', p. 125 and Kärkkäinen, 'David's Sling', pp. 148–49.

While Dabney rejoices in the centrality of pneumatology in current theological discussion, and is eager for Pentecostals to formulate their own distinctive theology, Kärkkäinen is not so sure.[36] He would prefer a less fragmenting, and more collaborative approach from Pentecostals, as they make their contribution to a common Christian Trinitarianism.[37] Furthermore, Kärkkäinen fears that placing primacy on pneumatology might displace the Christological centre on which all agree, especially Pentecostals whose identity surely focuses on Jesus Christ as the prime actor in the four- (or five-) fold gospel.[38]

I wish, in what follows, to give voice to both Kärkkäinen's and Dabney's concerns. I believe that Pentecostalism is supremely centred around Jesus; that his roles as Saviour, Baptizer, Healer and Soon-Coming King are fundamental to Pentecostal theology. In addition, I am persuaded that the pneumatological impulse in Pentecostalism is an essential, and defining aspect of Pentecostal reality. Dabney claims that as heir to the Wesleyan legacy, Pentecostalism belongs to 'a movement whose inner logic' has 'always . . . rejected the triumphalism and formalism that so often plagued the theologies of the first and second article championed by the established churches'. If this is true, it must be hastily added that Pentecostalism, in particular, and Wesleyanism in general have forged their own less formal triumphalism and bequeathed it to the broader Evangelical world.[39] It is this triumphalism, implicit in the very genesis of the fourfold gospel, and engendered by a pneumatology not adequately articulated in Christological terms, that drives the current crisis of Pentecostal spirituality.

The theology of the cross offers a meaningful reply to both Dabney and Kärkkäinen. For instance, Dabney raises the issue of immediate and uninterpreted experience in Pentecostal self-definition.[40] The possibility of immediate experiences of the Spirit raises fundamental epistemological questions about Christian formation. It is a fair question to ask whether Pentecostals are the heirs of Luther or the *Schwärmer*. A pneumatology rooted in the cross (a proposal of which Dabney heartily approves!) places a kenosis of the Holy Spirit in relation to the self-emptied Christ, and opens a discussion on the limitations of human experience of the Spirit.[41] On the other hand, Kärkkäinen indicates that Pentecostal theologians

36. Dabney, 'Saul's Armor', p. 131.

37. Kärkkäinen, himself, admits that this concern may reflect his bias as a scholar in the field of ecumenics; Kärkkäinen, 'David's Sling', p. 150.

38. Ibid., pp. 150–52.

39. Dabney, 'Saul's Armor', p. 139. I take it Dabney refers to the post-Constantinian relation between church and state. Regardless, it is difficult to deny the triumphalism already outlined in these pages.

40. Ibid., p. 123.

41. Thus Moltmann comments, '[T]he story of the suffering of the messianic Son of God is the story of the suffering of God's Spirit too'; Moltmann, *The Spirit of Life*, p. 64. Dabney proposes this very thing; Lyle Danby, '*Pneumatologia Crucis*: Reclaiming *Theologia Crucis* for a Theology of the Spirit Today', *SJT* 53 (2000), pp. 511–24.

in dialogue with Catholic academics defined the 'essence of Pentecostalism' as the experience of the Holy Spirit, which reveals the risen and glorified Christ and empowers the believer with the abundant life of Acts and the epistles.[42] Efforts to define Pentecostalism in these terms founder on Douglas John Hall's notion of resurrectionism, which calls into question an over-enthusiastic 'already'-ness often implicit in charismatic rhetoric. Confusion surrounding here-and-now potentials of the 'Soon-Coming King' and the 'powers of the age to come' create unsustainable expectations among Pentecostals that are often dashed by harsh reality. And yet, surely *Pentecost* heralds some kind of existential encounter with the Spirit.[43] A middle-ground between unrealistic expectancy and the genuine possibilities of Pentecostal experience may be discoverable by application of an *eschatologia crucis*.

Thus this chapter seeks to chart implications of the theology of the cross that respond to essential problems of Pentecostal identity, both historically and theologically. In so doing, it addresses matters at the level of Pentecostal spirituality and the popular doctrinal infrastructure that sustains it. Historically, Pentecostalism has been shaped by its restorationist tendency to reach into the past to find the primitive key to present-day repristination of the church. It has also exhibited an opposite perfectionist tendency to reach into the future to access the fullness of the age to come. This retrospective and prospective triumphalism may be replaced by two theological trajectories that arise from the theology of the cross. First, I propose to develop a *pneumatologia crucis* that reaches back to a cruciform *Pentecost*, that is a sending of the Spirit fully informed by cross and resurrection.[44] Second, I wish to construct an *eschatologia crucis* that apprehends 'the powers of the age to come' through the appropriate lens of the cross and resurrection. These two terms, emerging from Jürgen Moltmann's contemplation of Luther's theology of the cross, provide a useful means for tempering both Pentecostal expectation and experience.

II. Baptism in the Holy Spirit: Between Cross and Eschaton

The centrality of Spirit Baptism to Pentecostal identity has been questioned in recent years. A primary problem appears in the difficulty of offering a precise

42. Kärkkäinen, *Spiritus Ubi Vult Spirat*, p. 50.

43. By italicizing the words 'Pentecost' and 'Pentecostal', I wish to transform the referent from a historic movement to the actual theological sense of the Day of Pentecost, and its results as presented here.

44. The words 'cross' and 'resurrection' will be conjoined and collapsed into one another often in what follows. I mean them as a technical term for gathering the full range of the theology of the cross, as suggested in the previous chapter; see Moltmann, *Crucified God*, p. 204.

definition adhered to by all. Yet, however it is defined, it is difficult to avoid the category of 'Baptism in the Holy Spirit' when talking about Pentecostalism.[45] While exhaustive clarification of the full semantic, and theological domain of the term is beyond the scope of this discussion, its fundamental position in Pentecostal, charismatic and neocharismatic discussion indicates that it carries full theological freight in each circle.

My interest focuses on 'Baptism in the Holy Spirit' as the nexus between cross and *eschaton*. The fundamental question revolves around how *Pentecost* mediates both the cross event and the *eschaton* in the life of the contemporary believer. I contend that Spirit baptism acts as the pivotal experience by which both forward- and backward-looking historical trajectories meet, and this makes it significant in a thorough application of the theology of the cross to practical Christian experience.

The tendency among Pentecostals when thinking of Spirit baptism is to move too quickly to the fulfilment in the book of Acts, rather than to contemplate more fully the prediction in Luke 3. The result is to truncate Spirit baptism into an ecclesial empowerment with its principal locus in the present age.[46] The mistake here is to overlook a more biblically nuanced notion of the baptism in the Holy Spirit that sets its locus primarily as an eschatological event. As early as 1970, James Dunn noted that the baptism Jesus would offer was a baptism of Spirit-and-fire. This metaphor conjured Old Testament images of eschatological judgement and purification.[47] Indeed Frank Macchia indicates that 'if the Spirit is anything in the Bible, it is an eschatological gift (e.g., Ezek 39:10; Matt 12:18; Eph 1:13–14; Heb 6:5)'.[48] Taking this perspective into account, places the total Acts treatment of

45. On the one hand Kärkkäinen claimed in 1998 that '[t]he rise of Pentecostalism and the Charismatic Movement has lifted the issue of Spirit-baptism to the forefront of the theological agenda in modern theology'; *Spiritus Ubi Vult Spirat*, p. 198. On the other hand, though Frank Macchia provides a survey of recent work agreeing on the centrality of Spirit-baptism, he claims that it is 'no longer regarded as the most distinctive Pentecostal doctrine or as having central significance to Pentecostal theology without qualification or even rejection among leading Pentecostal theologians and historians today' and notes that it has received little theological elaboration since the early 1980s; Frank D. Macchia, *Baptized in the Spirit: A Global Pentecostal Theology* (Grand Rapids Zondervan, 2006), pp. 23 and 20–28. Henry Lederle, *Treasures Old and New: Interpretations of 'Spirit-Baptism' in the Charismatic Renewal Movement* (Peabody, MA: Hendrickson, 1988), offers a vast and diverse pallet of interpretations of Spirit baptism across the Christian tradition. Allan Anderson, *Introduction*, pp. 192–96, suggests that this diversity of opinion implies that Pentecostalism might better be evaluated from a different perspective than theological. As noted above, both Land and Chan (among others) have proposed spirituality as a more appropriate domain for discussion.

46. Macchia, *Baptized in the Spirit*, p. 85.

47. James D. G. Dunn, *Baptism in the Holy Spirit*, pp. 10–14.

48. Macchia, *Baptized in the Spirit*, p. 48.

Spirit baptism against a more firmly eschatological horizon. While Peter's sermon in Acts 2 continues the eschatological motif, it presents Spirit baptism as the fulfilment of Joel's prophecy, as though the *eschaton* were already upon his hearers. But is *Pentecost* intended as the complete fulfilment of the Spirit-and-fire baptism Luke looks forward to in his gospel? Or is it a partial fulfilment, an anticipation of the great end-time conflagration? Remembering the Baptist's foundational statements reminds us that the *Pentecost* event may be only one stage along the journey to the culminating eschatological event. In so doing it brings a corrective to Pentecostal resurrectionism, and an overemphasis on the 'Already' dimensions of spiritual experience.[49]

The forward-looking perspective of the baptism in the Holy Spirit is matched by a backward-looking dynamic, which anchors it to the Day of Pentecost along with the cross and resurrection accounts that give rise to it. A useful way to access this reality is to track, with Richard Bauckham, the path of Moltmann's initial trilogy. Bauckham unpacks the author's programmatic statement that '*Theology of Hope* began with a *resurrection* of the crucified Christ, and I am now [in *The Crucified God*] turning to look back at the *cross* of the risen Christ.'[50] Bauckham relates the three works as follows: the first book treats the resurrection in eschatological perspective, interpreting it in terms of dialectical promise – hope and mission; and in the second Moltmann contemplates the cross with regard to theodicy as interpreted by dialectical love – suffering and solidarity.[51] Both of these motifs are consistent expressions of Luther's theology of the cross as it has been elaborated in the previous chapter. The *theologia crucis*, I have argued, includes the twin dynamics of *katabasis* and *anabasis*. The synthesis of Moltmann's concerns in the first two volumes, he explores in the third, *The Church in the Power of the Spirit*. Here he consciously works out his pneumatology in Trinitarian terms.[52] As Bauckham summarizes it, 'the Spirit whose mission derives from the cross and resurrection, moves reality towards the resolution of the dialectic, filling the godforsaken world with God's presence, and preparing for the coming of the kingdom.'[53]

49. Arie W. Zwiep, 'Luke's Understanding of Baptism in the Holy Spirit', *PentecoStudies* 6 (2007), pp. 127–49 (pp. 132–33).

50. Moltmann, *Crucified God*, p. xxi.

51. Richard Bauckham, *The Theology of Jürgen Moltmann* (London: T&T Clark, 1995), p. 5. Bauckham enlarges on the dialectics of both resurrection and cross later in the chapter, pp. 9–13, and later in the book, pp. 33–35 and 120–21.

52. Moltmann is particularly forceful here: '[T]he doctrine of the Trinity will have to be newly formulated in such a way that the personhood of the Spirit and the Spirit's independent workings in concert with the Father and the Son can be seen and grasped.' In this 1990 preface, Moltmann claims to have begun the work in 1975 in *Church in the Power of the Spirit*, and to have continued it in 1980s *Trinity and the Kingdom: The Doctrine of God* (trans. Margaret Kohl; Minneapolis: Fortress, 1993); Moltmann, *Church in the Power*, p. xv.

53. Bauckham, *The Theology of Jürgen Moltmann*, p. 5.

The baptism in the Holy Spirit, then, becomes the nexus of backward- and forward-looking dynamics of Christian ontology. The Christian is that person in whose being the possibilities of the eschaton and the realities of cross and resurrection meet as mediated by Spirit baptism. The Holy Spirit fills the gap between godforsakenness as it is experienced in the broken reality of this age and the fulfilment of eschatological promise as it exists in the age to come. This takes place individually in the believer, as *Pentecostal* being, and corporately or socially in the church as *Pentecostal* community. Simultaneously acknowledging godforsakenness and embracing eschatological expectation places such a formulation of Spirit baptism firmly within the domain of the theology of the cross. As Luther stated with such eloquent bluntness: *A theologian of the cross calls the thing what it actually is.*[54] In the context of the crisis of contemporary Pentecostalism, the 'thing' is the triumphalism that denies godforsakenness in the life of the Spirit-filled believer, and anticipates the fullness of eschatological fulfilment in the here-and-now. That particular genre of triumphalism, I have contended, received its impetus from the peculiar interaction of backward-looking restorationism and forward-looking perfectionism as they coalesced in the early Pentecostal movement. But *Pentecost* as formulated here replaces those historic dynamics with cross and resurrection; and eschatological promise, respectively. These trajectories demand an already/not yet dialectic to function realistically within a theology of the cross. Describing that dialectic in terms of Pentecostal spirituality, doctrine, and theology forms the remainder of this chapter.

III. Pneumatologia Crucis *and* Eschatologia Crucis

The key to integrating the perspectives of *Pentecost* and the promise of the *eschaton* with the theology of the cross is to rephrase pneumatology and eschatology as *pneumatologia* and *eschatologia crucis*. These two terms occur seminally in Moltmann, but both have undergone further development.[55] My purpose is to reorient them to Luther's thought and apply them more directly to the issue of Pentecostal triumphalism. This restatement of pneumatology and eschatology in terms of the theology of the cross not only provides a critique of Pentecostalism, but allows it to be reformulated in more rigorously Trinitarian terms. Moreover,

54. 'Heidelberg Disputation: Thesis 21' (1518), *LW* 31:40–53.

55. In point of fact, *pneumatologia crucis* was originally developed by Lyle Dabney in his doctoral dissertation for Moltmann; Lyle Dabney, *Die Kenosis des Geistes: Kontinuitat zwischen Schopfung und Erlosung im Werk des Heiligen Geistes* (Neukirchener Beitrage zur systematischen Theologie Band 18; Neukirchen-Vluyn: Neukirchener Verlag, 1997). Moltmann credits Dabney and his other doctoral students with contributing to the publication of *The Spirit of Life* in the Foreword to the published edition, *Die Kenosis*, p. viii.

it frees scholarship from anachronistic readings of Pentecostal history while still honouring the historic roots of Pentecostal formation: experience of the Holy Spirit and eschatological anticipation.

a. *Pneumatologia Crucis*

Lyle Dabney doubts that a pneumatology of the cross can be discovered in Luther's writings. He charges Luther with maintaining a static medieval concept of the Holy Spirit, while proposing a dynamic notion of the Father and the Son's involvement in the cross.[56] In Luther's thought, the work of the Spirit is defined primarily in terms of his creation of faith in the hearers of the Word while his activity in the cross event proves to be a null set.[57] While this may be so, it must also be noted that Luther could still speak of 'the crucified God'.[58] By a creative application of the Chalcedonian communication of attributes (*communicatio idiomatum*), Luther was able to speak of 'the God who crucifies and the crucified God; the God who is dead and yet is not dead; between the manifest God in Christ and the hidden God above and beyond Christ'.[59] For instance, in his commentary on John 14.14, Luther applied the principle that the external works of the Trinity are indivisible.[60]

> For since Christ, who is one undivided Person, God and man, speaks thus, it is certain that God the Father and the Holy Spirit, that is, the whole Divine Majesty, is also present and speaking. Thus God is entirely contained in this one Person, and you need not and dare not search further and ask: 'How and where is He to be found or encountered?'[61]

56. As Dabney rightly indicates, 'What is striking, however, about Luther's account of the third member of the trinity, the Holy Spirit, is that otherwise than is his habit with the Father and the Son, he fails to speak of the Spirit in terms of "the humility and shame of the cross"'; Dabney, '*Pneumatologia Crucis*', pp. 514–15.

57. Ngien points out that the theology of the cross 'applies just as completely to God the Holy Spirit as it does to God the Son'. But his presentation of Luther's treatment of the Spirit's work demonstrates that it focuses on the subjective nature of that ministry in the believer, rather than the Spirit's involvement with the cross event; Ngien, *Suffering of God*, pp. 153–61. See also Dabney, '*Pneumatologia Crucis*', pp. 516–17.

58. See, for instance, Luther's comments on Psalm 118.28; 'Commentary on Psalm 118' (1530) *LW* 14:105.

59. Moltmann, *Crucified God*, p. 235.

60. Moltmann, *Crucified God*, pp. 231–35. See also Ngien's extended discussion of Luther's use of the *communicatio idiomatum* and his application of the principle '*opera trinitatis ad extra indivisa sunt*' (the external works of the Trinity are indivisible) to the question of Trinitarian involvement in the cross; Ngien, *Suffering of God*, pp. 68–86 and 142–53.

61. 'Sermons on the Gospel of St. John' (1537), John 14.14, *LW* 24:98.

Thus the trajectory of Luther's thought anticipates a pneumatology of the cross, even if he fails to explicitly develop one. The Reformer's curious silence on the matter may be a function of his battles with the Radical Reformation. Much of his elucidation of the doctrine of the Holy Spirit took place in dispute with the *Schwärmer*, and, as will become apparent, in its own way reflects the theology of the cross.[62]

Moltmann defines the primary locus of the cross as an event in the history of the Trinity.[63] The suffering of the cross involves each person of the godhead.[64] The Trinity, for Moltmann, is an essential corollary of the cross. Indeed, '[t]he theological concept for the perception of the crucified Christ is the doctrine of the Trinity. The material principle of the doctrine of the Trinity is the cross of Christ'.[65] He hypothesizes,

> If the central foundation of our knowledge of the Trinity is the cross, on which the Father delivered up the Son for us through the Spirit, then it is impossible to conceive of any Trinity of substance in the transcendent primal ground of this event, in which cross and self-giving are not present.[66]

The Spirit, then, is a necessary predicate of the theology of the cross, yet Moltmann's early treatment of the Spirit's role does not advance much further than Luther's. While much of his discussion of the cross centres on the separation between Father and Son, his account of the Spirit's involvement begins as a result of the cross:

> What proceeds from this event between Father and Son is the Spirit which justifies the godless, fills the forsaken with love and even brings the dead alive,

62. Prenter, *Spiritus Creator*, p. 206; Lohse agrees that Luther generally accepted the tradition of the Fathers and of Western theology with regard to the Holy Spirit and the Trinity; Lohse, *Luther's Theology*, p. 232. See Luther's comments on John 16.14 for an example of how he couched his doctrine of the Spirit between Catholic and enthusiast extremes; 'Sermons on the Gospel of St. John' (1537) *LW* 24:362 and 363.

63. Moltmann, *Crucified God*, pp. 235–49. Significant debate has arisen around various dimensions of Moltmann's Trinitarianism; Thomas G. Weinandy, *The Father's Spirit of Sonship: Reconceiving the Trinity* (Edinburgh: T&T Clark, 1995); and Thomas G. Weinandy, *Does God Suffer?* (Edinburgh: T&T Clark, 2000); Dennis J. Jowers, 'The Theology of the Cross as Theology of the Trinity: A Critique of Jürgen Moltmann's Staurocentric Trinitarianism', *TB* 52 (2001), pp. 245–66; and D. G. Attfield, 'Can God Be Crucified? A Discussion of J. Moltmann', *SJT* 30 (1977), pp. 47–57, are among those that speak to the issues raised here.

64. Moltmann, *Crucified God*, pp. 245–46.

65. Ibid., pp. 240–41.

66. Moltmann, *Trinity and the Kingdom*, p. 160; Moltmann makes clear here that he transcends Luther's notion of '*opera trinitatis ad extra indivisa sunt*' and proposes that '*opera trinitatis ad extra*' correspond to '*passiones trinitatis ad intra*' (the internal feelings of the Trinity).

> since even the fact that they are dead cannot exclude them from this event of the cross; the death in God also includes them.[67]

How the Spirit is actually involved in the cross, Moltmann does not at this point engage. The Spirit proceeds from the cross to bring its benefits to humankind.[68] In this regard, then, Moltmann's pneumatology of the cross is a direct amplification of Luther's implicit notions.

It is not until *The Spirit of Life* (1991) that Moltmann enlarges his thoughts regarding a *pneumatologia crucis*.[69] Here, he begins to tease out the implications of a Trinitarian theology of the cross for the doctrine of the Holy Spirit. He starts with Old Testament adumbrations of the Spirit's New Testament ministry, and finds help in the immense physicality of the *ruach* concept, the semantic domain of which includes breath, wind and the storm.[70] He amplifies these metaphors of immanence by calling on the development of *Shekinah* theology, a notion shaped in part by later rabbinical reflection.[71] In its fullest dimensions the *Shekinah* includes an empathy with Israel's shame, and a sharing in Israel's suffering. Moltmann goes so far as to suggest that the *Shekinah*, who suffers because he loves, points to a kenosis of the Spirit.[72] Such thinking does not parallel directly Abraham Heschel's notion of divine pathos in the prophets, but is reminiscent of it, and possibly originates there.[73]

Kenosis is normally a Christological category, but Dabney makes it a pneumatological one as well. According to Dabney, 'The self-emptying of the

67. Moltmann, *Crucified God*, p. 244.

68. See Dabney, '*Pneumatologia Crucis*', pp. 520–21. In 1976 Carl Braaten commented in his review of *The Crucified God*, 'Whereas the relations between the Father and the Son are spelled out in the event of the cross, the Spirit goes along for a free ride. Would not a binitarian concept of God work as well?'; Carl E. Braaten, 'A Trinitarian Theology of the Cross', *JR* 56 (1976), pp. 113–21 (pp. 117–18). Dabney reacts to this binitarianism by suggesting two moves that summarize his pneumatologia crucis: first an elevation of the Spirit and a de-emphasis of the Word (the Second Person) in an anti-*filioque* bid, and second, an eschatological understanding of the Trinity, *Die Kenosis*, pp. 112–15.

69. Peter Althouse, 'Implications of the Kenosis of the Spirit for a Creational Eschatology: A Pentecostal Engagement with Jürgen Moltmann', in *The Spirit Renews the Face of the Earth: Pentecostal Forays in Science and Theology of Creation* (ed. Amos Yong; Eugene, OR: Wipf and Stock, 2009), pp. 155–72 (p. 163); and Moltmann, *Spirit of Life*, p. 62. Peter Althouse traces developments in Moltmann's growing theology of the kenosis of the Spirit.

70. Moltmann, *Spirit of Life*, pp. 40–43.

71. Ibid., pp. 47–51.

72. Ibid., pp. 49 and 51.

73. Abraham J. Heschel, *The Prophets, 2 Vols* (New York: Harper Torchbooks, 1975), 2:4, presages some of Moltmann's concerns. Richard Bauckham, '"Only the Suffering God Can Help": Divine Passibility in Modern Theology', *Themelios* 9 (1984), pp. 6–12 (pp. 9–10), notes the influence of Heschel on Moltmann's thought. Already, in *The Crucified God*,

Spirit is accordingly a precondition for the self-humiliation of the Son. The Spirit of God is the spirit of kenotic self-surrender.'[74] As Moltmann puts it, 'the Spirit is the transcendent side of Jesus' immanent way of suffering.'[75] Interestingly, the kenosis of the Spirit has a venerable history in Orthodox theology. In the twentieth century, the theme was explored at length by Sergius Bulgakov in his master work *The Comforter* (1936).[76] Like Moltmann and Dabney, Bulgakov's Orthodoxy rejects the *filioque* clause. He sees two kenotic Dyads as accounting for the Christ event: a Father-Son incarnation, and a Father-Spirit procession.[77] For Bulgakov, the kenosis of the Son is met by that of the Spirit. The kenotic self-emptying of the Spirit does not represent an abandonment of divinity, but a self-diminishment of his power.[78]

1. A Lucan Development of Pneumatologia Crucis The *katabasis* of the Spirit is seen particularly clearly in Luke-Acts.[79] The Son of God is conceived by the 'coming upon' Mary of the Spirit. Thus the kenotic motif begins with a work of the Spirit (Lk. 1.35). The downward journey of the Spirit is implied by the fact the Virgin is 'overshadowed by the power of the Most High'. Later at his baptism, the Spirit 'descends' on Jesus (Lk. 3.22), an event given eschatological significance by John the Baptist's description of Jesus' future ministry as the one who will 'baptize

pp. 270–73, Moltmann reflects on Heschel's divine pathos, and begins to form his concept of the *Shekinah*.

74. Dabney, *Die Kenosis* cited in Moltmann, *Spirit of Life*, p. 64.

75. Ibid., p. 62.

76. Sergei Bulgakov, *The Comforter* (trans. Boris Jakim; Grand Rapids: Eerdmans, 2004), forms the central contribution of a trilogy entitled *On Divine Humanity*. Moltmann acknowledges his debt to the Orthodox notion of kenosis in *Crucified God*, pp. 206–7.

77. Both Dyads serve the revelation of the Father, and each does so in its own way. The Second hypostasis reveals the Father as Word, or content; the Third 'as the actualization of this content, *beauty*'. Bulgakov goes on to expand this thought: 'In the Third hypostasis, God not only *knows* Himself as the absolute Truth or the Word of all and about all, but He also *lives* in this hypostasis and *feels* it, with the reality of the felt truth being beauty'; Bulgakov, *The Comforter*, p. 182.

78. Ibid., p. 351.

79. Dabney and Moltmann pay particular attention to Mark's gospel. Donald Moessner, though, detects a distinct theology of the cross in Luke-Acts marked by the rejection/suffering/death motif in the life of the Messiah that in turn brings the final release of sins to Israel and the nations; Donald Moessner, '"The Christ Must Suffer," The Church Must Suffer: Rethinking the Theology of the Cross in Luke-Acts', in *Society of Biblical Literature 1990 Seminar Papers* (Society of Biblical Literature Seminar Paper Series, Number 29l; ed. David J. Lul; Atlanta: Scholars Press, 1990), pp. 165–95 (p. 195). The following outline is informed by Martin Mittelstadt's treatment of the convergence of Spirit and suffering in Luke-Acts; Martin Mittelstadt, *The Spirit and Suffering in Luke-Acts: Implications for a Pentecostal Pneumatology* (London: T&T Clark, 2004).

with the Holy Spirit and fire' (Lk. 3.16). The Spirit leads Jesus into the wilderness temptation at the beginning of his ministry, perhaps intimating his role in leading Jesus to the cross (Lk. 4.1–2). But it was the Spirit-filled Simeon who gave the first hint of crisis in the birth narrative when he spoke to the rejection of the Messiah and the sword that would pierce his mother's heart (Lk. 2.34–35).

At the inauguration of Jesus' public ministry in Nazareth, the proclamation of the Spirit-anointed liberation of the poor and the oppressed is met with opposition and the threat of death (Lk. 4.16–29). The fulfilment here of Isaiah 61 immediately thrusts Jesus in the role of eschatological Messiah who proclaims 'the year of the LORD's favour and the day of God's vengeance' (Isa. 61.2). The messianic ministry of Jesus is represented by the downward movement of the Davidic King to a Servant who 'in the power of the Spirit' (Lk. 4.14; Acts 10.38) expends himself rather than expanding himself, like other kings.[80] Jesus' power is not for himself, but for people of declining social position: the sick, the poor, the outcast and the dying. The servant of the Lord goes on to become the Suffering Servant.[81] For it is this Spirit-anointed Son of Man who 'must suffer many things, and be rejected by the elders, the chief priests and the teachers of the law, and he must be killed and on the third day be raised to life' (Lk. 9.22). In Luke 12, Jesus warns his disciples of persecutions they too must face, and assures of the Spirit's accompaniment (Lk. 12.12).

We see the motif repeated throughout the book of Acts: in the ministries of Peter, and the Twelve (Acts 3–5); Stephen (Acts 6–7); and Paul (Acts 20). 'The disciple's experience of the Spirit will lead some of them to the same fate as Jesus himself.'[82] The Spirit-led disciples find themselves at odds with the religious authorities in the same way Jesus did, through their Spirit-inspired acts and words, ultimately leading to the martyrdom of James (Acts 12.2). Similarly, Luke's presentation of Stephen as a Spirit-filled prophet ends with his martyrdom (Acts 7.57–60). Ananias is sent to pray for Saul of Tarsus to 'be filled with the Holy Spirit'. When he balks, he is admonished to go, because Saul, like the Suffering Servant is God's specially chosen instrument, and 'I will show him how much he must suffer for my name' (Acts 9.15–6). And we discover that this is his fate: success, opposition, rejection, imprisonment and the pregnant uncertainty of martyrdom. Yet Paul embraces suffering as a means by which the gospel may be proclaimed. 'Compelled by the Spirit', he moves towards Jerusalem, unsure what to expect,

80. See Kazuhiko Yamazaki-Ransom, *Roman Empire in Luke's Narrative* (Library of New Testament Studies 404; London: T&T Clark, 2010), where all power, including Jewish political and religious authorities are seen as under the Roman Empire which, in turn, is under demonic control.

81. For a concise but vigorous presentation of Jesus as the Suffering Servant in Luke; see Joel B. Green, 'Death of Jesus', in *DJG*, pp. 146–63 (pp. 161–62).

82. Mittelstadt, *Spirit and Suffering*, p. 6. See also Roger Stronstad, *The Prophethood of All Believers: A Study in Luke's Charismatic Theology* (London: Sheffield Academic Press, 1999).

but warned by the Spirit that prison and hardships await him. In spite of it all, though, he will continue 'the task of testifying to the good news of God's grace' (Acts 20.22–24). The counterintuitive result is that each episode of persecution and suffering results in the furtherance of the gospel.

2. The Silence of the Passion Narratives In endeavouring to construct a pneumatology of the cross, one might have expected a more complete discussion of the Spirit's role in the cross event itself. One looks mostly in vain through the synoptic passion narratives for a description of the Spirit's place. Two episodes suggest themselves. One is Jesus' chiding of Peter, James and John when they find themselves unable to stay awake at prayer in the dramatic moment of Gethsemane: 'The Spirit is willing', Jesus says, 'but the flesh is weak'. If this is indeed a reference to the Holy Spirit, it gives deeper pathos to Jesus' prayer, '*Abba*, Father' (Mk 15.36, 38). As Moltmann points out, the Spirit's presence at Jesus' baptism, leads to the Father's 'my beloved Son' (Mk 1.11), and his presence in Gethsemane to the reciprocating *Abba*.[83] This prayer dynamic is carried into Pauline thought as the work of the Spirit by whom we cry '*Abba*, Father' (Rom. 8.15), and who helps believers in their weakness, 'interceding for the saints in accordance with God's will' (Rom. 8.26–7).

The other possible reference to the Spirit's role at the cross involves all four gospels. Matthew, Luke and John offer the deliberately spare, even pathetic dismissal of Jesus' spirit (Mt. 27.50; Lk. 23.46; Jn 19.30). Mark notes that with a loud voice Jesus *exepneusen*: expired or breathed his last (Mk 15.37; cf. Lk. 23.46). The significance of this statement, if it, too, can be taken as a reference to the Holy Spirit, lies in the indication it gives that the Spirit accompanied Jesus through the entire ordeal of the cross.[84] Returning for a moment to the Hebrew concept of the *Shekinah*, one is reminded of the departure of the divine glory prior to the destruction of the temple (Ezek. 10). Not so here, as Jesus' temple is destroyed. In this regard, Dabney raises the question of the pneumatological significance of the cry of dereliction (Mk 15.34). What can godforsakenness mean in view of the Spirit of Life's presence in Christ's death on the cross?

Dabney's answer comes close to Luther's notion of the hiddenness of God. Dabney states, '[T]he Spirit of the Cross is *the presence of God with the Son in the eschatological absence of the Father*.'[85] The kenotic movement of the Spirit follows Jesus down to the depths of the grave, before he becomes the Spirit of the resurrection. But the Spirit is hidden in Christ during the passion. As these two ambiguous episodes imply, the Spirit's presence is at best only obliquely suggested. This is the nadir of self-effacement in the Spirit's kenosis. Bulgakov sees

83. Moltmann, *Spirit of Life*, p. 64.

84. Moltmann's comments here are ambiguous. Does he imagine that Jesus 'breathed the Spirit out'? Or that in Jesus' loud cry, the Spirit 'interceded for him, with inexpressible groanings, helping his weakness, also'; ibid., p. 64, quoting E. Vogelsang, *Der angefochtene Christus bei Luther*, p. 66

85. Dabney, *Die Kenosis*, p. 155 and '*Pneumatologia Crucis*', p. 524.

the forsakenness of Christ as limiting the action of the Spirit within Him to 'a completely potential state' and in his death reaching 'a kenotically depotentialized form in which it approaches inactivity, without, of course, ever becoming inactive'.[86] The Spirit's kenosis is asymptotic, tending to the limit of complete oblivion. But the relative silence of the passion narratives regarding the Spirit's involvement, far from raising questions regarding a pneumatology of the cross, actually reflects Luther's basic emphasis on divine hiddenness in his *theologia crucis*.[87] Bulgakov anticipates this hiddenness, for the Third hypostasis is known to humanity as '*the hypostatic revelation not concerning itself*'.[88] The hiddenness of the Spirit is fundamental to his kenotic ministry of revealing the Son, and 'manifesting the kingship of the Logos in creation and in salvation history'. As Orthodox theologian John Meyendorff expresses it, 'the personal existence of the Holy Spirit thus remains a mystery'.[89]

The above may explain the scarcity of explicit textual testimony to the Spirit's participation in the cross event. Still, perhaps the most striking statement of a *pneumatologia crucis* is to be found in the letter to the Hebrews, which Moltmann calls the first complete early Christian sermon we have.[90] In Hebrews 9.14, Christ is said to have 'offered himself unblemished to God'. It is not simply the offering of his life, Moltmann indicates, but the means by which it was offered: Christ's sacrifice was given 'through the eternal Spirit'. Neither Jews nor Romans, not even death itself, could take his life, but through the ultimate self-limitation of the Spirit, Jesus was the 'determining subject' of his suffering and death.[91]

3. The Kenosis of the Spirit in the Resurrection and the Church But the same Spirit through which the Christ offered himself, is also the power which was at work in the resurrection. Paul reminds us that Jesus was descended from David, but 'through the Spirit of holiness was appointed the Son of God in power by his resurrection from the dead' (Rom. 1.4). Often Paul attributes the resurrection to the power or glory of God, terms which Dabney and others take as circumlocutions for the Spirit.[92] Peter explains that 'he was put to death in the body but made alive in the

86. Bulgakov, *The Comforter*, pp. 252–53.

87. Luther makes a distinction at times between the Holy Spirit in his nature and essence (Spirit as Person) and as he is given to us (Spirit as Gift). This too implies a distinction between the hidden and revealed God; Lohse, *Luther's Theology*, p. 233.

88. Bulgakov, *The Comforter*, p. 188.

89. John Meyendorff, *Byzantine Theology: Historical Trends and Doctrinal Themes* (New York: Fordham University Press, 1974), pp. 168–69.

90. Moltmann, *Spirit of Life*, p. 62.

91. Ibid., p. 63.

92. The concept of the Spirit as 'the eschatological power' of the resurrection is the setting for Paul's understanding of the resurrection of Christ as promise, and the relationship between the Spirit and 'power'; Lyle D. Dabney, 'Naming the Spirit: Towards a Pneumatology of the Cross', in *Starting with the Spirit: The Task of Theology Today II* (ed.

Spirit' (1 Pet. 3.18). Such images hearken back to the eschatological valley of dry bones, which were revivified by the prophesied breath, and to its application in a renewed Israel.[93] God promises to open the graves of the Israelites, and that he will 'put [his] Spirit in you and you will live' (Ezek. 37.13–4). The Spirit's kenosis in Christ ends with the first event of the *eschaton*, the resurrection of Christ. Thus the full *pneumatologia crucis*, just as the full *theologia crucis*, must include the resurrection, and the beginning of the age to come. So on the day of *Pentecost*, that great eschatological moment, Peter proclaims 'Exalted to the right hand of God, [the Ascended Christ] has received from the Father the promised Holy Spirit and has poured out what you now see and hear' (Acts 2.33).

The kenosis of the Spirit continues now in the *Pentecostal* church. At one level, this returns us to the locus of Luther's theology of the Holy Spirit.

> I believe that by my own reason or strength I cannot believe in Jesus Christ, my Lord, or come to him. But the Holy Spirit has called me through the Gospel, enlightened me with his gifts, and sanctified and preserved me in true faith, just as he calls, gathers, enlightens, and sanctifies the whole Christian church on earth and preserves it in union with Jesus Christ in the one true faith. In this Christian church he daily and abundantly forgives all my sins, and the sins of all believers, and on the last day he will raise me and all the dead and will grant eternal life to me and to all who believe in Christ. This is most certainly true.[94]

Luther's emphasis on *solus Christus* casts the Spirit's primary role as bringing people to Christ.[95] This corresponds to the *pneumatologia crucis* of John's gospel where the Spirit's principal task is to testify to the meaning of the cross event. Gary Burge envisions a further self-limitation in the Spirit's kenosis. He emphasizes that the believer's experience of Jesus is actually to be identified with the experience of the Spirit: 'the Spirit assumes the role of Christ and *effects a personal epiphany of Jesus to the believer*'.[96] This resonates with Bulgakov's notion of the Spirit's kenosis: '[t]he hypostasis of the Spirit is eclipsed here in its transparence for the Word, is identified with Word, as it were'.[97] Max Turner claims that John's concept of salvation is by revelation, and specifically a revelation that focuses primarily on Jesus' cross and his resurrection. This is where the bulk of the Spirit's revelatory activity must take place, particularly as Paraclete. Turner argues the Paraclete functions as Teacher and Revealer, connecting Jesus' teaching to the profound realities of crucifixion

Stephen Pickard and Gordon Preece; Hindmarsh, SA: Australian Theological Forum, 2001), pp. 28–58 (pp. 41–42).

93. Moltmann, *Spirit of Life*, pp. 67–70; cf. Dabney, *Die Kenosis*, pp. 144–45; and Dabney '*Pneumatologia Crucis*', p. 522.

94. 'The Small Catechism' (1529), *BC* 345.

95. Lohse, *Luther's Theology*, p. 234.

96. Burge, *Anointed Community*, pp. 147–48 (emphasis added).

97. Bulgakov, *The Comforter*, p. 188.

and exaltation.[98] The Holy Spirit's ministry in John, then, is clearly recognized as revelatory, whether internally within the believer or as proclamation of the words of God through the believer.

The kenotic Spirit further expresses himself as mediator of the *eschaton* through the charismatic ministry of the church. Scripture uses rich imagery to describe the kenotic movement of the Spirit: 'pouring', 'filling' and 'flowing'. The typical results of such verbs are signs and wonders (Acts 2.22, 2.43, 5.12, 6.8, 14.3; Rom. 15.19; 2 Cor. 12.12; Heb. 2.4), and the profoundly Christian character of the new person and the new community (Eph. 5.18–6.9; Acts 2.42–46). But these are not simply proofs and testimonies, they are eschatological harbingers. These 'powers of the age to come' that we taste are mediated by the same Spirit who led Christ into his messianic mission, and calls the *Pentecostal* church to its eschatological mission as messianic community.[99] Moltmann offers this axiom: '[p]neumatological christology leads to a charismatic ecclesiology.' But, he continues, 'pneumatic christology is only realistic when it is developed into the trinitarian theology of the cross.'[100] Thus, the messianic mission bears the marks of the kenotic Spirit, for it, too, represents the self-emptying of the Spirit, expressed through the church as it embodies its calling as the anointed Servant of the Lord, continuing in all Jesus began to do and teach (Lk. 4.18–20; Acts 1.1, 5, 8).[101]

A summary of this *pneumatologia crucis* is in order and will prove useful for assessing Pentecostal spirituality, doctrine and theology. It consists in at least four elements:

- *The Spirit leads into suffering . . . and suffers with us.* In Luke-Acts, the Spirit's ministry leads the Messiah to the cross and clearly reproduces that work in the church as messianic community. However, the Spirit does not abandon the suffering disciple, just as he did not depart from Christ or Stephen (Acts 7.55–56).
- *The Spirit helps us in our weakness.* The phrase is Paul's (Rom. 8.26) but its resonance is felt in the gospels and Acts where the disciples will be taught what to say, or will find wisdom to withstand their oppressors (Lk. 12.12; Acts 6.10).
- *The Spirit testifies, reveals and convicts.* As Luther and John concur, it is the Spirit of the Cross who reveals the Crucified, creates faith and causes us to remember his words.
- *The Spirit quickens what is dead . . . and inaugurates the eschaton.* The same Spirit that raised Christ from the dead dwells in Christ's followers

98. Turner, *The Holy Spirit*, pp. 75 and 85–87.

99. Moltmann perceives continuity between Jesus' mission and the church's; *Church in the Power*, p. 11.

100. Ibid., pp. 36 and 37.

101. This paragraph is deeply indebted to Althouse's comments in 'Implications of the Kenosis of the Spirit', pp. 168–69 and 171–72.

and brings on the first fruits of the Coming Kingdom. The charismatic community is an eschatological expression of the new creation in this age. This last item anticipates the next section, the development of an *eschatologia crucis*.

b. Eschatologia Crucis

In a particularly capacious passage in *God in Creation*, Moltmann explains his notion of theology within the scope of created reality. He claims that all theology is one, because God is one; that our concepts of 'natural theology' and 'revealed theology' present a false dichotomy because theology can only be expressed in terms of the conditions in which it exists.[102] For instance in the era of human innocence all theology was natural theology, unmediated and clear. The fall brought the disruption of nature; and along with it, sin and death. Under these conditions all theology must be the theology of the cross, whose nemesis in this age is the theology of glory. Here all theology is necessarily mediated through the dialectical revelation/hiddenness of God in the cross. But in the day of consummation, the promises of innocence and the cross will be fulfilled, Moltmann says, in a true theology of glory: the beatific vision; unmediated knowledge of God where 'the whole earth is full of his glory' (Isa. 6.3).[103] Standing as we do, in the in-between time of the divine narrative, the recourse of humanity is to the theology of the cross, what Moltmann in this context calls Messianic theology, the distinguishing characteristic of which is its Janus-like awareness of our 'forfeiture to transience' and our 'hope of liberation to eternity',[104] These correspond to the forward- and backward-looking tendencies of Pentecostalism, and indeed all Christian theology. For Moltmann as much as Luther, the cross and the resurrection are simultaneous realities. All eschatology must be rooted in the cross or else it descends to mere triumphalism, yet the cross discloses no hope without eschatology and becomes only anguish.[105] Thus all eschatology must be *eschatologia crucis*.

1. Moltmann's Eschatologia Crucis Moltmann coined the term *eschatologia crucis* in his *Theology of Hope*. By it, he signifies an eschatological dialectic between the cross of suffering and the resurrection of hope. Within this concept, the consummation has offered a foretaste of glory, but has not fully disclosed it. Moltmann calls it an '*open* dialectic', which ultimately finds its resolution only in the *eschaton*.[106] 'The

102. Moltmann, *Jürgen Moltmann, God in Creation: A New Theology of Creation and the Spirit of God* (trans. Margaret Kohl; Minneapolis: Fortress, 1993), p. 60.

103. Ibid., pp. 59–60.

104. Ibid., p. 60.

105. Don Schweitzer, 'Douglas Hall's Critique of Jürgen Moltmann's Eschatology of the Cross', *SR* 27 (1998), pp. 7–25 (p. 18).

106. Moltmann, *Theology of Hope*, p. 201.

hope that is born of the cross and the resurrection', he asserts, 'transforms the negative, contradictory and torturing aspects of the world into terms of "not yet", and does not suffer them to end in "nothing"'. Thus the resurrection is not only a historical reality, but an eschatological expectation.[107] In fact, Moltmann perceives the resurrection as a proleptic event and has difficulty harmonizing any doctrine of expiation or justification with the cross as 'the form of the coming, redeeming kingdom'. The ultimate significance of the cross for Moltmann must be defined by the resurrection.[108] Hope is the treasure yielded by the resurrection to the believing, suffering and broken. The promise of hope is the negation of the present darkness and the affirmation of the coming kingdom.[109]

Some have suggested that Luther's *theologia crucis* and Moltmann's bear only superficial resemblance.[110] While significant differences exist between Moltmann's and Luther's theologies of the cross, particularly around the soteriological centre of Luther's use of the concept, the divergences between the two are not so much incompatibilities, as variations in emphasis and extensions of thought. Pastoral theologian Daniël Louw distinguishes between the two, suggesting they approach the cross from opposite perspectives. Luther's model is more existential, concerned about epistemology and God's identification with human suffering. Moltmann's is more '*theo*-logical' implying that the cross provides insight to God's being, and his experience of suffering.[111] Heinrich Bornkamm reflects a synthesis of these two notions in direct terms of Luther's theology of the cross.

> We can bear the ebb and flow of history, its unpredictability, and its seeming meaninglessness only if we entrust it to the God who is hidden within it, in order that he may lead us upon new paths when we no longer see the path at all. The key to this mystery is provided by the cross. Luther said, 'Behold, Christ became powerless on the cross, and yet there performed his mightiest work and vanquished sin, death, world, hell, devil, and all evil.' For those who believe, the cross of Christ

107. Ibid., p. 197.

108. Moltmann, *Crucified God*, pp. 184–86. Moltmann mollifies his views somewhat in *The Way of Jesus Christ*, pp. 185–89, where he reiterates his view of expiation but sees the entire soteriological enterprise in terms of justification.

109. Ryan Neal charges Moltmann with neglecting to establish his notion of hope on the cross event in his writings from the early to mid-1960s. Without wading into this debate, I choose a more diachronic view, synthesizing Moltmann's larger opus, particularly including *The Crucified God*; Neal, *Theology as Hope*, pp. 21–23.

110. Among these is Jowers, who asserts, 'One should not infer from Moltmann's use of the phrase "theology of the cross" any real similarity between his theology and the theology of Martin Luther'; Jowers, 'Staurocentric Trinitarianism', p. 245. See also Burnell F. Eckardt, 'Luther and Moltmann: The Theology of the Cross', *CTQ* 49 (1985), pp. 19–28.

111. Daniël Louw, *Meaning in Suffering: A Theological Reflection on the Cross and the Resurrection for Pastoral Care and Counselling* (International Theology, vol. 5; Frankfurt am Main: Peter Lang, 2000), p. 74.

> is the assurance that God really works where, from the human point of view, everything in the life of the individual, the church or the world is lost.[112]

Bornkamm's reference to Luther underscores the implicitly eschatological nature of the Luther's *theologia crucis*, and places Luther's existential concerns and Moltmann's theological interest in tandem.

With Moltmann, eschatology is not about some apocalyptic 'final solution', whether by divine fire or nuclear destruction. For Moltmann, the 'Christian hope is the remembered hope of the raising of the crucified Christ, so it talks about beginning afresh in the deadly end . . . Christian eschatology follows the christological pattern in all its personal, historical, and cosmic dimensions: *in the end is the beginning*.'[113] Parallel to this concept is the distinction Moltmann makes between *futurum* and *adventus* or *zukunft*. *Futurum* is what arises from the past and present, and as Moltmann claims, 'offers no special reason for hope'. But the Christian is captivated by *adventus*, a term signifying the coming of a person. It translates the Greek *parousia* that means presence, but is never used of Christ's fleshly presence nor his post-ascension presence through the Spirit: it is reserved for the coming presence of Christ in glory, what Luther called *zukunft Christi*.[114] The main category of eschatological interest, then, is not the future, and the minutiae of apocalyptic expectation, but rather the category of *adventus* which introduces the *novum*. Moltmann sees the *novum* as the historical side of the eschatological expectation. So, resurrection, the new community, and the new heaven and new earth carry a newness about them that is not implicit in the old. Rather than abandoning the old, the *novum* transcends it, implying both continuity and discontinuity between this age and the age to come.[115]

2. Luther's Eschatologia Crucis Luther's eschatology balances both apocalyptic and existential dimensions. Luther had a vivid sense of the apocalyptic. As demonstrated in the third chapter, his sense of imminence was palpable at times. The apocalyptic form, David Tracy explains, is concerned with systemic evil, and innocent suffering, and as a result with time and history. Whether de-literalized (as Tracy suggests), or not, the very nature of apocalyptic 'fragments any triumphalist totality system for understanding history and time'.[116] Thus apocalyptic calls on Luther's theology of the cross, seeking for the God hidden in the midst of

112. Heinrich Bonkamm, *The Heart of Reformation Faith: The Fundamental Axioms of Evangelical Belief* (trans. John W. Doberstein; New York: Harper & Row, 1965), p. 55.

113. Jürgen Moltmann, *The Coming of God: Christian Eschatology* (trans. Margaret Kohl; Minneapolis: Fortress, 1996), pp. xi–xii.

114. Ibid., p. 25. See Neal's description *Theology as Hope*, pp. 27–32.

115. Moltmann, *The Coming of God*, p. 25; and Anthony T. Thiselton, *The Hermeneutics of Doctrine* (Grand Rapids: Eerdmans, 2007), p. 575.

116. Tracy, 'Form and Fragment', p. 112.

suffering. This apocalyptic vision drives the political/liberationist declaration of God's presence *sub contrariis* in the lives of the marginalized and oppressed. Such a vision calls for social action.[117]

Though Luther's eschatology shares in the apocalyptic imagination of the middle ages, it also displays the existential anticipation of the coming kingdom we have associated with Moltmann. This is enshrined within the *simul*s which emerge from the theology of the cross: *simul justus et peccator*; and *simul gemitus et raptus*. Gordon Rupp called Luther's approach an 'eschatology of faith'.[118] The *eschaton* for the believer has begun in the act of justifying faith. 'We do not wait for forgiveness and all the graces as though we would not receive them until the life to come; rather they are now present for us in faith, even though they are hidden and will be revealed only in the life to come.'[119] This perspective provided for Luther a dialectical notion of time and eternity that located the church as eschatological community between two kingdoms. The believer's experience and anticipation of the life to come in the spiritual kingdom is balanced by his calling in the secular kingdom as an agent of social transformation through love of neighbour. Thus, both through the apocalyptic imagination, and existential experience, believers have a social responsibility to work for righteousness and justice in this age, though they anticipate their ultimate fulfilment only in the age to come.[120]

3. The Eschatological Community But how does the church as eschatological community accomplish this task? In one sense this is the burden of Peter Althouse's *Spirit in the Last Days*. By setting Pentecostal theologians in dialogue with Moltmann, Althouse teases out what he calls a transformational eschatology, the kind of affective orthopraxy Stephen Land had called for in a Pentecostalism shaped by Latter Rain anticipation.[121] The budding social vision Althouse finds in Land, Eldin Villafañe, Miroslav Volf and Frank Macchia arises in varying ways from the same kind of *eschatologia crucis* and *pneumatologia crucis* Moltmann espouses. More or less rooted in a theology of the cross, the transformational eschatologies that shape these seminal thinkers have sociopolitical consequences that Althouse claims restore the original social vision of William Seymour for a Spirit-filled community of faith that transcends racial and gender barriers.[122]

117. Ibid., p. 110.

118. Gordon Rupp, *The Righteousness of God: Luther Studies* (London: Hodder and Stoughton, 1953), p. 255.

119. 'Sermon on Judica Sunday', *WA* 17 II 229, as cited in Althaus, *Theology of Martin Luther*, p. 404.

120. Brian Hebblethwaite, *The Christian Hope: Revised Edition* (New York: Oxford University Press, 2010), pp. 71–72.

121. Peter Althouse, *The Spirit of the Last Days: Pentecostal Eschatology in Conversation with Jürgen Moltmann* (Journal of Pentecostal Theology Supplement Series, 25; London: T&T Clark, 2003), pp. xi–xii and 193–97.

122. Ibid., pp. 34–35 and 193.

More germane to the content of this chapter, is the charismatic nature of the eschatological community of the church.[123] Already intimations of this appeared in the discussion of a *pneumatologia crucis*, and, as the following discussion makes clear, this charismatic, eschatological community forms a threefold nexus between eschatology, pneumatology and ecclesiology. The *Pentecostal* community is empowered to proclaim its liberating message of the coming kingdom by the charismatic endowment of the Spirit.[124] The visible signs of this eschatological community include Word and sacrament, for both baptism and the Lord's Table carry a fundamentally eschatological significance; but these signs also include the charismatic ministry of each believer. Seen in this way, the *Pentecostal* church, as the community of Word and sacrament, as well as charismatic fellowship is even now a sign of the *eschaton* and the beginning of the new creation.[125]

Conclusion

The Pentecostal expectation of 'Victory in Jesus' normally undergoes some significant revision in the lifespan of most Pentecostals. The cycle of expectation and experience eventually moderates what congregants actually believe, even if it fails to lessen their rhetoric. For most Pentecostals, this is a loss of innocence. At some profound level, whether consciously or not, they have changed something fundamental in their degree of genuine expectation, so that they can live with the reality of their experience. But surely there is some kind of demonstrable victory in Jesus! The danger of throwing out the *Pentecostal* baby with the Pentecostal bathwater is real, and a threat to the future. One way of conceiving this chapter's contribution to the overall argument presented in this volume is to ask in what way believers can genuinely anticipate victory in Jesus.

Spirituality, doctrine, and theology provide categories for interpreting Pentecostalism. Each domain is essential for a full appreciation of the current situation, and indeed each area intersects with the others. The best topic around which to observe this intersection is the baptism in the Holy Spirit. Since Pentecostalism can best be apprehended as lived experience, and Spirit baptism is a highly existential phenomenon, and it has received multiple interpretations at the level of popular spirituality. Doctrinal formulations have created the convenient boundaries that demarcate the three waves of Pentecostalism, and even among classical Pentecostals there has not been doctrinal consensus.

123. This reflects Macchia's concern that a renewed paradigm for Spirit baptism 'must have a strong eschatological component and be connected to healing or the renewal of creation as well'; Frank D. Macchia, 'Baptized in the Spirit: Towards a Global Theology of Spirit Baptism', in *The Spirit and the Word: Emerging Pentecostal Theologies in Global Contexts* (ed. Veli-Matti Kärkkäinen; Grand Rapids: Eerdmans, 2009), pp. 3–20 (p. 23).

124. Moltmann, *Church in the Power*, pp. 218–19.

125. Ibid., p. 198.

The most fundamental issues, though occur at the level of underlying theology. Surveying the biblical development of the term, I offer an interpretation of Spirit baptism as the nexus between cross and eschaton. As such, it offers both backward- and forward-looking perspectives that can replace the restorationism (retrospective triumphalism) and the perfectionism (prospective triumphalism) that I have argued provide the dynamic of Pentecostal development historically. These Janus-like perspectives that merge in the baptism in the Holy Spirit may be described in terms of the theology of the cross. I propose a *pneumatologia crucis* and an *eschatologia crucis* as theological dynamics to propel Pentecostal theologizing. These twin trajectories allow Pentecostalism to retain a concept of victory that comes to terms with cruciform reality: the call to struggle against brokenness and injustice because of the assurance of the coming kingdom, and the joy and victory of prosecuting that struggle as partial participants already in a kingdom that is still coming.

Chapter 6

'He Lives within My Heart': Pentecostal Triumphalism and the Theology of the Cross

In all the world around me I see His loving care,
And tho' my heart grows weary I never will despair;
I know that He is leading through all the stormy blast,
The day of His appearing will come at last.

He lives, He lives,
Christ Jesus lives today!
He walks with me and talks with me
Along life's narrow way.
He lives, He lives,
Salvation to impart!
You ask me how I know He lives?
He lives within my heart.

—Alfred H. Ackley (1887–1960)

Therefore it is well with those who find water breaking into their ship, for this moves them to seek help from God. Wherefore, observe how Christ in all things is seeking our profit and is serving us even while he sleeps. The while he abandons us he is upholding us and while he is allowing us to go through storms in terror he is bringing us forward. Thus he brings it about that we do not perish but rather turn back to him, so that more and more we are constantly being saved . . . For he for whom Christ is not sleeping will not perish. He who does not perish does not cry out. He who does not cry out will not be heard. He who is not heard receives nothing. He who receives nothing has nothing. And he who has nothing will perish. So it happens that he who does not perish really perishes; and he for whom the Lord does not sleep never rightly wakes him. Therefore, sleep on, Lord Jesus, that thou mayest awake, and let us perish, that thou mayest save us.

Martin Luther, 'Sermon on the Fourth Sunday after the Epiphany, Matt. 8:23–27, February 1, 1517', *LW*, 51.24–5

Throughout this book triumphalism has been diagnosed as the underlying problem of contemporary Pentecostalism. The Pentecostal story has traditionally followed the form of 'testimony'.[1] Pentecostal testimony has often been enshrined in its hymnody, and Pentecostals like other Fundamentalists and Evangelicals took great joy in their gospel songs. I will mix a few metaphors in what follows, and a few hymns, but the existentialism of Alfred Ackley's 'He Lives' invites a certain intertextuality. Ackley's protagonist was weary, tempted to despair against 'all the stormy blast', but anticipation of Christ's soon coming and awareness of his presence within provides the needed stamina to persevere. And then Reason's daunting query: but how do you really know he lives? Any Pentecostal knows the answer, for surely the person with an experience is never at the mercy of the one with an argument: 'You ask me how I know he lives? He lives within my heart!' What questions could possibly remain?

Storms are a common hymnic metaphor for the vicissitudes of life, and they provide no end of opportunity for testimony. The gospel song 'Love Lifted Me' opens with this premise. 'I was sinking deep in sin, far from the peaceful shore.' First comes the tale of desperation that led to the cross. 'Then the Master of the waves, heard my despairing cry. From the waters lifted me, now safe am I.' Second was the joyful discovery of Jesus' saving power.[2] This was the standard Fundamentalist/Evangelical narrative arc. But the Pentecostal (like the Deeper Life, or Holiness saint) added one more stage. Shamelessly mixing metaphors, 'He plunged me to victory/Beneath the cleansing flood.' It is the victory-in-Jesus dimension that completes the Pentecostal narrative, and presents the central problem of Evangelical, and in its most aggravated state, Pentecostal triumphalism.[3] Pentecostal spirituality must find more authentic expression in terms that eschew the triumphalist assumptions of its metanarrative if it is to thrive in the postmodern ethos. I wish to suggest three dimensions of this disquiet for consideration. These include a concern for the place of experience in defining Christian reality; the nature of salvation as human perfectibility, whether instantaneous or progressive; and the role of the miraculous within Christian spirituality.

1. 'Much of Pentecostal/charismatic preaching and testimony-giving is meant to increase and strengthen faith, and consequently to heighten the expectation of miracles. Faith is often understood in power categories: the more faith one has, the more one has the right to expect from God'; Kärkkäinen, 'Theology of the Cross', p. 151.

2. 'Love Lifted Me', a hymn, lyrics written by James Rowe in 1911.

3. Land, applauding testimony as a means of oral theologizing, traces the narrative arc of a typical testimony as follows: 'I'm so thankful the Lord has saved me, sanctified me, and filled me with the blessed Holy Ghost. I'm thankful to be part of His Church and on my way to heaven.' In a footnote he adds 'I am determined to hold on to the end'; Land, *Pentecostal Spirituality*, pp. 80–81.

I. Replacing Restorationism: Experience as Penultimate[4]

Russell Spittler judges that 'by far the most pervasive' value of Pentecostal spirituality is experience. He declares, 'Pentecostals consider personal experience the arena of true religion.'[5] Daniel Albrecht claims that in the churches he surveyed, Pentecostal worship rituals allowed congregants to believe that 'they are actually experiencing God in an intimate, immediate, mystical way'.[6] Indeed as Albrecht perceives it, charismatic speech acts in particular, along with other charismatic rites, encourage participants to believe that they have enjoyed immediate access to the divine.[7] In what follows, I wish to argue that in the long-term development of Pentecostalism, restorationism has increasingly edged experience into a position of ultimacy. This has not always been the case among Pentecostals, but inasmuch as passion for apostolic restoration has grown in Pentecostal circles it has become a reality.

As already demonstrated, Luther himself anticipated the value of spiritual experiences in confirming faith. Unguarded, before his controversy with the Radicals, he is even able to elevate the role of immediate experience of the Spirit. In his exposition of the *Magnificat*, Luther asserts boldly of experience that,

> No one can correctly understand God or His Word unless he has received such understanding immediately from the Holy Spirit. But no one can receive it from the Holy Spirit without experiencing, proving, and feeling it. In such experience the Holy Spirit instructs us as in His own school, outside of which nothing is learned but empty words and prattle.[8]

4. Peter Althouse offers a useful catalogue of scholarly appraisals of Pentecostal experience; then offers a typology, rooted in the work of Catholic scholar George P. Schner, for systematizing the underlying basis of the appeal to experience. A few examples include 'the appeal constructive', 'the appeal immediate or mystical', and 'the appeal confessional'. Althouse argues that the prime Pentecostal appeal to experience is 'confessional'; that is the narrative, the testimony and its potential to 'inaugurate similar experiences'. While I do not deny that this is one legitimate facet of the Pentecostal appeal to experience, I am inclined to lean towards Land's notion of transformative encounter, that Althouse places under the appeal constructive, because as Schner says, '[e]xperience is, then, not unqualifiedly the "source" of theological construction.' It is primarily the 'appeal immediate or mystical' with which this section of my work takes exception; George Schner, 'The Appeal to Experience', *TS* 53 (1992), pp. 40–59 (p. 54); and Peter Althouse, 'Toward a Theological Understanding of the Pentecostal Appeal to Experience', *JES* 38 (2001), pp. 399–411 (pp. 401 and 410–11).

5. Spittler, 'Spirituality', p. 1097.

6. Albrecht, *Rites in the Spirit*, p. 159.

7. Ibid., p. 175.

8. 'The Magnificat' (1521), *LW* 21:299.

Even here, though, Luther is clear that while 'experience alone makes the theologian', he does not mean bare experience, but, as Oswald Bayer points out, '*experience with Scripture*'.[9]

a. Luther, the Enthusiasts and the Penultimacy of Experience

After his dismissive encounter with the Zwickau prophets early in 1522, his disappointing on-again-off-again dispute with his former colleague Andreas Bodenstein von Karlstadt (1521–25), and the tragic case of Thomas Müntzer (1522–25), Luther had learned all he needed about dissenting attitudes surrounding the sacraments and the role of God's Word.[10] These skirmishes had each become progressively vituperative, had resulted in deepening challenges to Luther's core concerns around *sola fide* and *sola Scriptura*, and had increasingly called upon experiences of divine immediacy as their epistemological basis. Not unlike the radical Evangelicals of the nineteenth century, the enthusiasts were given to both restorationist and perfectionist tendencies. By 1535, with the ill-fated Münster debacle, Luther's position towards dissenters had hardened. No form of Anabaptism, whether extreme, or evangelical could be tolerated. And while he was loath to call on state help to expunge them, Luther certainly took up the sword of the Word against them.[11]

As a result he appears to have become highly resistant to claims of unmediated encounters with the Holy Spirit. His statement in the Smalcald Articles (1537) represents a guarded position against the twin dangers of enthusiasm and Romanism, both of which share a similar emphasis on the internal Word.[12]

> In these matters, which concern the external, spoken Word, we must hold firmly to the conviction that God gives no one his Spirit or grace except through or

9. 'Table Talk No. 46: Value of Knowledge Gained by Experience, Summer or Fall, 1531', *LW* 54:7. This table talk starts with Luther lamenting the illiteracy of theologians as follows: 'A doctor of the Scriptures ought to have a good knowledge of the Scriptures and ought to have grasped how the prophets run into one another'; Oswald Bayer, *Martin Luther's Theology: A Contemporary Interpretation* (trans. Thomas H. Trapp; Grand Rapids: Eerdmans, 2008), p. 22.

10. When he finally had interactions with moderate Anabaptists, such as Conrad Grebel (1524), or was asked what he made of rebaptism by two pastors, Luther's responses indicated that he was indeed aware of the difference between these evangelical Anabaptists and the more radical kind, though he had not formulated a full response to them. With Melanchthon he believed that the moderates had arisen from the radicals; Loewen, *Luther and the Radicals*, pp. 70–71.

11. Ultimately, Luther and the Wittenberg theologians inclined increasingly to a position that advocated banishment and use of the sword by redefining the boundaries between the two kingdoms and contemplating the social ramifications of religious dissent; ibid., pp. 135–43.

12. In Richard Bucher, *The Ecumenical Luther: The Development and Use of His Doctrinal Hermeneutic* (St Louis: Concordia Academic, 2003), Bucher rethinks the Smalcald Articles

> with the external Word which comes before. Thus we shall be protected from the enthusiasts – that is, from the spiritualists who boast that they possess the Spirit without and before the Word and who therefore judge, interpret and twist the Scriptures or spoken Word according to their pleasure. The papacy, too, is nothing but enthusiasm, for the pope boasts that 'all laws are in the shrine of his heart', and he claims that whatever he decides and commands in his churches is spirit and law, even when it is above and contrary to the Scriptures or spoken Word.[13]

These 'enthusiasts' had threatened to undermine Luther's measured approach to reformation because, to their minds, it was neither adequately spiritual, nor sufficiently thorough.[14] Their claim against the sacrament of communion was its external focus in Luther's theology. For Luther, outward sign and external Word of promise together form the sacrament. In this sense it is literally a means of grace when received in faith.[15] For Karlstadt, '[i]t is totally impossible for any external thing whatsoever to be righteous or correct if the heart is not justified beforehand.'[16] The more radical enthusiasts, like Müntzer, rejected the mere letter of Scripture, believing that an inspired interpreter was necessary for clear understanding, and, of course, the individual must be instructed by the Spirit, himself. While the written Word for Luther was the revealed will of God, and the highest court of appeal, for Müntzer the Bible remained a record of God's revelation to specific individuals, and a testimony of Christian experience. Such ideas made Luther chary about his own earlier views because they left them open to misinterpretation. Luther's earlier words in his exposition of the Magnificat had promoted the indispensible necessity of existential encounter with the Holy Spirit: 'immediate understanding', 'experiencing, proving, and feeling'. These words almost imply the inner Word theology of the enthusiasts.

It is tempting, and perhaps even justified to read Luther diachronically here. Luther's position on immediacy underwent apparent change by the time of the Smalcald Articles because of his confrontation with enthusiasm. However, an

as an ecumenical document, in which the mature Luther sets forth his case for essential doctrine in any ecumenical discussion. Luther's dependence on the canon of Scripture and the gospel of justification were central controls for determining necessary doctrine, hence his concern regarding the methods of the enthusiasts and Romanists; ibid., pp. 28–57; 115–20 and 128–29.

13. 'Smalcald Articles' (1537): III, art. viii, par. 3–4, *BC* 312.

14. See, for instance Karlstadt's 'Whether One Should Proceed Slowly' (1524) in which he argues that reform should be as immediate and thorough as a local church can make it; Roland J. Sider, *Karlstadt's Battle with Luther: Documents in a Liberal-Radical Debate* (Philadelphia: Fortress, 1978), pp. 50–71.

15. 'The Babylonian Captivity of the Church' (1520), *LW* 36:92.

16. Karlstadt, 'Misuse of the Lord's Bread and Cup', (1524), cited in Sider, *Karlstadt's Battle with Luther*, p. 77.

argument could be made for a possible synchronic approach to the matter. There is no real inconsistency between the two statements. Both argue that the objective, external and divinely given revelation is ultimate. Both claim a penultimate experience with the Spirit. In the Smalcald Articles, Luther denies that the Spirit gives revelation outside or beyond the external Word. In *The Magnificat*, he affirms that the Word cannot properly be understood without the Spirit. His language in the wake of his encounters with the enthusiasts is particularly cautious, but not necessarily incompatible with his views in 1521. The immediacy he embraces in *The Magnificat* does not preclude the previous instrumentality of the Word, while that which he rejects in 1537 is one which by-passes not simply the primacy, but the ultimacy of Scripture.

b. Luther and Early Pentecostals on the Penultimacy of Experience

Imagine the anachronism of early Pentecostals adjudicating on this specific matter between Luther and the extreme enthusiasts. It seems clear they would have sided with Luther.[17] One of the iconic tales of the Pentecostal visitation was the story of Charles Fox Parham leaving his Topeka Bible School the assignment of discovering the biblical evidence of the baptism of the Holy Spirit while he went to Kansas City for services. On returning, 'to [his] astonishment' all 40 of his students had agreed that 'the indisputable proof on each occasion [when the Pentecostal blessing fell] was, that they SPAKE WITH OTHER TONGUES'. That night, the eve of the new century, Agnes Ozman asked Parham to lay hands on her 'to receive the Holy Spirit'. At first he demurred, 'not having the experience [him]self', but after he prayed, 'a glory fell upon her' and she spoke in tongues, not being able to speak in English for three days.[18]

The significance of the story is not so much its historicity, details of which are in doubt, but its mythic status in the recounting of Pentecostal origins. Indeed one of the divergences between the Ozman retelling and Parham's is the search for biblical evidence. Parham sets his Bible assignment as the triggering event of the new Pentecost. Ozman, on the other hand, adds the biblical search as her personal effort to understand her experience after the fact. On either reading, the mythic significance of the tale is the ultimacy of Scripture as objective standard. The fact

17. This is not to suggest the support would be unanimous. Represented among early Pentecostals was every stripe of Holiness come-outer, the most extreme of whom were virtually completely given to guidance by immediate impressions; Charles E. Jones, 'Anti-Ordinance: A Proto-Pentecostal Phenomenon?' *WTJ* 25 (1990), pp. 7–23 (pp. 11, 13 and 15–16).

18. Parham's testimony is recorded in Gordon Atter's *The Third Force*, pp. 24–26. Agnes Ozman's recollection of the event is found in Frodsham, *With Signs Following*, pp. 19–21. Goff outlines the troubles with synchronizing both accounts; *Fields White Unto Harvest*, pp. 66–75. An early account appears in the first issue of *The Apostolic Faith* from Azusa Street; 'Pentecost Has Come', *AF* 1 (September, 1906), p. 1.

that the story is most often told with Scripture as the primary motivator for seeking the biblical experience that magical night in Topeka, enshrines the Pentecostal attitude towards literal fulfilments of what are seized as external, divine promises.

Whatever early Pentecostals thought of their experience of Spirit baptism, and the supernatural, they did not imagine it to be ultimate; rather, they understood what they were experiencing as Scriptural, and took great confidence from the fact that 'this is that which was spoken of by the prophet Joel'. Before hastily rejecting such an approach as simplistic, self-aggrandizing and demonstrably a theology of glory; the received interpretation of Luther's ideas, institutionalized in the Formula of Concord bears examination. The Form urges 'the elect' not to oppose the Spirit, but rather to 'confirm their call and election' so that *the more they experience the power and might of the Spirit within themselves, the less they will doubt their election*. For the Spirit testifies to the elect that they are 'children of God' (Rom. 8.16). And if perchance they should fall into such grave temptation that they feel that they are no longer experiencing any power whatever of the indwelling Spirit of God and say with David, 'I had said in my alarm, I am driven far from thy sight' (Ps. 31.22), then, regardless of what they experience within themselves, they should nevertheless join David in the next words, 'But thou didst hear my supplications when I cried to thee for help.'[19]

The argument seems clear. Spiritual experiences of power are authenticating, confirming gifts of grace. As such, they fit Bonhoeffer's criterion of the penultimate: they prepare the way for the coming of the Lord. 'The penultimate, therefore, does not negate the freedom of the ultimate; instead the freedom of the ultimate empowers the penultimate.'[20] But, when experience fails, when it is tested, and overwhelmed by temptation, crisis and circumstance, the Formula of Concord advises recourse to God's Word, 'regardless of what they experience within themselves'.[21]

Pentecostalism as it institutionalized, and in its later permutations, in the charismatic and neocharismatic movements, has had a struggle maintaining this balance. On the one hand, Peter Neumann has shown that at the theological level, a hallmark of maturing of Pentecostal study has been the increasing embrace of the notion of mediated experience, which in turn has enabled it to interact more ecumenically in theological conversation.[22] On the other, Pentecostalism, as currently configured, at least at the popular level, will always be open to claims

19. 'The Formula of Concord: Solid Declaration' (1577), art. xi, par. 73, *BC*, p. 628.

20. Bonhoeffer, *Ethics*, p. 160.

21. 'The Formula of Concord: Solid Declaration' (1577), art. xi, par. 73, *BC*, p. 628. It should be noted that while early Pentecostals, and other theologically conservative Christians used the terms 'Scripture' and 'Word' interchangeably, Luther did not. For the nuances of Luther's doctrine of the Word, see Althaus, *Theology of Martin Luther*, pp. 35–42; and Lohse, *Luther's Theology*, pp. 189–91.

22. Peter D. Neumann, 'Encountering the Spirit: Pentecostal Mediated Experience of God in Theological Context', (Ph.D. diss.; University of St. Michael's College, 2010), p. 17.

of immediacy. The Latter Rain Movement arose in 1948 as a reaction to the institutionalizing of Pentecostalism. Richard M. Riss suggests that it be interpreted against the background of a broader evangelical spiritual awakening occurring about mid-century, but its distinctly anti-denominational tone, and broadly restorationist agenda nevertheless pitted it in a showdown with Pentecostal denominations.[23] At the heart of the power struggle that the Latter Rain created, was the claim to embodying the true Latter Rain, and the restoration of the full panoply of spiritual gifting, including all nine charismata of 1 Cor. 12, and the offices of apostle and prophet as in Ephesians 4. One leader even saw the current movement as preparatory for a 'THIRD OUTPOURING which shall finally bring the FULLNESS . . . this third great work of the Spirit shall usher a people into full redemption – free from the curse, sin, sickness, death and carnality'.[24] These comments are illustrative of the unbridled restorationism (and perfectionism) of Pentecostal immediacy, and reflect its reaction against the attenuated immediacy of institutionalizing Pentecostalism. They also presage some of the recurring themes of popular Pentecostal spirituality.

c. Experience and the Restoration of Apostles and Prophets

Many leaders of the Latter Rain Movement were instrumental in the emergence of the charismatic renewal, and have had an influence in the neocharismatic Third Wave.[25] Paul Cain is a paradigmatic example. His Latter Rain pedigree is irreproachable. He was noted as a youngster to have inherited the prophetic enabling of his grandmother.[26] Eventually, as a young man, Cain's prophetic gifting earned him a role with William Branham, the power of whose services, David Edwin Harrell said, 'remains a legend unparalleled in the history of the charismatic movement'.[27] Cain's ministry spans the charismatic movement and climaxed in

23. Richard M. Riss, *Latter Rain: The Latter Rain Movement of 1948 and the Mid-Twentieth Century Evangelical Awakening* (Mississauga: Honeycomb Visual Productions, 1987). For the Evangelical awakening, see chapter 2, pp. 17–47. For the essential anti-denominationalism of the movement, see pp. 76–78; for struggles with denominations, pp. 79–80, 93–95, 99–109 and 117–31. See also Riss' article, 'Latter Rain Movement' in *NIDPCM*, pp. 830–33.

24. Riss, *Latter Rain*, p. 143.

25. Peter Hocken, *The Challenges of the Pentecostal, Charismatic, and Messianic Jewish Movements: The Tensions of the Spirit* (Ashgate New Critical Thinking in Religion, Theology, and Biblical Studies; Aldershot, UK: Ashgate, 2009), pp. 43–49, summarizes the historical development of the current apostolic and prophetic movements.

26. David Pytches, *Some Said It Thundered: A Personal Encounter with the Kansas City Prophets* (Nashville: Oliver-Nelson, 1991), p. 24.

27. David Harrell, *All Things Are Possible: The Healing and Charismatic Revivals in Modern America* (Bloomington: Indiana University Press, 1979), p. 162; cf. Pytches, *Some Said It Thundered*, p. 28.

his involvement with a group of prophetic ministries emanating from the Kansas City Fellowship. Between 1988 and 1990, the 'Kansas City Prophets' exercised a significant influence over John Wimber, and the Vineyard, thus deepening the restorationist agenda in the Third Wave.[28] The emphasis on restoration, particularly, but not solely, among neocharismatics, becomes notably more pronounced after 1990. Bill Hamon, a leading prophetic voice, claims that the restoration of prophets was followed by that of apostles, begun in that year. These must precede the final stage, 'the Day of the Saints'. the release of a fully restored and empowered church to usher in the day of the Lord.[29] The similarities between the current Apostolic networks and the mid-century Latter Rain movement are apparent.

The power of these restored ministries flows from their claim to unmediated revelation from God. C. Peter Wagner, a pioneer in the current apostolic renewal points out that 'Apostles, when correctly related to prophets, receive revelation from God and consequently are able to say, "This is what the Spirit is saying to the churches right now." Making such a statement with credibility carries with it tremendous authority.'[30] Wagner's definition implies that an apostle is uniquely prepared by his personal experience with God: 'An apostle is a Christian leader, gifted, taught, commissioned and sent by God.'[31] Among the 12 tasks he lists for an apostle, the first that Wagner cites is that they receive revelation, some of which comes to them directly, some of which is received with prophets or in proper relation to prophets.[32] This emphasis has resulted in apostolic networks for the proper recognition of apostles, and the discernment of apostolic leading for the church.[33]

The theology of the cross reminds the believer that experiences and feelings are fickle, uncertain, requiring interpretation.[34] As William Hordern commented, 'Christian experience is not simply some inner, mystical, ecstatic feeling; Christian experience is any experience (including hauling manure) of a person who has faith in Christ.'[35] With its emphasis on the hiddenness of God, the theology of the

28. Bill Jackson, 'A Short History the Association of Vineyard Churches', in *Church, Identity, and Change: Theology and Denominational Structures in Unsettled Times* (ed. David A. Roozen and James R. Nieman; Grand Rapids: Eerdmans, 2005), pp. 132–40 (p. 147).

29. Bill Hamon, *The Day of the Saints: Equipping Believers for Their Revolutionary Role in Ministry* (Shippensberg, PA: Destiny Image, 2002), pp. 149–70.

30. Peter C. Wagner, *Apostles Today: Biblical Government for Biblical Power* (California: Regal Books, 2012), p. 24.

31. Ibid., p. 27.

32. Ibid., p. 28.

33. Ibid., pp. 94–95.

34. 'There is no such thing as uninterpreted experience, nor is there any "awareness" unmediated by the community of discourse to which those who claim such awareness belong'; Dabney, 'Saul's Armor', p. 123.

35. Hordern, *Experience and Faith*, p. 105.

cross encourages a self-critical hermeneutic of suspicion concerning the ultimacy of experience and personal interpretation.[36] Mary M. Solberg, writing from a distinctly feminist perspective suggests four significant questions.

1. What does this approach say about power?
2. What does it say about experience?
3. What does it say about objectivity?
4. What role does accountability play?[37]

These questions apply generally to epistemology, but particularly to an epistemology of the cross. They represent the kenotic trajectory of a *pneumatologia crucis*.

I wish to quickly survey Solberg's insights regarding these questions as they may be applied to the restorationist claim of unmediated revelation. First, Solberg claims that 'power-epistemology' resists the humiliation of doubt, ambiguity and limits of human knowledge.[38] Without an epistemology of the cross, knowledge becomes 'power-as-domination'. Among fallen humans, claims to unmediated revelation, if accepted, carry, as Wagner indicated, 'tremendous authority'. Without censuring specific individuals, it is not difficult to imagine the possibilities of abuse within such ecclesial systems.[39] Experience, also is a limited source of knowledge, because in our fallen world, and with our fallen interpretive grids, 'experience "lies"'.[40] This raises questions of objectivity for the knowledge of those in privileged positions. In kenotic fashion, an epistemology of the cross forces the critique of top-down knowing, and advocates knowledge from the foot of the cross, a knowing in solidarity with the marginalized. In charismatic communities where significant authority has been given to endowed leaders, significant openness to

36. Moltmann raises the epistemological consequences of embracing a theology of the cross: 'It does not promise the confirmation of one's own conceptions, hopes and good intentions. It promises first of all the pain of repentance and fundamental change. It offers no recipe for success. But it brings a confrontation with the truth. It is not positive and constructive, but is in the first instance critical and destructive. It does not bring man into a better harmony with himself and his environment, but into contradiction with himself and his environment'; Moltmann, *Crucified God*, p. 39.

37. Solberg, *Compelling Knowledge*, p. 109.

38. Ibid., p. 110. Solberg, of course, is considering power structures such as privileged white Western dominance in developing countries, and feminist concerns generally. The application of her observations within a charismatic context, I believe, is appropriate.

39. See Rodiguez, 'Biblical Oversight', who questions the authoritarian style of leadership among neopentecostal leaders in a manner that might be suggested by a theology of the cross.

40. Sandra Harding, *Whose Science? Whose Knowledge? Thinking from Women's Lives* (Ithaca, NY: Cornell University Press, 1991), p. 311, cited in Solberg, *Compelling Knowledge*, p. 109.

reflection from those outside the leadership cadre is an essential corrective.[41] For Solberg, accountability implies an admission of the 'knower's' complicity with the brokenness of the world and the church.[42]

These insights rest on the recovery of both a *pneumatologia crucis* and an *eschatologia crucis* in place of restorationism and perfectionism. Prophetic and apostolic gifts, if they are to be received as genuine, must come to terms with the limitations of human existence, and charismatic experience. A pneumatology of the cross begins with the profound foot-washing humility of servant-leadership. It acknowledges the gifting of others, as well as oneself, but recalls that at the best of times such gifts can only be mediated through flawed human vessels. These are among the limits of the New Testament gift of prophecy, which requires community evaluation (1 Cor. 14.29), but prophecy's limits have eschatological dimensions as well. The gifts are a foretaste, but only a distant shadow of what is to come. The believer in the present age sees only 'through a glass darkly' (1 Cor. 13.12 KJV). The metaphor conveys the incompleteness and indirectness of contemporary prophecy, since at best we can only know or prophesy 'in part'.[43] The partiality of New Testament prophecy will be done away in the *eschaton*, when the *teleion* comes. Thus, while always open to the power of religious experience, the theology of the cross denies the triumphalism that confidently asserts unmediated experiences of power, revelation and glory.[44] The cross and the Word remain ultimate; experience, prophecies, apostolic direction: these gifts must remain penultimate, if Pentecostalism is to experience a fruitful future.

d. Experience and the New Pentecostal Hermeneutic

Much of the current theological discussion regarding a Pentecostal hermeneutic involves a significant emphasis on the Holy Spirit and experience in the interpretative process.[45] Amos Yong writing in a non-Pentecostal context, and Kenneth Archer addressing Pentecostals both promote a similar three-sided process that involves the Word, the Holy Spirit, and the faith community in a trialectic (Yong) or tridactic (Archer) process of appropriating meaning. These strategies for negotiating

41. Ibid., p. 118.

42. Ibid., p. 123.

43. Wayne Grudem, *The Gift of Prophecy: In the New Testament and Today* (Eastbourne, UK: Kingsway, 1988), pp. 101–2.

44. Hordern, *Experience and Faith*, p. 93.

45. Lest one should imagine that such paradigms are exclusively in use among twenty-first-century Pentecostals, note, for example, the words of Mennonite theologian John Howard Yoder's written in 1985, '[I]n the juxtaposition of those [biblical] stories with our stories there leaps the spark of the Spirit, illuminating parallels and contrasts, to give us the grace to see our age in God's light and God's truth in God's words'; John Howard Yoder, 'The Use of the Bible in Theology', in *The Use of the Bible in Theology: Evangelical Options* (ed. Robert K. Jonston; Atlanta: John Knox, 1985), p. 113. Gabriel Fackre explores the

meaning owe much to semiotics and postmodern theory. Yong anticipates that the in-breaking of the Spirit 'enables us to break out of' our limited imaginations to offer 'alternative hermeneutical horizons and vistas by which we approach both tradition and the biblical text'.[46] Luther, himself an experiential theologian, also anticipates the necessity of the Spirit's work in existentially grasping the Word: 'It is not enough for someone to preach the word to me, but only God can put it into my heart. He must speak it in my heart, or nothing at all will come of it. If God remains silent, the final effect is as though nothing had been said.'[47] The key in Luther's thought is that Word is ultimate, experience must remain penultimate. To this, Yong appears to agree. Having come to a second naiveté has taught Pentecostal scholars that 'even their experiences of the Spirit are mediated by Scripture . . . and ecclesial traditions'.[48] Tridactic or trialectic methodologies may thus yield legitimate understandings according to the theology of the cross, inasmuch as they properly assess the power of experience for negotiating meaning as penultimate and the text of Scripture as ultimate.

The restorationist impulse in Pentecostalism has often resorted to the elevation of charismatic experience from penultimate to ultimate. It has made biblical interpretation a servant to experience, along the way accounting for some of the more bizarre extremes of Pentecostal spirituality, and at times, even doctrinal teaching. I have argued that the ultimacy of the Word functions as a proper safeguard against the vagaries of unmediated experience. But I have not done so at the expense of experience itself – nor does Luther. The place of experience as penultimate and preparatory, or perhaps better, in Luther's terms, interpretive, or quickening, is not in question, but rather is enhanced.

II. Replacing Perfectionism: Salvation and Human Perfectibility

Perfectionism casts a long shadow in the Pentecostal ethos. It informs significant dimensions of the development of spirituality, doctrine and theology. The Finished Work controversy of 1910 was the first major schism in the emergent Pentecostal movement. It pitted the Wesleyan notion of entire sanctification against a less definitive, more gradual appropriation. William Durham insisted that all the benefits of salvation, including sanctification flowed from the finished work of Christ on Calvary's cross, and were fully the believer's at regeneration, though

limitations and benefits of evangelical narrative theology in 'Narrative Theology from an Evangelical Perspective'. See also the fine article; Thomas A. Harvey, 'Narrative Theology', in *GDT*, pp. 598–602.

46. Yong, 'The Word and the Spirit', p. 248.

47. 'Sermons of 1522', *WA* 10.3, p. 260; 'Sermons of 1525', *WA* 17.2, p. 174, cited in Althaus, *Theology of Martin Luther*, p. 39.

48. Yong, 'The Word and the Spirit', p. 248. Archer explains Ricouer's notion of 'second naiveté' with his own hermeneutical journey in *Pentecostal Hermeneutic*, p. 10.

they must be appropriated by the individual progressively.[49] The controversy led to the emergence of three-step Holiness Pentecostal denominations (the Church of God, Cleveland, TN; the Pentecostal Holiness Church; and the Church of God in Christ) and two-step, Finished Work denominations (the Assemblies of God and the Pentecostal Assemblies of Canada).

a. Non-Wesleyan Pentecostal Perfectionism

Despite this outward division, both groups entertained optimistic notions of human perfectibility. Robert Mapes Anderson interpreted the Finished Work movement as, to some extent, an effort to relate Pentecostalism to emerging Fundamentalism. In fact, Anderson judged that Durham's view was largely similar to those of Torrey, Chapman, Simpson and other Keswick-Fundamentalists of their day.[50] As Peter Althouse summarizes the fundamental distinction, the two seem very close in their notion of human perfectibility: 'Wesleyanism taught that the soul itself was delivered from sin in sanctification, while Keswick taught that the believer was not made holy because sin remained in the heart, but that one could live a victorious life over sin.'[51] While Durham was adamantly opposed to a second sanctifying work of grace, there is no doubt that he anticipated that true salvation entailed victory over sin.[52] And for Durham this was essential because

49. Richard M. Riss, 'Finished Work Controversy', in *NIDPCM*, pp. 638–39.

50. Anderson, *Vision of the Disinherited*, p. 173. More recent study implies that Durham was in fact an eradicationist, the novelty of his approach surrounding his conviction that eradication occurred at conversion; Frank D. Macchia, 'Baptized in the Spirit: A Global Pentecostal Theology', in *Defining Issues in Pentecostalism: Classical and Emergent* (McMaster Theological Studies Series, vol. 1; ed. Steven M. Studebaker; Eugene, OR: Pickwick, 2008), pp. 13–28 (p. 6).

51. Peter Althouse, 'Wesleyan and Reformed Impulses in the Keswick and Pentecostal Movements', *The Pneuma Review* (1995). Online: http://pneumareview.com/peter-althouse-wesleyan-and-reformed-impulses-in-the-keswick-and-pentecostal-movements/ (Accessed 14 August 2014).

52. 'We agree with all who teach that without holiness no man shall see the Lord . . . but we do not agree with them that it takes two works of grace to make a man holy. . . . When God saves a man He does a complete work, not a halfway work.' Durham anticipated that professed Christians who sinned would have to come to God as unsaved sinners. 'If, through our weakness, we get from under the precious Blood, one or even more times, after conversion, it is necessary for us to humble ourselves before God and get back; but we can only approach Him, as at the first, through the precious Blood of Christ, as one who has sinned, and not as a justified person.' Durham held that God 'expects us to yield to the Holy Spirit continually, that He will have full control of our faculties'. This view is remarkably similar to the Keswick position in seeing the work tied to Christ and his cross, but not unlike the Holiness view in anticipating eradication of the sin nature, though not in a second experience. In some ways, Durham may be more extreme than both other

power followed purity, and God's purpose was to restore a powerful church at the service of humanity.[53]

Durham's perfectionism became somewhat attenuated over the period of institutionalization. Myer Pearlman, for instance, was able to speak of absolute and relative perfection, the former belonging to God alone, the latter to humans. 'That is relatively perfect which fulfills the end for which it was designed; this perfection is possible to man.' Indeed, Pearlman goes on to admonish, 'Both views, perfection as a gift in Christ and perfection as an actual work wrought in us, are taught in the Scriptures; what Christ has done for **us** must be wrought **in** us.'[54] Doctrinally inculcated in Bible Colleges, this notion of perfectibility filtered down to the popular spirituality of Pentecostalism. The charismatic movement, however, eventually tempered some of the soteriological perfectionism of Pentecostalism. Former Church of God in Christ pastor Conny Williams left her classical Pentecostal background because 'People were going to hell every Sunday and "getting saved" every Sunday. And the Charismatic movement moved in and said, "Hey . . . your salvation is secure. You are saved. God is excited about you!"'[55] Perfectionism, however, reared its head in other ways among charismatics, touching on healing and the life of faith.

Among Pentecostals, though, even the so-called Reformed-leaning Assemblies of God, perfectionism has remained a doctrinal category. Until 1961, the original Statement of Fundamental Truths (adopted in 1916) carried a statement on 'Entire Sanctification' though it steered from a second-work-of-grace position as the Wesleyan churches had adopted. This was in keeping with Finished Work theology.[56] As late as 1987, and again in a 1996 reprint, Stanley Horton could

viewpoints. All Durham citations from Jacobsen, *Thinking in the Spirit*, pp. 145, 157–58 and 159.

53. Ibid., p. 162.

54. Pearlman, *Knowing the Doctrines*, pp. 263 and 266.

55. Timothy Sims, *In Defense of the Word of Faith: An Apologetic Response to Encourage Charismatic Believers* (Bloomington, IL: AuthorHouse, 2008), p. 38. Many baby-boomers raised in Pentecostal circles can recall this as the unofficial soteriology of Pentecostal churches, both Wesleyan and non-Wesleyan.

56. Stanley M. Horton, 'The Pentecostal Perspective', in *Five Views on Sanctification* (ed. Stanley Gundry; Counterpoint; Grand Rapids: Zondervan, [1987] 1996), pp. 103–35 (pp. 110 and 112). The Canadian situation was interestingly somewhat different. PAOC's Statement of Fundamental and Essential Truths was not adopted until the 1927 General Conference; Miller, *Canadian Pentecostals*, p. 120. Both R. E. McAlister with Holiness roots, and Dr J. Eustace Purdie, who was educated by Keswick scholars at the Anglican Wycliffe College, claimed primary authorship of the document (R. E. McAlister, Letter to C. B. Smith, 22 January 1946, cited in Miller, *Canadian Pentecostals*, p. 120; Purdie, Letter to C. M. Wortman, 26 April 1955, 'Statement of Fundamental and Essential Truths File'). However the document arose, it managed a remarkable compromise between Holiness and Keswick paths. It calls entire sanctification 'the will of God for all believers', claims

still cite former General Superintendent Ernest Swing Williams who wrote in his systematic theology that the believer is empowered to live above sin and self-will. Horton asserts that the believer can live a life of victorious conquest over the temptation to sin by daily surrender.[57] How far this differs in practical terms from holiness eradication, or Keswick suppression is unclear.[58] What is clear, however, is that it is not a 'static plateau of perfectionism'. [59] Sanctification begun in this way is still an ongoing process of growth, understanding and struggle.

b. Perfectibility, Sanctification and the Cross

The precise nature of the Assemblies of God idea of sanctification is made confusing because of its reluctance to address the question and extent of sin in the believer. Pentecostalism appears to say with other Christian traditions that the believer is restored to a state of *posse non peccare* (able not to sin). But, by its ambiguity on the matter, it resists adjudicating on the question of whether the sanctified believer is also *non posse peccare* (not able to sin), and therefore liable to the loss of salvation in the event of sin, or conversely also *posse peccare* (able to sin), yet still retaining salvation.[60] And if the latter, at what point is salvation in danger? In this way Pentecostals experience Douglas John Hall's tension of expectancy and experience. At the popular level, the Spirit-filled believer lives with the anticipation of victory over temptation and sin, but the harsh experience of reality threatens her with defeat, unless she can redefine sin in ways that she remains unaware of the intransigence of human brokenness. For instance the sanctified North American believer may be unaware of his active complicity with oppressive systems of western injustice, but once made aware how will he extricate

that it is both instantaneous and progressive, and asserts that 'it is wrought out in the life of the believer by his appropriation of the power of Christ's blood and the person of the Holy Spirit'; Pentecostal Assemblies of Canada, *Constitution and By-Laws of the Pentecostal Assemblies of Canada* (London, ON: N.p. 1928), p. 17.

57. Horton, 'The Pentecostal Perspective', pp. 112, 114 and 124.

58. Representing the Keswick view, J. Robertson McQuilkin comments on Horton's paper with surprise at how little the Pentecostal position differs from Keswick; J. Robertson McQuilkin, 'Response to Horton', in *Five Views on Sanctification* (ed. Stanley Gundry; Counterpoint; Grand Rapids: Zondervan, [1987] 1996), pp. 143–45 (p. 144); Horton, 'The Pentecostal Perspective', pp. 131–32. On the other hand Melvin Dieter, writing from the Holiness position finds Horton's uses of the term 'entire sanctification' gratifyingly Wesleyan; Melvin Dieter, 'Response to Horton', in *Five Views on Sanctification* (ed. Stanley Gundry; Grand Rapids: Zondervan, 1987, 1996), pp. 136–38 (pp. 137–38).

59. William Menzies, 'The Spirit of Holiness', *Paraclete* 2 (1968), p. 15 cited in Horton, 'The Pentecostal Perspective', p. 124.

60. Horton admits that some Pentecostal writers believe that 'through the Holy Spirit we are able not to sin, even though we never come to the place where we are not able to sin'; ibid., p. 125.

himself from them? And if incapable of freeing oneself, is one still living in victory? If one's concept of sin does not include injustice, how biblical is such a notion theologically? If it does, how can one ever escape the essential incommensurability of the human predicament?

The problem is exacerbated by the plague of moral scandal that has attended a number of celebrity-status leaders in Pentecostal-Charismatic circles. When those perceived paragons of victorious Christian living, and especially those who claim supernatural attestation of their leadership, fall into public moral failure and yet continue in ministry, a measure of cognitive dissonance occurs at the level of popular spirituality. My concern here is not with church discipline or pastoral restoration, but rather with the tension between expectation and experience which is created. In the trickle-down formation of popular spirituality, so important among Pentecostals (and Evangelicals as well) the result is confusion on the topics of sanctification and charismatic leadership. Thus among believers generally the shift between older paradigms of holiness and contemporary ideas of spiritual freedom is furthered, at times eroding significant biblical principles.[61] As it concerns spiritual leadership, evaluations begin to be made more on pragmatic grounds of effectiveness or reputed claims to supernatural manifestation rather than character, spirituality and theological soundness.

The theology of the cross does not allow the believer to be delivered from the paradox of Christian holiness. On the one hand, it holds humanity to the highest and most perfectionist standard, on the other, it acknowledges that the only pure holiness comes from Christ. Luther's soteriology makes a distinction between grace (*gratia*, *favor*) and gift (*donum*). Finnish theologian Simo Peura points out that Luther sees these two as counteracting two evils. Grace deals with God's wrath by forensic righteousness, gift deals with human corruption by *renovatio*, the effective renewal of the sinner.[62] Luther clarifies how the two work in his 'Preface to Romans'.

> Between grace and gift there is this difference. Grace actually means God's favor, or the good will which in himself he bears toward us, by which he is disposed to give us Christ and to pour into us the Holy Spirit with his gifts. . . . The gifts and the Spirit increase in us every day, but they are not yet perfect since there remain in us the evil desires and sins that war against the Spirit, as he says in Romans 7[:5ff.] and Galatians 5[:17], and the conflict between the seed of the woman and the seed of the serpent, as foretold in Genesis 3[:15]. Nevertheless grace does so

61. For reference to the shift of traditional values among Pentecostals, see Poloma, *The Assemblies of God*, pp. 161–67 and 194–95.

62. Simo Peura, 'Christ as Favor and Gift: The Challenge of Luther's Understanding of Justification', in *Union with Christ: The New Finnish Interpretation of Luther* (ed. Carl E. Braaten, and Robert M. Jenson; Grand Rapids: Eerdmans, 1998), pp. 42–69 (pp. 42, 44 and 47). Peura argues that the Formula of Concord and modern Lutheranism have not adequately come to terms with Luther's concept of *donum*.

> much that we are accounted completely righteous before God. For his grace is not divided or parceled out, as are the gifts, but takes us completely into favor for the sake of Christ our Intercessor and Mediator. And because of this, the gifts are begun in us.[63]

The distinction between Christ's work *pro nobis* through forensic justification and his work *in nobis* by way of his presence within, through faith, by the Holy Spirit is a characteristic feature of the Finnish school of Luther studies. Inaugurated by Tuomo Mannermaa, the Finnish school links Luther's central soteriological affirmation with an ontological union with Christ by faith. '[Faith] takes hold of Christ in such a way that Christ is the object of faith, or rather not the object but, so to speak, the One who is present in the faith itself.'[64]

A fascinating, if controversial, aspect of Mannermaa's work is the thesis that a concept very similar in nature to the Orthodox concept of *theosis* is implicit in Luther's theology. According to Mannermaa, the patristic doctrine of *theosis*, asserts that (i) divine life has been manifested in Christ; (ii) in the body of Christ, the church, humans participate in this life; (iii) as leaven permeates dough, humans become partakers in the divine nature (2 Pet. 1.4) thereby restoring the divine image.[65] This idea of participation in Christ becomes a key to reinterpreting Luther's concept of justification and sanctification. Ed Rybarczyk has noted the parallel between Pentecostal spirituality and the mystical spirituality of Orthodoxy. He indicates that Orthodox teaching on *theosis* involves synergy between the Spirit's energy and the believer's energy.[66] What is fascinating in the present context, though, is the similarity and dissimilarity between Luther's idea of union with Christ and the Keswick idea of victorious Christian living.

Keswick places the provision for victorious Christian living in the believer's identification with Christ, offering 'the possibility of consistent success in resisting temptation to violate deliberately the known will of God'.[67] This occurs through

63. 'Preface to the Epistle of St. Paul to the Romans' (1522), *LW* 35:369. Stephan K. Turnbull, 'Grace and Gift in Luther and Paul', *W&W* 24 (2004), pp. 305–14, demonstrates the consistency of this paradigm across a varied sample of Luther's writings, over time and genre.

64. 'Lectures on Galatians, Chapters 1–4' (1535), *LW* 26:129. See Tuomo Mannermaa, *Christ Present in Faith: Luther's View of Justification* (trans. Kirsi Stjerna; Minneapolis: Augsburg Fortress, 2005).

65. Tuomo Mannermaa, 'Justification and *Theosis* in Lutheran-Orthodox Perspective', in *Union with Christ: The New Finnish Interpretation of Luther* (ed. Carl E. Braaten and Robert M. Jenson; Grand Rapids: Eerdmans, 1998), pp. 25–41 (p. 26).

66. Edmund Rybarczyk, 'Spiritualities Old and New: Similarities between Eastern Orthodoxy and Classical Pentecostalism', *Pneuma* 24 (2002), pp. 7–25 (pp. 10 and 13–14).

67. J. Robertson McQuilkin, 'The Keswick Perspective', in *Five Views on Sanctification* (ed. Stanley Gundry; Counterpoint; Grand Rapids: Zondervan, [1987] 1996), pp. 149–83 (pp. 154–55).

a mystical, existential living out of Christ's life through the believer, and that takes place only with total, moment-by-moment surrender to Christ.[68] Luther agrees that this ontological union is essential, but configures its expression very differently. 'Everything is forgiven through grace, but as yet not everything is healed through the gift.'[69] The Reformer recognizes the inherent weakness of the human constitution and takes a starkly realistic view of the situation. 'Sin is always present', he says, 'and the godly feel it'.[70] The struggle with sin is ongoing, but those who are aware of their weakness, because of their remaining internal uncleanness and actual failures, learn to find refuge in Christ, pleading for increasing faith and the supply of the Spirit by which they obtain victory.[71] When they fall into sin through weakness, or because, like Peter, David, and other saints, 'we are sometimes forsaken by the Holy Spirit [!]' there is always recourse to Christ: 'Therefore when the Law accuses and sin troubles, he looks to Christ; and when he has taken hold of Him by faith, he has present with him the Victor over the Law, sin, death and the devil – the Victor whose rule over all these prevents them from harming him'.[72] Victory for Luther, as with the Keswick view arises from Christ's ontological union with the believer, Christ's presence through faith, as Mannermaa has argued. But here the similarities end.

While Luther can use the word 'struggle', Keswick uses the term 'surrender'. The irony is how pitched a battle Keswick's surrender turns out to be, and how passive a strife is involved in Luther's struggle. Luther acknowledged a struggle with sin, and the believer's refuge in Christ. Keswick, however, sees struggle as part of the problem, offering faith in Christ's work as the solution.[73] The paradox of the matter is that Luther, in his talk of struggle, clearly affirms that Christians are saints 'not by active holiness but by passive holiness'; while the power of Keswick is found in the Christian's active participation in assuring that she lives in the full victory that is available to her.[74] Ontological union, Rybarczyk suggests, is not a typically Pentecostal category, thus while Luther, in comparative fashion to the Orthodox, roots transformation in the ontology of Christ, Pentecostals tend to focus on the work of Christ and the Christian's deliberate and active imitation

68. 'The unyielded person must surrender'; ibid., pp. 170–71; 'Any hope we have of demonstrating His glorious character through our lives is based on His living personally within us and providing us with all the resources of the God of the universe'; ibid., p. 174.

69. 'Against Latomus' (1521), *LW* 32:229.

70. 'Lectures on Galatians, Chapters 1–4' (1535), *LW* 26:133.

71. Struggle, 'Lectures on Galatians, Chapters 5–6' (1535), *LW* 27:86; weakness, 84, 86, 109 and 112; uncleanness, 86; refuge, faith, and Spirit, 86; victory, 82, 86.

72. 'Lectures on Galatians, Chapters 1–4' (1535), *LW* 26:133.

73. McQuilkin points to those who 'strive and struggle' for holiness of life, suggesting they have fallen short through self-dependence and a lack of faith; 'The Keswick Perspective', pp. 164–65. Likewise, he cites Steven Barabas chiding life-long struggle when what is needed is surrender, p. 154.

74. 'Lectures on Galatians, Chapters 5–6' (1535), *LW* 27:82.

of Christ through the power of the Spirit.[75] David Bundy cites early Pentecostal missionary Minnie Abrahams who, influenced by her Holiness background, wrote of the goal of life being 'union with Christ'. What is fascinating here is the essential upward movement of the spirituality Abrahams espouses: salvation, sanctification, baptism of the Holy Spirit and fire, spiritual struggle and eventually union with God. For Abrams, union with Christ still involves a theology of ascent.[76]

Sanctification through Christ's presence by faith is a predicate of the theology of the cross. This idea of ontological union with Christ implies first a 'nihilization' that destroys one's 'constant effort to make himself god and to justify himself'.[77] In the kenotic categories of *pneumatologia crucis*, this implies a self-emptying and a reduction of the self before the cross. 'It is impossible for a person not to be puffed up by his good works unless he has first been deflated and destroyed by suffering and evil until he knows that he is worthless and that his works are not his but God's.'[78] The Spirit of the cross prepares us for the reception of Christ as favour and gift. On the other hand, the *eschatologia crucis* turns the sanctification project upside down. The eschatological nature of sanctification is not so much that we are progressing to perfection, but rather that perfection is progressing towards us. Thus, sanctification is not the measure of our progress in grace, but grace's progress in us. The coming kingdom is overwhelming sin within us by the very grace that justifies completely.[79] The invasion of this eschatological grace, as it progresses within, causes the believer to love God more passionately and hate sin more thoroughly. The church is populated by Spirit people, God's people of the new age, becoming what they already are in Christ.[80]

For the Christian, questions of perfection are teleological. Ultimate perfection is wrapped in the *eschaton*, whose coming, since the day of Pentecost, has been upon us. Because the church is the Spirit-baptized eschatological community, it anticipates in experience the coming perfection as its incipient graces are bestowed. But whatever heuristic value concepts such as victory, surrender or consecration may have (and, certainly Luther is capable of using terms like them), they are not ultimately the agents of transformation. When theological paradigms make them such, they become tools of perfectionism. How total is my surrender? How absolute my victory? Have I consecrated myself enough? And if I have, how secure is my holiness, or

75. Rybarczyk, 'Spiritualities Old and New', pp. 17 and 18.

76. David Bundy, 'Visions of Sanctification: Themes of Orthodoxy in the Methodist, Holiness, and Pentecostal Traditions', *WTJ* 39 (2004), pp. 104–36 (pp. 129–31).

77. Mannermaa, 'Justification and *Theosis*', p. 39.

78. 'Heidelberg Disputation: Proof of Thesis 21' (1518), *LW* 31:53.

79. Gerhard O. Forde, 'The Lutheran View', in *Christian Spirituality: Five Views on Sanctification* (ed. Donald L. Alexander; Downers Grove: InterVarsity, 1988), pp. 13–32 (p. 29).

80. Gordon D. Fee, *God's Empowering Presence: The Holy Spirit in the Letters of Paul* (Peabody, MA: Hendrickson, 1994), p. 559; see pp. 803–6 for a fundamental understanding of Paul's emphasis on the 'eschatological Spirit'.

how profound? Does it search the inner recesses of my own self-doubt? The crisis of expectation and experience can only be fully defeated when 'Christ has become for us ... our righteousness, holiness and redemption' (1 Cor. 1.30). This is how the theology of the cross dispenses with the idea of human perfectibility in this age.

III. The Pentecostal Nexus: The Miraculous as Sign

Pentecost, I have proposed, is the nexus between cross and *eschaton*. It mediates, by way of a pneumatology of the cross, the benefits of the cross event, and it anticipates, through an eschatology of the cross, the full perfection of all things. A conception of Spirit-fullness nourished by the theology of the cross becomes the pivotal experience for synthesizing both the forward- and backward-looking dynamics of the Christian faith in a way that erodes the claim of restorationism and perfectionism as theological sources of Pentecostalism. In Chapter 4, Acts 10.38 was set out as a programmatic paradigm for the Spirit-filled church. '[You know] how God anointed Jesus of Nazareth with the Holy Spirit and power, and how he went around doing good and healing all who were under the power of the devil, because God was with him.' If Luke's gospel is all Jesus *began* to do and teach, and the Book of Acts is what he *continued* to do, how should one account for the supernatural element of this ministry of the church?

Both restorationist and perfectionist impulses strongly condition Pentecostal anticipation of the miraculous. Supernatural manifestations are often seen as vindicating signs in Pentecostal circles. In what follows I wish to reconfigure these events as sacramental signs in a fashion that appeals to the theology of the cross, and Luther's notion of sacrament. I will begin by laying out the salient background from Luther, then I will examine Pentecostal motifs of 'sign' and through a consideration of tongues and healing I will reposition them, not as sacraments or signs, but as sacramental signs.

a. Luther, the Hiddenness of God and Sacrament

Pentecostals don't do sacraments. They prefer to think in terms of ordinances.

Moltmann complains that the concept of sacrament has been liable to misunderstanding among the church's multiple traditions. Orthodoxy does not limit the number of sacraments (though it often speaks of seven). Catholicism espouses seven carefully defined sacraments. The Protestant church has generally limited the number of sacraments to the two ordained by Christ himself.[81] While sacraments were perceived as 'means of grace', conveying some divine blessing *to* the recipient, the term ordinance, originally preferred by Radicals and, later, the English Baptists, focused more on commitments being made *by* the recipient in the memorial act.[82]

81. Moltmann, *Church in the Power of the Spirit*, pp. 199–200.

82. Stanley J. Grenz, *Theology for the Community of God* (Grand Rapids: Eerdmans, 1994), pp. 513–17, provides an excellent discussion of the concept of *ordinance*.

Shorn of any vestige of divine grace, ordinances risk being undervalued.[83] At times in more extreme circles given to experiences of spiritual immediacy, they have been completely jettisoned, as in the short-lived anti-ordinance movement among Holiness come-outers.[84] Recently, however, Pentecostal scholarship has found good reason to revisit the notion of sacrament.[85]

I would like to enter this conversation by way of Luther's conception of sacrament. For Luther a sacrament involves three converging elements. They can be traced in the following statements from *The Babylonian Captivity of the Church.*

> But our signs or sacraments, as well as those of the fathers, have attached to them a word of promise which requires faith, and they cannot be fulfilled by any other work. Hence they are signs or sacraments of justification, for they are sacraments of justifying faith and not of works.
>
> Thus it is not baptism that justifies or benefits anyone, but it is faith in that word of promise to which baptism is added. This faith justifies, and fulfils that which baptism signifies.
>
> For to constitute a sacrament there must be above all things else a word of divine promise, by which faith may be exercised. [86]

A sacrament, then, involves, first the promise of Scripture; second the outward sign; and finally the faith of the recipient. Sacrament, for Luther, is yet another predicate of the theology of the cross. The connection between the two is found in the notion of divine hiddenness. In a passage denying the sacramental nature of marriage, Luther clarifies this concept, discoursing on the idea of 'mystery' in Ephesians 5, translated in the Vulgate as 'sacrament'. Paul uses the word differently than the Roman church does, Luther says. '[W]herever it occurs [in the Holy

83. Ibid., pp. 514–15.

84. See the fascinating treatment by Charles Edwin Jones, 'Anti-Ordinance: A Proto-Pentecostal Phenomenon?'

85. The development of sacramental theology among Pentecostals is indebted to John Christopher Thomas who began sacramental exploration in *Footwashing in John 13 and the Johannine Community* (JSNTS 61; Sheffield: JSOT Press, 1991); and *The Devil, Disease, and Deliverance: Origins of Illness in New Testament Thought* (JPTSup 13; Sheffield: Sheffield Academic Press, 1998). He encouraged his colleagues to recover the sacramental in his presidential address to the Society of Pentecostal Studies; 'Pentecostal Theology in the Twenty-First Century', *Pneuma* 20 (Spring, 1998). Two of Thomas' students have produced significant monographs on the topic: Daniel Tomberlin, *Pentecostal Sacraments: Encountering God at the Altar* (Cleveland, TN: Center for Pentecostal Leadership and Care, Pentecostal Theological Seminary, 2010); and Chris E. W. Green, *Toward a Pentecostal Theology of the Lord's Supper: Foretasting the Kingdom* (Cleveland, TN: CPT Press, 2012).

86. 'The Babylonian Captivity of the Church' (1520), *LW* 36:65, 66 and 92.

Scriptures] it denotes not the sign of a sacred thing, but the sacred, secret, hidden thing itself.'[87]

> [S]acrament, or mystery, in Paul is that wisdom of the Spirit, hidden in a mystery, as he says in I Cor. 2[:7–8], which is Christ, who for this very reason is not known to the rulers of this world, wherefore they also crucified him. . . . Therefore, a sacrament is a mystery, or secret thing, which is set forth in words, but received by the faith of the heart.[88]

The two signs Luther will allow are baptism and communion. And in these common things, water, bread and wine, the God who has hidden himself from bare reason and immediate experience makes himself known. 'We teach not that the body and blood of Christ are visibly present in external things, but that they are hidden in the sacrament.'[89] As Steven Paulson puts it, 'God hides in order *not to be found* where humans want to find God. But God also hides *in order to be found* where God wills to be found.'[90] As opposed to the upward motif of worship expressed in ordinance as commitment, Luther's theology of sacrament captures the downward motif of the theology of cross. Thus, worship involves what Dennis Ngien has called a radical reversal. 'Hidden in the cross, where God is revealed not as most powerful but most weak, is the condition of the possibility of worship.'[91] The human tendency is to delight in the power and the glory, but the cross reminds that worship begins where God has shown himself to be *for us*, that he has entered into our pain and deigns in Word and sacrament to be found by faith.

One need not buy into Luther's entire theology of sacrament in order to enjoy his profound insights regarding the hiddenness and revelation of God in sacrament. It is well beyond the scope of this discussion to enter into the '*hoc est corpus meum*' debate or the issue of paedobaptism. Suffice to say here that God is in some way both hidden and active in sacraments, and that these religious rites become sacraments and make their power real through faith in the preached Word that accompanies them. The sign remains mere bread, wine, or water without Word and faith.

b. The Role of 'Sign' in Pentecostal Experience

The connection between Luther's theology of sacrament and the miraculous trades on word play around the concept of 'sign' in Pentecostal experience. The essential

87. Ibid., 36:93.

88. Ibid., 36:94; see also 36:32 where Luther claims that Christ is hidden under the 'accidents' or visible dimensions of the sacrament.

89. 'Against the Heavenly Prophets in the Matter of Images and Sacraments' (1525), *LW* 40:221.

90. Steven D. Paulsen, 'Luther on the Hidden God', *W&W* 19 (1999), pp. 363–71 (p. 366).

91. Dennis Ngien, *Gifted Response: The Triune God as the Causative Agency of Our Responsive Worship* (Milton Keynes, UK: Paternoster, 2008), p. 126.

role of signs was to confirm the correctness of the Pentecostal message and to give evidence of its continuity with the apostolic experience. In the first issue of *The Apostolic Faith*, William Seymour wrote concerning the role of signs.

> We that are the messengers of this precious atonement ought to preach all of it, justification, sanctification, healing, the baptism with the Holy Ghost, and signs following. 'How shall we escape if we neglect so great salvation?' God is now confirming His word by granting signs and wonders to follow the preaching of the full gospel in Los Angeles.[92]

In an article on the same page titled 'Tongues as a Sign', the argument proceeds to show how tongues in the Book of Acts provided evidence of Spirit baptism: 'We have been running off with blessings and anointings with God's power, instead of tarrying until Bible evidence of Pentecost came.'[93] This restorationist appeal to signs among early Pentecostals is illustrated by Charles Parham, who, seeking apostolic evidence, claimed, '[T]he chief evidence if you get the same experience is, that they "spake in tongues".'[94]

An argument can be made that there is currently a return to 'sign' talk as a better designation for tongues than 'initial evidence'. Frank Macchia suggests that 'sign' is a more appropriate term, citing voices as diverse as Michael Welker and Jack Hayford who prefer to avoid speaking of tongues as proof, whether as forensic evidence or scientifically empirical datum. 'Sign', in contemporary usage, carries a sacramental sense of God being made dynamically present in experience.[95] For early Pentecostals, though, signs were more evidential (as suggested above) and more prophetically indicative, than this sacramental view conveys. Allen Anderson rightly claims that Spirit baptism and the accompanying tongues were primarily a sign indicating that the end times had arrived.[96] Steven Land says, 'It was a sign to the whole church of the restoration of the "early rain" of apostolic power and gifts being restored in a "latter rain" for missionary activity.'[97]

But, as John Christopher Thomas and Kimberly Alexander show convincingly, early Pentecostals also saw manifestations of the Spirit as confirming signs. Citing Mark 16, they expected the driving out of demons, the healing of the sick, and

92. Seymour, 'The Precious Atonement', *AF* 1 (September, 1906), p. 2.

93. 'Tongues as a Sign', *AF* 1 (September, 1906), p. 2.

94. Parham, *Selected Sermons,* pp. 66 and 70; cited in Archer, *Pentecostal Hermeneutic,* p. 108.

95. Frank D. Macchia, 'Groans Too Deep for Words: Towards a Theology of Tongues as Initial Evidence', *AJPS* 1 (1998), pp. 149–73. Online: http://www.apts.edu/aeimages// File/AJPS_PDF/98-2-macchia.pdf (Accessed 15 August 2014). Roger Stronstad, writing in 2008, speaks of tongues as 'the attesting sign', the 'supernatural sign of being baptized in the Holy Spirit'; Stronstad, '*Charismatic Theology*', pp. 121–22.

96. Anderson, *Introduction*, p. 217.

97. Land, *Pentecostal Spirituality*, p. 111.

for some, even the handling of serpents as signs, indicators of the age to come.[98] As such these miraculous proofs were foretastes of the coming kingdom, but, more importantly, they provided confirmation of the truthfulness of Pentecostal assertion. If the full gospel was preached by sanctified, Spirit-filled vessels, then faith would anticipate the confirming signs. In time, this became a matter of faith assertion where the empirical evidence was lacking in the moment. Carrie Judd Montgomery saw the sign as a confirmation of a work already done, and recommended that faith affirmation be made, for instance, of receiving one's healing: 'I believe the sign of healing now follows or accompanies the laying on of hands in Thy Name.'[99] Thus the sign became not only an empirical demonstrator of the kingdom, and a confirmation of the truth of the full gospel, but also an assertion of faith of something not yet fully visible. Understood in these ways, one can readily see how the sign nature of these gifts played into triumphalist assumptions of Pentecostal immediacy. They were at once restorationist in their claimed continuity with the apostolic age, and perfectionist as they anticipated the here-and-now fullness of the *eschaton*.

The notion of 'sign' underwent further development in two apparently divergent directions in the Latter Rain Movement of the late 1940s and early 1950s. A large-scale charismatic revival arose in those years through a preponderance of healing evangelists, Oral Roberts, W. V. Grant, A. A. Allen and William Branham who were among the most popular. Historian David Edwin Harrell notes their admiration and imitation of D. L. Moody, Billy Sunday, and pre-eminently their contemporary, Billy Graham; but he indicates a fundamental difference: 'theirs was a signs-gift-healing, a salvation-deliverance, a Holy Ghost-miracle revival.'[100] Ministries such as those of William Branham and Hobart Freeman, for instance, were seen to be accredited by astounding signs and wonders, and their fame gave them increasingly large platforms for ministry.[101] While this was not unheard of in the day of Maria Woodworth-Etter, or F. F. Bosworth, or even later, Aimee Semple MacPherson, Smith Wigglesworth and Charles Price (the last two of whom died within a few days of each other in 1947); the Latter Rain emphasis on a decisively new move of God and all the gifts of the Spirit, especially prophecy, made this revival different.[102] In particular, it seemed to take 'signs' out of the province of the multitude, and place special callings and anointings on the elite.[103] Leaders were not those appropriately educated, nor those in positions of authority, but those with

98. Thomas and Alexander, 'And the Signs', pp. 152–53.

99. Montgomery, *Triumphs of Faith* 28 (May 1908), p. 99; cited in Thomas and Alexander, 'And the Signs', p. 155.

100. Harrell, *All Things Are Possible*, pp. 5–6.

101. Ibid., pp. 28–29 and 76.

102. Ibid., p. 20.

103. Branham's 'small band of followers [by the end of World War II] believed he was a man of destiny'; ibid., pp. 29; see also 27 and 37. Evangelists generally required some supernatural sign of accreditation. 'The evidence of his anointing was different for each

the most impressive anointing. In the independent churches (and megachurches) of the charismatic movement this continues to form a significant dimension of the leadership narrative.

On the other hand, the Latter Rain movement also promoted the vision of an anointed community of latter day men and women with unction to evangelize the world and overcome sickness, disease and demons.[104] They received the impartation of gifts through the laying on of hands, leading to increasingly radical offshoots such as the 'Manifested Sons of God' and 'Joel's Army', and in the 1980s, Earl Paulk's Kingdom Now, or dominion theology.[105] These were all expressions of the possibility that a group of 'overcomers' would receive 'redemptive bodies' that might even escape death, and bring about the kingdom here and now. Such a plan had an understandably limited shelf-life, and the deaths of leaders such as Branham undercut their growth. But here was prophetic triumphalism at the extreme: a restoration that went beyond the apostolic age, and a perfectionism that rivalled the *eschaton* itself! These were all minority motifs through early Pentecostalism, but they had now returned with a vengeance to challenge institutionalized Pentecostalism.[106]

It was the Third Wave, exemplified by John Wimber's Association of Vineyard Churches that most significantly democratized the notion of 'sign'. Rather than seeing sign as a vindicating or accrediting concept, or a matter of evidence or proof, signs and wonders acquired more fully the sense of proleptic markers of the kingdom.[107] Signs and wonders, according to Wimber and the early proponents of the Third Wave, were to be the normative experience of all believers, because all had been translated into the kingdom. This democratized Spirit-empowerment had been part of the original impulse of Azusa, it had been lost to some extent through the era of institutionalization, and while overshadowed by the emergence of divinely appointed superstars, was still advanced by the Latter Rain movement.[108]

evangelist – a feeling in his hand, an audible voice speaking to him, a vision, the presence of an angelic helper, or some other miraculous circumstance'; ibid., p. 86.

104. Riss, *Latter Rain*, p. 96.

105. Althouse, *Spirit in the Last Days*, pp. 58–59, see especially n. 141; see also Michael G. Moriarty, *The New Charismatics: A Concerned Voice Responds to Dangerous Trends* (Grand Rapids: Zondervan, 1992), pp. 74–76, who takes up the matter into the 1960s and 1970s, and pp. 92–95, 161–62 and 176–79 where he charts the perfectionist claims of dominion theology, a kind of charismatic postmillennialism.

106. Edith Blumhofer, *The Assemblies of God: A Chapter in the Story of American Pentecostalism* (2 vols; Springfield, MO: Gospel Publishing House, 1989), vol. 2, pp. 54, 62.

107. The first footnote in Wimber's *Power Evangelism* acknowledges his debt to George Eldon Ladd for whom the inaugurated eschatology of the kingdom represents the organizing principle of New Testament theology; Wimber, *Power Evangelism*, pp. 16, n. 1, see 175.

108. Poloma, 'Charisma and Structure', pp. 49–53. The General Council of the Assemblies of God passed resolutions in 1949 and 1999 condemning the perceived excesses of the

It received fresh impetus in the charismatic renewal with its emphasis on deploying one's spiritual gifts, but it is arguably demonstrable that Wimber has been the most prolific democratizer of signs and wonders.[109]

This latter notion of 'sign' proves to be more theologically fruitful than earlier constructs. Evidential signs are an end in themselves, and fail to offer further insight into the value or benefit of the sign. Whether forensic in the sense of providing proof that one has indeed been included in the eschatological community, or empirical in the sense of providing an objective datum of the Spirit's activity, such notions are hopelessly modern, and anachronistic to the first-century context. Still more limited is the conception of sign that must be affirmed by faith. But sign as '"proleptic foretaste" of the kingdom', takes on the sacramental feature of mediating the divine presence, without insinuating a triumphalist restoration of immediacy with the apostolic age, or a perfectionist ideal of the overcomer who has achieved sufficient sanctity to be the master of the charism.

c. Tongues as Sacramental Sign

The quintessential mark of twentieth-century Pentecostalism has been glossolalia. Yet Frank Macchia indicated in 1998 that tongues-speech had received little theological attention.[110] The situation has improved somewhat, and a few significant pieces have appeared that provide a basis for the reconsideration of glossolalia. I wish to propose an account of tongues, not as a sacrament, but sacramental. I mean by this that while glossolalia does not meet Luther's criteria for a sacrament, I will show that, as a sign, it possesses truly sacramental qualities.

Macchia, pre-eminently, has explored the sacramental nature of tongues-speech. He cites Morton T. Kelsey, in his ground-breaking *Tongue-Speaking*, and Karl Rahner's affirmation of religious enthusiasm as proponents of tongues as an unmediated experience of the divine that bypasses intellect and institutionalized

Latter Rain Movement, including the impartation of spiritual gifts at the hands of leaders, Commission on Doctrinal Purity, 'Endtime Revival – Spirit-Led and Spirit-Controlled', *EJ* (Spring, 2001). Online: http://enrichmentjournal.ag.org/200102/088_endtime_revival.cfm (Accessed 14 August 2014).

109. Wimber claimed, '[O]ur ministry style does not flow from the pre-war (sic) model of the faith healers. We are a body ministry.... The ministry is for everyone', John Wimber, 'Zip to 3,000', in *Signs and Wonders Today: The Story of Fuller Theological Seminary's Remarkable Course on Spiritual Power, New Expanded Edition* (ed. Peter Wagner; Altamonte Springs, FL: Creation House, 1987), pp. 27–39 (p. 34). Ronald Kydd commented, 'Most striking in his teaching was Wimber's "democratization" of healing. In the cases of most outstanding healing figures, their ministries were tied to them personally'; 'Healing in the Christian Church', in *NIDPCM*, pp. 694–711 (p. 702); see also Ronald Kydd, *Healing Through the Centuries: Models for Understanding* (Peabody, MA: Hendrickson, 1998), pp. 54–55.

110. Macchia, 'Groans to Deep'.

religion.[111] While Macchia adds a sacramental view of tongues alongside these ideas of immediacy, I wish to propose the notion of sacrament as mediated encounter as a replacement to these views. Macchia cuts through 'neo-scholastic Catholic' views of sacrament, appealing rather to Rahner and Edward Schillebeeckx and a theology of sacrament that focuses primarily on encounter with God.[112] Luther makes three requirements of a sacrament: biblical promise, humble sign and active faith. I believe Luther's definition of sacrament, as a development of the Augustinian view, offers valuable insight to Pentecostal reflection on the meaning of tongues.

Tongues-speech certainly has the biblical imprimatur of a diverse and confusing array of varied data. The Pentecostal experience undoubtedly involves biblical precedent, though one would be hard pressed to claim a biblical promise, or an ordinance of the Lord (Mark 16?) to accompany it. Neither does glossolalia carry a soteriological dimension in the way baptism or communion do. But the narrative accounts of divine encounter surrounding tongues in the Book of Acts, where it appears as a sign of Spirit baptism, and no less in 1 Corinthians 14, where Paul terms it 'utter[ing] mysteries by the Spirit', clearly bear witness to the presence of God experienced through an otherwise common medium: the sign of linguistic expression. Beyond this there is a faith dimension to tongues-speech. One speaks in tongues believing that the Word and sign imply that something divine is afoot. Some sort of mystery, occurs in the transcendence of tongue-speech. 'We do not know what we ought to pray for, but the Spirit himself intercedes for us through wordless groans' (Rom. 8.26).[113] God is present, hidden in the humility of tongues.

The term Macchia uses is theophany.[114] Bread and wine become, through promise and faith, theophanic signs that transmit body and blood; and water corresponds to death, grave and resurrection. The Day of Pentecost was marked by theophanies of a mighty rushing wind, and tongues of fire; and the Last Day promises blood, fire and billows of smoke. The chief theophanic sign of *Pentecost* is tongues. Just as the Last Supper, and the Lord's baptism, were literal episodes that foreshadowed his passion, glossolalia was present at *Pentecost*. But like the signs of bread, wine and water, it, too, continues as theophanic sign. Glossolalia then represents a tangible sign of the *eschatologia crucis*. It represents the eschatological

111. Frank D. Macchia, 'Tongues as a Sign: Towards a Sacramental Understanding of Pentecostal Experience', *Pneuma* 15 (1993), pp. 61–76 (p. 62).

112. Ibid., pp. 62–63.

113. See Frank D. Macchia, 'Sighs Too Deep For Words: Toward a Theology of Glossolalia', *JPT* 1 (1992), pp. 47–73 (pp. 59–60), and notes 37 and 38 to substantiate a consensus among some scholars (Gunkel, Käsemann, and Stendahl) that the sighs or groans of Romans 8 refer to glossolalia.

114. 'The kind of Pentecostal sacramental spirituality implied in tongues as initial sign arises from a theology that seems more "theophanic" than incarnational'; Macchia, 'Tongues as a Sign', p. 73 and 'Groans Too Deep'.

already and not yet which comes with signs and wonders displayed through the freedom of God. It also captures the mystery and awe of new life in the Spirit, disclosed in the existential encounter with Christ.[115]

But tongues also have a kenotic dimension, for the Spirit helps us with our weakness in these groans beyond utterance. Glossolalia is exceptionally well suited as a mark of the *pneumatologia crucis* as well. In the description of human frailty to contain the divine, the sacramental nature of tongues is once more conveyed.

> The closer one draws to the divine mystery, the more urgent it becomes to express oneself and, concomitantly, the less able one is to find adequate expression. This is the crisis out of which tongues breaks forth. Any attempt rationally to communicate the experience ends it, for to reflect upon and rationally communicate an experience is to distance oneself from it already. Tongues is a way of expressing the experience without ending it. The experience and the expression become one.[116]

Tongues is transrational prayer. These mysteries spoken by the Spirit transcend the natural cognitive process of communication (1 Cor. 14.14).[117] But the context of Romans 8 provides more profound resonances with our own weakness, and the groaning of creation itself. Once more, glossolalia finds itself in dialogue with the theology of the cross. For in the cross, the believer is not only invited into solidarity with the suffering of Christ, but with the suffering of the surrounding world. Charles Cousar captures this movingly:

> Even in their prayers, which might seem to offer moments of escape, the Spirit provokes an intercessory litany of groaning, joining the Christian's voices with the moans of the terminally ill who long for death, with the angry raging of the oppressed who seek freedom, with the whispers of the hopeless who have no strength left to cry.[118]

Tongues, then, becomes the unifying sign of the suffering, and the reminder that there is an eschatological end of anguish in which we already participate.

115. Frank D. Macchia, 'The Tongues of Pentecost: A Pentecostal Perspective on the Promise and Challenge of Pentecostal/Roman Catholic Dialogue', *JES* 35 (1998), pp. 1–18 (p. 11); 'Groans Too Deep'.

116. Macchia, 'Sighs Too Deep', p. 62.

117. See Randy Holm's discussion of Abraham Heschel's examination of *Kavanah* prayer as a kind of post-language; and Martin Buber's interest in the relation between spirit and language; Randy Holm, 'Tongues and a Postmodern Generation' (Unpublished paper, delivered at 'The Many Faces of Pentecostalism', McMaster University, 25 October 2008). Online: http://www.mts.net/~rfholm/spiritmcmaster.htm (Accessed 14 August 2014).

118. Cousar, *A Theology of the Cross*, p. 173. Cousar notes that whether glossolalia is in view here or not, is irrelevant to his point.

It is this dialectic of the eschatological and pneumatological in glossolalia that provides it with a revolutionary edge as power critique. Philosopher James K. A. Smith, contemplating tongues through the lens of speech-act theory, conceives of speaking in tongues as an act of resistance. Philosophically, he sees it as a 'limit-case' on the margins of language, but more salient to the present discussion, Smith imagines tongues as a kind of politically subversive language in critique of power-structures that dominate the oppressed.[119] Against the dissolution of the particularity of the colonized into the normativity of the oppressors' culture; tongues becomes a means of hallowing ethnicity, and multilinguality and multiculturalism as part of God's plan for the liberation of the dominated.[120] Much has been written about Pentecostalism as a movement of the disenfranchised both in North America and in the world.[121] This is in keeping with the kenotic movement of the Spirit, but also with the eschatological hope he brings. In this context speaking in tongues expresses itself as sacramental sign of the nexus between both cross and *eschaton*, that is, the sign of Spirit baptism.

d. Healing as Sacramental Sign

Perhaps healing provides a more incisive test case for transposing supernatural intervention from the historical model of Pentecostal triumphalism to a paradigm rooted in the *theologia crucis*. While the Pentecostal rationale for tongues, both as initial evidence, and as gift leaned primarily on restorationist assumptions, the practice, if not the theology of healing has drawn more on perfectionist motifs in the Pentecostal heritage. Yet, in a manner similar to that applied to glossolalia, I will propose a view of healing that sees it, too, as sacramental sign.

For Pentecostals, healing came as a form of divine immediacy made possible by the Pentecostal experience. A typical article by Assemblies of God charter member S. A. Jamieson appearing in the June 1923 *Pentecostal Testimony* claimed, 'Many sick ones are not healed because they fail God in not complying with the conditions as laid down in God's word. Please notice the following requisite to

119. James K. A. Smith, *Thinking in Tongues: Pentecostal Contributions to Christian Philosophy* (Pentecostal Manifestos; Grand Rapids: Eerdmans, 2010), pp. 147 and 149.

120. Samuel Solivan, *The Spirit, Pathos and Liberation: Toward and Hispanic Pentecostal Theology* (Journal of Pentecostal Theology Supplement Series, 14; Sheffield: Sheffield Academic Press, 1998), pp. 115–16. Perhaps with Paul's mention in 1 Corinthians 14.21 of Isaiah 28 and the lips of Assyrian invaders coming to conquer Israel, he also thinks of tongues as a sign of judgement on Israelite oppressors, and not only a sign of liberation of the oppressed.

121. A short bibliography would include Anderson, *Vision of the Disinherited*; Solivan, *Spirit, Pathos, and Liberation*; Martin, *Tongues of Fire: The Explosion of Protestantism in Latin America* (Oxford: Blackwell, 1990); Martin, *The World Their Parish*; Miller and Yamamori, *Global Pentecostalism*; and for a contemplation of the political theology of Pentecostalism, Yong, *In the Days of Caesar*.

obtain Divine healing.' He then listed the standard litany of texts and imperatives: receive the prayer of faith, believe that healing is in the atonement; believe God gives the supplicant what is asked; stand firm against the Enemy and look to Jesus, not symptoms; confess all known sin; and pursue union with Christ. 'If the above directions are followed Jesus will make himself manifest by healing them', Jamieson concludes rather bluntly.[122] The matter, for early Pentecostals, was quite simple. Under the proper conditions, and of course with 'faith, nothing doubting', healing was assured.

The failure of healing, at least for the purist, could mean only one thing . . . human failure. Pentecostals anticipated that properly Spirit-filled believers would entertain such an intimacy with God that literally 'nothing' was impossible. This kind of confident assertion betrays the triumphalism of early Pentecostal spirituality. Breaking it down to its constituent parts, such a notion of divine healing assumes a number of things. First it asserts human certainty regarding the will and purposes of God. Beyond this, it depends on two kinds of perfection: a perfectly unshakeable faith; and a perfectly full confession of sin, perhaps even within the entire community of faith. But the height of its hubris is the kind of human agency it posits that renders it impossible for God to act otherwise than to comply with the request. The theology of the cross calls this sort of pride into question. It raises serious objections about the possibility of human faith of such quality that it must obtain its object. Above all, it asserts, to the contrary of this full renunciation of sin, that believers at their spiritually passionate best, and at their defeated and overwhelmed worst are never anything more or less than *simul justus et peccator*. Perhaps the most accurate summary of the human posture for healing is 'Lord, I believe, help my unbelief' (Mk 9.24, NKJV).

While the above description of divine healing is appropriate for early Pentecostals, it would be inaccurate to suggest that contemporary Pentecostalism retains the same ethos, at least in its denominational incarnation. This is the preserve of independent Pentecostal churches, and some of the more extreme charismatic churches in the word of faith movement. Joyce Meyer is a good case in point. She outlines a typical approach to the matter in *Be Healed in Jesus' Name*. Most charismatic approaches to healing have moderated the moral perfectionism of early Pentecostals, but still hold to the necessity of perfected faith. 'Many people believe God is **able** to heal them but aren't sure he **will** heal them.'[123] One might

122. 'Divine Healing', *PT* 4 (June 1923), p. 6.

123. Meyer, *Be Healed in Jesus' Name* (New York: Warner, 2000), pp. 1 and 35–37. An excellent example of the earlier influence of the healing revival of the 1950s upon contemporary charismatics is found in T. L. Osborn, *Healing the Sick* (Tulsa: T.L. Osborn Evangelistic Association, 1959). For a thorough overview, see D. R. McConnell, *A Different Gospel: A Historical and Biblical Analysis of the Modern Faith Movement, Updated Edition* (Peabody, MA: Hendrickson, 1995). The neocharismatic view of healing would represent a broad spectrum from John Wimber's less emphatic obsession with the absoluteness

find such attitudes within the popular spirituality of Pentecostal congregations, or at special events, such as camp meetings or services with a healing evangelist, but this paradigm for healing runs counter to the official statements of Pentecostal denominationalism, which tend to retain a sense of mystery regarding healing, without any theological infrastructure to support it.[124] Denominations like the Assemblies of God and the Pentecostal Assemblies of Canada have managed to institutionalize their success by distancing themselves from the more extreme forms of the charismatic movement, and to some extent from the roots that have nourished their triumph.

John Wimber moved meaningfully towards abandoning a triumphalist idea of the supernatural in three specific ways.[125] First, his emphasis on the already/not yet dimension of eschatological anticipation, freed his model of supernatural intervention from overly restorationist presuppositions.[126] Second, he explicitly acknowledged that the miraculous was not tied to his personal 'power to be good'.[127] Finally, the clear acknowledgement of the outright failure of healing prayer, and

of human faith; John Wimber and Kevin Springer, *Power Healing* (San Francisco: San Francisco, 1987), pp. 147–66, to Billy Joe Daugherty, deceased pastor of Victory Christian Center, a charismatic megachurch founded in 1981 in Tulsa OK, who claimed, 'Sickness is an invasion of an outlaw force seeking to rob you of your health. The knowledge of your covenant rights and privileges for being whole will enable you to stop the destruction of sickness and the power of God will heal you'; Billy Joe Daugherty, *You Can Be Healed: How to Believe God for Your Healing* (Shippensburg, PA: Destiny Image, 2006), pp. 9–10. The church's statement after his passing affirmed that Daugherty had 'experienced his ultimate healing by entering into the presence of God'; 'Pastor Billy Joe Daugherty'. Online: http://www.victory.com/pastor_letter/pl_home.asp (Accessed July, 2010, no longer accessible). See also Adrienne S. Gaines, 'Billy Joe Daugherty Dies at 57'. Online: http://www.charismamag.com/site-archives/570-news/featured-news/8133-billy-joe-daugherty-dies-at-57 (Accessed 15 August 2014).

124. The Assemblies of God, 'Divine Healing: An Integral Part of the Gospel'; and The Pentecostal Assemblies of Canada, 'Miracles and Healings'.

125. Don Carson points out, however, that '[Wimber's] framework is just not large enough. He tries to establish a theology of healing and power encounter without a theology of suffering; he has a theology of victory without an adequate theology of the cross; he has a theology of life without a proper reflection on the place of death. He sees the triumph of the kingdom when sickness is overthrown, and cannot see the triumph of the kingdom when people are transformed in the midst of sickness. He discusses God's power, but rarely wrestles with God's predilection for displaying his power in the context of continuing weakness'; D. A. Carson, *How Long, O Lord? Reflections on Suffering and Evil, 2nd Edition* (Grand Rapids: Baker Academic, 1990), p. 124.

126. Wimber and Springer, *Power Healing*, pp. 36–37 and 157.

127. Wimber and Springer, *Power Evangelism*, pp. 25–26. See also Charles H. Kraft's comments in 'Five Years Later', in *Signs and Wonders Today: The Story of Fuller Theological Seminary's Remarkable Course on Spiritual Power, New Expanded Edition* (ed. C. Peter

acknowledgement of its sporadic success remove the pressure of performance. These last two points undercut the assertion of perfectionism.[128]

Yet back at Azusa Street, particularly if interpreted as the heart rather than the infancy of Pentecostalism, triumphalist perfectionism is not so easily done away. William Seymour, speaking out of his Holiness background was able to say, 'Not only is the atonement for the sanctification of our souls, but for the sanctification of our bodies from inherited disease.'[129] Just as the sin issue was dealt with at the cross, not just the penalty but the power and presence of sin, so the matter of sickness could be entirely dispensed with. The sound of such pronouncements reverberates through all of Pentecostalism in its various permutations, and raises questions that must be addressed.

In her award-winning work on *Pentecostal Healing*, Kimberly Alexander suggests that healing models differed between Holiness Pentecostals and the Finished Work Pentecostals. She proposes a disjunction between Wesleyan and Reformed soteriologies. The Wesleyan view involved a relational soteriology motivated by love resulting in a recapitulation view of salvation. The Reformed perspective was primarily juridical, motivated by justice, and promoting a forensic view of salvation. Interestingly though, Alexander sees the essential deviation between the two as arising within the Holiness movement itself, and Phoebe Palmer's 'altar theology' where sanctification was to be received by faith and acted upon as though it had been received. This 'shorter way' short-circuited Wesleyan notions of assurance, and the emotive, relational dynamic of sanctification.[130] Carrie Judd Montgomery translated this notion of healing into the Pentecostal movement, and in so doing, along with Palmer, and against Wesley, pushed the paradigm of sanctification, and divine health as entry experiences to the Christian life, rather than goals towards which one lived. Healing, then, like holiness, was simply appropriated by faith.

Healing on this view was Christological, obtained once and for all 'by his stripes' and imparted by Christ's life in the believer through the Holy Spirit. It was a promise to be claimed.[131] As Durham had suggested about reckoning

Wagner; Altamonte Springs, FL: Creation House, 1987), pp. 115–23, where he traced a paradigm shift between his initial reluctance to pray for healing because 'maybe I . . . was "too sinful for God to use me in this way" to the place where he acknowledged that honours our "weak attempts" in spite even of scepticism and fear'; ibid., pp. 117 and 121.

128. Wimber tells the story of failed prayer in the case of his friend and British evangelical leader David Watson; Wimber and Springer, *Power Healing*, pp. 147–49, and explains that he continues to pray for healing in spite of failure, pp. 179–80. Wimber suggests the standard hindrances to healing (unconfessed sin, unbelief, etc.), but he also acknowledges that people who persist in prayer may not be healed; ibid., 149–52.

129. Seymour, 'The Precious Atonement', *AF* 1 (September, 1906), p. 2.

130. Kimberly Ervin Alexander, *Pentecostal Healing: Models in Theology and Practice* (Journal of Pentecostal Theology Supplement Series; Blandford Forum, UK: Deo, 2006), p. 47.

131. Ibid., pp. 154–58.

oneself dead to sin, one might also reckon oneself healed from sickness. In her analysis of early Pentecostal literature, Alexander found remarkable parallels to practices of the 'faith movement', such as 'acting one's faith'; not talking about symptoms or pains; commanding or rebuking intransigent illnesses; and claiming one's healing in the name of Jesus, and testifying to it. Similar prescriptions were given by Palmer to those seeking sanctification. As Finished Work salvation, offered in Reformed categories, was primarily forensic, so was healing. Finished work theology was primarily present appropriation of a work that was completed on the cross, and thus intrinsically involved a backward-looking dynamic.[132]

A more relational, growth-oriented paradigm was implicit among Holiness Pentecostals. Just as one maintained one's sanctification by a continuing growth of faith, similarly, healing came by recurring faith encounters with God. Wesleyan perfection in spirit, soul and body was to be understood as a continual drawing by the Spirit into the coming kingdom. Grace, now, rather than being a judicial attitude of favour, was to be seen as the power of God liberating his children to increasing, deepening freedom. The life of the believer is an upward journey into the heavenlies, and into the *eschaton*. It is to be an active, seeking engagement with God. Thus prayer for healing; seeking God at the altar; and 'praying through', that is praying beyond whatever barriers may be hindering the relationship between the believer and God; all these were seen as part of a transformative relational process. Alexander considers that Wesleyan-Pentecostals eschewed the immediacy of Palmer's altar theology, returning to Wesley's original vision of '*crisis-process*, at least where healing is involved'. The Holiness-Pentecostal model of healing, then, was a forward-looking paradigm that fundamentally sought healing as a proleptic experience of the resurrection.[133]

While Alexander's breadth of research is impressive, two factors raise questions about a strict application of her two models. First, while there are clear connections between the Finished Work theology and a Reformed concept of forensic righteousness, there can be little doubt that the Finished Work doctrine that created division in early Pentecostalism reflected the extreme perfectionist bent in Durham's thought that was clearly out of line with Reformed theology, and a remnant of Holiness theology, whether Wesleyan or Higher Life. Durham was convinced that the sin nature was eradicated at the moment of conversion. In fact, Thomas Farkas called his position 'single-work perfectionism'.[134] The abiding value of Durham's work, according to Macchia, is the provision of a link between Spirit baptism as an inner work, and an external forensic righteousness through the

132. Ibid., pp. 209–15.

133. Ibid., pp. 198–209.

134. Thomas George Farkas, *William Durham and the Sanctification Controversy in Early American Pentecostalism 1906–1916* (unpublished dissertation; Southern Baptist Theological Seminary, Louisville, 1993), p. 21; cited in Macchia, 'Baptized in the Spirit', p. 6.

person and work of Christ.[135] But the perfectionist heritage, though significantly moderated, remains, even in the Finished Work denominations.[136]

Whether ideas of 'forensic healing' as Alexander charges them to the Finished Work teachers derive from Reformed soteriology is not immediately clear. Durham also came under the influence of E. W. Kenyon in the formative years of the Finished Work paradigm.[137] Scholarly discussion of Kenyon has been limited, but centres around the blending of esoteric (New Thought, Christian Science, etc.) and Higher Life influences. D. R. McConnell's early work cast Kenyon as a propagator of clearly metaphysical ideas.[138] Geir Lie challenged McConnell, asserting that while there may have been such influences, Kenyon was a Higher Life Baptist, more dependent on Moody, Gordon, Simpson and Cullis.[139] Dale Simmons places Kenyon in a mediating position, evangelicalizing New Thought concepts and holding to a basic Higher Life framework.[140] The fact of Kenyon's influence on early Pentecostals, Latter Rain healing revivalists and the charismatic Word of Faith movement is unquestioned, though the extent and direct influences are still matters of debate, but it appears that many of the attitudes that Alexander laid at the feet of Finished Work find parallels in Kenyon as well as Palmer's followers. Lie suggests there is 'a surprising degree of doctrinal correspondence' between esoteric philosophy and the Higher Life movement. These observations at least mitigate Alexander's charges against the allegedly Reformed nature of Finished Work Pentecostalism.

Second, while, Alexander asserts that her Wesleyan-Pentecostal sources indicate that failure in healing was perceived within the freedom of a sovereign God, this does not appear to reflect the general consensus of the divine healing movement before 1900. Heather D. Curtis multiplies examples from Dr Charles Cullis, R. Kelso Carter, Robert Livingston Stanton, Carrie Judd Montgomery and

See also Thomas A. Fudge, *Christianity without the Cross: A History of Salvation in Oneness Pentecostalism* (Parkland, FL: Universal Publishers, 2003), pp. 256–66.

135. Macchia, 'Baptized in the Spirit', p. 7.

136. Though Macchia is correct in claiming that none of Durham's followers taught a similar 'single-work perfectionism'; ibid., p. 7.

137. While Alexander, *Pentecostal Healing*, pp. 45–46, 151 sees the origin of Finished Work theology in the ministry of Carrie Judd Montgomery; Jacobsen finds its sources in the work of E. W. Kenyon, whose writings prove to be foundational to the Word of Faith wing of the Pentecostal/Charismatic movement; Jacobsen, *Thinking in the Spirit*, see note 42, 380–81; and note 47, 397–98. See also Dale H. Simmons, *E. W. Kenyon and the Postbellum Pursuit of Peace, Power, and Plenty* (Lanham, MA: Scarecrow Press, Inc. 1997), pp. 292–93 and 312; and Geir Lie, *E. W. Kenyon: Cult Founder or Evangelical Minister?* (The Refleks-series, No. 2; Oslo: Refleks Publishing, 2003), pp. 117–18.

138. D. R. McConnell, *A Different Gospel*, pp. 24–26, 42–51.

139. Lie, *E. W. Kenyon*, p. 153.

140. Simmons, *E. W. Kenyon*.

A. B. Simpson to the effect that the fault for not appropriating healing is human. 'Many of the leading advocates of divine healing asserted that failure to receive healing was in some measure a result of insufficient trust in God's promises.'[141] She demonstrates how Montgomery applied Palmer's altar theology, but parallels to claiming one's healing, acting faith, and refusing to pray further also occur in other Palmer disciples including Cullis, Elizabeth Baxter and A. B. Simpson, who became a life-long associate of Montgomery's.[142] The characteristics of perfectionist healing among Finished Work proponents appear to have been widespread among late-nineteenth-century faith healers, most of whom were Wesleyans.

It is possible, as Alexander argues, that Holiness-Pentecostals who adhered to a perfectionist notion of sanctification, held a kinder, gentler concept of human limitation in divine healing. It may still be demonstrable that 'though healing was expected and anticipated, instances when healing did not occur were not necessarily viewed as defeat or as a failure of faith'.[143] It is clear, however, that the majority of Pentecostalism followed the Finished Work theology, and while mellowing from Durham on the matter of entire sanctification, continued to advocate perfectionist motifs as it touched healing.

The forgoing discussion raises the question of healing as sacramental sign. What I find compelling in Alexander's discussion of Wesleyan and Finished Work theologies of healing is the basic perspective she suggests as driving each. Alexander sees the Wesleyan view as essentially forward-looking, drawing from the eschatological horizon, while she perceives the Finished Work viewpoint as fundamentally backward-looking, reaching back to the cross. She wishes to assert the basically relational nature of Wesleyan theology against a static, and forensic Reformed paradigm, thus she sees the Spirit as the living link between the *eschaton* and Christ's Finished Work as a colder, more stagnant model for relational theologizing. On this view, the Pentecostal Holiness perspective provides an adequate posture for formulating a truly Trinitarian theology.[144]

I propose the opposite. It is the dynamic of the *pneumatologia crucis* emanating from the crucifixion of the Resurrected One mediated through *Pentecost* that animates an experiential encounter with Christ in us by faith. And it is the eschatology of the cross, equally mediated through *Pentecost*, which portrays the Resurrection of the Crucified as the dynamic of the eschatological already and not yet. To speak of forensic notions of righteousness as though they exhausted Luther's concept of justification is to limit perspective to half the story. Philip Watson, for instance, concluded that the *Christus Victor* metaphor was the most characteristic one which Luther used to describe the work of Christ. Luther typically pictured

141. Heather D. Curtis, *Faith in the Great Physician: Suffering and Divine Healing in American Culture, 1860–1900* (Lived Religions; Baltimore: Johns Hopkins University Press, 2007), pp. 87–94, quotation, 89.

142. Ibid., pp. 90, 92–93 and 94.

143. Alexander, *Pentecostal Healing*, p. 208.

144. Ibid., pp. 230–32.

Christ in mortal combat against sin, death, the devil, the Law and the Wrath of God (these last two, Luther saw as aspects of God's alien work).[145] This is the victory we share in today, though we still relate to it through the Crucified Christ, in a world of brokenness, sorrow and pain. As I have asserted, the nexus of these two dynamics in Spirit baptism forms the environment of sacramental expectation.

Anointing with oil exists as a sacrament in both the Roman Catholic and Orthodox tradition. The Roman Catholic sacrament of extreme unction has as its goal to arouse within the recipient an awareness in the passage to death that Christ is Lord over sickness and death.[146] In Orthodoxy, the sacrament of healing has as its goal the healing of spirit and body.[147] Luther denies that anointing with oil can be considered a sacrament for the promise is not dominical, and chastises the Roman church for denying its healing value.[148] But inasmuch as he had issues with the epistle of James, questioned its apostolicity and placed it at the end of his Bible, he did not reject James' wisdom on anointing with oil. 'If unction were practiced in accordance with the gospel, Mark 6[:13] and James 5[:14], I would let it pass.'[149]

> Therefore I take it that this unction is the same as that practiced by the apostles, of whom it is written in Mark 6[:13]: 'They anointed with oil many that were sick and healed them.' It was a rite of the early church, by which they worked miracles on the sick, and which has long since ceased. . . . There is no doubt at all that, even if today such a prayer were made over a sick man, that is, made in full faith by older, graver, and saintly men, as many as we wished would be healed. For what could not faith do?[150]

One cannot fault Luther for lacking either boldness to believe for the miraculous; or the meekness to acknowledge no corner on full faith.

Luther also anticipated healing through another ancient practice of the church, the laying on of hands. Asked by a pastor how to visit a person whom Luther appraised as 'melancholy' to the point of 'madness', Luther claims that this is 'an affliction that comes from the devil', and 'must be counteracted by the power of Christ and with the prayer of faith'. He recommends that the pastor go with a deacon and 'two or three good men'. He urges confidence in his ministerial authority, and encourages the pastor to lay hands upon the man, and greet him

145. Philip S. Watson, *Let God Be God! An Interpretation of the Theology of Martin Luther* (Eugene, OR: Wipf and Stock, [1947] 2001), pp. 116–25, especially 116–18. For wrath and the terror Law produces as aspects of God's alien work, see Althaus, *Theology of Luther*, pp. 171–73.

146. Thomas Talley, 'Healing: Sacrament or Charism?', *Worship* 46 (1972), pp. 518–27 (p. 526).

147. Stanley Harakas, 'The Sacrament of Healing', *IRM* 90 (2001), pp. 81–86 (p. 83).

148. 'Babylonian Captivity of the Church' (1520), *LW* 36:117–20.

149. 'Confession Concerning Christ's Supper' (1528), *LW* 37:370.

150. 'The Babylonian Captivity of the Church' (1520), *LW* 36:121.

with peace. Then he is to recite the Creed and the Lord's prayer, and then to pray after a form he gives him, including

> we unworthy sinners, relying on these thy words and commands, pray for thy mercy with such faith as we can muster. Graciously deign to free this man from all evil, and put to nought the work that Satan has done in him, to the honor of thy name and the strengthening of the faith of believers.[151]

The pastor is then to leave, but not before laying hands again and pronouncing, 'These signs shall follow them that believe; they shall lay hands on the sick, and they shall recover.' He recommends this be done on three successive days, and that 'meanwhile prayers be said from the chancel of the church, publicly, until God hears'.[152] Once more, Luther exemplifies the theology of the cross, combining holy boldness with holy meekness. Lest one should imagine Luther speaks without benefit of experience or success, he mentions to this beleaguered pastor the episode of a cabinetmaker he dealt with who was similarly afflicted and who was cured 'by prayer in Christ's name'.[153]

As Luther experiences healing and deliverance, he is conscious of what I have termed *pneumatologia crucis*, the utter emptying of self (unworthy sinners, such faith as we can muster), and the hope of the *eschatologia crucis*, the crucified Christ's resurrection power to vanquish the works of Satan and sickness. While such rites cannot be termed sacraments, they combine God's Word of promise with a humble physical sign (oil and hands), and call for faith to invoke God's presence. In this way, I call them sacramental signs, since, like baptism and eucharist, they incorporate the backward- and forward-looking dimensions of Christian reality. Something holy and transcendent takes place in moments where such prayers are offered, and particularly when they are met with that eschatological in-breaking of power that provides actual, demonstrable healing. But when they are not, when healing does not occur, they become tangible reminders that God is hidden here, too, in suffering and the cross. Suffering is not to be embraced in some fatalist resignation. It is to be resisted, reproved and rebuked in prayer. But like all God's alien works, it still has a purpose, and it may not always be so quickly dispatched.[154]

Those who see healing as larger than physical, those who acknowledge the nexus of the pneumatology and eschatology of the cross, may discern God's sacramental presence even when the outward manifestation does not occur. For these people, what Talley says of the Roman Catholic sacrament may be true. 'Situating me between the life I have lived and the life I am for, sickness is *liminal*

151. 'To Severin Schulze, June 1, 1545', *LSC*:52.

152. Ibid.

153. Ibid.

154. 'The cross reveals that the senseless suffering of this sorry existence has a point in God and that this point is penultimate – God's first alien work clears the way in us for God's proper work of salvation'; Wengert, '"Peace, Peace . . . Cross, Cross"', p. 200).

in an unusually personal and bodily way. And it is just that liminality which calls forth the sacrament of anointing for the illumination of its ambiguity and the articulation of the transition it marks and demands.'[155] In this way healing prayer serves as a sacred reminder of the already/not yet dialectic in which we are caught. And the touch of loving hands and empathetic hearts, as we wait, imparts its own healing.

e. Tongues and Healing as Tokens of Embodied Spirituality

I have proposed that tongues-speech and healing are sacramental signs of the kingdom of God and I believe that it is precisely here that the genius of Pentecostalism lies. Steven Land has asserted the potential of Pentecostalism to properly integrate orthodoxy, orthopraxy and orthopathy into a productive whole; and that Pentecostalism is most motivated to this integration in light of the coming kingdom.[156] I concur most heartily, and suggest that Pentecostal experiences (tongues, healing, *charismata*, generally) are models of this integration. At their best, they integrate these three modes of being with Scripture-informed and -bounded experiences that result in Spirit-led actions, and they do this in ways that anticipate and indeed depend on the active in-breaking of the divine. As sacramental signs, they are expressions of the spirituality of embodiment that is central to Pentecostalism.

James K. A. Smith points to the distinction between Reformed spirituality as he has come to experience it and the embodied spirituality of Pentecostalism. 'Reformed worship so often treats human beings as if we're brains-on-a-stick. All week long we talk about how good creation is, how good embodiment is. But then we have habits of worship that merely deposit great ideas in our heads, making us rather cerebral disciples.'[157] Smith does not see the two as mutually exclusive spiritualities, but suggests that Pentecostal spirituality embodies an expectation of the sovereignty of God in its spontaneity of expression and openness to the possibility of divine surprises . . . not unlike the Calvinist, Jonathan Edwards, who gave *A Faithful Narrative of the Surprising Work of God in Northampton*.

The sign dimension of these 'sacramental signs', the hands laid, the oil anointed, the tongues spoken; these all point to the embodied nature of Pentecostal experience and thus Pentecostal theology. Embodiment may well be another distinguishing mark of Pentecostalism. Hollenweger hints at this when he speaks of the 'body/mind relationship which is informed by experiences of correspondence between body and mind'.[158] Indeed Smith calls Pentecostalism a distinctly embodied practice of Christianity. Smith sets the incarnational realities of Pentecostal

155. Talley, 'Sacrament or Charism?', p. 526.

156. Land, *Pentecostal Spirituality*, pp. 41–44.

157. James K. Smith, 'Teaching a Calvinist to Dance', *CT* 52 (May, 2008), pp. 42–45 (p. 44).

158. Hollenweger, 'Pentecostals and the Charismatic Movement', p. 552.

spirituality against the sterility of Enlightenment rationalism, and its suspicion of other modes of knowing.[159] The postmodern posture of this embodied spirituality places a Pentecostalism shorn of its triumphalist metanarrative in a most favourable position for addressing the culture. The drift from 'Evidence-That-Demands-a-Verdict Evangelicalism' to a more pentecostalized form is perhaps as much a function of the postmodern cultural shift as it is a consequence of the proximity of Pentecostalism and Evangelicalism.

Very few aspects of Pentecostal spirituality escape this dimension of embodiment, which in turn is accounted for by the literalness of the early Pentecostal hermeneutic. These saints took so seriously the corporeal return of Christ to the earth that they imagined the Latter Rain outpouring they received and its bodily manifestation, xenolalia, would empower them to embody the gospel of material signs and wonders around the world. The residue of this spirituality is found in the demonstrative dimension of Pentecostal worship, and its continued practice of sacramental signs. The physicality of prophetic speech, the laying on of hands, the anointing with oil all reveal a consecration of materiality, or embodiment unknown in neo-Platonic thought or Gnosticism, and to some extent shunned in modernist, rationalist Evangelicalism. As Smith notes, '[T]here is a sacramentality of pentecostal worship that sees the material as a good and necessary mediator of the Spirit's work and presence.'[160] The removal, then, of triumphalism from Pentecostal spirituality will allow it to incarnate an anticipation appropriate to the theology of the cross, and to reinterpret its embodied nature consistently with it. Furthermore, it will make sense of its premillennial expectation as more than 'Left-Behind triumphalism' but a motive to embody the justice of the coming kingdom in the here-and-now.

Much has been said by those who wish to posit Pentecostalism as some kind of *tertium quid*, neither Fundamentalist nor Evangelical, neither Catholic nor Protestant – a theology of the Third Article. The fear, of course, is that Pentecostals have given in too much to the Enlightenment rationalism that has coloured both evangelical and liberal forms of Christianity; that they have begun to institutionalize the Spirit in ways that sacramental traditions have institutionalized their worship.[161] The accusation might be levelled against the view suggested here of sacramental signs of the kingdom. One must acknowledge the genuine concern for true Pentecostal spirituality in the bulk of denominational Pentecostal churches. An easy answer is to claim that Pentecostalism has been evangelicalized. I am not sure that the problem is so forthright. I suggest, instead, that the triumphalism of Pentecostal expectation has brought Pentecostals to this place. The failure of heightened expectation to produce experiences that live up

159. Smith, *Thinking in Tongues*, pp. 59–60.

160. Ibid., pp. 81–82.

161. James K. A. Smith sees the legacy of the Cartesian *cogito* in the Enlightenment 'valorization of *thinking* as the core of human identity and a devaluation of *embodiment* as a source of deception and distress'; Smith, *Thinking in the Spirit*, p. 54.

to the promise has debilitated both proper faith, and experience. And while I do not deny that Pentecostalism shorn of its anticipation of kingdom manifestation looks as much like the broader evangelical paradigm as any other variety of Evangelicalism, I do not imagine the solution is in a historical revisionism which de-evangelicalizes Pentecostalism, or the imposition of postmodern hermeneutics on early Pentecostals, as though this distances them from their evangelical roots.

I believe the way forward is a revisioning of the future. The notion of embodied spirituality as suggested by Smith is a good start, and may be a way that Pentecostals can bring more than the relish to the theological banquet.[162] But without the corrective of the theology of the cross, embodiment risks repeating the folly of Pentecostal triumphalism. Tongues-speech without the theology of the cross becomes a badge of superiority, but with a kenotic resonance it becomes a 'broken language for a broken body until perfection comes'.[163] The promise of healing without the theology of the cross becomes the cry of victory for those who are healed: prevailing prayer, overcoming faith, victorious vindication. But for those who are not healed it can only give way to tears of disappointment and despair. The *theologia crucis* reminds believers of the inescapable limitations of fallen life, and the reality that there is much of the kingdom that is not yet. And it reminds us that the Hidden God meets us where we least expect him, even in the place of suffering, despair and sin. Pentecostalism must ever come face up with the mystery of our existence in the dialectic of Spirit-filled life in a broken world.

Conclusion

Beginning with two components that derive genuinely from Luther's theology of the cross, and applying them to some major issues in Pentecostal spirituality, it is possible to elaborate a Pentecostalism that is no longer a theology of glory. The *pneumatologia crucis* and *eschatologia crucis* developed in the last chapter prove useful tools for revisioning at least three key areas central to Pentecostal theologizing: the place of experience, the perfectibility of humanity and the experience of the miraculous.

The theology of the cross raises a hermeneutic of suspicion against human pretensions to know God immediately. While Evangelicalism, Reformed theology and Luther all receive rough treatment at times by Pentecostals for their excessive rationalism, Luther, in particular. must be seen as a profoundly experiential theologian. Apart from his battles with the enthusiasts, Luther sounds remarkably Pentecostal at times. But Luther offers a dictum about the ultimacy of God's Word as *extra nos* standard to mediate all spiritual experience. Experiences are to be

162. Terry L. Cross, 'The Rich Feast of Theology: Can Pentecostals Bring the Main Course or Only the Relish?', *JPT* 8 (2000), pp. 27–47.

163. Russell Spittler, 'Glossolalia', in *NIDPCM*, pp. 670–76.

enjoyed as penultimate preparation for the ultimate, God as he is encountered in Word, sacrament, and justification, these *extra nos* realities that make the *in nobis* experiences possible.

The method has been to resolve these three dimensions of Pentecostal spirituality into forward-looking and backward-looking components, then to ask how the application of an eschatology and pneumatology of the cross might redefine them. Thus spiritual experience is reconceived as penultimate but necessary. Regarding human perfectibility, the divine standard of perfection is not abrogated, but rather strengthened, and on the other hand, the cross, having decimated human pretension, offers Christ as both favour and gift. Turning to the miraculous, a constructive approach to the theology of 'sign' suggests that tongues and healing might be reinterpreted as sacramental signs: the broken language of tongues, and the gentle touch of healing hands mediating God's divine and miraculous presence within the limitations of an inaugurated but not fully realized eschatology. Turning to a consideration of human perfectibility, the notion of perfectionism was traced, particularly in the non-Wesleyan stream of Pentecostalism. Against this, a consideration of the *theologia crucis* showed that, on the one hand, the divine standard of perfection is not abrogated, but rather strengthened, and on the other, the cross, having decimated human pretension, offers Christ as both favour and gift. Christ's alien righteousness turns away God's just wrath, and Christ himself within us imparts the gift of actual holiness, impeded by the not yet aspects of creaturely fallenness, but not paralysed by it.

Finally, a constructive approach to the theology of 'sign' provides a fresh look at the Pentecostal expectation of the miraculous. While Pentecostals have traditionally seen 'sign' in evidentiary categories, under the Third Wave, it has been increasingly seen as a proleptic taste of the kingdom. Reworking Luther's concept of sacrament as involving promise, faith and humble sign, it was suggested that tongues and healing might be reinterpreted as sacramental signs: the broken language of tongues, and the gentle touch of healing hands mediating God's divine and miraculous presence within the limitations of an inaugurated eschatology.

CONCLUSION: THE VALUE OF THIS STUDY TO THE CHURCH

The contemporary Pentecostal church in North America has come to a crisis of truth. The tired paradigm of expectation and experience has lost credibility and Pentecostalism, whether denominational or independent, is in danger of fading into the oblivion of institutionalism, whether that of denominations or megachurches. The current generation of young charismatics are no longer buying the rhetoric of Pentecostal triumphalism. They are demanding a spirituality that 'calls the thing what it actually is'. Yet as much as they are longing for authenticity, they are also yearning for a genuine encounter with God. Somehow these two dynamics must be attended to in any Pentecostal synthesis that will meet the need of the day. This is particularly true in the postmodern interstice in which we find ourselves. The spirit of the age appears to reject metanarrative and the linear reasoning that made Evangelicalism such a persuasive form of Christianity in the period of high modernity. Instead, the more existential qualities that contributed to the success of Pentecostalism in late modernity are in demand. Thus, Pentecostalism must rephrase its linear models of initial evidence, faith formulae and quid pro quo spirituality. It must embrace the ambiguity of existence in the here-and-now, and rearticulate its narrative in ways that acknowledge human limitation and divine possibility. In short Pentecostalism must shed its triumphalism if it is to thrive. It can do so by an application of Luther's theology of the cross.

At the level of spirituality, the theology of the cross provides a suitable epistemology for Pentecostal experience. The cross acknowledges reality, life as it is encountered with all its inscrutability. But it also breathes a spirit of mystery into the in-breaking of the divine on the everydayness of human existence. As a result, it raises an appropriate hermeneutic of suspicion around charismatic claims of certainty, particularly in the areas of healing, prophetic utterance and divine guidance. This reconstituted Pentecostalism will undercut the overly optimistic anthropology of the nineteenth century, and provide a realistic assessment of the *cor curvum in se* and personal complicity in systems of oppression. A redefinition of Pentecostalism that reckons with the sacramentality of the God's presence in an embodied spirituality will lead to a recovery of anticipation properly nuanced within the limits of here-and-now actuality. Stock concepts such as 'power', 'victory' and holiness will all require revision. Pentecostal narrative and 'testimony' will take on a less strident, more transparent tone, offering more genuine glimpses of life in Christ.

Rephrased in terms of Luther's theology of the cross, Pentecostalism offers tremendous possibilities. First, it becomes a spirituality expressed in meaningful theological categories, rather than one shaped by the forces of perfectionism and restorationism that cast such a long and dubious shadow in American religious history. Pneumatology and eschatology are inherent to Pentecostal theology, as is Christology, as a central integrating principle. Informed by the cross both pneumatology and eschatology gain a fuller Christological focus, and express a healthier, more holistic theology that encompasses the totality of human experience. Second, by applying the *theologia crucis*, Pentecostalism sheds a hopeless triumphalism from its metanarrative. The long-term effects of triumphalism lead in one of two directions, personal despair, in the face of failed experience, or the deflection of painful reality by sustained rhetoric. In either case, triumphalism presents an insuperable obstacle to the formation of a workable Pentecostal theology. Third, a Pentecostal theology of the cross assumes a position that allows it to propose an equidistant critique of both unbridled expectation and unrelenting experience, and it does this spiritually, ecclesiastically and culturally. It should be recalled that it was its critique of the status quo in the churches and society that gave Pentecostalism its original impetus. A posture of protest is native to Pentecostalism. The theology of the cross reorients that protest, including a significant dynamic of self-criticism, and gives it fresh momentum. Finally, the existential, Pietist bent in Pentecostalism has already led to an increasing pentecostalization of Evangelicalism, as a result of the postmodern shift in popular culture. A refitted Pentecostalism, unencumbered by the rationalistic apparatus of the more Reformed side of Evangelicalism, will even better speak the language of the age. Pentecostalism reconstructed by the theology of the cross will then find a voice that *can* be heard, and *must* be heard in the midst of the postmodern din.

Finally, the revisioning of Pentecostalism in terms of an *eschatologia crucis* and a *pneumatologia crucis* offers fresh perspectives for rethinking the Pentecostal project. It not only sustains a bold Pentecostal spirituality which comes to terms with life as it is lived; it not only provides a deep infrastructure for Pentecostal theologizing, in terms that relate to the broader Christian enterprise, thus loosening its hardened doctrinal categories; but it invites something more. If the theology of the cross can be properly applied to the nature of Pentecostal experience, then it calls for a rethinking of ecclesiology in these terms, since this is the context in which a truly Pentecostal theology must be lived. Indeed, this may be the most enduring benefit of the preceding study. And so this author wonders what would a Pentecostal ecclesiology of the cross look like? How would it refashion the presuppositions of church life, and redeploy the gifts of the Spirit, and the resources of the church? Could an *ecclesiologia crucis* applied to a particularly Pentecostal conception of the church revolutionize the future? Questions worth pondering in the days to come, if, as our fathers used to say, 'the Lord tarries . . .'

BIBLIOGRAPHY

Ahlstrom, Sydney E., *A Religious History of the American People* (New Haven: Yale University Press, 1972).

Albanese, Catherine L., *America: Religions and Religion, 3rd Edition* (Belmont, CA: Wadsworth, 1999).

Albrecht, Daniel E., *Rites in the Spirit: A Ritual Approach to Pentecostal/Charismatic Spirituality* (Sheffield: Sheffield Academic Press, 1999).

Alexander, Kimberly Ervin, *Pentecostal Healing: Models in Theology and Practice* (Journal of Pentecostal Theology Supplement Series; Blandford Forum, UK: Deo, 2006).

Allen, Richard, *The Social Passion: Religion and Social Reform in Canada, 1914–28* (Toronto: University of Toronto Press, 1971).

Althaus, Paul, *The Theology of Martin Luther* (trans. Robert C. Schultz; Philadelphia: Fortress, 1966).

Althouse, Peter, 'Implications of the Kenosis of the Spirit for a Creational Eschatology: A Pentecostal Engagement with Jürgen Moltmann', in *The Spirit Renews the Face of the Earth: Pentecostal Forays in Science and Theology of Creation* (ed. Amos Yong; Eugene, OR: Wipf and Stock, 2009), pp. 155–72.

—, *The Spirit of the Last Days: Pentecostal Eschatology in Conversation with Jürgen Moltmann* (Journal of Pentecostal Theology Supplement Series, 25; London: T&T Clark, 2003).

—, 'Toward a Theological Understanding of the Pentecostal Appeal to Experience', *JES* 38 (2001), pp. 399–411.

—, 'The Influence of Dr. J. E. Purdie's Reformed Anglican Theology on the Formation and Development of the Pentecostal Assemblies of Canada', *Pneuma* 19 (1996), pp. 3–28.

—, 'Wesleyan and Reformed Impulses in the Keswick and Pentecostal Movements', *The Pneuma Review* (1995). Online: http://pneumareview.com/peter-althouse-wesleyan-and-reformed-impulses-in-the-keswick-and-pentecostal-movements/ (Accessed 14 August 2014).

Anderson, Alan, *Spreading Fires: The Missionary Nature of Early Pentecostalism* (Maryknoll, NY: Orbis Books, 2007).

—, *An Introduction to Pentecostalism: Global Charismatic Christianity* (New York: Cambridge University Press, 2004).

Anderson, Robert Mapes, *Vision of the Disinherited: The Making of American Pentecostalism* (Oxford: Oxford University Press, 1979).

Appleby, R. Scott, 'Primitivism as an Aspect of Global Fundamentalism', in *The Primitive Church in the Modern World* (ed. Richard T. Hughes; Urbana and Chicago: University of Illinois Press, 1995), pp. 17–33.

Archer, Kenneth, 'Horizons and Hermeneutics of Doctrine: A Review Essay', *JPT* 18 (2009), pp. 150–6.

—, *A Pentecostal Hermeneutic: Scripture, Spirit and Community* (Cleveland, TN: CPT Press, 2009).

—, *A Pentecostal Hermeneutic for the Twenty-first Century: Spirit, Scripture and Community* (London: T&T Clark, 2004).

Arrington, French L., 'The Use of the Bible by Pentecostals', *Pneuma* 16 (1994), pp. 101–7.

Arthur, William, *The Tongue of Fire or, The True Power of Christianity, New and Revised Edition* (New York and Nashville: Abingdon-Cokesbury, n.d.).

Assemblies of God, *Divine Healing: An Integral Part of the Gospel* (Position Paper; Springfield, MO, 2010). Online: http://ag.org/top/Beliefs/Position_Papers/pp_downloads/PP_Divine_Healing.pdf (Accessed 15 August 2014).

—, 'Apostles and Prophets', (Position Paper, AG, 2001). Online: http://ag.org/top/Beliefs/Position_Papers/pp_downloads/pp_4195_apostles_prophets.pdf (Accessed 14 August 2014).

Atkinson, William, 'Pentecostal Hermeneutics: Worth a Second Look?', *Evangel* 21 (2003), pp. 49–54.

Atter, Gordon F., *The Third Force. 3rd Edition* (Caledonia, ON: Acts, 1970).

Attfield, D. G., 'Can God Be Crucified? A Discussion of J. Moltmann', *SJT* 30 (1977), pp. 47–57.

Bainton, Roland H., *Here I Stand: A Life of Martin Luther* (New York: Abingdon-Cokesbury Press, 1950).

Barnes, Robin Bruce, *Prophecy and Gnosis: Apocalypticism in the Wake of the Lutheran Reformation* (Stanford: Stanford University Press, 1988).

Bartleman, Frank, *Azusa Street (How 'Pentecost' Came to Los Angeles – How It Was in the Beginning* (Plainfield, NJ: Logos, [1925] 1980).

Bassett, Paul Merritt, 'The Fundamentalist Leavening of the Holiness Movement', *WTJ* 13 (1978), pp. 65–91.

Bauckham, Richard, 'Preface', in *The Crucified God: The Cross of Christ as the Foundation and Criticism of Christian Theology* (by Jürgen Moltmann, trans. R. A. Wilson and John Bowden; London: SCM, 2001), pp. ix–xvi.

—, *The Theology of Jürgen Moltmann* (London: T&T Clark, 1995).

—, '"Only the Suffering God Can Help": Divine Passibility in Modern Theology', *Themelios* 9 (1984), pp. 6–12.

Bayer, Oswald, *Martin Luther's Theology: A Contemporary Interpretation* (trans. Thomas H. Trapp; Grand Rapids: Eerdmans, 2008).

Baylor, Michael, G., *Action and Person: Conscience in Late Scholasticism and the Young Luther* (Leiden: Brill, 1977).

Bebbington, David, *Evangelicalism in Modern Britain: A History from the 1730s to the 1980s* (London: Unwin Hyman, 1989).

Bellah, Robert N., 'Civil Religion in America', in *American Civil Religion* (ed. Russell E. Richey and Donald G. Jones; New York: Harper & Row, 1974), pp. 21–44.

Bence, Clarence L., 'A Response to Luke Keefer', *WJT* 19 (1984), pp. 36–38.

Bercovitch, Sacvan, *The American Jeremiad* (Madison: University of Wisconsin Press, 1978).

Bethge, Eberhard, *Dietrich Bonhoeffer: Theologian, Christian, Man for His Times* (ed. Edwin Robertson; trans. Eric Mosbacher, et al. Second revised and unabridged version. ed. Victoria Barnett; Minneapolis: Fortress, 1999).

Bevins, Winfield H., 'A Pentecostal Appropriation of the Wesleyan Quadrilateral', *JPS* 14 (2006), pp. 229–46.

Bingham, June, *Courage to Change: An Introduction to the Life and Thought of Reinhold Niebuhr* (New York: Scribner, 1961).

Blumhofer, Edith, 'Revisiting Azusa Street: A Centennial Retrospect', *IBMR* 30 (2006), pp. 59–64.

—, 'William Durham: Years of Creativity, Years of Dissent', in *Portraits of a Generation: Early Pentecostal Leaders* (ed. James R. Goff and Grant Wacker; Fayetteville, AR: University of Arkansas Press, 2002), pp. 123–42.
—, 'For Pentecostals, a Move toward Racial Reconciliation', *CC* 111 (1994), pp. 444–46.
—, *Restoring the Faith: The Assemblies of God, Pentecostalism and American Culture* (Champaign: University of Illinois Press, 1993).
—, *The Assemblies of God: A Chapter in the Story of American Pentecostalism* (2 vols; Springfield, MO: Gospel Publishing House, 1989).
Bonhoeffer, Dietrich, *Ethics* (German Edition, 1949, Dietich Bonhoeffer Works, vol. 6, Minneapolis: Fortress, 2005).
—, *Act and Being* (Dietrich Bonheoffer Works, vol. 2; Minneapolis: Fortress, [1931] 1996).
Bonino, José Míguez, *Doing Theology in a Revolutionary Situation* (Minneapolis: Fortress, 1975).
Borlase, Craig, *William Seymour: A Biography* (Lake Mary, FL: Charisma House, 2006).
Bornkamm, Heinrich, *The Heart of Reformation Faith: The Fundamental Axioms of Evangelical Belief* (trans. John W. Doberstein; New York: Harper & Row, 1965).
Boyd, Frank M., *Ages and Dispensations* (Springfield, MO: Gospel Publishing House, n.d.).
Braaten, Carl E., 'A Trinitarian Theology of the Cross', *JR* 56 (1976), pp. 113–21.
Brauer, Jerald C., 'Revivalism Revisited', *JR* 77 (1997), pp. 268–77.
Brecht, Martin, *Martin Luther: His Road to the Reformation, 1483–1521* (trans. James L. Schaff; Minneapolis: Fortress, 1985).
Brock, Rita Nakashima, 'And a Little Child Will Lead Us: Christology and Child Abuse', in *Christianity Patriarchy and Abuse: A Feminist Critique* (ed. Joanne Carlson Brown and Carole R. Bohm; New York: Pilgrim, 1989), pp. 42–61.
—, *Journeys by Heart: A Christology of Erotic Power* (New York: Crossroad, 1988).
Brown, Joanne Carlson and Rebecca Parker, 'For God So Loved the World?', in *Christianity Patriarchy and Abuse: A Feminist Critique* (ed. Joanne Carlson Brown and Carole R. Bohm; New York: Pilgrim, 1989), pp. 1–30.
Brown, P. S., 'Nineteenth Century American Health Reformers and the Early Nature Cure Movement in Britain', *MH* 32 (1988), pp. 174–94.
Brumback, Carl. *Suddenly . . . From Heaven: A History of the Assemblies of God* (Springfield, MO: Gospel Publishing House, 1961).
Bruner, Frederick Dale, *A Theology of the Holy Spirit: The Pentecostal Experience and the New Testament Witness* (Grand Rapids: Eerdmans, 1970).
Bucher, Richard P., *The Ecumenical Luther: The Development and Use of His Doctrinal Hermeneutic* (St Louis: Concordia Academic, 2003).
Bulgakov, Sergei, *The Comforter* (trans. Boris Jakim; Grand Rapids: Eerdmans, 2004).
Bundy, David, 'Visions of Sanctification: Themes of Orthodoxy in the Methodist, Holiness, and Pentecostal Traditions', *WTJ* 39 (2004), pp. 104–36.
Burgess, Stanley M. and Ed M. Van der Maas (eds), *The New International Dictionary of Pentecostal and Charismatic Movements* (Grand Rapids: Zondervan, 2002).
Burgess, Stanley M., McGee, Gary B. and Patrick H. Alexander (eds), *Dictionary of Pentecostal and Charismatic Movements* (Grand Rapids: Zondervan, 1988).
Butler, Jon, *Awash in a Sea of Faith: Christianizing the American People* (Studies in Cultural History; Cambridge: Harvard University Press, 1990).
—, 'Enthusiasm Described and Decried: The Great Awakening as Interpretative Fiction', *American History* 69 (1982), pp. 305–25.

Bynum, Carole Walker and Paul Freedman, 'Introduction', in *Last Things: Death and the Apocalypse in the Middle Ages* (ed. Carole Walker Bynum and Paul Freedman; Philadelphia: University of Pennsylvania Press, 2000), pp. 1–17.

Campbell, Ted, 'Close Encounters of the Pietist Kind: The Moravian-Methodist Connection', *CV* 45 (2003), pp. 67–80.

Cargal, Timothy B., 'Beyond the Fundamentalist–Modernist Controversy: Pentecostals and Hermeneutics in a Postmodern Age', *Pneuma* 15 (1993), pp. 163–87.

Carpenter, Joel, A. *Revive Us Again: The Reawakening of American Fundamentalism* (New York: Oxford University Press, 1997).

Carson, D. A., *How Long, O Lord? Reflections on Suffering and Evil, 2nd Edition* (Grand Rapids: Baker Academic, 1990).

Cartledge, Mark, 'Empirical Theology: Inter- or Intra-disciplinary?', *JBV* 20 (1999), pp. 98–104.

Carwardine, Richard, *Transatlantic Revivalism: Popular Evangelicalism in Britain and America, 1790–1865* (Studies in Evangelical History and Theology; London: Paternoster, [1978] 2007).

Cerillo, Augustus, 'The Beginnings of American Pentecostalism: A Historiographical Overview', in *Pentecostal Currents in American Protestantism* (ed. Edith L. Blumhofer, Russell P. Spittler and Grant A. Wacker; Urbana: University of Illinois Press, 1999), pp. 229–59.

Chan, Simon, *Pentecostal Theology and the Christian Spiritual Tradition* (London: Sheffield Academic Press, 2000).

Chudacoff, Howard P., Judith E. Smith and Peter C. Baldwin, *The Evolution of American Urban Society, Seventh Edition* (Boston: Prentice Hall, 2010).

Clouse, Robert G., 'Millennium, Views of', *EDT* (YEAR), pp. 714–18.

Coleman, Simon, *The Globalisation of Charismatic Christianity* (Cambridge: Cambridge University Press, 2000).

Commission on Doctrinal Purity, 'Endtime Revival – Spirit–Led and Spirit–Controlled', *EJ* (Spring, 2001). Online: http://enrichmentjournal.ag.org/200102/088_Endtime_revival.cfm (Accessed 14 August 2014).

Conforti, Joseph, *Jonathan Edwards, Religious Tradition, and American Culture* (Chapel Hill: University of North Carolina Press, 1993).

Conklin, Paul K., *Cane Ridge: America's Pentecost* (Curti Lecture Series; Madison: University of Wisconsin Press, 1990).

Cousar, Charles B., *A Theology of the Cross: The Death of Jesus in the Pauline Letters* (Minneapolis: Fortress, 1990).

Cousins, Ewert H., 'What Is Christian Spirituality?', in *Modern Christian Spirituality: Methodological and Historical Essays* (ed. Bradley C. Hanson; Atlanta: Scholars Press, 1990), pp. 39–44.

Covington, Dennis, *Salvation on Sand Mountain: Snake–Handling and Redemption in Southern Appalachia* (New York: Penguin, 1995).

Cox, Harvey, *Fire from Heaven: The Rise of Pentecostal Spirituality and the Reshaping of Religion in the Twenty–first Century* (Reading, MA: Addison–Wesley, 1995).

Craig, James Dunlop, '"Out and Out for the Lord" – James Eustace Purdie: An Early Anglican Pentecostal' (Unpublished MA thesis). Online: https://paoc.org/docs/default-source/paoc-family-docs/Archives/Academic-Resources/j-craig---purdie-thesis.pdf (Accessed 14 August 2014).

Creech, Joe, 'Visions of Glory: The Place of the Azusa Street Revival in Pentecostal History', *CH* 65 (1996), pp. 405–24.

Cross, Robert D. (ed.), *The Church and the City, 1865–1910* (American Heritage Series, vol. 61; Indianapolis: Bobbs-Merrill, 1967).

Cross, Terry L., 'The Rich Feast of Theology: Can Pentecostals Bring the Main Course or Only the Relish?', *JPT* 8 (2000), pp. 27–47.

Cunningham, Raymond J., 'From Holiness to Healing: The Faith Cure in America, 1872–1892', *CH* 43 (1974), pp. 499–513.

—, 'Ministry of Healing: The Origin of the Psychotherapeutic Role of the American Churches' (Ph.D. diss.; Johns Hopkins University, 1965).

Curtis, Heather D., *Faith in the Great Physician: Suffering and Divine Healing in American Culture, 1860–1900* (Lived Religions. Baltimore: Johns Hopkins University Press, 2007).

Dabney, D. Lyle, 'Naming the Spirit: Towards a Pneumatology of the Cross', in *Starting with the Spirit: The Task of Theology Today II* (ed. Stephen Pickard and Gordon Preece; Hindmarsh, SA: Australian Theological Forum, 2001), pp. 28–58.

—, 'Saul's Armor: The Problem and the Promise of Pentecostal Theology Today', *Pneuma* 23 (2001), pp. 115–46.

—, '*Pneumatologia Crucis*: Reclaiming *Theologia Crucis* for a Theology of the Spirit Today', *SJT* 53 (2000), pp. 511–24.

—, *Die Kenosis des Geistes: Kontinuitat zwischen Schopfung und Erlosung im Werk des Heiligen Geistes* (Neukirchener Beitrage zur systematischen Theologie Band 18; Neukirchen-Vluyn: Neukirchener Verlag, 1997).

Daugherty, Billy Joe, *You Can Be Healed: How to Believe God for Your Healing* (Shippensburg, PA: Destiny Image, 2006).

Davis, Kenneth R., 'Anabaptism as a Charismatic Movement', *MQR* (1979), pp. 219–34.

Dayton, Donald W., 'Preface', in *The Heart of the Gospel: A. B. Simpson, the Fourfold Gospel, and Late Nineteenth-Century Evangelical Theology* (Princeton Theological Monograph; ed. Bernie Van De Walle, Eugene, OR: Wipf and Stock, 2009), pp. ix–xvi.

—, 'The Limits of Evangelicalism: The Pentecostal Tradition', in *The Variety of American Evangelicalism* (ed. D. W. Dayton and R. K. Johnston; Downers Grove: InterVarsity, 1991), pp. 36–56.

—, *Theological Roots of Pentecostalism* (Grand Rapids: Zondervan, 1987).

—, 'The Rise of the Evangelical Healing Movement in the Nineteenth Century America', *Pneuma* 4 (1982), pp. 1–18.

—, 'From "Christian Perfection" to "Baptism of the Holy Ghost"', in *Aspects of Pentecostal-Charismatic Origins* (ed. Vinson Synan; Plainfield, NJ: Logos, 1975), pp. 40–54.

—, 'Asa Mahan and the Development of American Holiness Theology', *WJT* 9 (1974), 60–69.

Dempster, Murray W., Byron D. Klaus and Douglas Petersen (eds), *The Globalization of Pentecostalism, A Religion Made to Travel* (Irving, CA: Regnum Books International, 1999).

Deppermann, Klaus, *Melchior Hoffman: Social Unrest and Apocalyptic Visions in the Age of Reformation* (ed. Benjamin Drewery; trans. Malcolm Wren; Edinburgh: T&T Clark, 1989).

Deppermann, Klaus, Werner O. Packull and James Stayer, 'From Monogenesis to *Polygenesis*: The Historical Discussion of Anabaptist Origins', *MQR* 49 (1975), pp. 83–121.

Dieter, Melvin Easterday, 'Response to Horton', in *Five Views on Sanctification* (ed. Stanley Gundry; Grand Rapids: Zondervan, 1987, 1996), pp. 136–38.

—, 'The Development of Nineteenth Century Holiness Theology', *WTJ* 20 (1985), pp. 61–77.

—, *The Holiness Revival of the Nineteenth Century* (Studies in Evangelicalism, No. 1; Metuchen, NJ: Scarecrow, Press, 1980).

Dobson, Ed and Ed Hindson, *The Fundamentalist Phenomenon: The Resurgence of Conservative Christianity* (ed. Jerry Falwell; Garden City, NY: Doubleday–Galilee, 1981).

Dolan, Jay, *Catholic Revivalism: The American Experience, 1830–1900* (Notre Dame, IN: University of Notre Dame Press, 1978).

Dreyer, Frederick, *The Genesis of Methodism* (Cranbury, NJ: Lehigh University Press, 1999).

Duffield, Guy P. and Nathaniel M. Van Cleave, *Foundations of Pentecostal Theology* (Los Angeles: L.I.F.E. Bible College, 1983).

Dunn, James D. G., *Jesus and the Spirit: A Study of the Religious and Charismatic Experience of Jesus and the First Christians as Reflected in the New Testament* (London: SCM, 1975).

Dyrness, William, Veli–Matti Kärkkäinen and Juan Francisco Martinez (eds), *Global Dictionary of Theology: A Resource for the Worldwide Church* (Downers Grove: InterVarsity Press, 2008).

Eastern Canada Superintendents, 'Education for the Next Generation', N.p.: N.p., 1999.

Eckadrt, Burnell F., 'Luther and Moltmann: The Theology of the Cross', *CTQ* 49 (1985), pp. 19–28.

Edwards, Jonathan, 'A Faithful Narrative', in *Jonathan Edwards, The Great Awakening* (ed. C. C. Goen; The Works of Jonathan Edwards, vol. 4; New Haven: Yale University Press, 1972), pp. 99–211.

Edwards, Mark U., *Luther's Last Battles: Politics and Polemics, 1531–46* (Leiden: E. J. Brill, 1985).

Eire, Carlos M. N., 'Major Problems in the Definition of Spirituality as an Academic Discipline', in *Modern Christian Spirituality: Methodological and Historical Essays* (ed. Bradley C. Hanson; Atlanta: Scholars, 1990), pp. 53–61.

Elton, Terri Martenson, 'Corps of Discovery', in *The Missional Church in Context: Helping Congregations Develop Contextual Ministry* (ed. Craig van Gelder; Grand Rapids: Eerdmans, 2007), pp. 143–45.

Ely, Richard T., *Studies in the Evolution of Industrial Society* (New York: Chatauqua Press, 1903).

Erb, Peter (ed.), *Johann Arndt: True Christianity* (Classics of Christian Spirituality, trans. Peter Erb; New York: Paulist, 1979).

Erdman, Charles. R., 'The Church and Socialism', in *The Fundamentals: A Testimony to the Truth, Volume XII* (ed. R. A. Torrey; Chicago: The Testimony Publishing Company, n.d), pp. 108–19.

Ervin, Howard M., *Conversion–Initiation and the Baptism in the Holy Spirit: A Critique of James D. G. Dunn's Baptism in the Holy Spirit* (Peabody, MA: Hendrickson, 1984).

Eslinger, Ellen, *Citizens of Zion: The Social Origins of Camp Meeting Revivalism* (Knoxville: University of Tennessee Press, 1999).

Evensen, Bruce J., *God's Man for the Gilded Age: D.L. Moody and the Rise of Modern Mass Evangelism* (New York: Oxford University Press, 2003).

Farkas, Thomas George, *William Durham and the Sanctification Controversy in Early American Pentecostalism 1906–1916* (Unpublished dissertation; Southern Baptist Theological Seminary, Louisville, 1993).

Faupel, William D., *The Everlasting Gospel: The Significance of Eschatology in the Development of Pentecostal Thought* (Sheffield: Sheffield Academic Press, 1996).

—, 'Whither Pentecostalism? 22nd Presidential Address, Society for Pentecostal Studies, November 7, 1992', *Pneuma* 15 (1993), pp. 9–27.
Fee, Gordon D., *God's Empowering Presence: The Holy Spirit in the Letters of Paul* (Peabody, MA: Hendrickson, 1994).
—, 'Hermeneutics and Historical Precedent – A Major Problem in Pentecostal Hermeneutics', in *Perspectives on the New Pentecostalism* (ed. Russell P. Spittler; Grand Rapids: Baker Book House, 1976), pp. 118–32.
Fiddes, Paul S., *The Creative Suffering of God* (Oxford: Clarendon Press, 1988).
Findlay, James F. Jr, *Dwight L. Moody: American Evangelist, 1837–1899* (Grand Rapids: Baker, [1969] 1973).
Finney, Charles G., *Lectures on Revivals of Religion* (ed. William G. McLoughlin; Cambridge: Belknap Press of Harvard University Press, 1960).
—, *Finney's Lectures on Systematic Theology* (ed. J. H. Fairchild; Grand Rapids: Eerdmans, [1878] 1957).
Flower, J. R., 'The Present Position of Pentecost', *PE* 601 (13 June 1925), pp. 7–8, 13.
Fogarty, Robert S., *All Things New: American Communes and Utopian Movements, 1860–1914* (Chicago: University of Chicago Press, 1990).
Föller, Oskar, 'Martin Luther on Miracles, Healing, Prophecy and Tongues', *SHE* 31 (2005), pp. 333–51.
Forde, Gerhard O., *On Being a Theologian of the Cross: Reflections on Luther's Heidelberg Disputation, 1518* (Grand Rapids: Eerdmans, 1997).
—, 'The Lutheran View', in *Christian Spirituality: Five Views on Sanctification* (ed. Donald L. Alexander; Downers Grove: InterVarsity, 1988), pp. 13–32.
Foster, Charles I., *An Errand of Mercy: The Evangelical United Front 1790–1837* (Chapel Hill: University of North Carolina Press, 1960).
Fowler, C. H., 'The Higher Life-An Entire Consecration', *CMM* 6 (July–December, 1877), pp. 80–83.
Fraser, Brian J., *The Social Uplifters: Presbyterian Progressives and the Social Gospel in Canada, 1875–1915* (Waterloo: Wilfrid Laurier University Press, 1988).
Frodsham, Stanley, *'With Signs Following': The Story of the Latter Day Pentecostal Revival* (Springfield MO: Gospel Publishing House, 1926).
—, 'Disfellowhiped!', *PE* 601 (1925), p. 8.
—, 'Dear Evangel Reader', *PE* 541 (1924), p. 15.
Froelich, Karlfried, 'Luther on Vocation', in *Harvesting Martin Luther's Reflections on Theology, Ethics, and the Church* (Lutheran Quarterly Books, ed. Timothy Wengert; Grand Rapids: Eerdmans, 2004), pp. 121–33.
—, 'Charismatic Manifestation and the Lutheran Incarnational Stance', in *The Holy Spirit in the Life of the Church: From Biblical Times to the Present* (ed. Paul D. Opsahl; Minneapolis: Augsburg, 1978), pp. 136–57.
Fudge, Thomas A., *Christianity without the Cross: A History of Salvation in Oneness Pentecostalism* (Parkland, FL: Universal Publishers, 2003).
Fuller, Daniel P., 'The Holy Spirit's Role in Biblical Interpretation', *IJFM* 16 (1997), pp. 91–95.
Gaines, Adrienne S., 'Billy Joe Daugherty Dies at 57'. Online: http://www.charismamag.com/site-archives/570-news/featured-news/8133-billy-joe-daugherty-dies-at-57 (Accessed 15 August 2014).
Gaster, Theodor, 'Myth and Story', in *Sacred Narrative: Readings in the Theory of Myth* (ed. Allen Dundes; Los Angeles: University of California Press, 1984), pp. 110–36.
Gerrish, Brian, '"To the Unknown God": Luther and Calvin on the Hiddenness of God', *JR* 53 (1973), pp. 263–92.

Goff, James R., Jr, *Fields White Unto Harvest: Charles F. Parham and the Missionary Origins of Pentecostalism* (Fayetteville, AR: University of Arkansas Press, 1988).
Graham, Stephen R., '"Thus Saith the Lord": Biblical Hermeneutics in the Early Pentecostal Movement', *EA* 12 (1996), pp. 121–35.
Granquist, Mark A., 'Between Pietism, Revivalism and Modernity: Samuel Simon Schmucker and American Lutheranism in the Early Nineteenth Century', in *Pietism, Revivalism and Modernity, 1650–1850* (ed. Fred van Lieburg and Daniel Lindmark; Newcastle upon-Tyne: Cambridge Scholars Publishing, 2008), pp. 256–73.
Green, Chris E. W., *Toward a Pentecostal Theology of the Lord's Supper: Foretasting the Kingdom* (Cleveland, TN: CPT Press, 2012).
Grenz, Stanley J., *Theology for the Community of God* (Grand Rapids: Eerdmans, 1994).
Gresham, John L., *Charles G. Finney's Doctrine of the Baptism of the Holy Spirit* (Peabody, MA: Hendrickson, 1987).
Gritsch, Eric W., *Martin-God's Court Jester* (Grudem, Wayne. *The Gift of Prophecy: In the New Testament and Today* (Eastbourne, UK: Kingsway, 1988).
Guelzo, Allen C., 'Oberlin Perfectionism and Its Edwardsian Origins, 1835–1870', in *Jonathan Edwards' Writings: Text, Context, and Interpretation* (ed. Stephen J. Stein; Bloomington, IN: Indiana University Press, 1996), pp. 159–73.
Hall, Douglas J., *The Cross in Our Context: Jesus and the Suffering World* (Minneapolis: Fortress, 2003).
—, *Confessing the Faith: Christian Theology in a North American Context* (Minneapolis: Fortress, 1996).
—, *Professing the Faith: Christian Theology in a North American Context* (Minneapolis: Fortress, 1993).
—, *Thinking the Faith: Christian Theology in a North American Context* (Minneapolis: Fortress, 1989).
—, *God and Human Suffering: An Exercise in the Theology of the Cross* (Minneapolis: Augsburg, 1986).
—, *Lighten Our Darkness: Toward an Indigenous Theology of the Cross* (Philadelphia: Westminster, 1976).
—, 'The Theology of the Cross: A Usable Past', n.p., n.d. Online: http://www.bradschrum.com/wp-content/uploads/2011/10/TheTheologyoftheCross_pdf.pdf (Accessed 14 August 2014).
Haller, John S., *American Medicine in Transition, 1840–1910* (Urbana: University of Illinois Press, 1981).
Hamm, Berndt, 'An Opponent of the Devil and the Modern Age: Oberman's View of the Luther', in *The Work of Heiko A. Oberman: Papers from the Symposium on His Seventieth Birthday* (ed. Thomas A. Brady, Katherine G. Brady, Susan Karant Nunn and James D Tracy, Kirkhistoriche Bijdragen, vol. 2+0; Leiden: Brill, 2003), pp. 31–49.
Hamon, Bill, *The Day of the Saints: Equipping Believers for Their Revolutionary Role in Ministry* (Shippensberg, PA: Destiny Image, 2002).
Handy, Robert T., *A Christian America: Protestant Hopes and Historical Realities* (New York: Oxford University Press; 2nd ed. rev. and enlgd.; [1971] 1984).
Hanegraaff, Hank, *Christianity in Crisis: 21st Century* (Nashville: Thomas Nelson, 2009).
Hanson, Bradley C., 'Spirituality or Spiritual Theology', in *Modern Christian Spirituality: Methodological and Historical Essays* (ed. Bradley C. Hanson; Atlanta: Scholars, 1990), pp. 45–51.
Harakas, Stanley, 'The Sacrament of Healing', *IRM* 90 (2001), pp. 81–86.

Hardesty, Nancy A., *Faith Cure: Divine Healing in the Holiness and Pentecostal Movements* (Peabody, MA: Hendrickson, 2003).
Harding, Sandra, *Whose Science? Whose Knowledge? Thinking from Women's Lives* (Ithaca, NY: Cornell University Press, 1991).
Hardman, Keith J., *Seasons of Refreshing: Evangelism and Revivals in America* (Grand Rapids: Baker, 1994).
Harrell, David Edwin, Jr, 'Bipolar Protestantism: The Straight and Narrow Ways', in *Re-Forming the Center: American Protestantism, 1900 to the Present* (ed. Douglas Jacobsen and William Vance Trollinger, Jr; Grand Rapids: Eerdmans, 1998), pp. 15–30.
—, *All Things Are Possible: The Healing and Charismatic Revivals in Modern America* (Bloomington: Indiana University Press, 1979).
Harrington, Hannah K. and Rebecca Patten, 'Pentecostal Hermeneutics and Postmodern Literary Theory', *Pneuma* 16 (1994), pp. 109–14.
Hebblethwaite, Brian, *The Christian Hope: Revised Edition* (New York: Oxford University Press, 2010).
Hefner, Robert W. (ed.), *Global Pentecostalism in the 21st Century* (Indiana: Indiana University Press, 2013).
Hempton, David, 'John Wesley (1703–1791)', in *The Pietist Theologians: An Introduction to the Theology of the Seventeenth and Eighteenth Centuries* (ed. Carter Lindberg; Oxford: Blackwell, 2005), pp. 256–72.
Heschel, Abraham J., *The Prophets, 2 Vols* (New York: Harper Torchbooks, 1975).
Hocken, Peter, *The Challenges of the Pentecostal, Charismatic, and Messianic Jewish Movements: The Tensions of the Spirit* (Ashgate New Critical Thinking in Religion, Theology, and Biblical Studies; Aldershot, UK: Ashgate, 2009).
Hoffman, Bengt R., *Luther and the Mystics: A Re-examination of Luther's Spiritual Experience and His Relationship to the Mystics* (Minneapolis: Augsburg, 1976).
Holl, Karl, *What Did Luther Understand by Religion?* (ed. James Luther Adams and Walter F. Bense; trans. Fred W. Meuser and Walter R. Weitzke; Philadelphia: Fortress, 1977).
Hollenweger, Walter J., *Pentecostalism: Origins and Developments Worldwide* (East Lynn, MA: Hendrickson, 1997).
—, 'Pentecostals and the Charismatic Movement', in *The Study of Spirituality* (ed. Cheslyn Jones, Geoffrey Wainwright and Edward Yarnold; London: SPCK, 1986), pp. 549–54.
—, *The Pentecostals: The Charismatic Movement in the Churches* (trans. R. A. Wilson; Minneapolis: Augsburg, 1972).
Holm, Randy, 'Tongues and a Postmodern Generation' (Unpublished paper, delivered at 'The Many Faces of Pentecostalism', McMaster University, 25 October 2008). Online,: http://www.mts.net/~rfholm/spiritmcmaster.htm (Accessed 14 August 2014).
Holmes, Peter R., 'Spirituality: Some Disciplinary Perspectives', in *A Sociology of Spirituality* (Theology and Religion in Interdisciplinary Perspective; ed. Kieran Flanagan and Peter C. Jupp; Farnham, UK: Ashgate, 2007), pp. 23–42.
Hood, Ralph W. Jr, 'When the Spirit Maims and Kills: Social Psychological Considerations of the History of Serpent Handling Sects and the Narrative of Handlers', *IJPR* 8 (1998), pp. 71–96 (p. 73).
Hood, Ralph W. and David L. Kimbrough, 'Serpent-Handling Holiness Sects: Theoretical Considerations', *JSSR* 34 (1995), pp. 311–22.
Hordern, William, *Experience and Faith: The Significance of Luther for Understanding Today's Experiential Religion* (Minneapolis: Augsburg, 1983).
Horton, Stanley M., 'The Pentecostal Perspective', in *Five Views on Sanctification* (ed. Stanley Gundry; Counterpoint; Grand Rapids: Zondervan, [1987] 1996), pp. 103–35.

Hughes, Richard T., 'Preface: The Meaning of the Restoration Vision', in *The Primitive Church in the Modern World* (ed. Richard T. Hughes; Urbana and Chicago: University of Illinois Press, 1995), pp. ix–xviii.

—, 'Are Restorationists Evangelicals?', in *The Variety of American Evangelicalism* (ed. D. W. Dayton and R. K. Johnston; Downers Grove: InterVarsity, 1991), pp. 109–34.

—, 'Christian Primitivism as Perfectionism: From Anabaptists to Pentecostals', in *Reaching Beyond: Chapters in the History of Perfectionism* (ed. Stanley M. Burgess; Peabody, MA: Hendrickson Publishers, 1986), pp. 213–55.

Hurka, Thomas, *Perfectionism* (New York: Oxford University Press, 1993).

Hutchison, William R., *Errand to the World: American Protestant Thought and Foreign Missions* (Chicago: University of Chicago Press, 1987).

Institute for Ecumenical Research. Lutherans and Pentecostals in Dialogue (Strasbourg: Institute for Ecumenical Research, 2010). Online: http://strasbourginstitute.org/wp-content/uploads/2012/08/Lutherans-and-Pentecostals-in-Dialogue-Text-FINAL.pdf (Accessed 16 August 2014).

Israel, Richard D., Daniel Albrecht and Randall McNally, 'Pentecostals and Hermeneutics: Texts, Rituals and Community', *Pneuma* 15 (1993), pp. 137–61.

Jackson, Bill, 'A Short History the Association of Vineyard Churches', in *Church, Identity, and Change: Theology and Denominational Structures in Unsettled Times* (ed. David A. Roozen and James R. Nieman; Grand Rapids: Eerdmans, 2005), pp. 132–40.

Jackson, Thomas, *Memoirs of the Life and Writings of the Rev. Richard Watson, Late Scecretary of the Wesleyan Missionary Society, Second Edition* (London: John Mason, 1834).

Jacobsen, Douglas, *Thinking in the Spirit: Theologies of the Early Pentecostal Movement* (Bloomington, IN: Indiana University Press, 2003).

—, 'Knowing the Doctrines of Pentecostals: The Scholastic Theology of the Assemblies of God, 1930–55', in *Pentecostal Currents in American Protestantism* (ed. Edith L. Blumhofer, Russell P. Spittler and Grant A. Wacker; Urbana: University of Illinois Press, 1999), pp. 90–107.

Jacobsen, Douglas and William Vance Trollinger, Jr, 'Introduction', in *Re-Forming the Center: American Protestantism, 1900 to the Present* (ed. Douglas Jacobsen and William Vance Trollinger, Jr; Grand Rapids: Eerdmans, 1998), pp. 1–14.

Jacobsen, Douglas and William Vance Trollinger, Jr (eds), *Re-Forming the Center: American Protestantism, 1900 to the Present* (Grand Rapids: Eerdmans, 1998).

Jenkins, Philip, *The Next Christendom: The Coming of Global Christianity* (New York: Oxford University Press, 2002).

Johns, Jackie David, 'Yielding to the Spirit: The Dynamics of a Pentecostal Model of Praxis', in *The Globalization of Pentecostalism: A Religion Made to Travel* (ed. Murray W. Dempster, Byron D. Klaus and Douglas Petersen; Oxford: Regnum, 1999), pp. 70–84.

Johnson, Luke Timothy, *Religious Experience in Earliest Christianity: A Missing Dimension in New Testament Studies* (Minneapolis: Fortress, 1998).

Jones, Charles Edwin, 'Reclaiming the Text in Methodist-Holiness and Pentecostal Spirituality', *WTJ* 30 (1995), pp. 164–81.

—, 'Anti-Ordinance: A Proto-Pentecostal Phenomenon?', *WTJ* 25 (1990), pp. 7–23.

—, *Perfectionist Persuasion: The Holiness Movement and American Methodism, 1867–1936* (ATLA Monograph Series, No. 5; Metuchen, NJ: Scarecrow, 1974).

Jowers, Dennis W., 'The Theology of the Cross as Theology of the Trinity: A Critique of Jürgen Moltmann's Staurocentric Trinitarianism', *TB* 52 (2001), pp. 245–66.

Kärkkäinen, Veli-Matti, 'Theology of the Cross: A Stumbling-Block to Pentecostal-Charismatic Spirituality?', in *The Spirit and Spirituality: Essays in Honor of Russell P. Spittler* (ed. Wonsuk Ma and Robert P. Menzies; London and New York: T&T Clark, 2004), pp. 150–63.

—, 'Identity and Plurality: A Pentecostal-Charismatic Perspective', *IRM* 91 (2002), pp. 500–3.

—, *An Introduction to Ecclesiology: Ecumenical, Historical, & Global Perspectives* (Downers Grove: InterVarsity, 2002).

—, *Pneumatology: The Holy Spirit in Ecumenical, International, and Contextual Perspectives* (Grand Rapids: Baker Academic, 2002).

—, 'David's Sling: The Promise and the Problem of Pentecostal Theology Today: A Response to D. Lyle Dabney', *Pneuma* 23 (2001), pp. 147–52.

—, *Ad Ultimum Terrae: Evangelization, Proselytism and Common Witness in the Roman Catholic Pentecostal Dialogue (1990–1997)* (Studies in the Intellectual History of Christianity, vol. 117; Frankfurt-am-Main: Peter Lang, 1999).

—, 'Authority, Revelation, and Interpretation in the Roman Catholic-Pentecostal Dialogue', *Pneuma* 21 (1999), pp. 89–114.

—, *Spiritus Ubi Vult Spirat: Pneumatology in Roman Catholic-Pentecostal Dialogue (1972–1989)* (Schriften der Luther-Agricola-Gesellschaft 42. Helsinki: Luther-Agricola-Society, 1998).

—, 'Pentecostal Hermeneutics in the Making: On the Way from Fundamentalism to Postmodernism', *JEPTA* 8 (1996), pp. 76–115.

Keefer, Luke L. Jr, 'John Wesley: Disciple of Early Christianity', *WJT* 19 (1984), pp. 23–32.

Kelly, Robert, 'Successful or Justified? The North American Doctrine of Salvation by Works', *CTQ* 65 (2001), pp. 224–54.

Kidd, Thomas S., *The Great Awakening: The Roots of Evangelical Christianity in Colonial America* (New Haven: Yale University Press, 2007).

Kitamori, Kazo, *Theology of the Pain of God* (Richmond: John Knox, 1965).

Kolb, Robert and Charles Arand, *The Genius of Luther's Theology: A Wittenberg Way of Thinking for the Contemporary Church* (Grand Rapids: Baker Academic, 2008).

—, 'Luther on the Theology of the Cross', *Lutheran Quarterly* XVI (2002), pp. 443–67.

Kostlevy, William, *Holy Jumpers: Evangelicals and Radicals in Progressive Era America* (New York: Oxford University Press, 2010).

Kraft, Charles H., 'Five Years Later', in *Signs and Wonders Today: The Story of Fuller Theological Seminary's Remarkable Course on Spiritual Power, New Expanded Edition* (ed. C. Peter Wagner; Altamonte Springs, FL: Creation House, 1987), pp. 115–23.

Kraus, C. Norman, 'Evangelicalism: The Great Coalition', in *Evangelicalism and Anabaptism* (ed. Norman Kraus; Scottdale, PA: Herald, 1979), pp. 39–61.

Kuo, David, *Tempting Faith: An Inside Story of Political Seduction* (New York: Free, 2006).

Kydd, Ronald A. N., *Healing Through the Centuries: Models for Understanding* (Peabody, MA: Hendrickson, 1998).

Kyle, Richard G., *Evangelicalism: An Americanized Christianity* (New Brunswick, NJ: Transaction Publishers, 2006).

Lambert, Frank, *Inventing the 'Great Awakening'* (Princeton, NJ: Princeton University Press, 1999).

Land, Steven Jack, *Pentecostal Spirituality: A Passion for the Kingdom* (Journal of Pentecostal Studies Supplement Series; London: Sheffield Academic Press, 1993).

Lawrence, B. F., *The Apostolic Faith Restored* (St. Louis: Gospel Publishing House, 1916).

Lederle, Henry, *Treasures Old and New: Interpretations of 'Spirit-Baptism' in the Charismatic Renewal Movement* (Peabody, MA: Hendrickson, 1988).

Lewis, Alan, *Between Cross and Resurrection: A Theology of Holy Saturday* (Grand Rapids: Eerdmans, 2001).

Lie, Geir, *E. W. Kenyon: Cult Founder or Evangelical Minister?* (The Refleks-series, No. 2; Oslo: Refleks Publishing, 2003).

Lindberg, Carter, 'Introduction', in *The Pietist Theologians: An Introduction to the Theology of the Seventeenth and Eighteenth Centuries* (ed. Carter Lindberg; Oxford: Blackwell, 2005), pp. 1–20.

—, *The Third Reformation? Charismatic Movements and the Lutheran Tradition* (Macon: Mercer University Press, 1983).

Loewen, Harry, *Luther and the Radicals: Another Look at Some Aspects of the Struggle between Luther and the Radical Reformers* (Waterloo: Wilfrid Laurier University, 1974).

Lohse, Bernhard, *Martin Luther's Theology: Its Historical and Systematic Development* (trans. Roy A. Harrisville; Minneapolis: Fortress, 1999).

—, *Martin Luther: An Introduction to His Life and Work* (trans. Robert C. Schultz; Philadelphia: Fortress, 1986).

—, *A Short History of Christian Doctrine: From the First Century to the Present-Revised American Edition* (trans. Ernest F. Stoeffler; Minneapolis: Fortress, 1985).

Louw, Daniël, *Meaning in Suffering: A Theological Reflection on the Cross and the Resurrection for Pastoral Care and Counselling* (International Theology, vol. 5; Frankfurt am Main: Peter Lang, 2000).

Lovett, Leonard, 'Black Origins of the Pentecostal Movement', in *Aspects of Pentecostal-Charismatic Origins* (ed. Vinson Synan; Plainfield, NJ: Logos, 1975), pp. 123–41.

Lummis, Adair T., 'Brand Name Identity in a Post-Denominational Age: Regional Leaders Perspectives On Its Importance for Churches' (Delivered at The Annual Meetings of the Society for the Scientific Study of Religion Columbus, Ohio, October, 2001). Online: http://hirr.hartsem.edu/bookshelf/lummis_article1.html#return1 (Accessed 15 August 2014).

Lutheran Church-Missouri Synod, 'The Charismatic Movement and Lutheran Theology' (A Report of the Commision on Theology and Church Relation of Lutheran Church-Mussouri Synod, 1972). Online: www.lcms.org/Document.fdoc?src=lcm&id=426 (Accessed 14 August 2014).

Lyotard, Jean François, *The Postmodern Condition: A Report on Knowledge* (trans. Geoff Bennington and Brian Massumi; Theory of History and Literature, vol. 10; Minneapolis: University of Minnesota Press, [1979] 1984).

Macchia, Frank D., 'Baptized in the Spirit: Towards a Global Theology of Spirit Baptism', in *The Spirit and the Word: Emerging Pentecostal Theologies in Global Contexts* (ed. Veli-Matti Kärkkäinen; Grand Rapids: Eerdmans, 2009), pp. 3–20.

—, 'Baptized in the Spirit: A Global Pentecostal Theology', in *Defining Issues in Pentecostalism: Classical and Emergent* (ed. Steven M. Studebaker; McMaster Theological Studies Series, vol. 1; Eugene, OR: Pickwick, 2008), pp. 13–28.

—, *Baptized in the Spirit: A Global Pentecostal Theology* (Grand Rapids: Zondervan, 2006).

—, 'Groans Too Deep for Words: Towards a Theology of Tongues as Initial Evidence', *AJPS* 1 (1998), pp. 149–73. Online: http://www.apts.edu/aeimages//File/AJPS_PDF/98-2-macchia.pdf (Accessed 15 August 2014).

—, 'The Tongues of Pentecost: A Pentecostal Perspective on the Promise and Challenge of Pentecostal/Roman Catholic Dialogue', *JES* 35 (1998), pp. 1–18.

—, 'Tongues as a Sign: Towards a Sacramental Understanding of Pentecostal Experience', *Pneuma* 15 (1993), pp. 61–76.
—, 'Sighs Too Deep For Words: Toward a Theology of Glossolalia', *JPT* 1 (1992), pp. 47–73.
Maddox, Randy L., *Responsible Grace: John Wesley's Practical Theology* (Nashville: Abingdon, 1994).
Madsen, Anna M., *The Theology of the Cross in Historical Perspective. Distinguished Dissertations in Christian Theology* (Eugene, OR: Pickwick, 2007).
Mahan, Asa, *The Baptism of the Holy Ghost* (New York: George Hughes, 1870).
Mannermaa, Tuomo, *Christ Present in Faith: Luther's View Of Justification* (trans. Kirsi Stjerna; Minneapolis: Augsburg Fortress, 2005).
—, 'Justification and *Theosis* in Lutheran-Orthodox Perpective', in *Union with Christ: The New Finnish Interpretation of Luther* (ed. Carl E. Braaten and Robert M. Jenson; Grand Rapids: Eerdmans, 1998), pp. 25–41.
Marsden, George M., *Understanding Fundamentalism and Evangelicalism* (Grand Rapids: Eerdmans, 1991).
—, *Reforming Fundamentalism: Fuller Seminary and the New Evangelicalism* (Grand Rapids: Eerdmans, 1987).
—, *Fundamentalism and American Culture: The Shaping of Twentieth Century Evangelicalism, 1870–1925* (New York: Oxford University Press, 1980).
Martin, David, *Pentecostalism: The World Their Parish* (Oxford: Blackwell, 2002).
—, *Tongues of Fire: The Explosion of Protestantism in Latin America* (Oxford: Blackwell, 1990).
Martin, Roger, *R.A. Torrey: Apostle of Certainty* (N.p.: Sword of the Lord Press, 1976).
Marty, Martin E., *A Nation of Behavers* (Chicago: University of Chicago Press, 1976).
—, *Righteous Empire: The Protestant Experience in America* (New York: Dial Press, 1970).
McConnell, D. R., *A Different Gospel: A Historical and Biblical Analysis of the Modern Faith Movement, Updated Edition* (Peabody, MA: Hendrickson, 1995).
McGee, Gary B., '"More Than Evangelical": The Challenge of the Evolving Identity of the Assemblies of God', in *Church, Identity, and Change: Theology and Denominational Structures in Unsettled Times* (ed. David A. Roozen and James R. Nieman; Grand Rapids: Eerdmans, 2005), pp. 35–44.
McGinn, Bernard, 'Introduction', in *Christian Spirituality: Origins to the Twelfth Century* (ed. Bernard McGinn, John Meyendorff and Jean Lelerq; World Spirituality, vol. 16; London: Routledge and Kegan Paul, 1986), pp. xv–xxiii.
McGrath Alister E., *Luther's Theology of the Cross: Martin Luther's Theological Breakthrough* (Oxford: Basil Blackwell, 1985).
McLean, Mark D., 'Toward a Pentecostal Hermeneutic', *Pneuma* 6 (1984), pp. 35–56.
McLoud, Sean, *Divine Hierarchies: Class in American Religion and Religious Studies* (Chapel Hill: University of North Carolina Press, 2007).
McLoughlin, William G., *Revivals, Awakenings, and Reform: An Essay on Religion and Social Change in America, 1607–1977* (Chicago History of American Religion; Chicago: University of Chicago Press, 1978).
—, 'Pietism and the American Character', *AQ* 17 (1965), pp. 163–86.
McQuilkin, J. Robertson, 'The Keswick Perspective', in *Five Views on Sanctification* (ed. Stanley Gundry; Counterpoint; Grand Rapids: Zondervan, [1987] 1996), pp. 149–83.
—, 'Response to Horton', in *Five Views on Sanctification* (ed. Stanley Gundry; Counterpoint; Grand Rapids: Zondervan, [1987] 1996), pp. 143–45.
Mead, Sidney E., *The Nation with the Soul of a Church* (New York: Harper & Row, 1975).

Menzies, Robert P., 'Jumping Off the Postmodern Bandwagon', *Pneuma* 16 (1994), pp. 115–20.
Menzies, William W., 'The Reformed Roots of Pentecostalism', *PentecoStudies* 6 (2007), pp. 78–99.
—, 'The Challenges of Organization and Spirit in the Implementation of Theology in the Assemblies of God', in *Church, Identity, and Change: Theology and Denominational Structures in Unsettled Times* (ed. by David A. Roozen and James R. Nieman; Grand Rapids: Eerdmans, 2005), pp. 97–131.
—, 'Non-Wesleyan Origins of the Pentecostal Movement', in *Aspects of Pentecostal-Charismatic Origins* (ed. Vinson Synan; Plainfield, NJ: Logos, 1975), pp. 81–98.
—, *Anointed to Serve: The Story of The Assemblies of God* (Springfield, MO: Gospel Publishing House, 1971).
—, 'The Spirit of Holiness', *Paraclete* 2 (1968), p. 15.
Meyendorff, John, *Byzantine Theology: Historical Trends and Doctrinal Themes* (New York: Fordham University Press, 1974).
Meyer, Joyce, *Power Thoughts: 12 Strategies to Win the Battle of the Mind* (New York: FaithWords, 2010).
—, *Be Healed in Jesus' Name* (New York: Warner, 2000).
Miller, Donald and Tetsunao Yamamori, *Global Pentecostalism: The New Face of Christian Social Engagement* (Los Angeles: University of California Press, 2007).
Miller, Perry (ed.), *Errand into the Wilderness* (Cambridge: Belknap Press of Harvard University Press, 1956).
Miller, Thomas, *Canadian Pentecostals: A History of the Pentecostal Assemblies of Canada* (Mississauga: Full Gospel Publishing House, 1994).
—, *The New England Mind: From Colony to Province* (Cambridge: Harvard University Press, 1953).
Mittelstadt, Martin William, *The Spirit and Suffering in Luke-Acts: Implications for a Pentecostal Pneumatology* (London: T&T Clark, 2004).
Moessner, Donald, '"The Christ Must Suffer," The Church Must Suffer: Rethinking the Theology of the Cross in Luke-Acts', in *Society of Biblical Literature 1990 Seminar Papers* (ed. David J. Lul; Society of Biblical Literature Seminar Paper Series, Number 29l; Atlanta: Scholars Press, 1990), pp. 165–95.
Moltmann, Jürgen, *A Broad Place: A Biography* (trans. Margaret Kohl; Minneapolis: Fortress, 2008).
—, *The Coming of God: Christian Eschatology* (trans. Margaret Kohl; Minneapolis: Fortress, 1996).
—, *God in Creation: A New Theology of Creation and the Spirit of God* (trans. Margaret Kohl; Minneapolis: Fortress, 1993).
—, *Trinity and the Kingdom: The Doctrine of God* (trans. Margaret Kohl; Minneapolis: Fortress, 1993).
—, *The Way of Jesus Christ: Christology in Messianic Dimensions* (trans. Margaret Kohl; Minneapolis: Fortress Press, 1993).
—, *The Spirit of Life: A Universal Affirmation* (trans. Margaret Kohl; Minneapolis: Fortress, 1992).
—, *The Church in the Power of the Spirit: A Contribution to Messianic Christology* (trans. Margaret Kohl; New York: Harper & Row, 1977).
—, *The Crucified God: The Cross of Christ as the Foundation and Criticism of Christian Theology* (trans. R. A. Wilson and John Bowden; New York: Harper & Row, 1974).

—, *Theology of Hope: On the Ground and the Implications of a Christian Eschatology* (trans. James W. Leitch; New York: Harper & Row, 1967).
Monge, David J., 'Contextuality in the Theology of Douglas John Hall', *dialog* 41 (2002), pp. 210–20.
Moore, R. Laurence, *Religious Outsiders and the Making of America* (New York: Oxford University Press, 1986).
Moorhead, James H., 'The Erosion of Postmillennialism in American Religious Thought, 1865–1925', *CH* 53 (1984), pp. 61–77.
Moriarty, Michael G., *The New Charismatics: A Concerned Voice Responds to Dangerous Trends* (Grand Rapids: Zondervan, 1992).
Morrow, Jimmy, *Handling Serpents: Pastor Jimmy Morrow's Narrative History of His Appalachian Jesus' Name Tradition* (ed. Ralph W. Hood; Macon: Mercer University Press, 2005).
Mumford, Bob, *Take Another Look at Guidance: A Study of Divine Guidance* (ed. Jorunn Oftedal Ricketts; Plainfield, NJ: Logos International, 1971).
Munroe, Myles, *The Purpose and Power of Praise and Worship* (Shippensburg, PA: Destiny Image, 2000).
Murray, Bruce T., *Religious Liberty in America: The First Amendment in Historical and Contemporary Perspective* (Amherst, MA: University of Massachusetts Press, 2008).
Murray, Iain, *Revival and Revivalism: The Making and Marring of American Evangelicalism, 1750–1858* (Edinburgh: Banner of Truth, 1994).
Myland, D. Wesley, *The Latter Rain Covenant* (Springfield, MO: Temple Press, n.d.).
Neal, Ryan A., *Theology as Hope: On the Ground and Implications of Jürgen Moltmann's Doctrine of Hope* (Princeton Theological Monograph Series 99; Eugene, OR: Pickwick, 2008).
Neumann, Peter D., 'Encountering the Spirit: Pentecostal Mediated Experience of God in Theological Context', (Ph.D. diss.; University of St. Michael's College, 2010).
Newman, Joe, *Race and the Assemblies of God Church: The Journey from Azusa Street to the 'Miracle of Memphis'* (Youngstown, NY: Cambria Press, 2007).
Ngien, Dennis, *Gifted Response: The Triune God as the Causative Agency of Our Responsive Worship* (Milton Keynes, UK: Paternoster, 2008).
—, *Luther as a Spiritual Adviser: The Interface of Theology and Piety in Luther's Devotional Writings* (Studies in Christian Thought and History; Milton Keynes, UK: Paternoster, 2007).
—, *The Suffering of God According to Martin Luther's 'Theologia Crucis'* (New York: Peter Lang, 1995).
Nienkirchen, Charles W., *A. B. Simpson and the Pentecostal Movement: A Study in Continuity Crisis, and Change* (Eugene, OR: Wipf and Stock, [1992] n.d.).
Noel, Bradley Truman, *Pentecostal and Postmodern Hermeneutics: Comparisons and Contemporary Impact* (Eugene, OR: Wipf and Stock, 2010).
—, 'Gordon Fee and the Challenge to Pentecostal Hermeneutics: Thirty Years Later', *Pneuma* 26 (2004), pp. 60–80.
Noll, Mark A., *The Rise of Evangelicalism: The Age of Edwards, Whitefield and the Wesleys* (A History of Evangelicalism: People, Movements and Ideas in the English-Speaking World; Downers Grove: InterVarsity, 2003).
—, *Turning Points: Decisive Moments in the History of Christianity. Second Edition* (Grand Rapids: Baker, 2000).
Numbers, Ronald L., *Prophetess of Health: A Study of Ellen G. White, Third Edition* (Grand Rapids: Eerdmans, 2008).

—, 'Sex, Science and Salvation: The Sexual Advice of Ellen G. White and William Harvey Kellogg', in *Right-Living: An Anglo-American Tradition of Self-Help Medicine and Hygiene* (ed. Charles E. Rosenberg; Baltimore: Johns Hopkins University Press, 2003), pp. 206–26.

Oberman, Heiko A., *Luther: Man between God and the Devil* (trans. Eileen Walliser-Schwarzhart; New York: Image Books, 1992).

—, 'Teufelsdreck: Eschatology and Scatology in the "Old" Luther', *SCJ* 19 (1988), pp. 435–50.

—, '*Simul Gemitus et Raptus*: Luther and Mysticism', in *The Reformation in Medieval Perspective* (ed. Steven Ozment; Chicago: Quadrangle Books, 1971), pp. 219–51.

—, *The Harvest of Medieval Theology: Gabriel Biel and Late Medieval Nominalism* (Cambridge: Harvard University Press, 1963).

O'Dea, Thomas and Janet O'Dea Aviad, *The Sociology of Religion, Second Edition* (Englewood Cliffs: Prentice-Hall, 1986, 1st edn, 1966).

O'Malley, J. Steven, 'The Influence of Gerhard Tersteegen in the Documents of Early German American Evangelicalism', in *Pietism, Revivalism and Modernity, 1650–1850* (ed. Fred van Lieburg and Daniel Lindmark; Newcastle-upon-Tyne: Cambridge Scholars Publishing, 2008), pp. 232–55.

Opp, James William, *The Lord for the Body: Religion, Medicine, and Protestant Faith Healing in Canada, 1880–1930* (Montreal and Kingston: McGill-Queen's University Press, 2005).

Opsahl, Paul D., *The Holy Spirit in the Life of the Church: From Biblical Times to the Present* (Minneapolis: Augsburg, 1978).

Osborn, T. L., *Healing the Sick* (Tulsa: T.L. Osborn Evangelistic Association, 1959).

Ostling, Richard N., 'Reporters Name Reformation Millennium's Top Religious Event', *Moscow-Pullman Daily News*, 10 December 1999, 9A.

O'Toole, Roger (ed.), 'Symposium on Religious Awakenings', *SA* 44 (1983), pp. 81–122.

Otto, Rudolf, *The Idea of the Holy: An Inquiry into the Non-rational Factor in the Idea of the Divine and Its Relation to the Rational* (trans. John W. Harvey, 2nd edn; London: Oxford University Press, 1950).

Outler, Albert, 'The Wesleyan Quadrilateral in John Wesley', *WTJ* 20 (1985), pp. 7–18.

Outler, Albert, (ed.), *John Wesley* (New York: Oxford University Press, 1964).

Oyer, John S., *Lutheran Reformers against Anabaptists: Luther, Melanchthon, and Menius, and the Anabaptists of Central Germany* (The Dissent and Nonconformity Series, No. 13; Paris, AR: Baptist Standard Bearer, 2000).

Ozment, Steven, 'Eckhart and Luther: German Mysticism and Protestantism', *The Thomist* 42 (1978), pp. 258–80.

Palmer, Phoebe, *The Way of Holiness with Notes by the Way; Being a Narrative of Religious Experience Resulting from a Determination to be a Bible Christian* (Printed for the Author; New York: N.p., 1854).

Pannenberg, Wolfhart, *Systematic Theology, Volume I* (trans. Geoffrey Bromiley; Grand Rapids: Eerdmans, 1991).

Parham, Robert, *Selected Sermons of Charles F. Parham, Sarah E. Parham: Co-Founders of the Original Apostolic Faith Movement* (Baxter Springs, KS: Apostolic Faith Bible College, 1941).

Parker, Stephen E., *Led by the Spirit: Toward a Practical Theology of Pentecostal Discernment* (Sheffield: Sheffield Academic Press, 1996).

Parsons, Michael, 'The Apocalyptic Luther: His Noahic Self-Understanding', *JETS* 44 (2001), pp. 627–45.

'Pastor Billy Joe Daugherty'. Online: http://www.victory.com/pastor_letter/pl_home.asp (Accessed July, 2010, no longer accessible).

Patterson, Eric and Edmund Rybarczyk (eds), *The Future of Pentecostalism in the United States* (Lanham, MD: Lexington, 2007).

Pauck, Wilhelm (ed. and trans.), *Luther: Lectures on Romans* (The Library of Christian Classics, Louisville: Westminster John Knox, 1961).

Paulsen, Steven D., 'Luther on the Hidden God', *W&W* 19 (1999), pp. 363–71.

Pearlman, Myer, *Knowing the Doctrines of the Bible* (Springfield, MO: Gospel Publishing House, 1937).

—, *Through the Bible Book by Book, 4 Volumes* (Springfield, MO: Gospel Publishing House, 1935).

Pentecostal Assemblies of Canada, *Rooted in Relationship: General Conference, 2010* (Mississauga: PAOC, 2010).

—, 'Contemporary Prophets and Prophecy' (Position Paper; Mississauga: PAOC, 2007). Online: https://paoc.org/docs/default-source/Fellowship-Services-Docs/credential-resources/Forms-Documents/contemporary-prophets-and-prophecy.pdf (Accessed 14 August 2014).

—, *Miracles and Healings* (Position Paper; Mississauga: PAOC, 2007). Online: https://paoc.org/docs/default-source/Fellowship-Services-Docs/credential-resources/Forms-Documents/miracles-and-healing---11-07.pdf?sfvrsn=0 (Accessed 14 August 2014).

—, *Constitution and By-Laws of the Pentecostal Assemblies of Canada* (London, ON: N.p., 1928).

Peters, Thomas J. and Robert Waterman, Jr, *In Search of Excellence: Lessons from America's Best-Run Companies* (New York: Warner Books, 1982).

Peura, Simo, 'Christ as Favor and Gift: The Challenge of Luther's Understanding of Justification', in *Union with Christ: The New Finnish Interpretation of Luther* (ed. Carl E. Braaten and Robert M. Jenson; Grand Rapids: Eerdmans, 1998), pp. 42–69.

Pieper, Francis, *Christian Dogmatics* (4 vols; St. Louis: Concordia Publishing House, 1950–53).

Pinnock, Clark H., 'The Work of the Spirit in the Interpretation of Holy Scripture from the Perspective of a Charismatic Biblical Theologian', *JPT* 18 (2009), pp. 157–71.

Podmore, Colin, *The Moravian Church in England, 1728–1760* (New York: Oxford University Press, 1998).

Poewe, Karla, *Charismatic Christianity as Global Culture* (Columbia: University of South Carolina Press, 1994).

Poirier, John C. and B. Scott Lewis, 'Pentecostal and Postmodernist Hermeneutics: A Critique of Three Conceits', *JPS* 15 (2006), pp. 3–21.

—, 'The Work of the Holy Spirit in Hermeneutics', *JPT* 2 (1993), pp. 3–23.

Poloma, Margaret M., 'The Symbolic Dilemma and the Future of Pentecostalism: Mysticism, Ritual, and Revival', in *The Future of Pentecostalism in the United States* (ed. Eric Patterson and Edmund Rybarczyk; Lanham, MD: Lexington, 2007), pp. 105–21.

—, 'The Future of American Pentecostal Identity: The Assemblies of God at a Crossroad', in *The Work of the Spirit: Pneumatology and Pentecostalism* (ed. Michael Welker; Grand Rapids: Eerdmans, 2006), pp. 147–65.

—, 'Charisma and Structure in the Assemblies of God: Revisiting O'Dea's Five Dilemmas', in *Church, Identity, and Change: Theology and Denominational Structures in Unsettled Times* (ed. David A. Roozen and James R. Nieman; Grand Rapids: Eerdmans, 2005), pp. 45–96.

—, *Main Street Mystics: The Toronto Blessing and Reviving Pentecostalism* (Walnut Creek, CA: Alta Mira, 2003).
—, 'The "Toronto Blessing": Charisma, Institutionalization, and Revival', *JSSR* 36 (1997), pp. 257–71.
—, *The Assemblies of God at the Crossroads: Charisma and Institutional Dilemmas* (Knoxville: University of Tennessee Press, 1989).
Prenter, Regin, *Luther's Theology of the Cross* (Philadelphia: Fortress, 1971).
—, *Spiritus Creator* (trans. John M. Jensen; Philadelphia: Muhlenberg Press, 1953).
Purdie, J. Eustace, Letter to C.M. Wortman. 26 April 1955. 'Statement of Fundamental and Essential Truths File' (Archive of the Pentecostal assemblies of Canada; Mississauga ON).
—, *What We Believe* (Toronto: Full Gospel Publishing House, 1954).
—, *Concerning the Faith* (Toronto: Full Gospel Publishing House, 1951).
Putney, Clifford, *Muscular Christianity: Manhood and Sports in Protestant America, 1880–1920* (Cambridge, MA: Harvard University Press, 2001).
Pytches, David, *Some Said It Thundered: A Personal Encounter with the Kansas City Prophets* (Nashville: Oliver-Nelson, 1991).
Quandt, Jean B., 'Religion and Social Thought: The Secularization of Postmillennialism', *AQ* 25 (1973), pp. 390–409.
Rauschenbusch, Walter, *Christianity and the Social Crisis* (New York: MacMillan, 1909).
Reed, D. A., '*In Jesus' Name*': *The History and Beliefs of Oneness Pentecostals* (Journal of Pentecostal Theology Supplement Series Number 31; Blandford Forum, UK: Deo, 2008).
Reid, Daniel G. (ed.), *Dictionary of Christianity in America* (Downers Grove: InterVarsity Press, 1990).
Reid, Darrel R., 'Toward a Fourfold Gospel: A. B. Simpson, John Salmon, and the Christian and Missionary Alliance in Canada', in *Aspects of the Canadian Evangelical Experience* (ed. G. A. Rawlyk; Montreal and Kingston: McGill-Queen's University Press, 1997), pp. 271–88.
Reimer, Sam, *Evangelicals and the Continental Divide: The Conservative Protestant Subculture in Canada and the United States* (McGill-Queen's Studies in the History of Religion; Montreal and Kingston: McGill-Queen's University Press, 2003).
Richery, Russell E. and Donald G. Jones (eds), *American Civil Religion* (New York: Harper & Row, 1974).
—, Riley, William Bell, *The Finality of the Higher Criticism or the Theory of Evolution and False Theology* (New York: Garland, [1906] 1988).
Riss, Richard M., *Latter Rain: The Latter Rain Movement of 1948 and the Mid-Twentieth Century Evangelical Awakening* (Mississauga: Honeycomb Visual Productions, 1987).
'The Significant Signs of the Times', in *The Coming and Kingdom of Christ: A Stenographic Report of the Prophetic Bible Conference Held at the Moody Bible Institute of Chicago, Feb. 24–27 1914* (Chicago: The Bible Institute Colportage Association, 1914), pp. 98–109.
Robeck, Cecil M., Jr, *The Azusa Street Mission and Revival: The Birth of the Global Pentecostal Movement* (Nashville: Thomas Nelson, 2006).
—, 'An Emerging Magisterium? The Case of the Assemblies of God', *Pneuma* 25 (2003), pp. 164–215.
—, 'Taking Stock of Pentecostalism: The Personal Reflections of a Retiring Editor', *Pneuma* 15 (1993), pp. 35–60.
—, 'Spotlight on The Society for Pentecostal Studies', *ET* 14 (1985), pp. 28–30.

Robins, Roger. G., *A. J. Tomlinson: Plainfolk Modernist* (Religion in America Series; New York: Oxford University Press, 2004).

Rogerson, J. W., 'Slippery Words: Myth', in *Sacred Narrative: Readings in the Theory of Myth* (ed. Allen Dundes; Los Angeles: University of California Press, 1984), pp. 62–71.

Roozen, David A. and James R. Nieman, *Church, Identity, and Change: Theology and Denominational Structures in Unsettled Times* (Grand Rapids: Eerdmans, 2005).

Rothstein, William G., *American Physicians in the Nineteenth Century: From Sects to Science* (Baltimore: Johns Hopkins University Press, [1972] 1992).

Ruge-Jones, Philip, *Cross in Tensions: Luther's Theology of the Cross as Theologico-social Critique* (Princeton Theological Monograph Series, Eugene, OR: Pickwick, 2008).

Rupp, Gordon, *The Righteousness of God: Luther Studies* (London: Hodder and Stoughton, 1953).

Rutz, James, *The Open Church: How to Bring Back the Exiting Life of the First Century Church* (Auburn, ME: Seedsowers, 1992).

Rybarczyk, Edmund, 'Spiritualities Old and New: Similarities between Eastern Orthodoxy and Classical Pentecostalism', *Pneuma* 24 (2002), pp. 7–25.

Sandeen, Ernest R., *The Roots of Fundamentalism: British and American Millenarianism, 1800–1930* (Chicago: University of Chicago Press, 1970).

—, *The Origins of Fundamentalism: Toward a Historical Interpretation* (Philadelphia: Fortress, 1968).

Sanders, Cheryl, *Saints in Exile: The Holiness-Pentecostal Experience in African American* (Religion in America; New York: Oxford University Press, 1996).

Sauter, Gerhard, 'Luther on the Resurrection', in *Harvesting Martin Luther's Reflections on Theology, Ethics, and the Church* (ed. Timothy Wengert; Lutheran Quarterly Books; Grand Rapids: Eerdmans, 2004), pp. 99–118.

Scaer, David P., 'Luther's Concept of the Resurrection in His Commentary on 1 Corinthians 15', *CTQ* 47 (1983), pp. 209–24.

Schmidt, Jean Miller, *Souls or the Social Order: The Two-Party System in American Protestantism* (Brooklyn: Carlson, 1991).

Schmidt, Leigh Eric, *Holy Fairs: Scotland and the Making of American Revivalism, Second Edition* (Princeton: Princeton University Press, 2001).

Schneider, Hans, *German Radical Pietism* (Pietist and Wesleyan Studies, No. 22, trans. Gerald MacDonald; Lanham, MD: Scarecrow, 2007).

Schneiders, Sandra M., 'Theology and Spirituality: Strangers, Rivals, or Partners?', *Horizon* 13 (1986), pp. 253–74.

Schner, George P., 'The Appeal to Experience', *TS* 53 (1992), pp. 40–59.

Schweitzer, Don, 'Douglas Hall's Critique of Jürgen Moltmann's Eschatology of the Cross', *SR* 27 (1998), pp. 7–25.

Shelton, R. L., 'Perfection, Perfectionism', *EDT*, pp. 839–43.

Shepard, W. E., 'The Meeting at Findlay, Ohio', *Nazarene Messenger* 6, No. 11 (12 September 1901).

Sheppard, Gerald T., 'Biblical Interpretation After Gadamer', *Pneuma* 16 (1994), pp. 121–41.

—, 'Pentecostals and Dispensationalism: The Anatomy of an Uneasy Relationship', *Pneuma* 6 (1984), pp. 5–33.

Sider, Ronald J., *Karlstadt's Battle with Luther: Documents in a Liberal-Radical Debate* (Philadelphia: Fortress, 1978).

Simmons, Dale H., *E. W. Kenyon and the Postbellum Pursuit of Peace, Power, and Plenty* (Lanham, MA: Scarecrow Press, Inc., 1997).

Simpson, A. B., *The Gospel of Healing, Revised Edition* (Harrisburg, PA: Christian Publications, [1915] n.d).

—, *The Gospel of the Kingdom: A Series of Discourses on The Lord's Coming* (New York: Christian Alliance Publishing Company, 1890).

Sims, Timothy, *In Defense of the Word of Faith: An Apologetic Response to Encourage Charismatic Believers* (Bloomington, IL: AuthorHouse, 2008).

Sloos, William, 'The Story of James and Ellen Hebden: The First Family of Pentecost in Canada', *Pneuma* 32 (2010), pp. 181–202.

Smail, Tom, 'The Cross and the Spirit: Towards a Theology of Renewal', in *Charismatic Renewal: The Search for a Theology* (ed. Tom Smail, Andrew Walker and Nigel Wright; Gospel and Culture; London: SPCK, 1995), pp. 49–70.

Smith, Hannah Whittall, *The Christian's Secret of a Happy Life: New and Enlarged Edition* (Chicago, New York and Toronto: Fleming H. Revell, 1888).

Smith, James K. A., *Thinking in Tongues: Pentecostal Contributions to Christian Philosophy* (Pentecostal Manifestos; Grand Rapids: Eerdmans, 2010).

—, 'Teaching a Calvinist to Dance', *CT* 52 (May, 2008), pp. 42–45.

Smith, Timothy L., 'Introduction', in *The Promise of the Spirit: Charles G. Finney on Christian Holiness* (ed. Timothy L. Smith; Minneapolis: Bethany House, 1980), pp. 3–6.

—, 'The Doctrine of the Sanctifying Spirit: Charles G. Finney's Synthesis of Wesleyan and Covenant Theology', 13 (1978), pp. 92–113.

—, *Revivalism and Social Reform: American Protestantism on the Eve of the Civil War* (New York: Harper & Row, [1957] 1965).

—, *Called Unto Holiness: The Story of the Nazarenes: The Formative Years* (Kansas City, MO: Nazarene Publishing House, 1962).

Snyder, Howard, 'Spirit and Form in Wesley's Theology: A Response to Keefer's "John Wesley: Disciple of Early Christianity"', *WJT* 19 (1984), pp. 33–35.

Soelle, Dorothee, *Suffering* (trans. Everett R. Kalin; Philadelphia: Fortress, 1975).

Solberg, Mary M., *Compelling Knowledge: A Feminist Proposal for an Epistemology of the Cross* (Albany: State University of New York Press, 1997).

Solivan, Samuel, *The Spirit, Pathos and Liberation: Toward and Hispanic Pentecostal Theology* (Journal of Pentecostal Theology Supplement Series, 14; Sheffield: Sheffield Academic Press, 1998).

Spener, Philip Jacob, *Pia Desideria* (trans. and ed. Theodore G. Tappert; N.p.: Fortress, 1964).

Spittler, Russell, 'Are Pentecostals and Charismatics Fundamentalists? A Review of American Uses of These Categories', in *Charismatic Christianity as Global Culture* (ed. Karla Poewe; Columbia: University of South Carolina Press, 1994), pp. 103–16.

—, 'Scripture and the Theological Enterprise: View from a Big Canoe', in *The Use of the Bible in Theology: Evangelical Options* (ed. R. K. Johnston; Atlanta: John Knox Press, 1985), pp. 56–77.

Stanley, Susie C., 'Wesleyan/Holiness Churches: Innocent Bystanders in the Fundamentalist/Modernist Controversy', in *Re-forming the Center: American Protestantism, 1900 to the Present* (ed. Douglas Jacobsen and William Vance Trollinger, Jr; Grand Rapids: Eerdmans, 1998), pp. 172–93.

Statistics Canada, *2001 Census: Analysis Series Religions in Canada*. Statistics Canada Catalogue no. 96F0030XIE2001015. (Ottawa, 2003). Online: http://www12.statcan.ca/english/census01/products/analytic/companion/rel/pdf/96F0030XIE2001015.pdf (Accessed 4 July 2014).

—, *National Household Survey, Canada, 2011* (Ottawa, 2014). Online:

http://www12.statcan.gc.ca/nhs-enm/2011/dp-pd/prof/index.cfm?Lang=E (Accessed 4 November, 2014) .

Stein, K. James, 'Philipp Jakob Spener', in *The Pietist Theologians: An Introduction to the Theology of the Seventeenth and Eighteenth Centuries* (ed. Carter Lindberg; Oxford: Blackwell, 2005), pp. 84–98.

Steinmetz, David C., 'Luther against Luther', in *Luther in Context, Second Edition* (Grand Rapids: Baker, 1996), pp. 1–11.

—, 'Luther and the Hidden God', in *Luther in Context, Second Edition* (Grand Rapids: Baker, 1996), pp. 23–31.

—, *Luther and Staupitz: An Essay in the Intellectual Origins of the Protestant Reformation* (Duke Monographs in Medieval and Renaissance Studies; Durham: Duke University Press, 1980).

Stoeffler, F. Ernest, 'Epilogue', in *Continental Pietism and Early American Christianity* (ed. F. Ernest Stoeffler; Grand Rapids: Eerdmans, 1976), pp. 266–71.

—, 'Pietism, the Wesleys, and Methodist Beginnings in America', in *Continental Pietism and Early American Christianity* (ed. F. Ernest Steoffler; Grand Rapids: Eerdmans, 1976), pp. 184–221.

—, *The Rise of Evangelical Piety* (Leiden: Brill, 1965).

Stout, Harry S., *The Divine Dramatist: George Whitfield and the Rise of Modern Evangelism* (Grand Rapids: Eerdmans, 1991).

Stronstad, Roger, '*The Charismatic Theology of St. Luke* Revisited (Special Emphasis on Being Baptized in the Holy Spirit)', in *Defining Issues in Pentecostalism: Classical and Emergent* (ed. Steven M. Studebaker; McMaster Theological Studies Series, vol. 1; Eugene, OR: Pickwick, 2008), pp. 101–22.

—, *The Prophethood of All Believers: A Study in Luke's Charismatic Theology* (London: Sheffield Academic Press, 1999).

—, *The Charismatic Theology of St. Luke* (Peabody, MA: Hendrickson, 1987).

Studebaker, Steven M. (ed.), *Pentecostalism and Globalization: The Impact of Globalization on Pentecostal Theology and Ministry* (McMaster Theological Studies Series, 2; Eugene, OR: Pickwick, 2010).

Sweeney, Douglas A., *Nathaniel Taylor, New Haven Theology, and the Legacy of Jonathan Edwards* (Religion in America Series; New York: Oxford University Press, 2003).

Synan, Vinson, *The Holiness-Pentecostal Tradition in the United States 2nd Revised Edition* (Grand Rapids: Eerdmans, [1971] 1996).

Synan, Vinson (ed.), *The Century of the Holy Spirit: 100 Years of Pentecostal and Charismatic Renewal 1901–2001* (Nashville: Thomas Nelson, 2001).

Szasz, Theodore Morton, *The Divided Mind of Modern Protestantism, 1880–1930* (Tuscaloosa, AL: University of Alabama Press, 1982).

Talley, Thomas, 'Healing: Sacrament or Charism?', *Worship* 46 (1972), pp. 518–27.

Taylor, George F., 'The Spirit and the Bride: A Scriptural Presentation of the Operations, Manifestation, Gifts and Fruit of the Holy Spirit in His Relation to the Bride with Special Reference to the "Latter Rain" Revival', in *Three Early Pentecostal Tracts* (vol. 14 of The Higher Christian Life; ed. Donald W. Dayton; New York: Garland, [1907] 1985).

Taylor, Nathaniel W., *Lectures on the Moral Government of God, Vol. II* (New York: Clark, Austin & Smith, 1859).

Thiselton, Anthony C., *The Hermeneutics of Doctrine* (Grand Rapids: Eerdmans, 2007).

Thomas, John Christopher, 'Reading the Bible from within Our Traditions: A Pentecostal Hermeneutic as Test Case', in *Between Two Horizons: Spanning New Testament Studies and Systematic Theology* (ed. Joel B. Green and Max Turner: Grand Rapids: Eerdmans, 2000), pp. 108–22.

—, *The Devil, Disease, and Delverance: Origins of Illness in New Testament Thought* (JPTSup 13; Sheffield: Sheffield Academic Press, 1998).

—, 'Pentecostal Theology in the Twenty-First Century', *Pneuma* 20 (Spring, 1998).

—, 'Women, Pentecostals and the Bible: An Experiment in Pentecostal Hermeneutics', *JPT* 2 (1994), pp. 41–56.

—, *Footwashing in John13 and the Johannine Community* (JSNTS 61; Sheffield: JSOT Press, 1991).

Thomas, John Christopher and Kimberly Ervin Alexander, '"And the Signs Are Following": Mark 16:9–20 – a Journey into Pentecostal Hermeneutics', *JPT* 11 (2003), pp. 147–70.

Tomberlin, Daniel, *Pentecostal Sacraments: Encountering God at the Altar* (Cleveland, TN: Center for Pentecostal Leadership and Care, Pentecostal Theological Seminary, 2010).

Tomlin, Graham, *The Power of the Cross: Theology and the Death of Christ in Paul, Luther and Pascal* (Paternoster Theological Monographs; Milton Keynes, UK: Paternoster, 1999).

—, 'The Medieval Origins of Luther's Theology of the Cross', *AR* 89 (1998), pp. 22–40.

Torrey, R. A. (ed.), *The Fundamentals: A Testimony to the Truth, Volume I-XII* (Chicago: Testimony Publishing Co., 1910–15).

Torrey, R. A., *The Baptism with the Holy Spirit* (New York: Fleming H. Revell, 1895).

Tracy, David, 'Form & Fragment: The Recovery of the Hidden and Incomprehensible God', in *The Concept of God in Global Dialogue* (ed. Werner G. Jeanrond and Aasuly Lande; Faith Meets Faith Series; Maryknoll, NY: Orbis Books, 2005), pp. 98–114.

Trask, Thomas E. and David A. Womack, *Back to the Altar: A Call to Spiritual Awakening* (Springfield: Gospel Publishing House, 1994).

Turnbull, Stephan K., 'Grace and Gift in Luther and Paul', *W&W* 24 (2004), pp. 305–14.

Tuveson, Ernest Lee, *Redeemer Nation: The Idea of America's Millennial Role* (Chicago: University of Chicago Press, 1968).

Van De Walle, Bernie A,. *The Heart of the Gospel: A. B. Simpson, the Fourfold Gospel, and Late Nineteenth-Century Evangelical Theology* (Princeton Theological Monograph; Eugene, OR: Wipf and Stock, 2009).

Van Die, Marguerite, *An Evangelical Mind: Nathanael Burwash and the Methodist Tradition in Canada, 1839–1918* (McGill-Queen's Studies in the History of Religion 3; Montreal: McGill Queen's University Press, 1989).

von Loewenich, Walther, *Luther's Theology of the Cross* (trans. Herbert J. A. Bouman; Minneapolis: Augsburg, 1976).

Wacker, Grant, *Heaven Below: Early Pentecostalism and American Culture* (Cambridge: Harvard University Press, 2003).

—, 'Travail of a Broken Family: Radical Evangelical Responses to the Emergence of Pentecostalism in America, 1906–1916', in *Pentecostal Currents in American Protestantism* (ed. Edith L. Blumhofer, Russell P. Spittler and Grant A. Wacker; Urbana and Chicago: University of Illinois Press, 1999), pp. 23–49.

—, 'Playing for Keeps: The Primitivist Impulse in Early Pentecostalism', in *The American Quest for the Primitive Church* (ed. Richard T. Hughes; Urbana: University of Illinois Press, 1985), pp. 196–219.

—, 'Searching for Eden with a Satellite Dish: Primitivism, Pragmatism, and the Pentecostal Character', in *The Primitive Church in the Modern World* (ed. Richard T. Hughes; Urbana: University of Illinois Press, 1985), pp. 139–66.

—, 'The Functions of Faith in Primitive Pentecostalism', *HTR* 77 (1984), pp. 353–75.
Wagner, Peter C., *Apostles Today: Biblical Government for Biblical Power* (California: Regal Books, 2012).
—, *The Third Wave of the Holy Spirit* (Ann Arbor: Vine Books, 1988).
Waite, Gary K., 'David Joris' Thought in the Context of the Early Melchiorite and Münsterite Movements in the Low Countries, 1534–1536', *MQR* 62 (1988), pp. 296–317.
Waldvogel, Edith, 'The "Overcoming" Life: A Study in the Reformed Evangelical Contribution to Pentecostalism', *Pneuma* 1 (1979), pp. 7–19.
Ware, S. L., *Restorationism in the Holiness Movement in the Late Nineteenth and Early Twentieth Centuries* (Studies in American Religion; Lewiston, NY: Edwin Mellen Press, 2004).
Warfield, Benjamin Breckinridge, *Studies in Perfectionism, Volumes I and II* (Grand Rapids: Baker, [1932] 2003).
Watson, Philip S., *Let God Be God! An Interpretation of the Theology of Martin Luther* (Eugene, OR: Wipf and Stock, [1947] 2001).
—, 'Wesley and Luther on Christian Perfection', *ER* 15 (1963), pp. 291–302.
Webber, Robert, *Common Roots: A Call to Evangelical Maturity. Contemporary Evangelical Perspectives* (Grand Rapids: Zondervan, 1978).
Weber, Max, *The Theory of Social and Economic Organization* (trans. A. M. Henderson and Talcott Parsons; New York: Free Press, 1947).
Weber, Timothy B., *Living in the Shadow of the Second Coming: American Premillennialism, 1875–1982* (Contemporary Evangelical Perspectives; Grand Rapids: Academic Books, 1983).
Weinandy, Thomas G., *Does God Suffer?* (Edinburgh: T&T Clark, 2000).
—, *The Father's Spirit of Sonship: Reconceiving the Trinity* (Edinburgh: T&T Clark, 1995).
Weinlick, John R., 'Moravianism in the American Colonies', in *Continental Pietism and Early American Christianity* (ed. F. Ernest Stoeffler; Grand Rapids: Eerdmans, 1976), pp. 123–63.
Weisberger, Bernard, *They Gathered at the River: The Story of the Great Revivalists and Their Impact upon Religion in America* (Boston and Toronto: Little, Brown and Company, 1958).
Wengert, Timothy J., '"Peace, Peace . . . Cross, Cross": Reflections on How Martin Luther Relates the Theology of the Cross to Suffering', *TT* 59 (2002), pp. 190–205.
—, 'The Priesthood of All Believers and Other Pious Myths' (Institute of Liturgical Studies, 2005), pp. 1–36. Online: http://www.valpo.edu/ils/assets/pdfs/05_wengert.pdf (Accessed 14 August 2014).
Westhelle, Vitor, *The Scandalous God: The Use and Abuse of the Cross* (Minneapolis: Fortress, 2006).
Whitaker, Alexander, 'Good News from Virginia', in *American Christianity: An Historical Interpretation with Representative Documents, Vol. 1. 1607–1820* (ed. H. Shelton Smith, Robert T. Handy and Lefferts A. Loetscher; New York: Scribners, 1960), pp. 45–48.
White, Charles Edward, *The Beauty of Holiness: Phoebe Palmer as Theologian, Revivalist, Feminist, and Humanitarian* (Grand Raids: Francis Asbury Press, 1986).
Whitely, Marilyn Färdig, 'Sailing for the Shore: The Canadian Holiness Tradition', in *Aspects of the Canadian Evangelical Experience* (ed. G. A. Rawlyk; Montreal and Kingston: McGill-Queens University Press, 1997), pp. 257–70.
Whorton, James C., *Nature Cures: The History of Alternative Medicine in America* (New York: Oxford University Press, 2002).

—, *Crusaders for Fitness: The History of American Health Reformers* (Princeton: Princeton University Press, 1984).

Wicks, Jared, *Luther and His Spiritual Legacy* (Wilmington: Michael Glazier, 1983).

Williams, George Huntston, *The Radical Reformation: Third Edition* (Sixteenth Century Essays and Studies, vol. XV, Kirksville, MO: Truman University Press, 2000).

Wimber, John, 'Zip to 3,000', in *Signs and Wonders Today: The Story of Fuller Theological Seminary's Remarkable Course on Spiritual Power, New Expanded Edition* (ed. Peter Wagner; Altamonte Springs, FL: Creation House, 1987), pp. 27–39.

Wimber, John and Kevin Springer, *Power Healing* (San Francisco: San Francisco, 1987).

—, *Power Evangelism: Signs and Wonders Today* (London: Hodder and Stoughton, 1985).

Winthrop, John, 'John Winthrop's Model of Charity', in *American Christianity: An Historical Interpretation with Representative Documents, Vol. 1. 1607–1820* (ed. H. Shelton Smith, Robert T. Handy and Lefferts A. Loetscher; New York: Scribners, 1960), 98–102.

Woodworth-Etter, Maria, *A Diary of Signs and Wonders* (Tulsa: Harrison House, [1916] n.d.).

Wyckoff, John W., *Pneuma and Logos: The Role of the Spirit in Biblical Hermeneutics* (Eugene, OR: Wipf and Stock, 2010).

Yamazaki-Ransom, Kazuhiko, *Roman Empire in Luke's Narrative* (Library of New Testament Studies 404; London: T&T Clark, 2010).

Yoder, John Howard, 'Primitivism in the Radical Reformation: Strengths and Weaknesses', in *The Primitive Church in the Modern World* (ed. Richard T. Hughes; Urbana: University of Illinois Press, 1985), pp. 74–97.

—, 'The Use of the Bible in Theology', in *The Use of the Bible in Theology: Evangelical Options* (ed. Robert K. Jonston; Atlanta: John Knox, 1985).

—, 'Marginalia', *Concern* 15 (1967), pp. 77–80.

Yong, Amos, *In the Days of Caesar: Pentecostalism and Political Theology: The Cadbury Lectures, 2009* (Sacra Doctrina: Christian Theology for a Postmodern Age; Grand Rapids: Eerdmans, 2010).

—, 'Pentecostalism and the Theological Academy', *TT* 64 (2007), pp. 244–50.

—, *Spirit-Word-Community: Theological Hermeneutics in Trinitarian Perspective* (Ashgate New Critical Thinking in Religion Theology and Biblical Studies; Aldershot, UK: Ashgate, 2002).

—, 'The Word and the Spirit, or the Spirit and the Word? Exploring the Boundaries of Evangelicalism in Relationship to Modern Pentecostalism', *TJ* 23 (2002), pp. 235–52.

Zahl, Simeon, *Pneumatology and Theology of the Cross in the Preaching of Christoph Friedrich Blumhardt: The Holy Spirit between Wittenberg and Azusa Street* (London: T&T Clark, 2010).

Zwiep, Arie, W., 'Luke's Understanding of Baptism in the Holy Spirit', *PentecoStudies* 6 (2007), pp. 127–49.

PERSON INDEX

SUBJECT INDEX

COPYRIGHT ACKNOWLEDGEMENTS

The author and publishers are grateful for permission to reproduce the following copyright material:

CPSIA information can be obtained
at www.ICGtesting.com
Printed in the USA
LVOW10s1942260617
539421LV00007B/48/P

9 780567 67189